	DATE DUE		

THE
Changing
Politics OF
Education

PROSPECTS FOR THE 1980's

Edited by

EDITH K. MOSHER
and
JENNINGS L. WAGONER, Jr.

University of Virginia

PROCEEDINGS OF A SYMPOSIUM
SPONSORED AND DEVELOPED BY
THE UNIVERSITY COUNCIL FOR EDUCATIONAL ADMINISTRATION
AND THE UNIVERSITY OF VIRGINIA

A Phi Delta Kappa Publication
distributed by

McCutchan Publishing Corporation
2526 Grove Street
Berkeley, California 94704

ISBN 0-8211-1252-X

Library of Congress Catalog Card Number 77-75609

The essays in this volume were first presented at a national symposium convened at the University of Virginia in Charlottesville, November 14-17, 1976, as a bicentennial observance in honor of Thomas Jefferson as an educational statesman. The central purpose of the symposium, that of examining contemporary problems in education, derives from Jefferson's timeless proposition that:

If a nation expects to be ignorant and free, in a state of civilization, it expects what never was and never will be.

Preface

On November 14-17, 1976, more than two hundred professors, educational practitioners, government officials, and graduate students convened in Charlottesville, Virginia, for a symposium on "The Changing Politics of Education: Prospects for the 1980's." Cosponsored by the University of Virginia and the University Council for Educational Administration (UCEA), the symposium provided a forum in which scholars and practitioners from a variety of fields within and without education assessed varying perceptions of immediate and future currents in the political sphere of education. The symposium featured eleven speakers who focused attention on six major topics during general sessions. Following three of the general sessions, topic analysts presented briefing papers to small groups that examined in more detail some of the most pressing priority issues related to each topic. The three-day conference proved to be a searching, lively, and timely experience and pointed to the need for continuing attention to the relationship between educational and political questions by a much broader audience.

The enthusiasm generated on that occasion justifies the expectation that this volume, the published proceedings of the symposium, will further advance the purposes of the undertaking: first, to link relevant past events to significant trends in educational governance and policy making; and, second, to contribute to an understanding of the influences and demands that will shape educational policy analysis in future research, teaching, and practice of educational administration.

Several considerations dictated the substance and the timing of the symposium and this publication about the changing politics of education. The first was the unparalleled opportunity, as a part of the bicentennial observances, both to commemorate Thomas Jefferson as an educational statesman and to put contemporary problems into the context of enduring purposes of, and challenges to, the American system of education. The second was the critical state of the American polity as it struggled through the aftermath of the Vietnam War, domestic scandal and public disillusionment, and economic recession. As a counterpoise to the emotionalism of election year politics, sober, constructive, long-range thinking about the shape of future governmental action was, and still is, very much in order.

A third and more immediate stimulus is the turbulent state of the educational enterprise itself, an arena in which the study of politics has never been more urgent. Consensual and low-visibility forms of political involvement no longer characterize any of its sectors. Competition with other public services has intensified. The processes and outcomes of schooling have become more controversial and many sided. Faced with an avalanche of social change, educational professionals can no longer rely on earlier mappings of the political terrain.

A fourth consideration is the status of the study of educational politics. In 1963, the UCEA contributed to a significant beginning of this cross-disciplinary area by its sponsorship of a conference of political scientists, sociologists, and educators. This produced a seminal publication, *The Politics of Education in the Local Community*, edited by Robert S. Cahill and Stephen P. Hencley (Danville, Ill.: Interstate Printers and Publishers, 1964). Subsequent developments in the study of both precollegiate and higher education have been rapid, but somewhat chaotic. Scholars from the parent fields have conducted research, written numerous books and reports, formed collegial groups, caught the attention of legislators and government executives, and begun to offer specialized instruction in the politics of education at a number of universities. Practitioners are finding some of the results of these activities in professional journals, books, and conference programs. Yet much remains to be done: to identify underresearched and novel problems, to gain broader acceptance of policy-oriented forms of inquiry, and to integrate research-based findings into educational practice and professional training.

All of these reasons—the desire for historical perspective, the need to confront contemporary malaise in the political realm and in the educational sector, and the possibility of advancing a fledgling field of study—converged to indicate that the time was opportune for a searching look at the prospects for educational politics in the 1980's.

This volume is thus designed for two audiences: educators, especially those in policy-making positions, who wish to gain greater understanding of the political forces that shape their work; and students of educational policy making who need to relate specialized lines of inquiry to a broader, yet pragmatic, frame of reference. Within these very general guidelines, the various authors were invited to write about their topics as they saw fit. Several drew heavily on the research literature in politics of education; this book does not, however, purport to provide a systematic assessment of that area of study. It seeks, rather, to bridge the worlds of practice and research, an effort that must overcome some notable difficulties. Not the least of these is that both practitioners and researchers already possess, or rapidly tend to develop, specialized perspectives and prejudices that impede communication and mutual respect. Further, research activities in politics of education are still scattered, fragmented, and uneven in the sense that some topics have been intensively studied while others are as yet virtually untouched. Findings and generalizations vary widely in scope and level of analysis, as well as in their relevance for explaining and predicting events and trends that practitioners would consider to be most cogent.

In considering these gaps between research and practice, readers will find that Laurence Iannaccone offers a helpful framework for imposing some order on the diversity of research activities by suggesting three levels of analysis ("Three Views of Change in Educational Politics," *The Politics of Education,* ed. Jay D. Scribner [Chicago: University of Chicago Press, 1977], p. 285). At the least complex level, studies of the routine workings of the administrative policy system provide many generalizations about incremental policy changes in educational services. When more general questions are posed about the manner in which the political system manages conflict, then a more demanding study of the periodic political adjustments within educational governments is required. When even more profound questions are raised about the meaning and significance of widespread political controversies over education, then it is necessary to probe the ideological underpinnings of the whole system.

The recent upheavals in long-established attitudes, policies, and institutions indicate that we may well be witnessing a watershed period in American society and education. To those involved with the conceptualization of the symposium and subsequent published proceedings, it therefore seemed important to encourage analyses encompassing all three levels of inquiry suggested by Iannaccone. Thus, the opening chapters give consideration to basic values by examining the ideological foundations on which the house is built and asking, in essence, whether Jeffersonian political and educational views apply in the third American century. Other normative concerns are explored primarily in the first four chapters, while the remaining chapters exemplify the other levels of analysis projected by Iannaccone: the accomplishment of incremental policy and program changes and the methods by which the political system manages conflict.

In addition to trying to narrow the gap between research and practice, this volume also attempts to create a bridge connecting the preoccupations of educators and political analysts with those of professionals in other disciplines, particularly history, economics, and sociology. This linkage is designed to overcome the long-standing habit of viewing education as an autonomous field of action and study. Any such attempt, however, necessarily introduces great and sometimes frustrating complexity in treatment of values, missions, and policy. In a similar way, the book considers problems that bridge all sectors of education — elementary, secondary, and postsecondary. This combination is rare in the politics of education literature and makes for a more complicated but decidedly more realistic and fruitful engagement than is the case when the various levels are analyzed in isolation from each other.

Although each of the authors of the essays in this volume has focused attention on specific problem areas in the political realm of education, all have taken into account, in varying degrees, two major developments affecting the whole of the educational enterprise: the conflicts arising from the disaggregated state of power in American politics; and the challenges posed by a modified rather than a diminished educational universe. Pressures and responses in the elementary-secondary and in the higher-postsecondary arenas do not always reflect an even cadence or direction, but the authors of the essays treat constantly recurring themes and tensions that not only provide coherence to this volume but that also characterize the unsteady state of educational politics in a period of steady state economic realities.

Central among the repetitive themes that tie these essays together is the assumption that, in spite of conflicts and concerns occasioned by fluctuations in the economy and the instability of needs for educational services, change is likely to be of an incremental nature. Emphasized more in some essays than in others is an awareness of the constancy of the features basic to the policy-making process, features that, in operation, tend to foster caution, compromise, and conciliation and hence gradual rather than abrupt shifts in arrangements. At the same time, and as is stressed in many of these essays, the unclear relations between education and the state and federal governments encourage steps toward accommodation that are faltering and uncertain. Tensions are mounting between those who see the need for increased regulation, centralization, and accountability and those who fear a continuing erosion of institutional and professional autonomy and who thus are encouraging decentralization and adherence to informal or negotiated arrangements. Tensions are compounded by desires and pressures to distribute the benefits of education more equitably, to attract new clienteles, and to expand services without at the same time adding to the layers of bureaucracy or increasing institutional vulnerability to external controls. The unevenness of growth and of decline in the demand for educational services further exacerbates the tensions within the educational community as well as between the educational sectors and the political sphere in general.

Implicit in all the essays and explicit in the final chapters is the need for renewed attention to the preservice and in-service preparation of educational administrators. Changes taking place within the structure of the education profession as well as in its relations to the political arena make necessary a more sensitive, informed, and politically astute educational leadership. After reading these essays, only the most naive could feel comfortable in relying upon the traditional assumptions and conventional wisdom of academic administration associated with bygone years.

The conceptual framework of the book consists of a chapter-by-chapter progression from the historical, philosophical, demographic, and economic contexts of education, in Parts I, II, and III, to the more specific and central focus on political aspects in Parts IV and V. The reader will find variable modes of presentation in each of these sections. In Part I, historical perspective is provided by the two complementary essays by Stephen K. Bailey and Jennings L. Wagoner, Jr. In Part II, the chapters by Nathan Glazer and Frank Riessman are less

formal in tone and provide in a quasi-debate format contrasting sociological and educational programming points of view on the same
topic.

Parts III, IV, and V are comparable in structure; that is, the first
chapter in each is a comprehensive overview of a topic. This is followed by a second chapter consisting of several brief analyses of important aspects of the general topic. Jesse Burkhead's review of economic
and demographic aspects of the educational sector is found in Chapter
5, Michael W. Kirst's treatment of the politics of elementary and secondary education in Chapter 7, and Robert O. Berdahl's analysis of
the politics of higher education in Chapter 9. The intervening chapters — 6, 8, and 10 — consist of the "briefing papers" that amplify certain facets of these presentations.

Part VI deals with the implications of the changing politics of
education for various aspects of educational administration. In Chapter 11 Roald F. Campbell outlines a program for more adequate preentry preparation of a corps of high-level administrators. His proposal
is the subject of commentaries by Kenneth P. Mortimer, a specialist in
the study of higher education, and by Aubrey V. McCutcheon, a
lawyer experienced in educational policy-making roles. Chapter 12,
the concluding essay by Jack Culbertson, provides a brief analysis of
the import of the foregoing chapters of the book and a commentary on
the prospects for constructive action by educational administrators in
the years ahead.

The eighteen briefing papers in Chapters 6, 8, and 10 merit the
particular attention of readers seeking introductory-level information
and suggestions for further reading on topics of high priority in the
study of the politics of education. They are descriptive and analytical,
not prescriptive, in content, and the topics were selected by the principal authors from a longer suggested list of priority issues. By this and
other means, the editors of the volume sought to bring many contribu-
tors together in a coherent and unified form of collaboration. The
principal authors exchanged advance copies of the outlines of their
chapters, and, following the symposium, all the authors reviewed and
updated their contributions. In many instances, they strengthened the
relationship of the chapters to each other by cross-reference and supplementary commentary.

Summary introductions to each of the six parts of the book were
prepared by the editors, Edith K. Mosher and Jennings L. Wagoner,

Jr., who were jointly responsible for developing the symposium program and for the organization of the published proceedings. The editors wish to acknowledge with appreciation the assistance rendered by the members of the program advisory committee: Stephen K. Bailey, American Council on Education; William L. Boyd, University of Rochester; Jack Culbertson, University Council for Educational Administration; Joseph Duffey, then of the American Association of University Professors; Samuel Halperin, Institute for Educational Leadership; James Kirkpatrick, American Association of School Administrators; and Mike M. Milstein, State University of New York at Buffalo. William H. Seawell, Unversity of Virginia, also a member of the program advisory committee, rendered invaluable assistance in many capacities and is especially thanked for his continuing encouragement and counsel.

Officials at the University of Virginia were generous and enthusiastic in their support. President Frank L. Hereford, Jr., Dean Richard M. Brandt, and Dean B. F. D. Runk contributed greatly to the success of the symposium and the bicentennial celebration of the university's founder. Jack Culbertson and the staff of UCEA deserve special recognition for their helpful collaboration. Stanley Elam of Phi Delta Kappa and John McCutchan of McCutchan Publishing Corporation are due thanks for their role in making this volume possible.

Patricia Fox, our editor at McCutchan, proved to be an invaluable associate during the months devoted to manuscript revision and editorial refinement. Her professional judgment greatly enhanced the quality of this volume, and her sense of humor eased us through the strain of trying moments. We would like also to thank Leigh Kindler and Deborah Williams for typing and retyping many portions of this book and to acknowledge the conscientious editorial assistance provided by Ronald Hutchinson, Ronald Head, Gerald Murray, and Janice Wanner.

To all these, and others who are acknowledged below, we express appreciation. To Fritz Mosher and to Shirley, David, and Brian Wagoner, we owe no small measure of love and gratitude for their patience and understanding through all this.

Charlottesville, Virginia
November 1977

Edith K. Mosher
Jennings L. Wagoner, Jr.

The following faculty members and graduate students of the University of Virginia participated in the symposium program in November 1976.

Faculty members: Frank E. Barham, James H. Bash, Charles W. Beegle, M. Howard Bryant, Robert Lynn Canady (Arrangements Coordinator), James Ceasar, D. Larry Carmichael, Jay L. Chronister, Josué Cruz, Larry Decker, James P. Esposito, Alexander G. Gilliam, Jr., Peter Hackett, George W. Holmes III, Samuel E. Kellams, John L. Knapp, Donald H. Medley, Robert Montjoy, Lawrence O'Toole, Robert H. Pate, Jr., Walter Wadlington, and John S. Wright.

Students: Georgia Arrington, Sue Basdikis, Robert Bender, Ned Browning, Alfred Butler, Lyn Clay, Beverly Cox, Roger Gaunt, Robert Grymes, Jr., Carleen Hill, Robert Knighton, Martha Lawrence, Elizabeth Lowe, James McDowelle, Sherry Mullett, Richard Nicholson, Ronald Nunnery, Timothy O'Leary, Robert Oliver, Ramsey Seldon, William Spence, Sharon Turshen, and Earl Wheatfall.

Contributors

PRINCIPAL AUTHORS

Stephen K. Bailey, a distinguished political scientist with graduate degrees from Oxford and Harvard Universities, is now Professor of Education and Social Policy at Harvard University, having served as Vice-President of the American Council on Education until September 1977. Formerly Chairman of the Policy Institute of the Syracuse University Research Corporation and Professor of Political Science in the Maxwell School of Citizenship and Public Affairs of Syracuse University, he served from 1960 to 1969 as Dean of the Maxwell School. He was also Professor of Educational Administration in Syracuse University's School of Education. He was a founding member, and for a time Secretary-Treasurer, of the National Academy of Education; President of the American Society for Public Administration; and Vice-President of the American Political Science Association. He is the author of many books and articles on politics, government, and education, including: *Congress Makes a Law* (1950); *The New Congress* (1966); *ESEA: The Office of Education Administers a Law,* with E. K. Mosher (1968); *Congress in the Seventies* (1970); and *Education Interest Groups in the Nation's Capital* (1975).

Robert O. Berdahl holds a master's degree from the London School of Economics and Political Science and a doctorate in political science from the University of California, Berkeley. He has been Professor of Higher Education at the State University of New York at Buffalo since 1969, having previously been a member of the faculty at San Francisco State College. He was a Senior Fellow

at the Carnegie Council on Policy Studies in Higher Education
from mid-1974 to June 1976. He served as Director, Comparative
Higher Education, International Council for Educational Development, Western Europe, during 1972-1973. Among his notable
publications are: *British Universities and the State* (1959);
Statewide Coordination of Higher Education (1971); and *From
Elite to Mass to Universal Higher Education: The British and
American Transformations,* with T. R. McConnell and M. Fay
(1973).

Jesse Burkhead is Maxwell Professor of Economics at Syracuse University, where he has been a member of the faculty since 1948. He is
a specialist in public finance and urban economics, with a related
interest in economics of education dating from 1960 when he
directed the Carnegie Corporation-supported Syracuse Project
for Research in Educational Finance and edited the project summary, *Public School Finance—Economics and Politics* (1964). He
has published extensively in economics, public administration,
and educational journals. His most recent books include: *Inputs
and Outputs in Large City Education* (1967); *Public Expenditure*
(1971); and *Productivity in the Local Government Sector* (1974).

Roald F. Campbell is Emeritus Professor of Educational Administration, Ohio State University, where he was Fawcett Professor of
Educational Administration from 1970 to 1974. From 1957 to
1970, he was Reavis Professor of Education, and he also held
positions as Director of the Midwest Administration Center and
Dean of the Graduate School of Education at the University of
Chicago. Since retirement he has served as Adjunct Professor at
the University of Utah and as Visiting Professor at the University
of California, Santa Barbara, the University of Victoria, and
Stanford University. He is a noted consultant to school boards,
professional organizations, colleges, state departments of education, and the National Institute of Education. He was a charter
member of the National Academy of Education and was President of the American Educational Research Association,
1969-1970. Among his notable recent publications are: *Strengthening State Departments of Education* (1967); *Educational
Administration as a Social Process,* with J. W. Getzels and J. M.
Lipham (1968); *The Organization and Control of American
Schools,* with L. L. Cunningham, R. O. Nystrand, and M. D.

Usdan (1975); *State Policy Making for the Public Schools,* with
T. Mazzoni (1976); and *Introduction to Educational Administration,* with E. M. Bridges and R. O. Nystrand (1977).

Jack Culbertson received his A.B. degree from Emory and Henry College, his M.A. from Duke University, and his Ph.D. in educational administration from the University of California, Berkeley.
He has taught in elementary, junior high, and senior high
schools; he has served as a community school principal and as a
local school district superintendent of schools; he has taught at
the Universities of California and Oregon; and he has served as
Executive Director of the University Council for Educational
Administration since 1959. He has been a member of numerous
special committees and advisory boards and has served as adviser
to the U.S. Office of Education, the Ford Foundation, the W. K.
Kellogg Foundation, and the "Designing Education for the
Future" project. He was coauthor or coeditor of the following
publications: *Administrative Relationships: A Case Book* (1960);
Simulation in Administrative Training (1960); *Preparing Administrators: New Perspectives* (1962); *Educational Research:
New Perspectives* (1963); *The Professorship in Educational Administration* (1964); and *Performance Objectives for School Principals* (1974).

Nathan Glazer, a sociologist with research interests in the fields of urban social policy and ethnic and race relations, has been Professor of Education and Social Structure at Harvard University
since 1969. He was previously a Professor of Sociology at the University of California, Berkeley. Since 1973 he has been coeditor of
The Public Interest. Among his numerous publications are: *The
Lonely Crowd,* with D. Riesman (1952); *Remembering the
Answers: Essays on the American Student Revolt* (1970); *Ethnici-
ty: Theory and Experience,* with D. P. Moynihan (1970); *Beyond
the Melting Pot,* with D. P. Moynihan (1970); and *Affirmative
Discrimination* (1976).

Michael W. Kirst is Associate Professor of Education and Business
Administration at Stanford Unversity and Chairman of the
California State Board of Education. He has been the chief consultant to the Oregon and New Jersey legislatures on school
finance reform as well as to the Governor's Committee on Public

Education, State of Florida. Former Staff Director of the U.S.
Senate Subcommittee on Employment, Manpower, and Poverty
and Associate Director of the President's Commission on White
House Fellows, he has also served as Associate Director of the
Council on the Education of Disadvantaged Children. His teaching, research, and editorial and consulting activities range across
the spectrum of educational politics in the United States, and he
recently completed a nine-country comparison of educational
finance policy for the Organization of Economic and Cooperative
Development. He has edited and coauthored a number of books,
including *State, School, and Politics* (1972); *Political and Social
Foundations of Education*, with F. Wirt (1975); and *The New
Era of State Education Politics*, with J. Berke and M. Usdan
(1977).

Aubrey V. McCutcheon, Jr., now head of McCutcheon Associates, was
an executive in the Detroit Public Schools from 1966 to 1976, becoming Deputy Executive Superintendent in 1973. He was previously a hearing officer and counsel for the Detroit region of the
National Labor Relations Board. An attorney who is a specialist
in public and private employee bargaining and dispute settlement, he has also been extensively involved in educational and
community organizations and activities, including the National
Academy of Education, the American Association of School Administrators, the National Urban Coalition, and the University
Council for Educational Administration. He has conducted simulated collective bargaining seminars for the University of Michigan, Industrial Relations Research Association, and the American Management Association.

Kenneth P. Mortimer is Professor of Higher Education, Research
Associate, and Director of the Center for the Study of Higher
Education, Pennsylvania State University, where he has been a
member of the faculty since 1969. He is President of the Association for the Study of Higher Education. He has written extensively on academic governance and collective bargaining in higher
education. Recent publications for which he has been editor or
contributor include: *State-Institutional Relations under Faculty
Bargaining* (1976); *Sharing Authority Effectively*, with T. R.
McConnell (1977); and *Campus Employment Relations* (1977).

Edith K. Mosher, Associate Professor of Education, University of Virginia, was program coordinator of the symposium and coeditor of these published proceedings. A specialist in the politics of education, she received a Ph.D. in educational administration from the University of California, Berkeley, in 1967. She had administrative experience in the federal government and was formerly on the staff of the Far West Laboratory for Educational Research and Development. She was coauthor with S. K. Bailey of *ESEA: The Office of Education Administers a Law* (1968) and recently contributed chapters on intergovernmental relations in education to two books: *Politics of Education,* the 1977 Yearbook of the National Society for the Study of Education; and *Understanding School Boards,* the report of a research symposium of the National School Boards Association (1975).

Frank Riessman is Professor of Education, Queens College of the City University of New York, Codirector of the New Human Services Institute, and editor of *Social Policy.* From 1966 to 1972 he was Professor of Education and Director of New Careers Development Center at New York University. Previously he served as Associate Professor, Department of Psychiatry, Albert Einstein College of Medicine, and as Visiting Professor of Psychiatry at Columbia University. His many important publications include: *Social Class and Social Policy,* with S. M. Miller (1968); *The Service Society and the Consumer Vanguard,* with A. Gartner (1974); *The Inner City Child* (1976); and *Self-Help in the Human Services,* with A. Gartner (1976).

Jennings L. Wagoner, Jr., is Director of the Center for the Study of Higher Education and Associate Professor of Social and Historical Foundations of Education at the University of Virginia. He joined the faculty there in 1968 after receiving his Ph.D. from Ohio State University. He is active in campus governance, in the American Educational Studies Association, and is on the editorial board of *Educational Studies.* He has published in a variety of journals and is author of a Phi Delta Kappa Bicentennial Fastback, *Thomas Jefferson and the Education of a New Nation* (1976).

AUTHORS OF BRIEFING PAPERS

Carl R. Ashbaugh, Associate Professor, Educational Administration, University of Texas, Austin

Paul E. Barton, Senior Associate, National Manpower Institute

Patrick J. Bird, Associate Dean of Education, University of Virginia

William L. Boyd, Associate Professor of Education, University of Rochester

Harold J. Burbach, Associate Professor, Foundations of Education, University of Virginia

John J. Callahan, Director, Legislators' Education Action Project, National Conference of State Legislatures

William R. Carriker, Professor, Special Education, University of Virginia

Marjorie G. Elsten, Legislative Assistant to Assistant Secretary for Human Development, U.S. Department of Health, Education, and Welfare

Elmer H. Gish, Director of Planning and Development, Richmond, Virginia, Public Schools

Lawrence E. Gladieux, Director of the Washington Office, College Entrance Examination Board

Michael H. Kaplan, Assistant Professor, Educational Administration, University of Virginia

Jenni W. Klein, Director of Educational Services, Program Development and Innovation Division; Administration for Children, Youth, and Families; Office of Human Development Services, U.S. Department of Health, Education, and Welfare

David W. Leslie, Associate Professor, Higher Education, University of Virginia

Mike M. Milstein, Professor, Educational Administration, State University of New York at Buffalo

James F. Nickerson, Director, Servicemen's Opportunity Colleges Project, American Association of State Colleges and Universities

Richard W. Saxe, Professor and Chairman, Administration and Supervision, University of Toledo

Jacob O. Stampen, Senior Research Associate for Policy Analysis, American Association of State Colleges and Universities

Robert G. Templin, Assistant Professor, Higher Education, University of Virginia

Norman C. Thomas, Professor of Political Science, University of Cincinnati

Michael Timpane, Director, Center for Educational Finance and Governance, RAND Corporation

Virgil S. Ward, Professor, Foundations of Education, University of Virginia

John W. Warden, Center Associate, Mid-Atlantic Center for Community Education, University of Virginia

Eleanore C. Westhead, Associate Professor, Special Education, University of Virginia

David K. Wiles, Professor of Educational Administration, Miami University, Ohio

Contents

PART I
Education, Politics, and the
Jeffersonian Legacy

Thomas Jefferson was the first American statesman to give firm voice to the connection between public education and the basic tenets of democratic government. Thus the 1976 symposium honoring his achievements as an educational statesman and this volume, which comprises the papers prepared for that occasion, are not only commemorative of the values championed by Jefferson but dedicated, in their substance, to inquiry concerning fundamental if often neglected relationships between events in two worlds—the educational and the political.

In keeping with Jefferson's own belief in the inevitability of change and reflective of his faith in the necessity of critical inquiry, it seems especially important that his assumptions and priorities be evaluated in light of present educational and political circumstances and challenges. Moreover, by bringing into focus the dominant political concerns that gave purpose and direction to Jefferson's efforts in behalf of public education, it is hoped that pressing questions of our own day may be explored from a more enlightened and more meaningful perspective than otherwise might be the case.

In the opening chapter, Stephen Bailey directly confronts the issue of the appropriateness of Jeffersonian educational purpose for our own generation. Many of Jefferson's specific educational recommendations and concerns, Bailey observes, have lost their relevance in the context of the closing decades of the twentieth century. Also, cer-

1

tain issues that presently seem most compelling and perplexing in some cases received either scant attention from Jefferson or no mention at all. The gulf that separates our generation and our agenda from that of Jefferson's day must be measured in terms far more meaningful than the mere passage of time. Bailey cautions that only in violation of the Jeffersonian spirit and at great risk to ourselves can we "overlay our painful and attenuated predicaments with eighteenth-century poultices."

Even as we recognize that solutions to current problems cannot be discovered ready-made in the past, we can, and must, learn from our past. And, if in some particulars Jefferson's educational prescriptions no longer seem applicable, there yet remains in the Jeffersonian legacy much that is germane and instructive to those who would concern themselves with the role of education in a democratic society. It is through an analysis of timeless "beacons of the past" that Bailey examines the contemporary relevance of Jefferson and the purposes of education.

In Bailey's estimation, four themes emerge from Jefferson's life and writings that connect our educational past to the present and that hold meaning for prospects in the 1980's and beyond. First, Jefferson's insistence that education be useful, that it bear directly on the issues and problems of the living generation, remains as vital and demanding a purpose today as in Jefferson's time. Utility must, of course, be redefined with each succeeding generation, and, as Bailey pointedly notes, the psychological and social traumas of our own age can scarcely be eased by adherence to educational form and substance that remain blindly traditional and self-serving to educators and comfortable establishments.

That education is a just and necessary claimant of public support is a second Jeffersonian proposition that Bailey finds unchanging. Jefferson's persistent advocacy of a public system of education, even in the face of public apathy and repeated legislative resistance, was grounded in a third conviction he held as basic to the health and even to the life of a nation in which government rested with the people: education as "a necessary handmaiden to effective citizenship." Bailey finds Jefferson's own life as a citizen-statesman an instructive if all too rare an example for our own day, and he warns that the tenor of our politics and vitality of our national spirit will not likely be improved without some form of "refurbished commitment by educated people to public probity and to the public interest."

Bailey concludes his inquiry into the relevance of Jeffersonian purposes of education by again citing the legacy of Jefferson's own inquiring and extremely active style of life. Jefferson demonstrated, Bailey reminds us, that education can be both an end as well as a means. Education can and ought to be useful, it deserves public support and importantly contributes to the public weal, but it ought also be a means to psychic fullness, or as Jefferson phrased it, "the pursuit of happiness." "An educated life is itself a thing of beauty," Bailey writes. Certainly, the richness and fullness of Jefferson's life remain an enduring part of his legacy to us.

In Chapter 2, Jennings Wagoner examines Jefferson's attempts to translate educational and political ideas into institutionalized realities. Jefferson's firm belief in the necessity of an educated populace as a safeguard against tyranny and his concern for the liberties proclaimed in the Declaration of Independence led him to declare a "crusade against ignorance" and to champion various educational measures. Beginning in 1779, Jefferson engaged in a protracted struggle with a reluctant legislature in behalf of a plan for a unified system of public schooling. As Wagoner points out, however, Jefferson's carefully drawn proposals and fervent appeals proved unable to move legislators concerned with economy into favorable action. It was not until the closing years of Jefferson's life that he was able to realize part of his general plan, that which provided for the creation of a state university.

In describing Jefferson's advocacy of a public system of education and his efforts in establishing the University of Virginia, Wagoner provides a case study of educational politics that underscores the constancy of features basic to the policy-making process. The interaction of individuals, ideas, institutions, and interests provides the substance for analysis of Jefferson's political struggles. Competing ideologies, interest groups, sectional rivalries, economic stringencies, "staff work," committee maneuvering, lobbying, cost overruns, personal sacrifice, legislative inaction—these and other characteristics of policy making are found to be essential elements in the strategies and contests that surrounded the founding of the University of Virginia. Jefferson, the pragmatic statesman, knew from firsthand experience the demands associated with the political process, and he tasted both the bitterness of disappointment and the sweetness of victory in his engagements in the cause of education.

These opening essays, then, form the foundation and the frame-

work for the discussions and analyses that comprise the major portion
of this volume. Prospects for the 1980's are considered in the light of
enduring educational purposes and in a context of competing political
priorities and pressures.

1 Thomas Jefferson and the Purposes of Education

Stephen K. Bailey

Over the past months as I read into Jefferson's life and works as background for writing this piece, I was reminded of Plutarch's comment on why he wrote biography. "It was for the sake of others that I first began to write biography, but I find myself continuing to do it for my own." And he explained the reason. "The virtues of these great men . . . living daily with them [turns] my thoughts happily and calmly to the noble."[1]

Today the very concept of nobility seems archaic. Revisionism and sensationalism exploit the weaknesses of the traditionally revered. In such a context it is reassuring to sense from direct exposure the moral majesty of Jefferson's life and writings. Jefferson's was a beautiful mind. Denigrating him because of his occasional human weaknesses, or because of his perplexities and inconsistencies on such matters as race, academic freedom, or the proper uses of power, tells something about his detractors but little about Jefferson's essential role in history. His words and deeds will continue to inspire human attitudes and influence human behavior long after his foibles, uncertainties, and compromises have been forgotten. It is simply a doleful part of our contemporary intellectual and cultural malaise that, like a child with measles, we cannot stand bright lights—especially those beacon lights of the past that would, if we would let them, cast revealing beams into the veiled options of the future.

Until recently, I had done no systematic reading in Jefferson since graduate school. Then, in a seminar taught by Richard Gummere on "Classical Influences on American Colonial Literature," I became aware of some of Jefferson's ideas and of the profound influence on his thinking of his great teachers, James Maury, William Small, and George Wythe. But at that time I had no sense of the sheer richness of Jefferson's life, the extent to which his honed mind informed his total education — education used as Henry Adams later used the term to suggest total life experience.

Jefferson's mind was always in active voice. If reincarnated, he would, I think, be appalled by the passivity of life in contemporary American civilization. He would chide us and pity us for our lazy diversions and their attendant melancholy. He would be both fascinated and horrified by the endless proliferation of the gadgetry of our applied science, which is a development in part traceable to his own penchant for inventive tinkering. But I am confident that he never dreamed such gadgetry might someday clutter our psyches as well as our households.

Jefferson would be happier, I think, in observing the success of our constitutional and political system. The autocracies of most of the rest of the contemporary world would not surprise him. And he would be genuinely proud of the faithfulness of most Americans to the essential conditions of civility and political freedom, even if he would view with foreboding the growing cynicism that infects large sections of the contemporary body politic.

But these are all guesses and, in one sense, are futile fantasies. Jefferson had a great respect for modernity and believed that no generation should be bound by the dead hand of the past. This suggests that he would probably disown any attempts to use his concepts and precepts for either censure or praise of contemporary movements. The only thing of which we may be sure is that he would ask us to solve our own problems by using our minds creatively in the context of a politically free society. For Jefferson this was the ultimate purpose of education.

I wish to underscore this basic point. It is really the only central theme or theory in Jefferson's writings about education that appears to be still directly relevant. Most of Jefferson's specific educational assumptions and recommendations are, if taken in their appropriate historical context, starkly irrelevant to our present age. His task was to design an educational system to undergird political freedom in a wilderness. Ours is to design an educational system to preserve political freedom in a wildly elaborated technology. His task was to fashion an education suitable for national independence. Ours is to fashion an education suitable for a condition of global interdependence. His task was to construct an educational curriculum that would assist citizens in unlocking and exploiting natural resources. Ours is to remind citizens, through education, that, first, our natural resources are precious gifts that need prudent conservation, and, second, that we must live, not as exploiters of nature, but in loving symbiosis with other life and with nature generally. Jefferson's scientific tasks were largely empirical and taxonomic. Ours are largely analytic and syndetic. At the top of the agenda of his world was physical and legal engineering. Our agenda virtually begins and ends with psychological and social integration. His task was to discover laws and to affirm meaning. Ours is to rediscover law and to create meaning. Even his and our views of the relationship of education to social equality are at variance. He wanted geniuses raked annually from the "rubbish." We do not recognize human rubbish as a legitimate condition of a social order. He saw two classes, the laboring and the learned, deserving of differential schooling. We are beginning to see the baneful long-term consequences of this cruel and senseless dichotomy. Jefferson gave little thought to the education of women, blacks, Indians, or those who were handicapped. We could not ignore the educational needs of these segments of our population even if we were so disposed.

In terms of the philosophical matrix of educational purposes, he believed that advanced education should be tied solely to modernity and utility. We know, however, that, unless one is careful, the concepts of modernity and utility can be more stultifying than tradition and learning for the sake of learning. Daniel Boorstin points out in his book *The Lost World of Thomas Jefferson* that Jefferson's notions of modernity and usefulness tended to leave an educational legacy that was essentially "uncritical and conservative," whereas Harvard's more traditional emphasis on metaphysics and pure science made it "a center of intellectual ferment, a breeding ground for potent and revolutionary ideas, for new and pregnant systems of philosophy."[2] Whether Boorstin is right or wrong, Jefferson's notion of educational utility was far removed from the emerging concepts of educational utility today.

These are not minor gulfs that separate our world from the world of Jefferson. We pay him little homage by trying to overlay our painful and attenuated predicaments with eighteenth-century poultices.

To what, then, do we repair? What is there in Jefferson's life and letters that can, in some legitimate sense, become beacons of the past — beacons to illuminate our own possible future and the role of education in it?

I find four such beacon lights: first, Boorstin to the contrary notwithstanding, the general idea that education is a means, and must be related to what, in Jefferson's phrase, "is useful to us and at this day"; second, the idea that education is a highly legitimate claimant on public treasuries; third, the concept that education is a necessary handmaiden to effective citizenship; and, finally, the notion that education, as a lifelong encounter with the delights of the mind, is an end in itself.

Space permits only the briefest elaboration of these four propositions.

First, on education as a means, Jefferson would have resonated to the words of Alfred North Whitehead a century later: "Pedants sneer at an education that is useful, but if an education is not useful, what is it?"[3] Education for Jefferson was a utility. Why should one study history? Because it teaches of man's ambitions and their attendant dangers to the body politic. Why should one study Spanish? Because, as he wrote to his nephew Peter Carr, "Our future connection with Spain and Spanish America will render the language a valuable acquisition."[4] Why study medicine, anatomy, and surgery? Because they will help prepare doctors and will also help all students to live long and healthy lives.

Jefferson's proposed curriculum for the University of Virginia included botany, chemistry, zoology, agriculture, natural philosophy, geography, mathematics, astronomy, commerce, and law. This selection, bold in relation to the academic traditions of the eighteenth century, was directly related to Jefferson's views of utility. His compatriot, Benjamin Rush, put the matter succinctly: "We occupy a new country. Our principal business should be to explore and apply its resources, all of which press us to enterprise and haste. Under these circumstances, to spend four or five years in learning two dead languages is to turn our backs upon a goldmine in order to amuse ourselves catching butterflies."[5]

Boorstin is right that in his search for utility Jefferson tended to prescribe educational stereotypes. But Boorstin is, I believe, wrong in denigrating the generic concept of utility in education. In fact, Boorstin himself finds utility in seemingly inutile intellectual pursuits. The issue is not whether education should be useful, but what kinds of education are most useful for what ends.

Surely, if Jefferson were alive today, he would try to gear education to the frontiers of contemporary anxieties and opportunities. In my recent book, *The Purposes of Education,*[6] I have tried to indicate some of the contemporary needs that should be addressed by our educational and educative institutions and agencies. We know with increasing poignancy what our contemporary traumas and dangers include: loneliness, boredom, disaffection, the unfulfilling nature of work, a sense of uselessness among those young and old for whom society has no work, an absence of meaning in life for all too many people in their middle and older years, political cynicism, a surfeit of gadgets and diversions, continuing prejudice and injustice, only slightly contained global anarchy, a profligate waste of energy and resources, wanton disrespect for the health of the biosphere. And these are in addition to the daily frustrations of living in a technobureaucratic society in which simple coping is exasperating.

Educational utility today, if we would be true to Jefferson's spirit, is addressing these wildernesses of the soul and these malfunctions of our social order and discovering ways of overcoming them. That so many educational institutions and innovations are working on these frontiers is heartening. That so much education in our society remains traditional, and self-serving to educators and to comfortable establishments, is a cause for continuing reflection and anxiety.

What of the second proposition—Jefferson's concern for the public support of education? In 1779 Jefferson drafted a Bill for the More General Diffusion of Knowledge for the Virginia legislature. Perhaps the most dramatic and prescient aspect of the bill was his call for substantial public funding of the educational enterprise. It was, in truth, the predicted cost of his bill that killed it politically. The Virginia legislature in 1796 passed a bill that purported to provide free elementary education for all, but, as Jefferson reports, it was a fraud. The legislature "left it to the court of each county to determine for itself, when this act should be carried into execution, within [the] county. One provision of the bill was, that the expenses of these schools should be borne by the inhabitants of the county, everyone in proportion to his general tax rate. This would throw on wealth the education of the poor and [as Jefferson reported sorrowfully] the justices, being generally of the more wealthy class, were unwilling to incur that burden . . . ."[7] It is paradoxical that the legislature, by following Jefferson's own philosophy of decentralization, had effectively killed adequate financing for universal public schooling. This lesson clearly has modern implications for increased federal and state funding for education.

Later on, when Jefferson was President, he foresaw possible surpluses in the federal treasury. Public education headed Jefferson's list of targets for such a surplus, and he considered rewriting the Tenth Amendment to the Constitution to permit federal funds to help states and localities support education through what would today be called block-grant revenue sharing. Alas, neither the projected surplus nor the recommended adjustments in the Tenth Amendment materialized, but the vision and commitment were there.

Jefferson did, of course, win public funds to initiate the University of Virginia. None of this was easy. Jefferson's personal lobbyist on such matters in the state legislature, Joseph C. Cabell, wrote to his mentor time and again about the opposition of key legislators, like the chairman of the Committee of Schools and Colleges, to measures to finance the construction of the college buildings that Jefferson had designed. For some of us presently in the trade, the beginning of Cabell's letter of January 23, 1823, has a desolate familiarity: "You must be surprised at the slow progress of our bill. The tardiness of the movement is to be regretted."[8] But public money finally was approved for the university, following the example proximately set in time and place by the University of North Carolina.

Jefferson's passionate belief that the support of education is a legitimate and necessary public investment in the long-term freedom, prosperity, and well-being of the entire society is as needed today as it was during his lifetime. Agendas have changed; the generic proposition has not.

My third proposition relates to Jefferson's belief that education is a necessary handmaiden to effective citizenship—to political freedom. Many of Jefferson's most eloquent statements were directed at this theme. Jennings Wagoner has included a number of examples of such statements in his excellent pamphlet for Phi Delta Kappa, *Thomas Jefferson and the Education of a New Nation.* Following are three:

"I know of no safe depository of the ultimate powers of the society but the people themselves . . . if we think them not enlightened enough to exercise their control with a wholesome discretion, the remedy is not to take it from them, but to inform their discretion by education." Or, again, referring to political leadership, "these persons whom nature have endowed with genius and virtue, should be rendered by liberal education worthy to receive, and also to guard the sacred deposit of the rights and liberties of their fellow citizens." Or, most familiar of all, "if a nation expects to be ignorant and free, in a state of civilization, it expects what never was and never will be."[9]

One could dismiss such eloquence as facile sermonizing were it not for the luminous reinforcement of Jefferson's own life. Jefferson was always a reluctant politician. He hated what he called "the morbid rage of debate." The excesses of the political press, to use a modern idiom, "freaked him out." He frequently lamented that the calls of public service deflected him from what he called "the delightful paths of science." And yet he was a consummate citizen-statesman. Most of his mature life from the early 1770's to 1809 was spent in the service of his state and nation. He lacked flamboyant charisma, but he was an enormously effective committeeman. John Adams noted this ability during the Continental Congress. Though a silent member (on the floor), he was, according to Adams, "so prompt, frank, explicit, and decisive upon committee and in conversation, that he was soon acknowledged as one of the stronger members."[10]

Jefferson brought to his political tasks a wide-ranging and sharply honed mind. But he also brought a sense of noblesse oblige, of deep concern for the decent treatment of all, that, in Irving Howe's phrase, was "patrician in quality yet not aristocratic in bias."[11] I doubt that this nation can reassert its spirit or improve the tenor of its politics without some kind of Jeffersonian commitment to the public weal — some refurbished commitment by educated people to public probity and to the public interest. In this respect, Jefferson's own life is one of this nation's most precious legacies. I doubt that we ever needed the nourishment of its example more desperately than we do today.

Finally, what of Jefferson's demonstration that education is an end in itself — or, put in another way, that education is a means to psychic fullness and joy? He rarely articulated this particular theme. But, once again, his life was a vast laboratory experiment in the pursuit of happiness through the creative exercise of the mind. It was not that he lacked emotion. However arch and formal his well-known letter on "the battle between head and heart," there was nothing studied in the delightful abandon of his relationship with Maria Cosway in Paris, so sensitively described by Dumas Malone.[12] He was capable of far more varied aesthetic experiences than the classical geometry of his own architecture conveyed.

What is dazzling is the sheer energy of his constantly probing mind. He found the world of nature, the world of artifacts, and the world of ideas completely engrossing. His only book, *Notes on Virginia,* is a brilliant introduction to his virtuosity. But even a casual dip into his 50,000 letters gives one a sense of the richness of what the nineteenth century was to call "the furniture" of his mind. He was interested in the length of rainy seasons, the causes of disease, the strength of fabrics, the shape of ploughs, the structure of harpsichords, the properties of minerals. For eight years (in the 1790's), he tabulated with painful accuracy the earliest and latest appearance of thirty-seven vegetables on the Washington market. He was as fascinated by balloons as he was by butterflies. Not since Emperor Nero had a chief of state been more talented in both fine and practical arts.

Jefferson collected three impressive libraries during his lifetime. But he was neither an encyclopedist nor an antiquarian. He observed, he classified, he analyzed, in order to solve problems. Good Deist that he was, he believed that the universe was tidy and that science could unlock its mysteries to the endless instrumental benefit of mankind. But one gets the feeling that even if he could have predicted no practical outcomes, the sheer exhilaration of unlocking mysteries and classifying the helter-skelter of the cosmos would have kept him at it indefinitely. Why else would he have taken such pleasure at age seventy-six in noting "I am again a hard student"?[13] How else could one explain his endless delight in conversation and correspondence?

It is only strange that he did not articulate in terms of educational theory what was so deeply underscored by the example of his own life: the marvelously enriching effect upon human happiness of a full, lively, and aesthetically sensitive mind. Even when he confessed to being an enthusiast on the subject of the arts, he justified this intent on the grounds, not of intrinsic satisfaction, but of utility, of his objective "to improve the taste of [his] countrymen . . . ."[14] This leaves one with a sense of rationalization. Earlier in his life Jefferson thought that by going to college he would get "a more universal acquaintance which thereafter would be serviceable . . . ." But he failed to see what his brilliant life emphasized: that beyond facilitating direct service to others, an educated life is itself a thing of beauty, a hosanna to the Almighty, and, coming full circle, by its very example, a supreme indirect service to the happiness of the entire human race.

The four propositions — that education is a means to solving problems, a handmaiden to constructive citizenship, an end in itself, and an objective worthy of public support for all of these reasons — constitute the rich and pertinent legacy of Jefferson's life and letters to us. His memory does us honor. Let us honor it by appropriate word and deed.

NOTES

1. Plutarch, *Selected Lives and Essays* (Roslyn, N.Y.: Walter J. Black, 1951), p. xiv.

2. Daniel Boorstin, *The Lost World of Thomas Jefferson* (New York: Henry Holt, 1948), p. 225.

3. Alfred North Whitehead, *The Aims of Education* (New York: Macmillan, 1929), p. 2.

4. James B. Conant, *Thomas Jefferson and the Development of American Public Education* (Berkeley and Los Angeles: University of California Press, 1963), p. 100.

5. Boorstin, *Lost World of Thomas Jefferson,* p. 221.

6. Stephen K. Bailey, *The Purposes of Education* (Bloomington, Ind.: Phi Delta Kappa, 1976).

7. Cited in Conant, *Thomas Jefferson and the Development of American Public Education,* pp. 29-30.

8. *Ibid.,* p. 146.

9. Jennings L. Wagoner, Jr., *Thomas Jefferson and the Education of a New Nation* (Bloomington, Ind.: Phi Delta Kappa, 1976), pp. 20, 26, 39.

10. *Encyclopedia Britannica,* 1944 ed., s.v. "Jefferson, Thomas."

11. Irving Howe, *Politics and the Novel* (New York: Horizon Press, 1957), p. 162.

12. Dumas Malone, *Jefferson and His Time,* vol. 2, *Jefferson and the Rights of Man* (Boston: Little, Brown, 1951), pp. 70-75.

13. Wagoner, *Thomas Jefferson and the Education of a New Nation,* p. 15.

14. Malone, *Jefferson and the Rights of Man,* p. 87.

2 Thomas Jefferson and the Politics of Education

Jennings L. Wagoner, Jr.

Perhaps President John Kennedy came as close as anyone to capturing in one sentence the admiration most Americans have for Thomas Jefferson. Addressing an assembly of Nobel Prize laureates at a White House dinner, President Kennedy saluted his illustrious guests as representing "the most extraordinary collection of talents . . . that has ever been gathered together at the White House, with the possible exception of when Thomas Jefferson dined alone."[1]

President Kennedy was, of course, invoking an image of Jefferson as an exemplar of the American Renaissance man. As we look back across the centuries at Jefferson's many interests and accomplishments, we feel that little escaped his notice. Jefferson's greatness is compounded by the fact that he combined in one person the interests and talents of the scientist and the humanist, the political theorist and the shirt-sleeves politician, the agrarian and the cosmopolitan, the democrat and the aristocrat. Jefferson's taste for fine wines and good music was paralleled by his interest in improved farming techniques, the flora and fauna of the American wilderness, and the living conditions of men of all stations and races who inhabited the continent. His own love of freedom and desire for privacy were tempered by his willingness to devote his energies and his reputation to the demands and criticisms of public service. The meticulous detail that marked his architectural design of Monticello, the state capitol in Richmond, and eventually the buildings of the University of Virginia was equaled by

the care he gave to the drafting of numerous bills designed to eliminate privilege and to ensure the benefits of a republican form of government. Whether at any moment his attention was riveted on government, law, religion, education, architecture, or on the many branches
of science and philosophy, Jefferson devoted himself to practical detail
as well as to theory.

As varied as Jefferson's interests seemed to be, and as numerous as
were his activities and accomplishments, there was a pattern, a logic, a
unifying direction to his efforts, at least in the political sphere. Dumas
Malone has suggested that the best single clue to Jefferson's motives in
the Revolution and continuing throughout his entire career was his
concern for "the attainment and maintenance of liberty."[2] Indeed,
Jefferson's own epitaph, dictated by him, proclaims the three accomplishments of which he was most proud: author of the Declaration of
Independence, which proclaimed man's political freedom; author of
the Virginia Statute for Religious Freedom, which guaranteed religious liberty; and father of the University of Virginia, which was established as a shrine to intellectual freedom. Unlike the presidency or
other prestigious offices and honors that the people bestowed upon Jefferson, the achievements he considered his most important were his
benefactions to the people.

It is not difficult to concur with Jefferson's estimation of the real
and symbolic importance of the founding of the University of Virginia. One must, however, always keep in perspective both the political motivations and the long years of political struggle and numerous
defeats of larger education plans that preceded the university's founding. So revered is the Jeffersonian image in the popular mind today
that it becomes tempting to imagine that Jefferson "willed" that there
be a university and that his countrymen, out of deference to his status
and wisdom, were gratefully disposed to accept still another benefac-
tion from the Sage of Monticello. History records quite a different
story, however, and reveals that in Jefferson's day, no less than in our
own, politics, in terms both of purpose and process, was central to
educational considerations.

As Bailey has observed in Chapter 1, the political importance of
education was a matter of continuing concern to Jefferson. He was
convinced that neither declarations nor wars alone could ensure the
survival of a new nation founded upon lofty ideals of liberty, equality,
and popular government. A typical expression of this conviction is embodied in a letter to George Washington in 1786: "our liberty can

never be safe but in the hands of the people themselves, and that, too, of the people with a certain degree of instruction." It was no insignificant afterthought that prompted Jefferson to add: "This it is the business of the state to effect, and on a general plan."[3]

Jefferson's plan for a unified system of education in his native state was not realized during his lifetime. He first proposed a Bill for the More General Diffusion of Knowledge in 1779 and fought with a reluctant legislature for its passage for years thereafter. Arguments against the bill were many and varied, but then as now one consideration reigned supreme: money. James Madison informed Jefferson following a negative vote on the bill in 1786 that a leading objection to it was the expense, which was alleged to exceed the people's ability to pay.[4] Jefferson himself conceded that the reluctance of the people to bear the expense of the undertaking was doubtless a primary cause for the bill's defeat, but he remained convinced that the enlightenment of the people was too important to be so lightly dismissed. Within a year of the bill's rejection, Jefferson wrote to Madison: "I hope the education of the common people will be attended to; convinced that on their good sense we may rely with the most security for the preservation of a due degree of liberty."[5]

Jefferson could take little satisfaction from the passage in 1796 of a feeble bill that allowed the counties in Virginia the option of developing elementary schools if they so chose. He was no more successful in 1817 when he authored yet another comprehensive education bill that was also rejected by the state legislature. Jefferson's experiences with the Virginia legislature were paralleled by equally frustrating attempts to excite the federal Congress to action in behalf of education. As President, Jefferson expressed support for a constitutional amendment that could have made possible the creation of a national university. When the measure failed to win the endorsement of Congress, he rather philosophically consoled an advocate of the project by observing: "There is a snail-paced gait for the advance of new ideas on the general mind, under which we must acquiesce. A forty years' experience of popular assemblies has taught me that you must give them time for every step you take. If too hard pressed, they balk, and the machine retrogrades."[6] Through painful experience, Jefferson was giving voice to a fundamental lesson in the politics of education.

When Jefferson left the White House in 1809, he could boast no victories for any of his educational plans. He had gained in his knowledge of legislatures, however, and, even while involved in other affairs of state, had over the years kept abreast of educational currents and entertained varied strategies that gave promise of contributing at least in part to his larger plan. It might have been expected then that within a few years after retiring to Monticello Jefferson was again actively involved in the cause of education and in carrying through his plan to establish a high-quality university in his state.

It is possible here to provide only a brief glance at the sequence of events that eventually led to the founding of the University of Virginia. Enough can be said, however, to underscore our observation that Jefferson considered education as a political necessity in terms of the survival of the new nation. And perhaps we can get a glimpse as well of Jefferson as an astute politician, able at long last to realize an important segment of his larger educational plan and thus to render, as he termed it, his "last act of usefulness"[7] to his country.

The circumstances setting the stage for Jefferson's reentry into politics in behalf of education occurred during the spring of 1814. For some time a body of citizens in his native Albemarle County had periodically expressed interest in establishing a local academy. In 1803 a charter had been granted for an institution known as Albemarle Academy, but the school existed for years on paper only. The undertaking was being revived in 1814, and Jefferson was asked to join his nephew, Peter Carr, and others as a member of the board of trustees of the yet unborn institution. This Jefferson agreed to do, but it soon became apparent that he could not be content with the creation of an undistinguished secondary school. Jefferson confided to John Adams shortly after joining the board of Albemarle Academy: "When sobered by experience, I hope our successors will turn their attention to the advantages of education. I mean education of the broad scale, and not that of the petty *academies,* as they call themselves, which are starting up in every neighborhood . . . . I hope the necessity will, at length, be seen of establishing institutions, here, as in Europe, where every branch of science, useful at this day, may be taught in its highest degree."[8]

In the fall of 1814 Jefferson presented Carr with an elaborate proposal for a comprehensive educational system. Jefferson outlined in detail the range of studies he thought appropriate for each level or tier in his educational hierarchy and encouraged the trustees to envision not an academy but a college. The program of studies Jefferson felt appropriate for the college would at once encompass and surpass the work of the better secondary schools and colleges of the day and would reach into the realm of "professional" or university studies as well. Not only was Jefferson bypassing the proposed academy in favor of a college, but the college was to contain the seeds of a university, "in which each science is to be taught in the highest degree it has yet attained."[9]

Convincing the trustees of the Albemarle Academy of the merits of this more ambitious undertaking proved much easier than gaining legislative approval. Senator Joseph Cabell of Albemarle County carried the brunt of the legislative battles in behalf of Jefferson's measure. In February 1816, legislative assent was given a bill that changed the name of Albemarle Academy into a new institution, Central College.

James Monroe, James Madison, Cabell, and Jefferson were among those appointed by the governor as members of the board of visitors of Central College. The visitors took an option on a parcel of land on the outskirts of Charlottesville, literally within view of Monticello, and Jefferson quickly produced drawings for buildings and a layout of the grounds. Jefferson's design for an "academical village" with dormitories connected to distinct pavilions for each professorship and the whole arranged around an open square of grass and trees proved to be not hastily conceived. The idea had been in formation for at least fifteen years and was even suggested by Jefferson to the trustees of East Tennessee College in 1810 when they had sought his advice for the development of that institution.[10] There were to be further refinements of Jefferson's architectural and academic plans before the University of Virginia acquired its distinctive design, but there can be no question that Jefferson, long before charters began to give life to his vision, had been carefully at work considering both the style and substance worthy of the capstone of a complete educational system.

As construction began on Central College in 1817, Cabell continued his efforts in the legislature in behalf of Jefferson's total plan. Although Jefferson's comprehensive school bill was again defeated, Cabell did manage to win an authorization of $15,000 annually toward the support of a state university. The selection of an appropriate site for the proposed university and matters pertaining to governance were to be determined by a special commission appointed by the governor.

The governor, James Preston, a native of Albemarle County, did no disservice to Jefferson's ambitions for Central College when he appointed Jefferson and Madison to the commission charged with the task of organizing the institution and selecting a site. Jefferson, however, well aware of the difficulties that yet lay ahead, was dubious as to the wisdom of his now playing an overt role in a matter so crucial to the success of his plans. In a letter to Cabell, Jefferson confessed his anxieties:

As to myself, I should be ready to do anything in my power for the institution; but that is not the exact question. Would it promote the success of the institution most for me to be in or out of it? Out of it, I believe. It is still to depend ultimately on the will of the legislature; and that has its uncertainties. There are fanatics both in religion and politics who, without knowing me personally, have long been taught to consider me as a raw head and bloody bones, and as we can afford to lose no votes in that body, I do think that it would be better that you should be named for our district. Do not consider this as mock-modesty; it is the cool and deliberate act of my judgment. I believe the institution would be more popular without me than with me . . . .[11]

Jefferson had assumed a like posture a few years earlier when he recommended the name "Central College" to those who sought to honor him with "Jefferson College." In the instance of the nomination to the commission, however, Jefferson was prevailed upon to accept the appointment.

On August 1, 1818, the commission began its deliberations in a tavern at Rockfish Gap, a location west of Charlottesville and high in the Blue Ridge Mountains. Jefferson was chosen chairman of the group and immediately directed the commissioners' attention to the question of the best site. Those who, with Jefferson, favored Charlottesville and pointed with pride to nascent Central College as the logical foundation for the state university were not without opposition. Delegates from the Tidewater, loyal supporters of William and Mary, did not make the journey to Rockfish Gap, but supporters of Washington College in Lexington were there, and they were well prepared to fight for their location. Another faction favored Staunton, hoping that by capturing the university the city might also increase its chances of someday becoming the capital of the state.

Jefferson had anticipated the arguments advanced by the supporters of the other localities. During the months prior to the meeting, he had collected information from every county clerk in Virginia as to the distance between the local courthouse and other points, the condition of roads, and the population of each county. Jefferson laid before the commissioners a large map on which he had carefully charted the geographical and population centers of the state. With lines dividing the state from east to west and north to south, he demonstrated that, in terms of both distance and population, Charlottesville was the superior choice. Jefferson's earlier insistence that the new college be named

"Central" thus proved to be far more than an act of modesty. As if to clinch the matter, so at least tradition has it, Jefferson also produced a list of extraordinary length on which he had recorded the names of every person in Albemarle County who had reached the age of eighty. Not only was the area central, but it was an extremely healthy environment as well![12]

As to the other matters before the commission—developing a plan of governance, determining the number and description of professorships, recommending the range of studies appropriate to the university, and establishing a plan for the completion of the buildings—Jefferson again came forward with ideas already prepared. The final report signed by the twenty-one commissioners on August 4 had been in substance prepared by Jefferson months before.

The report was submitted to the General Assembly in December 1818, and Jefferson's fears about the uncertainties of legislative will proved well founded indeed. Sectional politics dominated the debates in the months that followed. Proposals and counterproposals of various combinations were put forward with the loyal Cabell, his health rapidly failing, endeavoring still to discharge Jefferson's behind-the-scenes strategies. In January 1819, a favorable vote finally gave birth to "Mr. Jefferson's University," to be completed under his watchful eye from the heights of Monticello.

Still another six years had to pass before Jefferson considered the institution ready to open. These years were marked by financial difficulties and continuing rounds of legislative battles for more appropriations. Jefferson's activity in superintending the construction of the university was matched only by his constant prodding of Cabell to secure more funds. Cabell's letters during this period reveal a loyal but often fatigued and embarrassed colleague, and he warned Jefferson that "The popular cry is, that there is too much finery and too much extravagance."[13]

Jefferson's plan was extravagant, and his buildings of studied classical design had run almost 50 percent above his estimate. Jefferson nonetheless held to his design, which blended the useful with the beautiful, and refused to compromise now that his efforts in behalf of a distinctive state university were so close to realization. His response in one instance to the possibility that excellence might have to yield to expediency was typical:

The great object of our aim from the beginning has been to make the establishment the most eminent in the United States, in order to draw to it the youth of every state, but especially of the South and West . . . . The opening of the institution in a half state of readiness would be the most fatal step which could be adopted. It would be an impatience defeating its own object by putting on a subordinate character in the outset, which never would be shaken off, instead of opening largely and in full system. Taking our stand on commanding ground at once will beckon everything to it, and a reputation once established will maintain itself for ages . . . . Courage and patience is the watchword.[14]

Jefferson's labors for over forty years gave ample testimony to his courage and patience as an educational statesman. He lived to see the university open its doors in March 1825 and, as rector, nursed the institution through its first year of life.

Although death ended Jefferson's activities in behalf of his university and his country on July 4, 1826, the institution he founded stands as a symbol of an accomplishment of singular importance, a living monument to his devotion to the cause of human liberty and happiness. Perhaps "Mr. Jefferson's University" can also serve as a constant reminder to all who labor in behalf of education that worthwhile struggles are seldom easily won and political considerations are never absent. New challenges dictate new responses in the political arena, and yet the challenges encountered by Jefferson reveal that political change is protean in nature: although the issues and context may change, the ingredients of the political process are constant.

NOTES

1. John F. Kennedy, as quoted by Merrill D. Peterson, *Thomas Jefferson and the New Nation: A Biography* (New York: Oxford University Press, 1970), p. 724.

2. Dumas Malone, *Jefferson and His Time*, vol. 1, *Jefferson the Virginian* (Boston: Little, Brown, 1948), p. 47.

3. Jefferson to Washington, January 4, 1786, in *The Papers of Thomas Jefferson*, ed. Julian P. Boyd, vol. 9 (Princeton, N.J.: Princeton University Press, 1950-   ), p. 151.

4. Madison to Jefferson, December 4, 1786, *ibid.*, vol. 10, p. 576.

5. Jefferson to Madison, December 20, 1787, *ibid.*, vol. 12, p. 442.

6. Jefferson to Joel Barlow, December 10, 1807, in *The Writings of Thomas Jefferson*, ed. Paul L. Ford, vol. 9 (New York: G.P. Putnam's Sons, 1892-1899), p. 169.

7. Jefferson to Judge Spencer Roande, March 9, 1821, *ibid.*, vol. 10, p. 189.

8. Jefferson to Adams, July 5, 1814, *ibid.*, vol. 9, p. 464.

9. Jefferson to Carr, September 7, 1814, in Nathaniel Francis Cabell, *Early History of the University of Virginia as Contained in the Letters of Thomas Jefferson and Joseph C. Cabell* (Richmond, Va.: J.W. Randolph, 1856), pp. 384-390.

10. Phillip Alexander Bruce, *History of the University of Virginia*, vol. 1 (New York: Macmillan, 1920), p. 179.

11. Jefferson to Cabell, February 26, 1818, in Cabell, *Early History of the University of Virginia,* p. 128.

12. Bruce, *History of the University of Virginia,* vol. 1, pp. 209-221. See also John S. Patton, *Jefferson, Cabell and the University of Virginia* (New York and Washington, D.C.: Neale Publishing Co., 1906), pp. 45-50; and Roy J. Honeywell, *The Educational Work of Thomas Jefferson* (Cambridge, Mass.: Harvard University Press, 1931), pp. 71-75.

13. Cabell to Jefferson, March 10, 1821, in Cabell, *Early History of the University of Virginia,* p. 211.

14. Jefferson to Cabell, December 28, 1822, *ibid.,* pp. 260-261.

PART II
Public Aspirations and Power Politics:
How Should the People Be Served?

The experiment fashioned by Jefferson and the other Founding Fathers, premised on the inalienable right of each citizen to enjoy life, liberty, and the pursuit of happiness, has endured. But there remains an uncomfortable awareness that for many in our nation the richness of the promise has not been realized, at least on a scale that seems adequate or just. The political dilemma of our time and in the years immediately ahead can thus be fashioned in terms of public aspirations and power politics: How much more can be done and should be done—given political and economic realities and uncertainties—toward providing competing segments of our population with the assistance each deems necessary to carry forward its interests? From what groups and toward what ends will future demands likely be made? Given present circumstances and guided by our best estimates of conditions in the decade ahead, what responses are likely from government to these demands and expectations? What is even more fundamental, how realistic is it to assume that public expectations can be met through existing structures and programs? In the simplest yet most demanding mode of framing the question, we must ask ourselves "how should the people be served?"

Nathan Glazer, coeditor of *The Public Interest,* and Frank Riessman, editor of *Social Policy,* undertake in the chapters that follow to examine, from their differing perspectives, how well or how badly basic values of a democratic society are being and might be served by existing public institutions and programs. As Glazer observes in his essay "On Serving the People," the role of the federal government has increased enormously in the area of social services since the early 1960's. In what would appear to be a response to the wishes of the people, government has undertaken in recent years to support massive programs designed to improve services to the people in such areas as education, housing, medical care, and employment. With the election of President Carter in 1976 and the continuing control of Congress by the Democratic party, additional increases in the level of federal spending seem likely in the years immediately ahead.

Glazer contends, however, that the tendency of the federal government to become more and more involved in our individual, institutional, and community affairs is not a direct consequence, election results not withstanding, of "public" wishes. Deficit spending, the power of the federal government to print more money, the responsiveness of various branches of government to different publics and agendas, and the growth in size and power of governmental agencies contribute in large measure to increased governmental activity in spite of public disillusionment with some recent human service programs and their attendant regulations and mounting costs.

Glazer argues that we are now at a crossroads in considering the scale and form of governmental actions. We are also, he maintains, uncertain about the fundamental principles that should guide public policy as we face the 1980's. In assessing recent trends, Glazer notes that governmental social policy has entered a new phase, one in which spending is being curtailed while regulation is being increased. Although the objectives of social programs are the same as in the earlier phase of massive spending, the tone of the "new age of regulation" is different in that intervention by regulation is frequently seen by those who must comply with federal directives as punitive and arbitrary as well as expensive and disruptive. We thus find ourselves, Glazer suggests, torn between competing impulses. While we are prone to resist further governmental intrusion into our lives and pocketbooks, we yet encourage government to continue its efforts to ensure a just and equal society. Glazer cautions that, as we struggle with this fundamental conflict, we weigh carefully the question of just how far government can be allowed to intrude into the lives of citizens before it expands to the point where the terms of the contest will be changed unalterably.

Riessman, who has focused his essay on "The Service Society and the Crisis in Education," shares many of the concerns expressed by Glazer. Both are concerned with the tendency of institutions and programs once established to become self-serving and expansive. Both lament the fact that increased expenditures, while politically designed to satisfy public aspirations, characteristically result in increased bureaucracies with disproportionately small results in terms of improved services.

Riessman explores the present state of ineffectiveness of agencies designed to serve the people by noting two major contradictions that beset human services in our society. The first contradiction is fashioned by the nature of our highly individualistic and competitive societal framework which "uses" programs designed to provide benefits to the people for other purposes such as social control, enhancing the power and prestige of government employees, and shoring up the economy. The second and interrelated contradiction derives from the bureaucratic formalism, impersonality, and rule-governed behavior that increasingly characterize the very agencies created for humanistic ends. The failure of many social programs has resulted, Riessman argues, from the adoption of methods of organization that may be suitable for business or the military, but seem counterproductive in the sphere of human service programs. Central, then, to Riessman's concern is the need to resolve the problem of organizing human service programs on a scale that will allow for efficiency and humaneness at the same time. Riessman holds that it is both possible and necessary for growth to occur in the "people services" or "human services" area at the same time that we experience contraction in industrial production. Not all growth, he argues, must be limited in the decade ahead.

To Riessman, the most promising avenue for improving human services lies in expanding opportunities for consumers or clients to become more directly involved in programs designed for their benefit. Outlining a "strength-based model" for improving human services, Riessman optimistically forecasts the possibility of using human resources more efficiently and meaningfully toward the end of a greatly improved quality of life. From Riessman's perspective, the tension surrounding increased governmental intervention and improved social services can be resolved by enabling the people themselves to play a greater role in managing their own affairs.

3 On Serving the People

Nathan Glazer

In the 1976 election campaign one message emerged sharply: Governor Carter (or if not Carter, then the Democratic party) believed in a more activist governmental role than did President Ford. The exact dimensions of this activism were unclear. Certainly it included governmental intervention in the economy to increase the number of jobs. Perhaps it meant direct provision of jobs by government. Certainly it meant national health insurance. And certainly—as reflected in Carter's confidence and Ford's uneasiness in appearing before groups of teachers and educators—it meant that the plateau we had reached a few years ago in the level of federal assistance to education, at all levels, would rise.

The closeness of the election also indicated that we were at a crossroads in considering what the next stage of governmental action would look like. We were unclear about its scale. We were unclear about its form. And, I would argue, we were unclear about the fundamental principles that should guide it. The first two issues are perhaps easier to deal with.

THE SCALE OF GOVERNMENTAL ACTION

We have arrived at a situation in this country in which approximately 44 percent of the gross national product is collected by government for governmental purposes and for redistribution at the federal,

state, and local levels. I would be the last to place in opposition to each
other in any crude way "government" versus "people," to say that what
"government" does not take in taxes to spend as "it" wishes, "people"
have to spend as "they" wish. Government—in this country, at
least—is people, and it reflects in broad measure what people want
and what people have decided can be done better collectively than individually. But, of course, government is not only people. The way in
which individual choices in the form of votes, organization, and
money aggregate to select and influence a group of representatives inevitably means that government, at the legislative level, is not a carbon copy of what people want; nor, of course, was it ever the intention
of the founders that it should be. Nor is it ever the case that the action
of the executive, elected by the people, is a carbon copy of majority
views; it could not be, for the majority that elects the executive is too
divided for its views to be reflected in any simple way. Nor is it ever the
case that the increasing number of those who work for government are
simply the servants of legislatures and executives; they develop their
own interests, their own values, their own outlook, and reflect the generations from which they were predominantly selected and the way
outlooks of those generations were shaped by education and by events.
Government employees are also subject to the direct and indirect
intervention of "people" aggregated in different ways for different
purposes.

All this, though undoubtedly too abstract, is perfectly obvious.
The consequence is that just as we must reject the simpleminded view,
which places government—and the governmental share of the
GNP—in opposition to the people, so must we reject the alternative
view, which asserts that, if government spends 44 percent of the GNP,
that is what people want. And if the share climbs to above 60 percent,
as it may have in Sweden, that is what people want, too.

In particular, the scale of government is being affected by the distinctive interests of the employees of government, of whom the largest
number are teachers. If we increase teachers' compensation, it is not
simply because the people have decided to spend more on education.
Indeed, increasing teachers' compensation is not exactly the same as
spending more on education. We have certainly been doing the first.
As teachers' income and power have risen, there has been a concurrent, striking change. I present it for the moment as a hypothesis, but
I believe it is true: when teachers were poorly organized, inadequately
paid, more closely under the thumb of school boards, and had fewer

rights, whether determined by union power or judicial rulings, public opinion perceived a harmony between the interests of teachers and students. As the power and income of teachers have risen, the public has increasingly seen a disharmony in those interests. Where teachers have become strongest — and best rewarded — the sense of disharmony, of almost a contradiction between the interests of teachers and parents and pupils, is strongest.

We may find the same attitudes toward doctors. When doctors' incomes were based on simple fees for service, balanced by some measure of free or charitable contribution, attitudes toward doctors seemed, on the whole, to be more positive than they are today. There has been a preception that teachers, and doctors, as they become more effectively organized to achieve a larger share of income and power, are less committed to their professional objectives. I leave aside the question whether this perception actually reflects any change in professional ethics. It appears clear, however, that if the main things people read in newspapers or hear on television are that teachers are striking, demanding a shorter day or smaller classes and resisting reduction in staffs as the number of students declines, or that the tax rate must increase because teachers are receiving higher wages, this will affect the public image of teachers. I am not suggesting, of course, that teachers should relinquish their organization and their power. Obviously they will not. I am describing what I think must happen if service-oriented public servants are increasingly seen as devoting their energy to their rewards rather than to their services. I would argue that this perception also reflects another reality: that these groups are truly powerful and that their interests can be placed in opposition to others' interests.

In Boston, while the schools were under court order, it seemed that the only way to get anything done was to add new personnel for new functions. Thus, as the number of children in the schools dropped, the resources demanded by the schools rose precipitously. In New York, teachers had sufficient power to have the state legislature mandate that their share of the city budget would never drop. Certain distortions have, in fact, developed by which the scale of government is affected so strongly by the employees of government — expanded in number, strengthened in organization, sophisticated in the uses of power — that the scale is no longer responsive, in the degree to which it perhaps once was, to what the electorate and their representatives broadly want.

One effect of this development has been to increase rapidly the rewards of public employees in comparison to those in the private sector. In addition to the greater security and fringe benefits of public employment, they have now generally achieved higher salaries. There is no reason to think that this process can be easily reversed. It has taken something akin to bankruptcy to reduce the scale of government in some central cities. The favored course has been to reduce the number of city employees rather than to reduce their salaries, benefits, and pensions to the levels that prevail in the private sector. This has many consequences. It reduces the services available. It tends to push the private sector into those parts of the country, particularly the South and the Southwest, where the strength of civic employee organizations is not yet so great, their benefits not yet so advantageous, and their impact on urban finances not yet so damaging.

The dynamics of the scale of government are quite different at the federal than at the state and local level. The reason is simple: the federal government can print money, and the states and cities cannot. By definition, the federal government cannot go bankrupt. If Congress and the President agree on the appropriation levels, there is no one to say nay, regardless of the size of the budget. Thus at the federal level we cannot expect those sharp reversals in the numbers of employees that we see at the state and municipal levels in some places. On the other hand, a nationally elected President and a nationally elected Congress are far more powerful in relation to federal employees than are mayors and councils—or even governors and legislatures—in relation to municipal and state employees. Thus, there is a considerable range of freedom at the federal government level. We can indeed increase the size of government, and perhaps we can decrease it (though we have seen no recent examples of this).

The question of the scale of government is not a simple matter, and I have argued that an increase in the scale does not necessarily mean that the people demand more services. The scale of government may increase because government employees (at the municipal and state level) have become already and insensibly so numerous, so well organized, and so clear in their objectives that the scale of government increases regardless of what the people want. At the federal level, scale increases for another reason: since the federal government can insouciantly run deficits of $60 billion dollars or more, there is little restraint on Congress to vote in a way that would satisfy its tastes, consciences, or constituents, and the President and the executive offices also find it difficult to restrain themselves. They would only look like curmudgeons insensitive to the pleas of the needy.

The increase in the scale of government has some unexpected consequences. In the state where I live, Massachusetts, one can cross the border to New Hampshire and escape both sales and income taxes. New Hampshire is considered a rockbound Republican state indifferent to human needs, but I am not aware that there is any more suffering in New Hampshire than there is in Massachusetts. Perhaps that is because those who would suffer under New Hampshire's refusal to provide handsome welfare and medicaid benefits, bilingual instruction, and special assistance for the handicapped child simply move across the border to Massachusetts to get all these benefits. If one extrapolates the effects, one sees that Massachusetts loses taxpayers and industry and acquires, in turn, those whose demands on the public resources are greatest. New York is in the same situation. By moving to Connecticut or New Jersey, one can considerably improve one's economic position, even if one cannot do quite as well as moving to New Hampshire. One can do best, overall, by moving to the South or the Southwest. The crisis of the Northeast is not only a crisis of old cities, cold winters, and high fuel costs, but also a crisis of the scale of government, which has become much greater than in the South and Southwest.

One answer to this problem is to increase the scale of government at the national level. It is suggested that the national government pick up the huge out-of-line costs for welfare and medicaid, for expanded systems of public higher education, for the public schools of such states as New York and such cities as Boston. But will it? Can the Carter administration really justify paying two or three times more in welfare and education costs to some cities and states than it pays to others? Can it possibly find the formulas that would justify the enormous costs of government in New York?

I recall an instructive demonstration by a brilliant young public policy analyst. He had been employed in the New York City Budget Bureau, which under Mayor John Lindsay became by far the largest and most sophisticated of its kind in any city in the country. The problem was to determine what formula for revenue sharing would bring New York City some appreciable relief. Should there be a double count for poverty? For age? For density? For tax effort? Everything was tried, and no matter what formula or combination of formulas was used, the federal contribution would be insignificant compared to the

already enormous size of the city budget. It was determined that the
only formula that would help New York was one that gave each city
and state federal aid in proportion to how much each had already
spent. To those who spent the most, the most aid would go. The
reasoned conclusion is not far from the current common wisdom concerning the way high-spending states such as New York may be
assisted. I do not believe, however, that this formula was ever seriously
proposed, and it is doubtful that any administration or Congress could
possibly go along with such a scheme. One recalls President Ford's asking why the rest of the country, which pays tuition to attend public
colleges and universities, should assist New York City when it refused
to charge tuition for its public higher education.

One suspects, nevertheless, that, despite these restraints, the irre-
sistibly attractive power to print money, combined with a new and activist administration, will lead to another increase in the level of federal spending. With what effect? It is necessary to turn to the next
issue—the effectiveness of services—to get some light on this matter.

THE FORM OF GOVERNMENTAL SERVICES

The issue of the scale of government at the federal level is determined in part by some judgment as to the effectiveness of government.
This is a large question on which mountains of research have accumulated in the past ten years. I would like to discuss this question from a
narrow point of view: effectiveness depends in part on the objectives
one sets. Some objectives, by their nature, are easy to attain, such as
the objective of increasing expenditures and employees to deliver
health or education services at a particular rate. Once we phrase objectives in another form—improving the actual level of public health
and education—our problem becomes much more difficult. Such objectives, which involve the attaining of real goals, seem to involve a
much greater intrusion into people's lives than objectives phrased in
terms of money and employees.

The question becomes, then, what should be the *form* of government services? How far into the reshaping of individuals, institutions,
and communities should government go? How far in truth can it go?
In the early 1960's, the form of federal government expenditures for
social services began to change rapidly. Thus, at first, a situation prevailed in which there were broad programs with a relatively low
threshhold of discretion by government agents. Then we moved into
programs designed specifically to attack complex problems that re-

quired high levels of discretion by government agents. Consider the pattern of federal government services in the early 1960's: unemployment insurance based on entitlement through work; public housing based on qualification by cities and entitlement through income by tenants; no significant federal role in health care; a relatively small reimbursement role to states in Aid to Families with Dependent Children; a very limited role of the federal government in education, and a more substantial role in supporting research in higher education. From these programs that entailed minimal discretion, we went on to programs that, on the whole, increased the discretion of governmental agents in order to increase, we thought, their effectiveness in attacking complex social problems. For example, the Social Security Administration became more than an insurance agency. It was given various social functions that were much more complicated than its earlier charter, in particular medicare. Public housing became elaborated into a complex of programs to achieve various objectives or at least attempt to: family problems, integration, neighborhood improvement. The Federal Housing Administration, too, became more than an insurance program as it was required to get involved in insuring socially beneficial projects at rates lower than those prevailing at the time. It was much less successful in this area than in performing its straight insurance functions. Totally new programs, such as the poverty program and the model cities program, showed the greatest degree of expansion of discretion. They took the form of "contests," in which communities and groups competed, and government employees decided who had won and who should be funded. Many new manpower training programs were launched, each of which involved great discretionary powers in their funding.

To some extent, the same thing happened in education, but in that area the expansion of federal funding was through fairly strict formulas which, whatever their limitations, actually reduced discretion. This was particularly true of Title I of the Elementary and Secondary Education Act and of the decision in the Nixon years to move toward student loans and grants in higher education. From the point of view of the individual school district and the individual student or college, there is still far too much discretion in the hands of federal officials. From a larger point of view, however, these programs, in particular the higher education programs, represent a withdrawal of government from the high ground in which it attempted to shape people and institutions to a lower ground on which it simply provides support.

There have been other evidences of the newer form of government services replacing those of the 1960's: for example, block grants to cities and states, for general purposes and for manpower and community development. Efforts by the Nixon and Ford administrations to replace the great degree of discretion on the part of federal officials in granting or withholding funds for social purposes turned out, however, to be extremely difficult. Congress—and many people putting pressure on it—still felt the need to get deeper into social problems and to attack them at ever more fundamental levels. Thus to each of the block-grant programs various requirements were attached that made it onerous for recipients to get and spend the money and for the government to distribute it.

We are now uncertain how to evaluate the great period of governmental discretion in the later 1960's, and this is reflected in our uncertainty over what kinds of programs we should launch. One point of view is expressed by Governor Edmund Brown of California: do less, exercise care in what we do, avoid new governmental bureaucracies because we will never get rid of them, and be particularly suspicious of strategies that provide services because this kind of support goes to the servicers, with doubtful and uncertain effect on those to be serviced.

We have moved through a number of interesting phases in our thinking about the form of social services, including education. The first notion was broad general support. In the sphere of education, in which there is a strong local and state tradition, this seemed to be the most reasonable way of tapping federal aid for schools. For higher education, on the other hand, there developed a system of specific grants and contracts, which became very important for the major institutions. This is where we stood in the earlier 1960's. The new thinking, which, many feel, reflected a premature hubris on the part of social policy analysts, was to direct programs toward specific problems, such as the poverty program, community action, model cities, and the like. When federal aid for elementary and secondary education materialized, it was, for the most part, general formula support, but was aimed at a specific target group, the poor. The degree of discretion exercised by federal officials in the area of higher education was reduced as the main volume of federal aid shifted from loans and grants for research and facilities to direct support of students.

Now a third phase seems to be developing, one suggested by my reference to Governor Brown. Many people today are against both new broad-gauged formula support (except for health care) and against throwing money at specific social problems. Does that mean that government simply withdraws from problems? It does not. It simply means that more and more people think the right approach is for government to require the ends it wants through regulation without supplying any more money for the purpose, except perhaps for regulation itself and the attendant litigation. Bob Kuttner caught the mood perfectly in a commentary in the *New York Times* on the eve of the presidential election (November 1, 1976):

Several state administrations now contain a new breed of reformer, properly skeptical of more programs and forced by a paucity of resources to become more resourceful.

California, for example, curbs spending but enacts laws recognizing farm-worker unions and protecting its coastline from exploitation. Vermont changes its tax code to discourage land speculation. A number of states—Colorado, primarily, but also Massachusetts—are trying to get more money into central cities and slum areas by forcing their banks to invest there.

Kuttner pointed out a number of reasons for this shift, from the absence of money and resistance by taxpayers to higher taxes. "Many of the social programs," he wrote, "are turkeys."

FUNDAMENTAL PRINCIPLES FOR GOVERNMENTAL ACTION

Thus we find social policy entering into a new phase—a phase of regulation, with some rather serious attendant problems. It is these problems that I have in mind when I speak of the "fundamental principles" that affect how the people will be served. In each area of regulation, of course, one person's fundamental principle is nothing of the sort to the next man or woman. The fact that we have extensive governmental regulation in the fields of occupational safety, environment, and auto and highway safety reflects a broad consensus that we should act in these areas. In the earlier phase of social policy, government intruded benevolently with its money in order to improve people and to overcome their problems. In the new phase, there is governmental regulation without money for new programs, though, of course, some programs have involved substantial quantities of money to assist in reaching the standards set by legislation or regulation.

We still think of these regulations as a way of improving people and society. There is little question, however, that the *tone* has changed. The new regulations are punitive and preemptory, even though the objectives are in one sense the same. There is, for example, a great difference between a work program that intends to improve the work effectiveness of minorities, and goals and timetables that tell employers how many individuals from minority groups they should be hiring. The new age of regulation seems to have produced innumerable examples of what appears to be arbitrary governmental power. These examples include the need for outdoor toilets in enormous western wheat fields, the banning of boys' choirs, and the closing of a subway station in the new system in Washington because it does not yet have access for the handicapped. In the last example the judge apparently acted on the principle that one way to get justice for the handicapped was to penalize both handicapped and unhandicapped equally. Oddity and excess are, of course, present in any government and in any system of bureaucratic rules. This brings us back to the fact that government is not exactly the people; that, as we move into the sphere of increased regulation, some people will become specialized as regulators, developing their own distinctive corporate outlook, and the general run of people, who may have supported the initial legislation enthusiastically, will get regulated.

In the new age of regulation, the government imposes a cost on an institution or individual, either on the basis of simple governmental authority (such as the need to keep records and submit income tax returns, to maintain occupational safety, and to adhere to environmental requirements) or as a necessary quid pro quo for governmental assistance or governmental business (for example, reporting to the Office of Civil Rights on racial and ethnic distribution of students in order to be eligible for federal funds or fulfilling Affirmative Action requirements to get government contracts). Institutions are not happy about this rising level of governmental intrusiveness, which is expensive, disruptive, troublesome, and may often, in the minds of the persons involved, have little relationship to the ends the requirements are intended to serve. And yet in the past ten years we have grown accustomed to an enormous increase in governmental power to regulate, and few people with any knowledge of the situation really believe there can be any rollback. If it did not happen under Nixon and Ford, can it possibly happen under Carter? It is interesting that this increase in power does not really reflect any increased faith in government, as did the extension of governmental powers during the New Deal. Thus, even though we became suspicious of government, we nevertheless increasingly gave it more power to regulate our lives. How did this come about?

We must disaggregate the "we's" in order to understand this situation. The "we" who became suspicious and cynical of government, according to the public opinion polls, were the people in general. The "we" who expanded the powers of government were, in the first place, the Congress, which passed into legislation the new demands for equality for racial and ethnic groups and for women, for a greater governmental role in safety, health, and environment. But, to even a greater extent, it was a different "we" that expanded the powers of government — the administrative agencies that formulated and then imposed the detailed requirements that implemented general legislation for equality. Congress often was upset by the regulations that implemented its legislation. It was never the case that the administrative agencies did *less* than Congress intended; it was always the case that they did *more*. Why was this so?

One reason was that after Congress acted, and the administrative agencies took over, pressure did not cease. But now the pressure came unrelentingly from those interest groups that wanted to see the greatest possible reach of government intervention. Thus, for example, when Congress decreed equality for women, it never expected that it meant that there could not be different regulations on campus for men and women, or that they would have to attend gym classes together. Indeed, when these regulations came back to Congress for review a number of people were shocked. But then women's groups put so much pressure on Congress, in what was called one of the great lobbying efforts, that it did the easier thing — nothing — and let the regulations come into play. Congressmen may even benefit from supinely accepting regulations they do not like. First, they do not have to face the difficult decision to resist a powerful lobbying effort. Then they can write nasty letters to the Secretary of the Department of Health, Education, and Welfare when a boys' chorus is banned, or mother-daughter events are outlawed, and appear to be heroes opposing the bureaucrats, whom they were not heroic enough to oppose at the time that it might have counted.

We have not fully disaggregated the "we" who do these things, for there is another group that is, in a sense, a "we": the judges and the courts. They, too, take the general statements of Congress and, apparently convinced by advocates, are willing to extend them far beyond what Congress intended and indeed even in direct contradiction to what Congress writes in its legislation. For this reason, the Civil Rights Act of 1964 is taken to support desegregation requirements whose objective is racial balance and employment requirements with the same objective, despite clear prohibitions against both interpretations.

Yet it would be "improper" to say the "we's" who oppose busing or racial requirements in employment are really different from the "we's" who require it. In most of us, there struggle two conceptions of the proper role of government. We have never quite resolved that struggle. Thus Congressman James O'Hara, who tried to limit the HEW regulations on sex equality in education and who has done the most to ventilate the issue of Affirmative Action in higher education, was defeated by Congressman Donald Riegle, who represents the liberal "we," despite the fact most voters probably agreed with O'Hara on these issues. Riegle then went on to defeat Congressman Marvin Esch for the Senate. Esch is the congressman whose name is attached to what is potentially the most effective legislation to date limiting judges' power to order large-scale assignment to schools on the basis of race. And all this took place in Michigan, which was a few short years ago so agitated by the issue of busing.

I have suggested that in this new stage of government regulation, to impose goals that, in some forms, most of us agree on — aid to minorities, the handicapped, women, the environment — fundamental principles are raised. I have not, however, said what they are. But, to speak of "fundamental principles" is only a way of saying one is worried. One has in mind the issue of how much government should take upon itself to correct. One has in mind the autonomy of certain institutions that bend willy-nilly to objectives that are declared overriding. One has in mind above all other matters the fine structure of society, present in families, ethnic groups, neighborhoods, and social groups. As a result of this structure, some people are ambitious, and others are not, some people think it is terrible to have illegitimate children, and others accept it as a norm, and some people like school and do well, and others dislike it and do badly.

We are impatient with this fine structure. We call on government to achieve things by fiat that in the past were achieved, if at all, at length and in mysterious ways. Of course, when I speak thus of "fundamental principles," I am expressing certain conservative points of view as to how much government can do, and how much it should do, though I realize I have barely gone into any argument that would permit me to draw a line asserting government should go so far and no further. (I have gone into greater detail, for some issues, in my book *Affirmative Discrimination.*) But for the summary purposes here it is perhaps enough to sound the note of caution with which I hope to restrain the overgenerous and oversanguine impulses of humanity.

And so we have the two "we's"—the "we" that says government should stay out of our business, stop spending our money, and stop intruding into our lives, and the "we" that says government must continue doing so in order to ensure a just and equal society. One must record that the second "we" scored a victory over the first "we" in November 1976. The two "we's" presumably still live within most American breasts, still struggle within the society, with at times one dominant, at other times the other. One can only hope that the struggle remains a fair one and that fears are unjustified that the terms of the combat will be changed unalterably if the government should become much expanded in response to the urgings of the second "we."

4 The Service Society and the Crisis in Education

Frank Riessman

Various appellations have been used to describe America since World War II. Such terms as "postscarcity" and "postindustrial," for example, seek to capture the essence of changes occurring in the economic and social life of the country. Other terms—the "service economy" or "human-service society"—perhaps more nearly reveal the basic concerns of our age.

The measurement criteria for labeling an era are hardly standardized, but one can note a variety of developments that make a case for the term "service." These include: the growing percentage of the labor force engaged in such work; the increase in such services (paid and unpaid) delivered in terms of both numbers of recipients and the amount they consume; the importance of such services in terms of their affording access to other benefits (for example, the role of education, or of at least the credential-granting role of educational institutions, in providing access to employment and thence to income); and the attention given by the public and the media to the human service institutions, their employers, and their consumers.

Victor Fuchs's working description of service "industries" captures much of our structure. He states that "most of the industries in it are manned [*sic*] by white-collar workers, that most of the industries are labor intensive, that most deal with the consumer, and that nearly all of them produce an intangible product." Fuchs is suggesting, in effect, four characteristics of services: the composition of their work

43

force, labor intensivity, closeness to the consumer, and lack of a tangible product. Closeness to the consumer and intangibility are key qualities. Sidney Fine's categorization of work as involving either people-to-people, people-to-data, or people-to-things relationships captures our meaning in its people-to-people formulation. One can see this best in the human services, where to these characteristics we add that of their beneficial intent, a quality aspired to though not always achieved.

The human service sector differs from the industrial sector in ways that are vitally important to the character and quality of the service sector. Its functions are ostensibly initiated to produce benefits for the recipient, and they are explicitly relational and interpersonal, creating a multiplier effect (that is, they produce an impact far beyond the numbers employed in the service area).

It is the common characteristics of the human service occupations that are the most interesting. Perhaps the best way to examine these characteristics is to juxtapose the human service occupations, which are largely in the public sector, against the private-goods-producing sector. At one level, these differences can best be seen in terms of the relationship of each sector's products to its consumers. In the human services, consumers have a right to the service and a right to participate in decisions affecting the service; there is a public concern for the quality of the service; and, increasingly, the quality of the service is not a function of an individual's ability to pay. For example, the right to an education, which has long been recognized, is now being expanded to include the handicapped; the role of consumers has been accelerated in a wide range of human service programs; and a new concept of state responsibility for equality of educational services is being developed. Part of this relates, of course, to the fact that those who deliver the service are supported through public funds, though they may not actually be public employees. Even when this is not the case, however, there is some sense of the rights of the service consumer.

For the workers, the central feature of the work is serving people. However poorly the function is performed, there is an ethos of service and commitment in the work. Though human service workers may sometimes fail to live up to proclamations of service to others, one could hardly deny that the attitude of a teacher toward a student is qualitatively different from that of a production-line worker toward an engine mount.

Services are essentially concerned with people and with interaction among people, and it is this simple dimension that subtly but pervasively affects major value themes of our era. These themes are deeply concerned with self and relationships with others: expression; inner life, growth, and development; expansion of consciousness; sex; participation; encounters. Services (and human services are the most pristine form of services) are characterized by individualization. Thus, the great reaction in our society today is directed against the impersonal, the cold, the formal, the bureaucratic, the rule-oriented action that is not flexible, individual, specific, personal.

MAKING THE HUMAN SERVICES PRODUCTIVE: WHY IS IT IMPORTANT?

It is difficult to conceive of a service society advancing very far without a significant qualitative improvement in the character of the human services. These services, after all, are the hub around which the ethos of the service society revolves. Thus far in the emergence of the service sector there has been a marked increase in consciousness about the services, particularly about their inadequacies, but there has as yet been no qualitative leap in the development of the services.

Two major contradictions beset human services and frame all their specific dimensions. The first contradiction is between the intrinsic thrust of the services, which is to provide benefits for people and improve their welfare, and the societal framework, which is highly individualistic and competitive and in which the services are used for all kinds of other purposes — shoring up the economy, controlling people's rebelliousness, providing status to a professional stratum, and so on. The second contradiction, which often interweaves with the first, is between the tremendous expansion in scope and scale of the services within a highly impersonal bureaucracy and the personal, human-oriented nature of the activities. Various bureaucratic characteristics, especially formalism, impersonality, and rigid rules, run counter to activities that have humanistic ends and require interpersonal processes. Methods of organization that are suitable in factories, the army, and offices may be particularly unsuitable for human services, even when these services grow to mammoth proportions.

It is obvious that the traditions, training, and historic experience of human service workers, which have been primarily in small, relatively autonomous settings, have not prepared them for functioning in large bureaucratic contexts characterized by hierarchy and strict controls. These workers resist in many ways the industrialization of their occupations. This industrialization involves attempts to organize their work along traditional lines; to measure it in these terms, as in the GNP; and to improve or reorganize it by using managerial techniques that are, at best, relevant for nonservice occupational spheres in which interpersonal relations are not the end product. It is not surprising, of course, that, as difficulties have appeared in the large-scale management of human services, countless attempts have been made to impose industrial modes on the service sectors.

One thing is quite clear: we have not resolved the problem of how to organize human services on a large scale, while at the same time maintaining their humaneness and increasing their efficiency. This problem is further magnified by the first contradiction, the fact that bureaucratization is taking place in a context characterized by anarchy, chaos, confusion, and the manipulation of the services for various purposes that have nothing to do with serving humanity.

It is necessary, therefore, to develop quite different perspectives in the area of human services. These perspectives must emphasize the consumer-intensive character of the services and build organization and management around this theme rather than either abstract managerial principles or principles derived from the industrial sector. We must develop, furthermore, a strategy for human services that relates to the societal contradictions in which the service society is emerging. Thus, we cannot simply project a vision of how the services could be more efficient, beneficial, and humanistic in the abstract. We must, rather, deepen our consciousness of service to include the need for major societal reorganization if the services are really to fulfill their potential.

In light of the growing environmental crises, it seems likely that, if we are to survive, increasing numbers of people will be employed in work that does not deplete our resources and pollute our surroundings. Service work, particularly human service work, fits this requirement. If the entire life-style of people changes drastically, there will be a greater need for services that are less dependent on automobiles, airplanes, and machines.

This new direction provides a whole new agenda for services — both their production and consumption. It should lead to a tremendous broadening of the growth and development services: lifetime education, new forms of recreation, new therapeutic forms, preventive medicine, marriage encounters, sex therapy, new religious mind-expanding experiences, special services for the dying, the development of all kinds of groups, family planning services, day-care centers. The services of the future will go far beyond health, education, and welfare and should involve the consumer to a greater degree than in the past.

INEFFECTIVENESS OF THE SERVICES

One can group the failures, ineffectiveness, and inefficiency of the services in four categories.

1. Large numbers of people who need services simply do not get them. The list of the unserved is almost as long as that of the services themselves. There are, for example, vast numbers suffering from chronic illnesses who are not treated (23 million suffering from hypertension,[2] the nearly 50 percent of diabetics who are "hidden,"[3] the 9 million alcoholics[4]).

2. Many who receive services do not benefit by them, as evidenced, for example, by the low reading and low achievement scores of growing numbers of schoolchildren.[5] Dropouts and pushouts,[6] too, are often a result of inadequacies in the service system. Recidivism among former prisoners is so high as to have produced the label "revolving door jails."[7] And, those few addicts who are treated rarely are rehabilitated.[8]

3. The services are poorly organized and designed. We have, at best, a hospital-based medical care system, not a community-based one (with the hospital as a backup resource for the relatively rare instances where its use is warranted). The welfare system makes dependent those who could be independent by failing to provide jobs for those who need them. Efforts that would serve people better are shunned because they do not fit the professional bureaucratic model, which stresses self-help efforts. Practices shown to be effective on a small scale usually are not expanded to a wider audience; in rare instances when expansion does occur, the practices are so watered down that they lose their effectiveness.

4. Much of the practice is inadequate and biased. In all the services, as in society as a whole, racism and sexism are dominant factors both in terms of how consumers are treated and in the roles servers play. The services are also overprofessionalized, self-serving, elitist, highly susceptible to jargon, and, at best, accountable to peers. The practice often ignores, when not actually acting counter to, the culture of the consumers.

Recognizing that human services are ineffective in many ways leads to the question of how to change and improve them, particularly in a society that does not encourage the fullest development of these services for the benefit of people. That is, the fact that these services are used for so many purposes besides the benefit of the recipient frequently produces effects that actually interfere with their potentially humane, beneficial qualities. These qualities are hampered to the extent that services are used to socialize people to the status quo, to quell dissent, to divert people with passive recreational activities, to enhance the status and power of those who provide the services, and to maintain class, race, and sex differentials.

In attempting to develop a strategy for reforming services in our society, we should consider carefully the basic context in which the services are performed. This context sets certain limits that will have to be overcome if the services are to flourish and if a genuine human service society is to emerge. Our strategy should, therefore, have two goals: to increase the quantity and improve the quality of the services performed; and to ensure against the use of services for other than the benefit of people.

WHY DO THE SERVICES FAIL?

Apart from the larger societal context discussed above, there are a number of specific reasons for the failure of the services.

1. We do not know enough; for example, we do not know how to cure neuroses.

2. Our training is inadequate. Even in areas where we do know something, we do not train people well with regard to what we do know. Thus, we do not instruct teachers in group management principles.

3. There is usually a gap in class and race between server and recipient. Most teachers, for example, are white and middle class, and large numbers of students are from poor families or minority groups.

4. A gap exists between the professional and the consumer. Professionals have too much power, are elitist, removed, and defensive, and they make their practice mystifying and difficult to comprehend. For these reasons, they fail to involve the consumer.

5. The service fails because it succeeds. Thus, intelligence tests that are used to categorize children succeed in doing just that, but fail in the development of children's learning.

6. Cross-pressures are operative, as when, for example, the goals of communities may differ from those of teachers, although both presumably are concerned with children's learning.

7. There is considerable confusion with regard to the organization of services; and management principles, particularly for large-scale enterprises such as school systems, are highly inadequate.

8. Resources are scarce. This is true in the fields of education, health, and mental health.

9. Cynicism concerning the role and value of services is prevalent among those who provide and those who receive services.

In the 1960's there was strong criticism regarding the cost of the services. This occurred primarily when large portions of increased funds for services were used principally for higher professional salaries and more professional jobs rather than improved services to consumers. The criticism was aimed at all the service fields, including education at each level, health, mental health, and social work, all of which seemed to be providing services in a traditional, nonvital manner. At least some positive steps were taken in the 1960's, however. For instance, discretionary power of the professionals was reduced, and they became more sensitive to consumers' needs, whether the consumers were blacks, participatory students, women, homosexuals, or patients without rights.

Various means were utilized to shift power to consumers: consumer advocates, paraprofessionals, decentralized neighborhood service centers, community boards, voucher systems, students on boards of trustees, and accountability measures such as competency- or performance-based training and certification. In addition, a variety of alternative institutions emerged; they included community schools, free universities, people's health clinics, women's counseling centers, hot lines, radical therapy groups, and growth centers.

These new institutions were largely led by new and unorthodox professionals, Young Turks, some noncredentialed professionals, and, in general, professionals who were outside or critical of the mainstream. They combined with the strong forces of minorities, youth, women, and affluent individuals who were strongly dissatisfied with such institutions as the traditional schools, which, they felt, would not educate their children for the society that was emerging, the work that the youngsters would probably do, and the leisure that they were likely to enjoy. Many of the developments that have their origins in alternative institutions are, to some extent, being utilized by traditional institutions. Examples include Catholic marriage encounter groups, the use of alternative schools, open classrooms in the public schools, and schools without walls. The popularity of professionals like R. D. Laing in psychiatry and John Holt, Neal Postman, Ivan Illich, George Leonard, Abraham Maslow, Carl Rogers, Bill Schutz, Fritz Perls, and Paul Goodman in education is a reflection of the influence of these alternative institutions. Most of these writers were strongly anti-institutional, were much concerned with deprofessionalization, deinstitutionalization, and deschooling, and were oriented toward the involvement of consumers and the reduction of distance between the professional and the consumer.

What clearly occurred in the 1960's was a changed conception of the relationship between the professional and the consumer in which the former was always boss ("doctor knows best") and the consumer was the passive recipient of the service.

It would be dangerous, however, if this change led to complete rejection of what the professional potentially has to offer: knowledge, perspective, and systematic practice based on theory. It is important, moreover, for the professional to be an ally since many are and will be resisting attempts at industrialization and further bureaucratization of their services. Large numbers of teachers, government employees, and health workers express, by their alienation and in various other ways, their resistance to the bureaucratization that is imposed upon them, and thus they are an important force in a progressive strategy for a service society.

One must remember, however, that professionals are always an ambivalent force because their own narrow self-interests and desire for control are not necessarily consonant with social change or the improvement of services.

Essentially, then, we need effective professionals. We must have not only a deprofessionalization, but a reprofessionalization combined with involvement of consumers both in the sense of their control and their immersion in the direct production of the service.

If we are to have an effective service society with a major redistribution of resources to the service sectors, these services must embody an ethic and must involve a spreading participation. Feelings related to helping, serving, sharing, joy, excitement, opening up, self-development, self-expression, autonomy, the expansion of experience and consciousness, growth, and breakthroughs are observed almost entirely in the alternate institutions. These sentiments must become part of the mainstream as much as possible, while continuing to expand on the perimeters. It is also going to be necessary to evaluate carefully, using many new indexes, what services actually do provide people at many levels. This evaluation will be essential not only as feedback for improving the service, but also to win new support for a service society.

During the 1960's the first steps were taken in this battle for changes in services. Control by the professionals was reduced, and the notion that the community should be involved in determining the amount and character of the services was put on the agenda. These changes have not, however, occurred without a battle. In the general backlash against service expenditures, the professionals have regrouped and have diverted some of the power of consumers. But much has been gained, and many new traditions and institutions have been established. The vanguards of consumers have helped to sensitize professionals to their needs. One of these vanguards—women—has been especially strong in questioning professional mystique and control. The problem now is for the consumers to regain the initiative in order to move out of the current period of decline. We must also move beyond the consumer-professional battle where the professional is the first line of defense for the welfare state. It is necessary to control, both locally and nationally, the direction of services in order to achieve a redistribution of national resources. We need some positive models and a specific national agenda.

Effectiveness of the services is both an issue intrinsic to them and central to the expansion of a human service society. We must recognize that the consumer, the central player in the service society, is the key to the improvement of services. It is important to recognize that the criteria of effectiveness are neither self-evident nor neutral, but need to be understood in terms of by whom (and how) they are set, whom they benefit, by whom they are paid, and by whom they are received.

We traditionally think of productivity as a function of technology—the more machinery, the more efficient production will be. This has certainly been characteristic in the manufacturing of goods. Services, on the other hand, are labor intensive; they use a high proportion of labor or human power in contrast to machinery or capital in order to produce the service product, whether it be education, health, safety, or personal services. To make the services more efficient, it has seemed natural to apply machinery so that they will perhaps become more like manufacturing.

According to traditional notions, productivity in human service work cannot be increased sharply because it is not amenable to capital-intensive inputs; moreover, as it is labor intensive, the work inputs are costly and potentially inflationary. Our point, however, is that human service work is consumer intensive; thus, the key to increasing productivity in this sector lies in effectively engaging and mobilizing the consumer.

We have already noted some of the broad concerns of consumers regarding the services, but, for the most part, the initial impact has been indirect or nonspecific. Thus, community advisory boards have been established on the assumption that such community involvement may make those who provide the service more responsive to the consumer. Paraprofessionals have been employed with the idea that they would bring a voice of the community into the service system, thereby affecting agencies and professionals. Voucher systems have been experimented with in order to capture some of the presumed power that the buyer of a service may possess. Decentralization has been applied in neighborhood service centers in order to reduce the distance between the client and the service.

Competency- or performance-based certification has been advocated in order to identify more closely what the practitioner is able to do. New methods of analyzing work (such as job or functional task analysis) are designed to demystify the services and to bring them under greater scrutiny and control. Advocates and expediters have been employed to cut through red tape and speed delivery of services. Much more developed training designs have been employed, stressing simulation, in the hope that sharper, more precise skills will emerge and thus improve the service. And, of course, such innovations as the open classroom and the community mental health center have been introduced on the grounds that they intensify the involvement of the client or consumer and will therefore produce a better service. The reorganization of roles, both professional and paraprofessional, has been proposed as a major device for increasing effectiveness, and the use of new types of personnel has been suggested as a way of representing clients better.

Fuchs points out that in the production of services, unlike in the production of goods, "the knowledge, experience, honesty, and motivation of the consumer affects service productivity."[9] Fuchs seems to be implying a new classification, which might be termed "consumer intensive"; that is, the more the productivity of the provider depends on consumer behavior, the more consumer intensive we could call that industry or activity. Some services can be seen as both labor intensive (that is, little capital) and consumer intensive; health outside the hospitals would be one and social services another. Other services might be consumer intensive and capital intensive: banking and insurance, for example. The human services, then, seem to be both consumer intensive and labor intensive.

Here, then, is a decisive factor that can affect education or any other human service. If we see students, for example, not as the passive recipients of teaching but as workers in the production of their own learning, then the organization of those learning activities becomes quite different.

Thus, the key to increasing children's learning is activities that make the student a more active and effective learner. Programs in which students learn through teaching other students make most efficient use of them. If students are key factors in the production of their own learning, then the other forces of production (teachers and equipment) must be directed toward maximizing the efficiency of students. One of the ways to do this is to enlist the consumers (that is, the students, their families, and the community), to give them a say in what is to be learned, who is to be employed, and how the learning is to be organized.

PARTICIPATION IS NOT ENOUGH

It is important to understand the role of community control in the process of educating students. While community participation may improve the input of consumers, it is not sufficient in and of itself. People may participate without any improvement in their learning; they may not become engaged in teaching themselves, learning how to learn, listening more carefully, or any cognitive mechanism related to a better performance. In many cases, participation may be a detour. Although it may be valuable on its own terms, it may fail in leading to increased productivity. Hence, it is important to consider carefully the mechanisms of connecting participation (or any other approach) to expanded involvement of consumers in the actual performance of the function, whether it be learning, health services, or whatever. Much attention must be given to the various mechanisms whereby a consumer's involvement increases productivity. Participation alone is not enough.

Most of what we are suggesting is not new, of course. Making learning self-directed, giving the students and their community a role in the school, and increasing the students' motivation are all well-known ideas. What is new is recasting these efforts in the context of seeing students as the key factors in their own learning.

The approach outlined above is potentially highly economical in that it vastly expands the service resources of the system and thereby increases the productivity of the producers—the teachers or other professionals and the agency. This is quite different from the current approach to increasing the productivity of teachers, which entails teaching more and more students. The danger in the latter approach, of course, is that the teaching may become less effective.

THE UNIQUE EDUCATIONAL CRISIS

What is the special crisis in education today, and how does it relate to the particular character of our service society? That schools fail large numbers of children both literally and figuratively is, of course, not new. Colin Greer documents in *The Great School Legend* that this situation has been characteristic of our society since the inception of public education.[10] In the early part of the twentieth century many immigrants, including Jews, Italians, Irish, and Swedes, were at various times labeled "uneducable and incorrigible,"[11] just as the newer urban immigrants of the present day—blacks—are so labeled. Today's immigrants, of course, are only migrating from one part of the United States to another, from the rural sectors to the urban. But the same difficulties persist, and there is some evidence that these problems are actually transnational; for example, the Cultural Revolution in China was directed most sharply at overcoming the tendency of the schools to serve the poor badly.

Since all of this is, of course, not new, why is there special concern today? Did not the old immigrants, after all, "make it" in society with or without education? The problem is that it is much more difficult now to "make it" in the service society without an education or, at least, an educational credential. A major finding of the Jencks study,[12] but one that is frequently overlooked, has important bearing here. Jencks found that, at each educational level, the credential was decisive in terms of future income.

Most of the routes to economic success that existed throughout the earlier part of the twentieth century are more or less closed now. Previously, if one failed in school, he had the opportunity to succeed by way of business and the general rapid expansion of the private sector. Today, many jobs are in the service sector—government, education, research, health, the professions. In all these areas, education, or at least an educational credential, is required. Sometimes the requirement is too stringent; that is, more education is required than is necessary to do the job. Thus, it is virtually impossible to fail in school and still be able to move into those occupations and professions. The school is, therefore, expected to do a bigger job than ever before, and its failure to do so is quite visible. This leads to an educational crisis that is considerably greater than that of the early years of the twentieth century when the schools were no more successful than they are today when dealing with the deprived.

The schools have always been relatively successful in responding to the needs of their middle-class clientele. Teachers tend to prefer students who are similar to themselves and whose school culture and home culture match. This is often formulated as the home reinforcing the school, but there is no reason why it could not be formulated in exactly the reverse fashion. That is, children from middle-class homes do well in school because the school reinforces the home and all the expectations that exist there.

Greer suggests that the earlier immigrants who "made it" economically had children who were indeed relatively successful in the schools. Here the school sanctioned what had occurred economically and culturally in the family. This is also true today among middle-class blacks and minorities.

It should be noted, of course, that there are other reasons in the service society for the special importance of the school. An increasing number of people are kept off the labor market for a greater period of time, and the school is a good place to spend this time. Education may, moreover, enable individuals to use more fruitfully the greatly increased amount of leisure time accumulated as a result of a highly productive economy. In addition, the educational establishment itself, professional associations, and all levels of government develop vested interests in maintaining high educational requirements, even in the absence of evidence that such requirements are necessary to do the job effectively.[13]

As part of this picture of the contemporary interest in education, one should note some pertinent statistics. First, there has been a vast increase in the number of individuals completing high school (while 6 percent of the population aged seventeen were high school graduates in 1900, nearly 80 percent had completed high school in 1970). Second, whereas those enrolled in college in 1900 constituted only 4 percent of the population aged eighteen through twenty-one, today well over half of this group attends college.

TWO APPROACHES TO THE EDUCATIONAL CRISIS

There are two approaches to the contemporary crisis in education. One is school centered and endeavors to provide intensive compensatory education, including preschool, Head Start programs, and special reading classes, for children in groups that typically have not responded well to the middle-class school system. The strategy has, for the most part, had only limited effect, largely because of its emphasis on the weaknesses of the students rather than on their strengths.

Without always directly stating as much, these measures were guided by the implicit assumption that the schools were all right as they were and that it was the children who needed to be remedied and changed. This is somewhat surprising in light of the tremendous criticism of the schools from many groups.

The 1960's demonstrated conclusively the failure of most of these compensatory measures. Currently, however, this approach has been revamped in what might be termed an intensive compensatory approach; that is, it has become more highly organized and can thus zero in on specific problems. Some evidence suggests that this intensive approach may be more beneficial than the broad-gauged approaches of the 1960's. But the emphasis is still negative, and the child continues to feel deficient and inadequate and must, therefore, become more like the middle-class child in order to please the teacher.

What is needed are approaches based upon the strengths of children. Youth tutoring youth programs provide a good example of a positive approach. Thus, disadvantaged youngsters in high school who are doing poorly themselves tutor youngsters in the elementary school who are also doing poorly. The message is clearly that the high school youngsters have something to give, something to teach. By utilizing their strengths, they can assume the role of helper. As a result of their contributions, their learning improves dramatically in a wide variety of areas. They improve on achievement tests, in reading, including the number of books they read, in their self-concept — in their total educational function both inside and outside the classroom. It may be that this type of approach, which is built on the strengths of the child, will be strategic in obtaining leaps in their learning. (In this context, intensive compensatory reading approaches can be beneficial. That is, if the child feels that he is good at something, then it is easier for him to accept improvements in his weak areas.)

The second approach is directed at changing the parents, but in some surprising ways, a number of which are work related and some community based. In the realm of work, there is an increasing tendency to provide new routes for jobs and careers for the adult disadvantaged who have been excluded from the educational system. Thus, a paraprofessional can acquire a job first as a teacher's aide and then use some of this experience and in-service training toward acquiring a college credential and a professional position. This strategy has two functions. First, it provides access to the system in newly created jobs (and it is extremely important that such jobs be created) without requiring that the traditional path to those positions be followed. Thus, one could fail in the schools and still acquire a semiprofessional or professional position. Second, and perhaps more important in relation to the point being made here, adults who are now involved in school themselves provide very different models for their children who may have been experiencing difficulty in school. Various studies of paraprofessional programs indicate that the paraprofessionals' educational know-how increases, and, thus, they are better able to help their children make their way through the system. Also, the aspirations of other members of the community are raised as they see their neighbors doing varied work and going to and completing college. The aspirations of the paraprofessionals themselves also increase as they progress through the program. In fact, many persons who felt that they could not complete college, once having done so, aspire to go even further.[14] Thus, they become more like the traditional parent who has "made it" and values education. In addition to the paraprofessionals, of course, increasing numbers of people among the disadvantaged are acquiring higher education via recurrent or continuing education, external degrees, open enrollment, and so on.

But there is another very different way for disadvantaged parents to affect, at least indirectly, their children's school performance: through community involvement in the schools, as, for example, through service on school boards. The direct intent of community involvement is to transform the schools and make them more educationally responsive to the disadvantaged youngsters by changing curriculum, personnel, and procedures. The indirect intent is to provide a new parental model that recognizes the importance of learning and that encourages the child to do the same. In this way, disadvantaged parents become similar to their middle-class counterparts in other communities where parents are constantly concerned with educational matters.

Changed career patterns for adults and their involvement in the community have, of course, powerful value in their own terms. We are noting here simply a latent function that potentially has important learning benefits for the disadvantaged child functioning even in a traditional school culture.

These strategies, by themselves, probably will not be sufficient to overcome the present crisis in education. They have, however, brought about some constructive changes.

TOWARD A STRENGTH-BASED MODEL FOR EDUCATION

Implicit within this model are three assumptions. First, the success of any program must be measured in terms of its effect on children's learning as measured by a variety of both cognitive and affective indicators. Improved performance of teachers without an improvement in the learning of children is insufficient. The decisive factor is the child.

Second, a program can be no more than partially successful unless it produces significant leaps in the child's desire and capacity to learn. Does a program make a child responsive to learning? Is it the first step in stirring his potential to be a true lifelong learner, not just a temporary statistic on a progress chart?

Third, the consumer (the child) can be the key producer in the school, and thereby increase output enormously. In such programs as cross-aged learning, peer teaching (and counseling), children teaching children, and youth tutoring youth, the child becomes a transmitter of information, ideas, and values.

These assumptions can become realities and, by extension, form the basis of sensible, responsive public policy. Without romanticizing "disadvantaged" children, those who frame national responses to their needs should nonetheless be aware of the underrated characteristics these children possess. Many, for example, are especially adept at coping, often quite successfully, with difficult physical or psychological stresses. Those whose native language is not English may effectively teach and communicate the complexities of a second language to their peers or to younger children. Inner-city children, as well as their rural counterparts, have often been raised by siblings, aunts, or grandmothers in extended families and have learned much about group living. Most have acquired the skills of survival, and many have learned and even contributed to the language and wisdom of the street.

But these strengths are often considered shortcomings that today's compensatory programs seek to reduce. They are not nurtured by the schools that serve these children. For example, instead of having the Spanish-speaking youngsters teach Spanish to the other children, their knowledge of the language is seen as a problem to be overcome.

In the search for altered directions, the following ideas and options suggest themselves:

1. Schools can make a difference, but they cannot do the whole job. Educational efforts must be supplemented by a national policy and program of full employment. To make the schools responsible for providing options and mobility is hypocritical if there is no place to go when students graduate.

2. Educational efforts must avoid labeling children. The stigma of a presumed handicap is often as damaging as the child's actual shortcomings. The child must develop a sense of self-worth that can come from such educationally sound processes as learning through teaching (youth tutoring youth); the reinforcing presence of trained, culturally similar paraprofessionals in the classroom; the encouragement rather than suppression of ethnic, racial, and other "pluralistic" traits and values; field-based, action learning; less dependence on tests that are oriented toward the majority of the society; and building on the learning styles of many children.

3. The importance of the staff must be recognized. It is unfortunate that most in-service staff development has failed. We propose that much more attention be given to the training and retraining of principals, as well as superintendents and administrators, particularly in relation to their roles as managers. Especially important is training the staff to maximize the resources of the school, particularly how to use the children as resources. In addition, the staff should be broadened to include community residents, older people, and so forth.

4. As school size increases, ostensibly for more economical management (although the data do not support this theory), the individuality of the underprepared child is quashed. The larger, more impersonal school no longer reaches the community or makes a community, and the people no longer feel a sense of ownership, access, control, participation, or pride in education.

5. A great many small-scale programs work, but fail when trans-

lated into large-scale ones. Better management practices might alter this considerably. These practices would include careful phasing; in-depth training of cadres; planned variation; the use of model demon-stration training sites; and a managerial perspective that integrates the need to develop participation, autonomy, decentralization, flexi-bility, and openness to the new with the obligation to ascertain that the program is carried through efficiently, in a well-coordinated fashion, and with quality control.

SERVICES AND GROWTH

In all the current discussion about growth, one basic misconcep-tion stands out above all others: one type of growth—industrial—is equated with total economic growth by practically all of those in-volved in the debate, whatever their viewpoint. A part is confused with the whole.

But the fact of the matter is that we may be able to have enor-mous growth in human services—health, education, recreation, art, culture, research, mental health—while at the same time shrinking industrial production is rapidly depleting the resources and energy of the earth. As has been said, these human services are labor and con-sumer intensive rather than capital and resource intensive, and, unlike the situation in the past, we are now long on human capital and short on all other resources. In other words, not all growth must be limited. Emile Benoit states the issue effectively:

What is needed instead is selective growth. We can look forward to a continued rise in per capita incomes and real welfare if there is a shift: (1) from goods production to services and leisure; (2) from status displaying goods to goods yielding mainly intrinsic satisfactions; (3) from resource wasteful and polluting goods to resource conserving and pollution combating goods; (4) from population growth to population decline; (5) from braking expenditures on higher education and research and development to maximum achievable expansion of this sector, plus a reallocation of resources to give new emphasis to environmental problems.

The advantage of services over goods is that they absorb little or no scarce raw materials and create little or no pollution. Most services, of course, have to be pro-vided by some physical mechanisms, and do require the production of some comple-mentary goods: hospitals, offices, and medical equipment for health services, class-rooms, offices, laboratories, etc., for education and research and so forth. But the relative strain on the environment over the long run is far lower than for the sale and consumption of goods, which not only require the construction of facilities and equipment but which use these facilities and equipment for the further transforma-tion of raw materials into products which will be used up and discarded.[15]

To achieve a human service society will require a major shift toward developing large-scale alternative life-styles. These life-styles will not constitute a new primitivism, a regression to an earlier stage of development, a communal society, a deinstitutionalization of society, or a return to the past based upon scarcity and a low level of technology. The service society requires, rather, that we organize our resources carefully so as to produce a high level of culture and aesthetics and new qualities of living that are not based upon waste and an increasing demand for things, which exhaust the world's resources and pollute the atmosphere. Continuous industrial growth is leading to unemployment and the underutilization of people. By contrast, growth of human services will lead to the fullest utilization of people. In addition, if we use our human resources efficiently and meaningfully, our quality of life will greatly improve.

NOTES

1. Victor Fuchs, *The Service Economy* (New York: Columbia University Press, 1969), p. 16.

2. *Heart Facts* (New York: American Heart Association, 1974).

3. U.S. Public Health Service, *Bulletin No. 1168* (Washington, D.C.: U.S. Government Printing Office, 1968).

4. U.S. Department of Health, Education, and Welfare, *First Special Report to the U.S. Congress on Alcohol and Health, from the Secretary of Health, Education, and Welfare* (Washington, D.C.: U.S. Government Printing Office, 1971), p. viii.

5. U.S. Department of Health, Education, and Welfare, *Digest of Educational Statistics* (Washington, D.C.: U.S. Government Printing Office, 1972), Tables 178, 182.

6. U.S. Bureau of the Census, *Current Population Reports*, Series P-23, No. 42 (Washington, D.C.: U.S. Government Printing Office, 1972).

7. National Council on Crime and Delinquency, "Two-Year Follow-Up," *Uniform Parole Reports*, No. 2 (February 1973); Federal Bureau of Investigation, *Crime in the United States, 1972*, Uniform Crime Reports (Washington, D.C.: U.S. Government Printing Office, 1973).

8. Few longitudinal studies report rehabilitation rates for users of hard drugs above 10 percent. See Drug Abuse Survey Project, *Dealing with Drug Abuse: A Report to the Ford Foundation* (New York: Praeger, 1972).

9. Fuchs, *Service Economy*, p. 17.

10. Colin Greer, *The Great School Legend* (New York: Basic Books, 1972).

11. For example, in 1912, Henry Goddard, one of the major innovators in IQ testing, studied immigrants arriving at Ellis Island and found, based upon the tests, that 83 percent of Jews, 90 percent of Hungarians, 79 percent of Italians, and 87 percent of Russians were "feeble minded." Henry H. Goddard, "The Benet Tests in Relation to Immigrants," *Journal of Psychoasthenics* 18 (1913): 107. For further discussion

of the past and present pernicious use of IQ tests, see Frank Riessman and Alan Gartner, "The New Hereditarians," review of *Educability and Group Differences,* by Arthur R. Jensen, in *Change* 6 (February 1974): 56-59.

12. Christopher Jencks *et al., Inequality: A Reassessment of the Effects of Family
and Schooling in America* (New York: Basic Books, 1973).

13. Ivar Berg's *Education and Jobs: The Great Training Robbery* (New York:
Praeger, 1970) is the best of several recent studies documenting the lack of correlation
between education and job performance. Indeed, Berg cites numerous instances
where the correlation is negative; that is, those with more education perform the work
less well.

14. See Alan Gartner, *Paraprofessionals and Their Performance* (New York:
Praeger, 1971).

15. Emile Benoit, "What Society for Spaceship Earth?" *Social Policy* 4
(November-December 1973): 17-22.

PART III
Financing Educational Services: Problems of Supply and Demand

The chapters in Part III focus on topics that underlie and, to an important extent, precede political analysis and action, since they may define the limits within which political choices are possible or probable. The basic concepts are economic and fiscal: the *resources* available for funding public programs, and *modes of allocation* for these resources in the light of existing commitments and changing service needs and demands. In short, the questions the authors address in various ways are: "What will be the size of the pie?" "How will it be sliced?" Educational professionals and their clients are only a few of the claimants who hungrily search for answers to these uncertainties. Unfortunately for their peace of mind and assurance of a sustaining diet, even the best-informed experts can seldom provide definitive answers. Economic analysis and forecasting can, nevertheless, help policymakers to put their own specialized areas into perspective, become aware of relevant short- and long-range trends in the larger world, and avoid unduly optimistic or pessimistic views of the future.

The reader will find that the authors, more or less explicitly, project educational developments, issues, and anticipated problems in education in broad contexts and conceptual terms, such as: the state of the economy, institutional and human investment perspectives, the structure of intergovernmental fiscal relations, and general tax and expenditure policy. They also display in various ways the complexity, interrelatedness, and instability of the environmental variables affecting the delivery of educational services. These include: economic factors, such as industrial productivity; demographic factors, such as birthrates and geographical distribution of total and school-age populations; and public value choices, such as the expansion of services to handicapped or preschool-age children.

In spite of their diversity of subject matter, the authors agree on some unifying themes. First, demands and costs for public services, including education, are increasing at a faster rate overall than are the economic resources to support them. Second, the aggregation and allocation of resources for education are presented as a highly fragmented process that occurs in many arenas: national, state, and local. Third, major and sudden shifts in resource allocation policies are not projected; rather, the shape of the future is seen as emerging from a ferment of prior debate and speculation about environmental change, citizens' preferences, and institutional capabilities. Finally, past assumptions about continuous growth of the educational sector are viewed as no longer tenable; yet currently popular fears of "dour and dire" retrenchment are also held in question because they take inadequate notice of anticipated realignments of needs, demands, and resources — human and fiscal — for educational services.

In Chapter 5, Jesse Burkhead provides a broad, nontechnical analysis of the state of the economy and its import for education. His view is one of "guarded pessimism for the near-term future of the entire educational sector." He first analyzes the factors that will contribute to a slow-growth economy, including related changes in regional economies and population age distributions. He then examines the budget outlook for the national government in the light of emerging constraints on resources. In this connection, he describes the effects of the general revenue sharing legislation on federal aid to education. He then considers the state-local component of the federal structure and comments on the outlook for more effective planning of educational resources. He notes that the effects of a slow-growth economy will be different at each level of the federal structure and that the past decade has witnessed a transformation in the fiscal, if not the administrative, roles of the three levels of government.

Burkhead's analysis of the school district budgeting from an economist's point of view offers a novel insight into this pervasive process of allocating resources. He does not foresee a strengthening of discretion by local school districts in fiscal management, but rather limited planning initiatives at federal and state levels that will contribute to greater centralization in the distribution of educational resources.

In the first two contributions in Chapter 6, by Norman C. Thomas and John J. Callahan, fiscal aspects of intergovernmental relations and state governance are examined in greater detail than in Burkhead's introductory essay. Thomas describes the divergent views that are held concerning the appropriate roles of authorities at the three levels of government and the effects that uncertainty, conflict, and complexity have on fiscal policies for education. He analyzes specific issues associated with financial assistance, control, and equalization. He concludes that two opposing influences are at work in determining the politics of intergovernmental activity: the pervasiveness and the strength of the value of local self-determination, and the imperative for cooperation and attainment of equality across the various sectors, in education as in all policy areas.

Callahan analyzes state-level education finance reform, which he, as well as Burkhead and Thomas, sees as potentially the most influential development of the past decade in changing the patterns of resource allocation in the direction of greater equity among school districts. He discusses the pros and cons of various state funding options and notes that policymakers have been more preoccupied with effects of the reforms on the tax system than on the levels or distribution patterns of school expenditures. In other words, it is still debatable whether taxpayers or schoolchildren will be the main beneficiaries of finance reform. He notes that educational program reforms have not been a major factor in school finance reform. It also remains to be seen whether current developments will produce new educational governance and administration policies that will enhance public confidence in school spending.

Although Paul E. Barton and David K. Wiles write on disparate topics, they are both concerned about the effects that will be associated with economic growth—or lack of it—and with challenges to the system of delivering educational services. They both suggest that retrenchment in the support of traditional educational functions will not necessarily eventuate in fewer of the same programs. Rather, they see in contemporary social and economic life the possibility that new imperatives will precipitate some basic changes in what schools do and how they complement other institutions. Barton points out that current views and practices concerning the relationship of education to vocational experiences are not in accord with the "life cycle" needs of individuals already in the work force or geared to the expanded opportunities required for the youth who will enter the labor market in the immediate future. Manpower policies are now inappropriately related to economic trends. One of the highest priorities for educational leaders is, therefore, to offer some guidance on how to bring the economy more in line with the skills of the people available to participate in it.

As a means of delineating the forms of program and organizational changes that might flow from a slow-growth economy, Wiles provides alternative interpretations of the economic future of schooling. He sets forth the economic assumptions that underlie an "institutional" model and a "human investment" model. The first defines schooling as a declining industry, utilizes quantitative methods of analysis that assume that all things of value ultimately have a price and are exchangeable, and assigns priority to the maintenance of institutional stability. To survive, the institutions must seek to negotiate or create needs and to establish "prices" for their products or services that do not reflect consumers' preferences but rather those of interests that manipulate the environment.

On the other hand, the human investment model addresses such concerns as the qualitative aspects of growth, the organizational adjustments made to cope with policy uncertainty and investment risk, and the effects of alterations of clients' choices for services. He concludes that such schemes for logically determining the most appropriate social and educational policies may provide a coherent intellectual framework for analyzing problems, but that recommendations for constructive action will remain very much a matter of a priori judgments of particular analysts and institutional decisionmakers.

The contributions of Eleanore C. Westhead and William R. Carriker and of Marjorie G. Elsten and Jenni W. Klein describe the rationales and issues associated with two major expansions of educational services that transcend traditional practice. The first deals with the legislation enacted by Congress in 1975, which seeks to assure to handicapped children the equality of educational opportunity that has already been extended in principle to other minority clienteles through various categorical grant-in-aid arrangements. The programmatic implications of this legislation are still to be fully understood, as are its eventual costs. The authors foresee a severe period of stress as commitments to provide equal and effective treatment for all forms of educational needs must be tailored to, and constrained by, available resources.

Preschool children are yet another clientele whose special needs have now been recognized by professionals and parents. Elsten and Klein describe the historical developments that have preceded recent attempts to enact broad federally supported programs. They anticipate that the trends in women's employment, among other influences, assure a continuing and active demand for well-designed flexible programs that will correct the shortcomings of existing day-care arrangements. The role to be assumed by the schools and other public agencies is, however, still highly controversial, as many persons view early childhood educational programs as improper interventions in family life.

5   The State of the Economy: Resources and Costs for Educational Services*

Jesse Burkhead

The word has somehow got around that the American economy, along with a number of other advanced industrial economies, has not been doing very well in the last few years. If gross national product is measured in constant dollars, the last year of decline in the U.S. economy was from 1957 to 1958, until the near catastrophic drop from 1973 to 1974 and the further serious decline in 1975. There was some upturn in the second quarter of 1975, and this has continued sporadically since that time. The recovery in GNP in terms of growth has not been smooth. In the first quarter of 1976 it was 9.2 percent (constant dollars), but in the second quarter it dropped to 4.4 percent, and to 4.0 percent in the third quarter.[1]

All of this could perhaps be expected after a sixteen-year uninterrupted growth in real GNP, but what is particularly disturbing is that the decline in the GNP and high unemployment have been accompanied by price inflation.[2]

The inflation started earlier than the decline in the GNP. The tax reductions of 1964-1965, followed by the rapid increase in expenditures for the Vietnam War, contributed to GNP price increases that were 2.2 percent in 1965 and mounted to 9.7 percent in 1974. The peak of 13.4 percent was reached in the fourth quarter of 1974. There has been some abatement since that time in GNP inflation rates.

*The author is indebted to his colleagues, Jerry Miner and Alan K. Campbell, for comments on an earlier draft of this chapter.

Unemployment reached its low point in 1973 at 4.9 percent, peaked at 8.9 percent in May 1975, and with some fluctuations has since receded to 7.8 percent, with teenage and black unemployment at several times this rate. One economist-journalist coined an ugly word to describe an ugly situation — "stagflation." It has indeed been an unpleasant economy.

The word is also around that the state of disarray in the economy is matched by the state of disarray in economic analysis. Indeed, my profession has been reduced to the point of writing books about how little economists now know, given the bankruptcy of neo-Keynesian remedies that seemed to work so well for so long.[3]

Although there are always optimists among the forecasters, and one might have expected to find them among the officials of the Ford administration, the economic assumptions of the Office of Management and Budget (OMB) are not particularly cheering. Relevant data are set forth in Table 5-1, compiled from the July 1976 *Mid-Session Review of the 1977 Budget.*

Table 5-1. The state of the economy, 1974–1981
(calendar years)

Economic indicators	Actual		Forecast		Assumed			
	1974	1975	1976	1977	1978	1979	1980	1981
GNP (current dollars in billions)	1,407	1,499	1,687	1,890	2,121	2,370	2,575	2,747
GNP change (percent, constant dollars)	-1.8	-2.0	6.8	5.7	5.9	6.3	4.4	3.7
GNP deflator (percent, annual)	9.7	8.8	5.3	6.0	6.0	5.1	4.0	2.9
Unemployment (percent)	5.6	8.5	7.3	6.4	5.7	5.1	4.8	4.7

Source: Office of Management and Budget, *Mid-Session Review of the 1977 Budget* (Washington, D.C.: OMB, 1976).

The projections assume that constant dollar GNP growth rates will rise moderately until 1979 and start to drop thereafter, descending to 3.7 percent in 1981. The OMB was somewhat more optimistic on prices and unemployment. By 1981 the GNP deflator is expected to drop to 2.9 percent and unemployment to 4.7 percent. Projections of the Congressional Budget Office (CBO) cannot easily be compared with those of the OMB. In its projections made in January 1976 the CBO described a Path A with an assumed 6 percent GNP real growth rate and a Path B with a 5 percent growth rate. Path A puts unemployment at 4.5 percent in 1981 with a 6.6 percent inflation rate.

Following this chapter's somewhat pessimistic beginning are: first, a brief examination of the factors that will contribute to a slow-growth economy in the near future; second, a discussion of the budget outlook for the federal government in the light of emerging constraints on resources; third, a consideration of the state-local component; and, finally, a comment on the outlook for more effective planning of educational resources. The mood of this chapter is one of guarded pessimism for the near-term future of the entire education sector.

A SLOW-GROWTH ECONOMY

In spite of some optimism about recovery from the recession of 1974-1975, and in spite of an economic performance in 1976 and 1977 that is an obvious improvement, it is most difficult to believe that the American economy will return to the stable growth rates that we enjoyed from 1958 to 1973. The basic forces that produced the unholy combination of high inflation and high unemployment seem to remain with us, although in a slightly modified form.

First, the demographic factor is extremely important. In 1955, seven employed persons paid social security taxes for one person collecting benefits. Today, the ratio is about three for one. This downward trend will continue into the 1990's until it is about two to one.[4] With a smaller proportion of the population in the work force, GNP growth per capita will also be smaller. An increasing proportion of our resources will be devoted to sustaining those who are retired. This will also contribute to inflation.

Second, there is no abatement in domestic or international pressures for additional expenditures for armaments, and it is by no means clear that such outlays contribute to productivity and technological progress in the civilian sector. This pattern of resource allocation adds to demand without adding to the supply of consumable resources, thus contributing both to inflation and to low growth rates.

Third, oligopolies continue their pattern of price fixing wherein prices are increased, but seldom reduced. Trade unions, of course, occasionally occupy such favored positions and contribute to inflationary pressures when wage settlements exceed economy-wide gains in productivity.

Fourth, prices of basic raw materials, particularly those controlled by the Third World, are likely to increase more than other prices. These nations are becoming increasingly restive under what is regarded as several centuries of exploitation with respect to their raw materials. The experience of the OPEC bloc in raising petroleum prices will not be lost on the producers of copper, tin, magnesium, bauxite, and lumber. It is likely that the costs of energy will be affected by environmental controls, adding a dimension to what promises to be an inflation-ridden area for the next decade or more.

Fifth, there is the phenomenon that has come to be called "Baumol's disease,"[5] wherein advanced industrial economies experience shifts from sectors of high productivity to sectors of low productivity. This typically involves a structural change in the economy from employment in the manufacturing and agricultural areas to that in the services area. Although it is difficult to measure productivity in the services sector, including government, conventional standards, such as output per person per hour, register much slower gains over time than in the nonservice sector. Hence, since wage rates tend to move together in all sectors of the economy, prices will inevitably rise.

Finally, expenditures for an improved environment are certain to increase. These long-term improvements in the quality of life will have the short-term effect of increasing costs to the consumer and occasionally threatening some jobs.

There are also some regional factors at work. The economic growth that does occur between now and, say, 1980 will not be spread evenly. New York City's fiscal problems are not due alone to "fiscal mismanagement" but to a serious decline in the city's economic base, by way of a loss of jobs and residence. This same phenomenon is occurring not only in the large cities of the Northeast and Midwest but also in their metropolitan areas.[6] The sun belt states or "the southern rim," as the area is sometimes called, is acquiring the new tax base and the employment opportunities that are being lost in the Northeast and Midwest. There is no evident public policy that can reverse these trends; nor, indeed, is it entirely clear that any such attempt should be made.

An additional factor that will have special impact on education, especially at the elementary and secondary levels, is the astonishing decline in the birthrate that has occurred in the last five years.[7] The baby boom turned into a baby bust as birthrates dropped from 23 per 1,000 of total population in the early 1960's to 15 per 1,000 in 1974. Demographers found this particularly startling since the number of potential mothers actually increased. No one seems to know why this occurred. Possible explanations include the increased availability of contraceptive techniques, legalized abortions, greater participation of women in the labor market, women's liberation, and changing lifestyles.

The educational implications of these drastic changes in the economy are explored by Michael Kirst in Chapter 7. Some of the resource allocation and economic impacts can be projected with reasonable confidence. The Census Bureau's estimates of probable population in 1985 suggest that there will be absolutely fewer in the population age group of five to twenty-one. Hence, the quantitative demand for education from kindergarten through college is certain to decline. (Some of the implications of this decreased "demand" will be explored in the last section of this chapter.)

The foregoing recital of the characteristics and implications of a slow-growth economy is, of course, not exhaustive. There are, nevertheless, the signposts along the way for the next several years, and none suggest that elementary, secondary, and higher education will enjoy the halcyon days of the 1950's and the 1960's when educational outlays constituted a larger and larger proportion of the GNP and when teachers' salaries at all levels were increasing more rapidly than average earnings in the noneducation sector.

Some implications of a slow-growth economy go well beyond our immediate concern for education. It is, of course, easier to resolve societal conflicts in a growth economy than in a nongrowth economy. Low growth rates will greatly exacerbate conflicts between capital and labor, among regions that are enjoying differential changes in economic activity, and among claimants on the resources that are available through federal, state, and local budgets. It is reasonable to anticipate that those persons and groups who are favorable to the educational enterprise will advance their claims with vigor, but realization of the claims will be very difficult to achieve. And certainly new tensions will emerge between the spokesmen for elementary and secondary education and those for higher education.

Slow growth with inflation will have differential impacts on the federal, state, and local sectors and hence on the costs and resources available for education. It is safe to say, however, that all sectors will be adversely affected.

THE FEDERAL SECTOR

In recent years the shares of financing from federal, state, and local governments for elementary and secondary education have been remarkably constant, as is shown in Table 5-2. The federal contribution reached its peak in 1971-1972 at 9.5 percent and has since receded to 8 percent. State governments picked up the lag as the federal governments receded, and the local share has remained constant at 52 percent of the total. These averages, of course, disguise great differences among states.

Table 5-2. Sources of current revenue, elementary and secondary education, selected fiscal years (in percent)

Years	Federal	State	Local
1969–1970	8.0	40.0	52.0
1971–1972	9.5	38.5	52.0
1973–1974	8.0	40.0	52.0
1975–1976	8.0	40.0	52.0

Source: Rochelle L. Stanfield, "Why Johnny Can't—The Problem of State School Financing," *National Journal* 8 (April 24, 1976): 556.

Federal Budget Projections

Perspectives on the federal budget to 1981 are set forth in Table 5-3. This outlook, prepared by the Office of Management and Budget in July 1976 presumably reflected the "official" stance of the Ford administration.[8] The Carter administration's budget proposals have not altered this outlook in any important dimension.

Table 5-3 emphasizes a number of interesting points. The first and most obvious is the effort by Nixon and Ford to restrict the size of the federal sector. It is assumed that the federal budget will drop from 27.5 percent of the GNP in fiscal 1975 to 21.3 percent of the GNP in fiscal 1981. In this shrinkage the broad category of education, training, employment, and social services will probably decline from $18.7 billion in current dollars in fiscal 1976 to $16.8 billion in fiscal 1981 — a drop from 4.6 percent to 2.9 percent of total budget authority, which is a 37 percent decline. At the same time, budget authority for national defense is expected to expand from $86.6 billion in fiscal 1975 to $142.5 billion in fiscal 1981 — a 9 percent increase.

**Table 5-3. Federal budget outlook, 1975–1981
(selected fiscal years)**

Budget components	Actual 1975	Forecast 1976	Assumed 1977	1981
Budget authority (billions of dollars)	412.1	409.9	431.4	586.2
Percent of GNP	27.5	24.3	22.9	21.3
Education, training, employment, and social services (billions of dollars)	15.2	18.7	18.4	16.8
Percent of budget authority	3.8	4.6	4.2	2.9
National defense (billions of dollars)	86.6	90.6	101.6	142.5
Percent of budget authority	21.0	22.1	23.6	24.3
Deficit or surplus (billions of dollars)	-43.6	-69.6[a]	-47.5	+ 36.1

[a] Actual deficit for fiscal 1976 was $65.6 billion.
Source: Office of Management and Budget, *Mid-Session Review of the 1977 Budget* (Washington, D.C.: OMB, 1976).

The ever elusive fiscal dividend is replaced by the OMB with the concept of "budget margin." This is expected to amount to $36.1 billion in fiscal 1981 measured simply as an anticipated budget surplus. Herein, of course, lies the possibility for increased outlays for elementary, secondary, and higher education, a possibility that will be further examined below.

Charles L. Schultze, of the Brookings Institution and now chairman of the Council of Economic Advisers, has an even more pessimistic set of projections than does the OMB.[9] Economic and budget projections are, of course, only as good as their underlying assumptions. Schultze assumes that between 1975 and 1981 (calendar year) the price increase measured in terms of the GNP will average 5.2 percent annually. He defines a nonrecession budget in terms of 5 percent unemployment. The real GNP growth rate is assumed at 3.7 percent annually from 1975 to 1981. Schultze is also heroic enough to attempt a projection for 1986: between 1981 and 1986 GNP prices are expected to increase by only 4.0 percent, but the constant dollar growth rate is projected to drop to 3.5 percent.[10]

Schultze then points out that, under existing legislation and given the country's demographic profile, medicaid, medicare, and other Social Security payments that are already indexed to the cost of living will increase sharply. He projects an expansion in expenditures for national defense roughly comparable to that in the foregoing OMB projections.[11] This generates a decline in the category "social investment and services," which includes federal aid to education, in constant dollars of $1.1 billion between fiscal 1977 and fiscal 1981 and the further decline of $3 billion from 1981 to 1986.[12]

Schultze finds, moreover, that there is virtually no leeway. If federal expenditures, including both goods and services and transfer payments, are held at 20 percent of the GNP, and unless existing commitments for national defense are repudiated, in fiscal 1981 there will be $6 billion "available leeway."[13] If federal tax rates are held at their current levels, revenue will increase with inflation. Only in these circumstances is the federal budget margin expanded substantially. This assumption implies, of course, that federal expenditures will increase beyond 20 percent of the GNP, and this would yield a $27 billion leeway in 1981 plus $10 billion for "contingencies."

The $6 billion minimum available in 1981 could easily be wiped out by a national health insurance program, by a modest increase in public service employment designed both for jobs for inner-city residents and for maintenance of urban government service delivery, or by the enactment of larger countercyclical general revenue sharing.

The $27 billion maximum leeway rests on the assumption that unemployment can and will be reduced to 5 percent and that taxpayers are willing to let inflation increase their effective tax rates. A reduction of a half percentage point in the unemployment rate appears to be worth about $11 billion in additional federal net revenue. But bringing the unemployment rate down to 5 percent is, to put it mildly, most difficult.

The second assumption concerning maximum leeway depends on a shift in citizens' preference for taxpaying, and this is perhaps the least likely prospect of all. There is, for example, mounting pressure for corporate tax relief, which is based on the argument that there is either a profit squeeze or a capital shortage or both. It will, therefore, be difficult for Congress to resist demands for tax reduction in the business sector. This will lead to further erosion of the federal tax base and further reduce the leeway that might otherwise be available.

Prospects for Federal Support

An appraisal of the prospects for future federal support of elementary and secondary education requires a brief recital of recent history.

Some would place the watershed of federal support with the National Defense Education Act of 1958. Others would argue that the Elementary and Secondary Education Act of 1965 was crucial. ESEA, of course, never reached its authorized funding levels, although Title I has given significant support to almost every school district in the nation.

The year 1972 was marked by two interesting developments that affected the role of the federal government in education. First was the culmination of long debate over general revenue sharing (GRS) and its ultimate adoption in October of that year. School districts were excluded from GRS; payments to local governments were restricted to those that had "general purpose responsibilities." There were some good administrative and technical reasons for this exclusion. For example, Congress had sufficient difficulty in writing this complicated legislation to provide for a workable pass-through to local governments without adding in school districts.[15] But there was an additional reason for excluding school districts from GRS. The supporters of a large federal role in education, sometimes called the education lobby, did not press for inclusion. They apparently hoped instead that there would be increased federal funding by way of special revenue sharing for education in accordance with President Nixon's proposal. This produced the second interesting development in 1972.

President Nixon's proposal was for a value-added tax to assist public elementary and secondary education and at the same time provide substantial relief for local property taxes.[16] But Congress was most unreceptive to special revenue sharing for education and even more unreceptive to the value-added tax.

Since 1972 every U.S. budget message has contained proposals for special revenue sharing for education up to and including that of January 1977. In only one case has a message been given serious consideration by Congress. President Ford's proposals in January 1976 were not even accorded the courtesy of a House or Senate committee hearing.

It is interesting that GRS probably helped education, not by direct payments, but through state aid from the one-third share received by the states. It has been estimated[17] that perhaps 20 to 25 percent of GRS monies assisted education. This estimate may be on the high side since state shares of GRS were only one-third, although cities with fiscally dependent school districts are, in effect, quite capable of diverting GRS funds to schools. But, if it is a reasonable estimate, it means that of the $30.2 billion distributed under GRS from 1972 to 1976 somewhere between $6 billion and $7.5 billion ended up in support of elementary and secondary education. In the extension of GRS in 1976 there was no visible effort to include school districts as local government recipients.[18]

Although prospects for major federal initiatives in education appear to be dismal, it may not be concluded that there will be no federal action in the next few years. Even in the past two years some modest programs have been adopted. Amendments to the Education Act of 1974 (P.L. 93-380) authorized additional outlays of about $7.5 million to state education agencies for "libraries, learning resources, educational innovation and support." The commissioner of education was given authority for grants up to $200 million for such experimental programs as education in the metric system, education of gifted and talented students, and consumer education. The National Reading Improvement Program was authorized to be funded up to $93 million in fiscal 1978. While these are not large sums, the actions indicate that Congress will continue to look at specific categorical programs. The administrative arrangements that accompanied the amendments of

1974 are perhaps of more interest and will be examined in the final section of this chapter.

The fact that the ESEA must be renewed in 1977 provides the occasion for a reexamination of both programs and administrative patterns. Although it is too early to indulge in informed speculation as to the outcomes, some idle speculation is possible. Education for the disadvantaged is likely to be given reasonably high priority; it might, in fact, receive authorizations of up to $700 million annually—an important addition to the federal aid package that now amounts to about $4.6 billion for elementary and secondary education.

PROSPECTS FOR STATE SUPPORT

As previously noted, the states have done reasonably well by education in recent years. Funds from GRS have helped; state revenue structures have become somewhat more elastic over the past decade; in most, but not all, states, the fiscal crisis has not been quite as severe as at the local level. And in the states where the fiscal crisis was severe, aid to education was not always the victim. Forced by court decision, New Jersey, after so many years, did adopt an income tax, and the schools are open in that state.

There is an obvious unused revenue potential at the state level. John Due, in a careful survey based on data from 1973, estimated that the underutilized tax capacity of the states amounted to $38.7 billion, most of which was in sales tax and personal income taxes.[19] During this year expenditures on public elementary and secondary education totaled $57.1 billion. The utilization of this untapped potential depends, however, not on its existence, but on the taxpayers' willingness to pay additional taxes and on the ability of the educational establishment to capture resources in the face of strongly competing demands.

One catalyst for additional state support of elementary and secondary education continues in the aftermath of the *Serrano* and *Rodriguez* cases. Although the Supreme Court's decision in the *Rodriguez* case was a serious disappointment to those who feel that equal educational inputs should be required under the Fourteenth Amendment, in fact the school finance reform movement in the states is far from dead. At least a dozen states have initiated major reforms to reduce inequities in the intrastate distribution of educational resources, and the reform movement will probably reach another twelve to fifteen states. These efforts will inevitably increase state shares.

Reform with new money is, of course, easier than reform without new money. Even as state aid was the incentive for many decades in the consolidation of school districts, so must state aid be the incentive for the reduction of intrastate disparities in educational resources.[20]

It may be noted in passing that the school reform movement in the states owes much to the grant policies of the Ford Foundation, which, in recent years, has supported many outstanding research projects in this area. It may also be noted that as this movement proceeds a most interesting phenomenon may occur: an improvement in property tax administration either by way of a state takeover or by way of new patterns of state supervision of local administration. This would be a most fortuitous outcome in an area that has so long resisted administrative reform.

State school finance reform to reduce intrastate disparities in inputs could proceed along any one or a combination of three possible paths. One path, perhaps the least likely, is to broaden the areal basis of support by metropolitanizing school districts. Another path is to remove industrial and commercial property from local tax rolls and transfer assessment, levy, and collection to the state. State collections would then be utilized for reducing disparities in school district revenues. A third path is a state-wide property tax levy as proposed a few years ago by the Fleischmann Commission in New York State. The pursuit of either of these latter two possibilities would, of course, require fundamental changes in the role of the states in property tax administration.

Intelligent generalizations about what will happen to school finance in fifty states and the District of Columbia over the next several years are, of course, impossible. The relative economic decline of the Northeast and Midwest, the relative prosperity of the Southeast and Southwest, and the resulting population shifts will have diverse effects on state resources that are available for education and on demands on state governments for educational support. We need fifty-one very good applied econometric models. We need fifty-one first-rate political analysts who are sensitive to the emerging impact of teachers' unions on state legislatures.[21] And we need a back-up of fifty-one very clear crystal balls.

PROSPECTS FOR LOCAL SUPPORT

The prospects for local support of elementary and secondary education must be appraised in terms of our peculiar system of fiscal federalism. As has been well said, "In a word, federalism is about conflict. Federalism is also about cooperation, that is, the terms and conditions under which conflict is limited."[22] The past decade has been characterized more by turmoil and conflict than by cooperation. It has been a decade of changes in intergovernmental relations where measures undertaken incrementally have added up to major transformations in the fiscal, if not the administrative, roles of national, state, and local governments.

In this peculiar system, local school districts, like all branches of local government, are the residual legatees. A school district, for example, budgets as if it were at the bottom of the hierarchy. The school board, in preparing its budget for the coming year, counts the anticipated aid from the federal and state governments, arranges its expenditures to give the appearance of fulfilling all matching requirements, and adds whatever miscellaneous revenue is to go into the general pot. Then, on the expenditure side, the school board looks at the projected enrollments and salary adjustments that have been mandated or arrived at through bargaining; makes an allowance for the impact of inflation on materials, supplies, and maintenance; adds in the bond amortizations and interest payments; and usually comes up with a gap between revenue and expenditure. This gap can be closed in one of two ways: the size of classes can be increased, thus reducing the requirements for instructional staff; or property tax rates can be increased. The possibilities for the latter depend, of course, on determining the preferences of citizens for elementary and secondary education over their preferences for other public goods and for private goods.

An economist who looks at school district budgeting, particularly as practiced in consolidated school districts in upstate New York, cannot help but be impressed by its congruence with what is known as neoclassical fiscal theory. In upstate New York the school board sends to each resident of the district a preliminary budget for the forthcoming year that indicates proposed increases in expenditures and their intended purpose. The budget also shows the proposed increase in the real property tax. The taxpayer can thus balance at the margin, equating marginal tax costs with marginal benefits in education. If he is dissatisfied, he can appear at the budget hearing and reveal his preferences. In response to the changes requested by citizens, the school board may then adjust its budget to reflect these preferences. The citizen finds it difficult in fiscally independent school districts to make direct comparisons between education and other public goods, such as police and fire protection. In fiscally dependent districts balancing education as against other public goods at the margin, usually with less direct input by citizens, is a more prominent part of budget procedure. In the economic model, and in the operating reality of making school district budgets, the crucial elements are the citizens' marginal valuations of educational outlays and their marginal valuations of educational tax-prices. These tax-prices are usually imposed in terms of property tax rate changes. Thus, at the local level the valuation process is translated into property tax-prices for education.

At some level of abstraction, there are three determinants of school district support from their own resources. The first, as noted, is the tax-price of education in terms of property tax rates. The second, also noted, is the generalized attitude of the citizenry toward public elementary and secondary education in comparison with the benefits to be derived from other local public goods and from private goods. The third determinant, which has not been discussed, is citizens' attitudes toward declining public school enrollments, which are now a reality in many central cities and even in some suburban districts.[23]

It has been observed that the size of the economic pie and its division are not the only factors of concern to the community. The method of slicing the pie may also be relevant.[24] Determining the size of the slices by property tax levies continues to be a most unpopular method. The rapid growth of state legislation favoring so-called "circuit breakers" that provide property tax relief to the elderly, sometimes to all low-income families, and sometimes to both owners and tenants is sufficient evidence of widespread discontent. It is somewhat contradictory that, in the past few years, when citizens' discontent about the property tax has been surfacing, a small but prominent group of economists is contending that the tax is not regressive for homeowners and tenants, but, where reasonably uniform in its impact on all real property is, in fact, progressive.[25] But, regardless of whether the tax is progressive or regressive, the fact of its unpopularity is real, and "Reducing the role of the property tax in school finance is not an easy task."[26]

The property tax will probably continue to serve reasonably well for the fiscal support of local elementary and secondary education in metropolitan areas that are still experiencing economic growth. It will serve very badly in the older central cities and in declining metropolitan areas. It is far easier, of course, to prescribe a solution for this state of affairs than to secure its political implementation. The solution is to tie the support of local schools to more elastic sources of revenue, such as income and sales, and, ideally, on a metropolitan-wide basis rather than on the basis of existing school district lines.

In regard to citizens' attitudes toward education, a reality and an anomaly are again present. The reality is that, for the past two years, even in those cities where the fiscal crisis has been most severe, employment cutbacks in education have been more modest than for police, fire, and sanitation departments. The next few years will probably bring the same kinds of pressures for employment cutbacks, particularly on large city school budgets, that other local government services have already experienced.

The anomaly is that education, as a cure for all manner of societal ills, has undoubtedly been oversold. There is little evidence that increased expenditures for education lead to higher quality education.[27] Education is, for example, an inferior instrument for the redistribution of income.[28] Special programs for education in the inner city have apparently made little if any contribution to reducing unemployment among inner-city youth. But the largely negative findings of researchers on this issue seem not to have affected prevailing opinion. Education continues to rank very high among citizens' preferences for public expenditures, in spite of increased rejection rates on school bond issues in the last several years.[29] Public evaluation of education, as compared to other public goods and private goods may change, however, as the proportion of voters with children of school age is reduced.

To project the response of 16,000 school districts to this set of complex factors is simply not possible. One is tempted to retreat to the device of contemporary social scientists and prepare alternative scenarios without attempting to give an award to the best playwright.

We can be reasonably certain of one thing: in the nation as a whole the number of school-age children will decline. This decline will be most severe in the large metropolitan areas of the Northeast and Midwest. The decline will not be offset at the secondary level by increased high school attendance in the age group that has been stable at 77 percent since about 1965.[30] Many school districts will face extremely difficult and controversial decisions in the utilization of school facilities. In what neighborhoods will schools be closed? Will taxpayers be willing to pay for teacher-student ratios that increase sharply in half-empty classrooms? Busing, which until now has been related to desegregation, will emerge as a controversial issue related to the reallocation of educational resources at the school district level. It may, in fact, be almost as controversial in this context as in the racial context.

All of this leaves the evaluation of prospects for local support very cloudy. It may be just as well to admit that we simply cannot predict for the next few years the outcomes in this sector.

EDUCATIONAL PLANNING

In 1975 there was great interest in national economic planning. A group of prominent economists, labor leaders, and businessmen organized an Initiative Committee for National Economic Planning. Its membership reflected a fascinating spectrum of political views from the moderately radical to the reasonably conservative. We have had a Humphrey-Javits bill and a Humphrey-Hawkins bill, with the latter endorsed in the Democratic party platform. But in recent months, as the economic situation has improved somewhat, interest has abated in new mechanisms for economic planning. That interest could revive quickly, however, if inflation or recession or both emerged with increased severity.

Such a development would, of course, dramatically change the economic outlook — for better or for worse. Federal spending priorities would certainly be altered, and at some point manpower planning would materialize. Though the point of entry would probably be well after the establishment of wage and price guidelines, manpower and, hence, national educational planning would inevitably be subject to some greater centralized control. This would extend to programs for continuing education and higher education. The form, content, and objectives of such increased centralized control provide the occasion for some interesting speculation, but at this juncture such speculation is rather fruitless.

In an ideal world of educational planning there would be close attention to the measurement and projection of educational needs of the type developed by the National Educational Finance Project and exemplified, in their final report, by the careful statistical work of Jordan and Stultz.[31] Here are estimates of needs, state by state, to 1980 for basic educational programs, for education for the handicapped, and for the culturally deprived, for vocational education, and for kindergarten. Projections from experiences for 1968-1973 would require additional outlays of $29.4 billion — a 64 percent increase over 1973 to meet the goals for 1980. It is simply not reasonable to anticipate that resources for public elementary and secondary education will be available—federal, state, or local—to come even close to these goals.

There is one area that demands immediate attention, where some kind of planning and some new initiatives are most pressing: unemployment among youth, in which rates are running above 40 percent in large-city ghettos. This is surely a case of multiple causation, including the failure of the educational system to provide employable skills, the failure of private and public employers to assume responsibility, a disequilibrium in the job market, and a tremendous alienation among affected youth. Public policy responses in terms of OEO programs such as the Neighborhood Youth Corps, the Job Corps, or the Youth Conservation Corps have been sporadic, underfunded, and of very limited success. Comprehensive Employment and Training Act (CETA) programs, except in a very few jurisdictions, have not even addressed the problem.

In 1975, 22.3 percent of the unemployment average of 7,800,000 were in the age bracket of sixteen to nineteen, and another 23.2 percent in the age bracket of twenty to twenty-four. Thus, almost half of those unemployed are in these age groups.[32] The future of 3.5 million young people is, therefore, in jeopardy.

This suggests that educational alternatives are not the sole solution. Any comprehensive program must be multifaceted, with numerous options and with public service employment high on the list of options.

In regard to less pressing problems, even if there are no major new federal programs for education in the next several years, there have been some recent developments at the federal level that suggest the possibility of modest reforms. These developments may be said to fall under the general rubric of educational planning.

The first development is contained in the Education Act Amendments of 1974 (P.L. 93-380). In this statute the National Reading Improvement Program was authorized with funding up to $93 million in fiscal 1978. To qualify for grants that are awarded at the discretion of the commissioner of education, each state must establish an advisory council on reading improvement to devise a state-wide plan. The grant is contingent on the commissioner's approval of the plan.

The amendments of 1974 provided for a similar type of state council and a state plan as a condition for the receipt of small grants for "libraries, learning resources, educational innovation and support." In the Education Amendments of 1975 (section 842) modest grants were made available to the states for the development of improved state equalization plans.

If this exemplifies the approach of the New Federalism to education, one cannot say that it is replete with local autonomy. But it will very likely be followed if there is federal legislation for disadvantaged children.

It should be stressed that until these recent developments in education federal aid has had virtually no impact on relationships between state and local agencies. Federal aid has not been contingent on school district reorganization, on state education planning, or on school finance reform. If the actions taken by Congress in 1974 and 1975 are the harbinger of the future, we may very well see further developments of this type. That is, Congress authorizes a categorical grant conditional on specified actions by the state. The state is then required to engage in program planning and may well be given resources to assist in this planning effort. The state, in cooperation with local school districts, then emerges with a plan devised within the guidelines laid down by the commissioner of education. When the commissioner approves the plan, grant funds are extended to implement it.

This approach to intergovernmental relations in education is roughly comparable to the patterns that have emerged for special revenue sharing under the CETA and special revenue sharing for community development. Although both of these programs have been accompanied by much rhetoric about transferring local decision making to localities, there is, in fact, a strong federal presence in this administrative relationship.

It is likely that this pattern will be followed in education planning in the next few years. A major special revenue sharing program, with substantial new federal funds, is not now in view. But a few existing categoricals may be consolidated, and in the process the states will be required to engage in new planning endeavors. This kind of device could be extended to such problems as state school finance reform or the metropolitanization of school districts, but this would appear to be a less likely outcome. One certain outcome is that Congress will continue to be involved in education, and the paperwork that accompanies the involvement will be massive.

NOTES

1. All data reported here, unless otherwise noted, are derived from the U.S. Department of Commerce, *Survey of Current Business,* various issues.

2. For an excellent review of recent stabilization experience and the frustrations that have been encountered in the use of conventional fiscal and monetary policy, see

George L. Perry, "Stabilization Policy and Inflation," in *Setting National Priorities for the Next Ten Years,* ed. Henry Owen and Charles L. Schultze (Washington, D.C.: Brookings Institution, 1976), pp. 271-321.

3. Robert Lekachman, *Economists at Bay* (New York: McGraw-Hill, 1976).

4. Alan K. Campbell, "The Politics and Economics of the Future Financing of Education," Institute for Chief State School Officers, Jackson Hole, Wyoming, 1974.

5. William J. Baumol, "Macroeconomics of Unbalanced Growth: The Anatomy of the Urban Crisis," *American Economic Review* 57 (June 1967): 415-426.

6. U.S. Bureau of the Census, *Population Estimates and Projections,* Series P-25, No. 618 (Washington, D.C.: U.S. Government Printing Office, 1976).

7. Peter A. Morrison, *The Demographic Context of Educational Policy Planning* (Santa Monica, Calif.: RAND Corporation, 1976).

8. The numbers presented in Table 5-3 are for budget authority. A slightly different set of numbers would emerge if budget outlays were used, but the general picture would remain the same.

9. Charles L. Schultze, "Federal Spending: Past, Present and Future," in *Setting National Priorities,* ed. Owen and Schultze, pp. 323-369.

10. *Ibid.,* p. 347.

11. On September 14, 1976, the Pentagon increased its request for fiscal 1978 to $130 billion. This is $9 billion more than the administration's estimate in February and $18 billion more than Congress has thus far authorized for the fiscal 1977 budget. (*New York Times,* September 15, 1976.)

12. Another pessimistic projection available is that provided by the Congressional Budget Office (CBO) in March 1976. Although current federal expenditures for education and academic research amount to about $23 billion, when that portion ($9.7 billion) devoted to early childhood, elementary and secondary, higher and "other" is isolated, the CBO finds that an extension of current policy will bring outlays from fiscal 1977 of $9.7 billion to $11.9 billion in fiscal 1981. With an annual inflation rate of 5 percent, this is equivalent to $9.7 billion in 1981. (Congressional Budget Office, *Budget Options for Fiscal Year 1977* [Washington, D.C.: U.S. Government Printing Office, 1976], pp. 223-224.)

13. Schultze, "Federal Spending," p. 352.

14. P. Michael Timpane, "Federal Aid to Schools: Its Limited Future," *Duke Law Review* (Winter 1974-1975): 493-512.

15. As an example, contemplate the difficulties inherent in devising a formula that would be "equitable" for school districts with both large and small nonpublic school enrollment.

16. The proposal did not actually reach congressional committees. Instead, the President asked the Advisory Commission on Intergovernmental Relations to study the suggestion; their response was largely negative. (Robert D. Reischauer, Robert W. Hartman, and Daniel J. Sullivan, *Reforming School Finance* [Washington, D.C.: Brookings Institution, 1973].)

17. Robert D. Reischauer, *General Revenue Sharing: Its Impact on and Relation to the Education Sector* (Washington, D.C.: Educational Policy Research Institute of the Educational Testing Service, 1975).

18. The politics of GRS in 1976 was almost as interesting as in 1972. In spite of some obvious defects in the law — particularly the ceiling provisions that worked against consolidated governments in large cities and the floor provision that provided for payments to insignificant governments such as New England counties and mid-

western townships—the governors and mayors who lobbied for the extension of GRS had no desire to make any major changes in the statute for fear of losing the support of constituents for a measure that has not enjoyed great popularity in Congress.

19. John Due, "Alternative State and Local Tax Sources for Education," in Kern Alexander and K. Forbis Jordan, *Educational Need in the Public Economy* (Gainesville: University Presses of Florida, 1976), pp. 257-298.

20. For an excellent survey of the history and current prospects for school finance reform, see Joel S. Berke and Jay H. Moskowitz, "Research in School Finance: A Concern with Equity and Equality," *1976 Review of Research in Education,* vol. 4, ed. Lee S. Shulman (New York: American Educational Research Association, 1977, pp. 309-337.

21. See Campbell, "Politics and Economics of the Future Financing of Education."

22. Aaron Wildavsky, "A Bias toward Federalism: Confronting the Conventional Wisdom on the Delivery of Governmental Services," *Publius* 5 (Spring 1976): 85-120.

23. There will be an abundance of general literature and case studies on this problem in the next few years. One such study is Citizens Research Council of Michigan, *The Management of Declining Public School Enrollments* (Detroit: the Council, 1976).

24. See Stephen A. Marglin, "Objectives of Water-Resource Development," in Arthur Maass *et al., Design of Water-Resource Systems* (Cambridge, Mass.: Harvard University Press, 1962), pp. 17-18.

25. See Henry J. Aaron, *Who Pays the Property Tax?* (Washington, D.C.: Brookings Institution, 1975).

26. Reischauer, Hartman, and Sullivan, *Reforming School Finance,* p. 56.

27. See Henry A. Averch *et al., How Effective Is Schooling? A Critical Review and Synthesis of Research Findings* (Santa Monica, Calif.: RAND Corporation, 1972).

28. See Christopher Jencks *et al., Inequality: A Reassessment of the Effect of Family and Schooling in America* (New York: Basic Books, 1972). An alternative approach that looks only at the "direct" benefits of education in terms of expenditures per pupil and tax payments by income class reaches the conclusion that elementary and secondary education is importantly redistributive. See Kern Alexander, Thomas Melcher, and Stephen Thomas, "Income Redistribution Effect of Public Schools on Low-Income Families," in Alexander and Jordan, *Educational Need in the Public Economy,* pp. 84-112.

29. The National Opinion Research Center found in 1973, 1974, and 1975 that about 50 percent of "the public" responded that too little money was spent on education, about 36 percent responded "about the right amount," and only 10 percent responded "too much money." (National Center for Education Statistics, *The Condition of Education 1976* [Washington, D.C.: U.S. Government Printing Office, 1976], p. 206.)

30. See Thomas F. Green, *The General Educational System* (Syracuse, N.Y.: Syracuse University, Cultural Foundations of Education, 1976).

31. K. Forbis Jordan and James R. Stultz, "Projecting the Educational Needs and Costs of Elementary and Secondary Education," in Alexander and Jordan, *Educational Need in the Public Economy,* pp. 163-211.

32. Congressional Budget Office, *Policy Options for the Teenage Unemployment Problem* (Washington, D.C.: U.S. Government Printing Office, 1976), p. 85.

6   Priority Issues in Educational Finance

The Politics of Intergovernmental Fiscal Assistance and Controls

Norman C. Thomas

The governance of American education occurs within the broader context of the federal system.[1] In this respect education is subject to the same intergovernmental forces that operate in other domestic policy areas. Education is somewhat distinctive, however, in that the delivery of most services in elementary and secondary education is a function of special rather than general governmental authorities. What is more important, the value of local self-determination appears to have greater influence over the design of administrative arrangements and the making of policy choices in education than in most other areas. A popular shorthand formulation holds that education is a local function, a state responsibility, and a federal concern. This condition is reflected in the proportion of support for public elementary and secondary schools in recent years borne by local (52 percent), state (40 percent), and federal (8 percent) governments.[2]

In spite of the apparent stability of this pattern of predominant reliance on local support and a relatively small amount of federal support, there are numerous conflicts over the appropriate roles of governmental authorities at the three levels and over the locus of control of educational operations. These disagreements stem in part from different understandings of the nature of American federalism. Two alternative models dominate the literature. On the one hand there is the traditional hierarchical view that conceives of an ordered layering of governmental levels, each performing specific functions. On the other

hand, the twentieth-century growth of federal activity through categorical grants-in-aid to state and local governments has given rise to
an alternative concept which sees the American system "as a matrix,
not a hierarchy . . . in which powers are not allocated by 'levels' but
are divided among different arenas—federal and state by primary
constitutional grant and local by derivation."[3] The matrix model re-
jects the superior-subordinate ranking of governmental levels and
holds that different arenas vary in importance by functional policy
area. Tensions between these approaches are reflected in conflicts over
the determination and implementation of policy. This condition has
been particularly acute in education since the passage of the Great
Society educational legislation in the mid-1960's.[4]

A related issue contributes further to uncertainty over the nature of
the federal system: at what point should the federal government intervene in an area, such as education, that hitherto has been the domain
of state and local governments? The "activist" view holds that federal
involvement is desirable if the proposed action will make a "timely
contribution . . . to the solution of a serious and persistent domestic
problem."[5] The "traditionalist" uses a more rigorous test that requires
a proposed federal initiative to meet two conditions: "The problem
that precipitated the demand for Federal intervention stems from a
head-on conflict—a serious undercutting of a major Federal program
objective by policies of most States. The intergovernmental conflict
can be resolved only by Federal government action."[6] It is thus an
open question if, when, what kind, and how much federal involvement in a policy area is appropriate. In education there are continuous pressures for and against an expanded federal role. Though the
prospect of additional funds is welcomed by most state and local officials, they disagree widely over the kind and degree of controls that accompany the aid.

A third aspect of the pattern of intergovernmental relations in
education that results in political controversy is its complexity. The
variety of the sources of income, the diversity of objectives, the numerous opportunities for multipocket budgeting, and the diversity of
channels of professional and citizen influence make it difficult to
establish accountability for performance.

The web of relationships has been portrayed graphically by David
O. Porter, who has developed a model of intergovernmental transactions (see Figure 6-1). Limitations of space preclude detailed explora-

Figure 6-1. Intergovernmental transactions in education

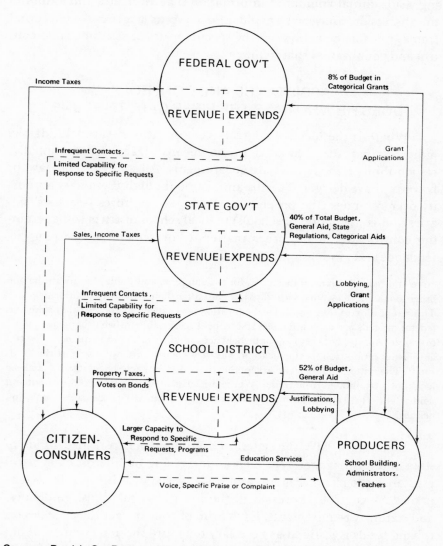

Source: David O. Porter, "Responsiveness to Citizen Consumers in a Federal System," *Publius, The Journal of Federalism* 5 (Fall 1975): 68.

tion of Porter's model. It is included here as a quick means of conveying a substantial amount of information that illustrates and amplifies the discussion above. It should also serve as a general conceptual framework for the analysis of the specific issues of assistance and control and equalization that follow.

ASSISTANCE AND CONTROL: DOES HE WHO PAYS THE PIPER CALL THE TUNE?

Where is the locus of control over education? Aaron Wildavsky indicates that the answer is by no means clear. Constitutionally, responsibility is lodged in state governments. All states except Hawaii, however, have delegated a substantial amount of discretionary authority over revenues (the property tax) and expenditures (teachers' salaries and construction of schools) to local school districts while retaining control over many other matters (requirements concerning attendance and graduation and certification).

State and federal financial incentives for teaching this and doing that mean that, in order to maximize income, local districts must alter their own order of priorities . . . . This temptation to tinker with local education is enhanced by the fact that state and federal officials are not, in the last resort, held responsible for what happens; judges may order busing, but they cannot be held accountable for the consequences. Central authorities cannot run local education, but they are not quite willing to let the locals run it. The center cannot devise acceptable trade-offs for each school district, and the localities are inhibited from trying. Whose priorities prevail? Both to some extent and neither entirely. Who is ultimately responsible? The answer is the same: both and neither.[7]

Since the 1950's the federal government has provided funds to state and local agencies through an increasing number of categorical assistance programs. Federal and state assistance is invariably accompanied by controls expressed in the form of regulations, guidelines, and statutory requirements. Each form of control over the agencies receiving funds is justified as necessary to ensure the achievement of national or state goals. Each objection to the controls is couched in appeals to the value of local self-determination.

The conflict between centralization and decentralization is related to the question of accountability. Whom can the citizen-consumers of education—students and their parents—hold responsible for the quality and quantity of the services they receive or fail to receive? How can that accountability be democratically exercised? Should control over the delivery of educational services be roughly correlated with the proportion of financial support that the three levels of government provide? How much leverage should the federal and state governments attempt to exert on local agencies in order to guarantee minimum standards of performance and to achieve more ambitious goals such as the equalization of educational opportunities on a national and a state-wide basis? These and similar questions permeate the politics of education as a consequence of the intergovernmental framework in which it occurs.

The conflict over control of education has been most intense when Congress has tried to determine the federal role. Pressures for general and relatively unrestricted assistance have yet to overcome the various forces arrayed against them.[8] A key element in the sustained opposition to general aid, at least between 1945 and 1965, was the fear that it would lead to a national system of education. In the face of its inability to form a winning coalition in support of general aid and confronted with rising demands for federal assistance, Congress enacted a series of categorical programs beginning in 1950. These programs were designed to meet special needs such as those of areas impacted by children of federal employees at nontaxable facilities (P.L. 874), instruction in science, mathematics, and foreign languages (NDEA, 1958), vocational education (Vocational Education Act, 1963), and economically disadvantaged children (ESEA, 1965).

These categorical aid programs cover approximately 8 percent of the cost of elementary and secondary education. They also carry with them a sizable amount of regulation, so much so, in fact, that Joseph Cronin, state superintendent of education in Illinois, claims that a federal takeover of education is "inevitable." "[S]lowly, inexorably, and incrementally, the federal government is taking over education. Especially since 1965, the country has moved — almost every year — toward a national system of education. Furthermore, the potential opposition has almost conceded the inevitability of the trend, if not all the details."[9] Illustrative of the federal regulations and controls that so distress Cronin are such things as: the comprehensive proposals, documentation, and formal evaluations that are required to secure funds; the reports and studies to which state and local agencies must respond (over twenty-four in the 1970's); the Buckley Amendment which imposed new record-keeping procedures and costs and provided access to students' records; costs of responding to federal environmental and safety regulations; documentation (upon request) of compliance with Title VI of the Civil Rights Act of 1964; and implementation of Title IX of the Education Amendments of 1972, which prohibits sexual bias in athletics, vocational education, and extracurricular activities. Cronin also observes that two of the principal traditional bulwarks against a federal takeover—the Education Commission of the States and state departments of education—receive most of their funding from Washington.[10] On the other hand, some critics of the U.S. Office of Education have charged that the agency has been lax in ensuring that state and local recipients comply with congressional requirements.[11] Still others have argued that approval by USOE of state plans required for participation in categorical federal programs tends to be a pro forma ritual.

THE QUEST FOR GREATER EQUITY: SCHOOL FINANCE REFORM

The system of financing public elementary and secondary education in the United States has been the target of extensive reform efforts since the mid-1960's. "The root of the question is money: who should pay how much for financing public elementary and secondary schooling. But the subsidiary questions are all important. What should the role of state governments be? How heavily should the schools rely on the local property tax? What formulas for equalization are equitable and politically feasible?"[12] The principal complaint is well known: the unequal amounts of resources available for education in local school districts.[13]

[T]he history of public school finance by local districts is the history of determined inequality. The traditional liberal, whom we now call conservative, focuses attention on the *processes* in the economy, desirous of maintaining freedom of the individual and of his freely entered into collectives. Some of these collectives are cities, suburbs, towns, and school districts; they exist to promote and to maintain inequality in the provision of public services. Modern liberals look more at the *results* of individual and collective freedom, particularly as exercised by the powerful. Since collectives designed to maintain schooling inequality are local in nature, liberals look to higher levels of government—state and federal—to promote their concept of justice, which entails preventing some individuals and collectives from maintaining inequalities.[14]

Disparities exist between states as well as within states. This condition, reformers claim, results in a denial of equality of educational opportunity. The root of the problem lies in the predominant reliance on local and state taxes that are based on the wealth and economic well-being of states and communities. Of foremost concern is the local property tax which varies according to the value of the residential, commercial, and industrial wealth of a community and the willingness of voters there to tax that wealth. The resources generated by the property tax, which accounts for 98 percent of local school revenues, are but infrequently related to the educational needs of children in a community; they tend more, in fact, to be inversely related, especially in depressed rural areas and aging central cities. Moreover, to the extent that state assistance to local school districts is based on local property tax revenues, it contributes little to the equalization of resources.

The periodic budgetary crises encountered by state governments and local school districts coupled with citizens' "revolts" against further property tax increases have led educators and elected officials to look to the federal government as a stabilizing source of support and for additional funds that will permit a reform of state and local tax systems. Such reforms would reduce dependence on the local property tax and substantially eliminate intrastate disparities in expenditures. They would also take into account such factors as the differing educational needs of some children (such as the handicapped), the existence of cost differentials between local school districts, and the variable pattern of demands for services on local governments (municipal overburden).

Advocates of school finance reform have recognized that interstate disparities can be eliminated only through federal action. This raises the question of whether the federal government should undertake to equalize expenditures between states that now vary by a ratio of greater than 2.5 to 1. If the answer is affirmative, then additional questions arise: What kinds of regulation and control will accompany the federal effort? Is it possible that such aid will lead to a national educational system? In light of the strong support given to the value of local control of education that is manifest in the legislation authorizing existing categorical programs, is it likely that support on the scale needed to overcome interstate disparities can be enacted in the face of its potential threat to this control? A more realistic question is whether education has the public support and political clout to prevail over the claims of other domestic programs in areas such as welfare, income maintenance, and health care.

Even if a quantum increase in federal aid is not in the offing,[15] it might still be possible to utilize existing federal support for leverage to stimulate greater state efforts toward eliminating intrastate disparities. To date the federal role in promoting equalization has been limited. Of the categorical aid programs, only ESEA Title I has had significant equalizing effects. The Education Amendments of 1974, however, authorized grants up to a maximum of $1 million to assist states in equalizing their school finance systems. In 1972, at the peak of the revolt against the property tax, President Nixon suggested the imposition of a federal value-added tax (VAT), the proceeds of which would finance local property tax relief, and the overhaul of state school finance systems. The VAT attracted little support, and the proposal faded away. More recently, the property tax has enjoyed a moderate gain in support among experts in public finance and politicians. After all, the burdens and inequities of an existing tax are known while a new tax is fraught with uncertainty. Since 1972, no President has expressed interest in reforming school finance through federal action. The brightest prospect for a major federal impact on school finance reform dimmed in 1973 when the Supreme Court rejected a challenge to the constitutionality of the Texas school finance system on the ground that it violated the "equal protection of the laws" clause of the Fourteenth Amendment.[16]

The most successful and extensive efforts to reform school finance have occurred at the state level. State courts have entertained challenges to school finance systems based on state constitutional provisions.[17] Between 1971 and 1975 legislatures in eleven states, responding to judicial decisions and a variety of other factors, enacted statutes reforming their school finance systems.[18] Attempts through referenda to achieve reform proved unsuccessful in five states, however, during 1972 and 1973.

Berke, Shalala, and Williams have identified the conditions associated with successful efforts to achieve reform through state legislatures.[19] These conditions include a prior history of reform efforts, which creates a favorable climate for reform; events outside the normal pattern of educational policy making, such as a judicial decision; committed political leadership, especially by legislators; and a favorable fiscal situation manifested either in a budget surplus or in the availability of funds from general revenue sharing. A successful reform package can only be created through compromises that lead to the formation of a winning legislative coalition. As a consequence, the statutes that have been adopted have not closely approximated either of the two basic types of reform options: full state funding and district power equalizing. Most reform statutes include such limiting features as minimum and maximum limits on aid to local districts and "save harmless" provisions guaranteeing that no district will receive less state aid after reform than it did before. Wealthy districts are unlikely to accept reductions in state support for their schools and are even more inclined to resist attempts to redistribute the resources generated locally through property taxes.

The ethic of local control operates largely to preclude full state funding. It also dominates consideration of reform legislation through such questions as: To what degree will educational resources be equalized among districts? Will voters in local districts be permitted to override limits on local property taxes? How much reward, if any, will be given to local tax efforts? What consideration will be accorded to municipal overburden and to differentials between cost and need? What role will the property tax play in funding education? Will additional state restrictions accompany reforms that bring greater state support?

Another issue that involves local control is the prospect that state legislation might govern the salaries, fringe benefits, and conditions of employment of teachers and school administrators. With or without substantially increased state aid, however, state control over labor negotiations in education appears likely to grow, in part because of the rise of teachers' unions. The extent to which state regulation of collective bargaining will reduce the autonomy of local school districts remains to be seen.

CONCLUSION

Two themes emerge from this brief and necessarily incomplete consideration of the political aspects of the intergovernmental financing of education. First, and most striking, are the pervasiveness and strength of the value of local self-determination. Whatever action the federal and state governments contemplate is sharply constrained by localism. Conflict continuously wages between centralization and decentralization and between localism and more general values, such as equity, efficiency, and accountability. How much ground the forces of local control have yielded is itself a matter of dispute. What is clear is that a national educational system is not likely to develop in the foreseeable future and that, within most state systems, local districts will retain substantial control over a wide range of matters including finance. All of this may prove frustrating to educators and politicians who make rational arguments for the need to reduce and manage locally based disparities and diversities. Movement in that direction will take place gradually and in the face of considerable opposition.

The second theme is in many respects the converse of the first. Although American federalism facilitates great diversity of activity and encourages fragmentation of political control, it also links the people of this nation together in an interdependent web of relationships. Intergovernmental cooperation is an imperative in education as in all policy areas. Education is an institutional service of vital significance to the nation and its people. Consequently, we can expect to witness continuing efforts to obtain equality of educational opportunities, services, and outcomes across the nation, within the states, and in the multitude of local school districts. Proponents of change, be it in financing systems, curriculum, instructional methods, or other aspects of the educational enterprise, will continue to press their cases in whatever professional forums they can find and through whatever political channels that are open to them.

This is not a neat, orderly, or ideal pattern, and few, if any, persons or groups involved in or concerned with education can expect to achieve more than a portion of their goals. But the tension between the centrifugal forces of localism and the centripetal forces of interdependence imparts a creative dynamic that has so far prevented development of a static equilibrium that stifles adaptation and change.

NOTES

1. See Edith K. Mosher, "Education and American Federalism: Intergovernmental and National Policy Issues," in *The Politics of Education,* Seventy-sixth Yearbook of the National Society for the Study of Education, Part II, ed. J. D. Scribner (Chicago: University of Chicago Press, 1977).

2. Rochelle L. Stanfield, "Why Johnny Can't—The Problem of State School Financing," *National Journal* 8 (April 24, 1976): 557.

3. Daniel J. Elazar, "Federalism: 'The Cardinal Question,' " in *Federalism, ed. Martin J. Macbin* (Washington, D.C.: National Journal Reprints, 1976), p. 1.

4. See Stephen K. Bailey and Edith K. Mosher, *ESEA: The Office of Education Administers a Law* (Syracuse, N.Y.: Syracuse University Press, 1968); and Norman C. Thomas, *Education in National Politics* (New York: David McKay, 1975).

5. Advisory Commission on Intergovernmental Relations, *Financing Schools and Property Tax Relief—A State Responsibility* (Washington, D.C.: the Commission, 1973), p. 125.

6. *Ibid.,* p. 126.

7. Aaron Wildavsky, "The Strategic Retreat on Objectives," *Policy Analysis* 2 (Summer 1976): 517.

8. See Frank J. Munger and Richard F. Fenno, Jr., *National Politics and Federal Aid to Education* (Syracuse, N.Y.: Syracuse University Press, 1962); Philip Meranto, *The Politics of Federal Aid to Education in 1965* (Syracuse, N.Y.: Syracuse University Press, 1967); Bailey and Mosher, *ESEA;* Eugene Eidenberg and Roy D. Morey, *An Act of Congress* (New York: W. W. Norton, 1969); and Thomas, *Education in National Politics.*

9. Joseph M. Cronin, "The Federal Takeover: Should the Junior Partner Run the Firm?" *Phi Delta Kappan* 57 (April 1976): 499-500.

10. *Ibid.*

11. See, for example, Milbrey W. McLaughlin, *Evaluation and Reform: The Elementary and Secondary Education Act of 1965/Title I,* RAND Educational Policy Study (Cambridge, Mass.: Ballinger Publishing Co., 1975).

12. Stanfield, "Why Johnny Can't," 556.

13. The literature of the school finance reform movement is extensive. Among the major works are: Arthur E. Wise, *Rich Schools, Poor Schools* (Chicago: University of Chicago Press, 1968); John E. Coons *et al., Private Wealth and Public Education* (Cambridge, Mass.: Belknap Press of Harvard University Press, 1970); Joel S. Berke, *Answers to Inequity: An Analysis of the New School Finance* (Berkeley, Calif.: McCutchan Publishing Corp., 1974); *Future Directions for School Finance Reform,* ed. Betsy Levin (Lexington, Mass.: Lexington Books, 1974); and the reports of the National Educational Finance Project directed by Roe L. Johns and Kern Alexander (Gainesville, Fla.: the Project, 1969-1971).

14. Stephan Michaelson, "What Is a Just System for Financing Schools? An Evaluation of Alternative Reforms," *Law and Contemporary Problems* 38 (Winter-Spring 1974): 436.

15. See P. Michael Timpane, "Federal Aid to Schools: Its Limited Future," *Law and Contemporary Problems* 38 (Winter-Spring 1974): 493-512.

16. *San Antonio Independent School District* v. *Rodriguez,* 411 U.S. 1 (1973).

17. See, for example, *Serrano* v. *Priest,* 5 Cal. 3d 584, 487 P. 2d 1241 (1971); *Robinson* v. *Cahill,* 118 N.J. Super. 223, 287 A. 2d 187 (1972), *modified and affirmed on other grounds,* 62 N.J. 473 303 A. 2d 273 (1973); and *Seattle School District No. 1* v. *State of Washington* (Jan. 14, 1977, No. 53950). Litigation is currently in progress in New York and Ohio.

18. See W. Norton Grubb, "The First Round of Legislative Reforms in the Post-*Serrano* World," *Law and Contemporary Problems* 38 (Winter-Spring 1974): 459-492.

19. See Joel S. Berke, Donna E. Shalala, and Mary Frase Williams, "Two Roads to School Finance Reform," *Society* 13 (January-February 1976): 67-72.

The Policy Dilemmas in New School
Finance Reforms within the States

John J. Callahan

From 1971 on, eighteen states have adopted major revisions in their school funding systems. Since that time two out of three new state and local dollars for education have come from the state level. Thus, school tax burdens have been eased in many poor communities across the country, and at least three states—Iowa, New Mexico, and Florida—have disparities in expenditures of less than 25 percent between districts whose expenditures are very high and those whose expenditures are low. More and more states are adopting compensatory education finance programs, and state funding for special education has increased from $900 million nation-wide in 1971-1972 to well over $2.5 billion in 1975-1976. All these circumstances indicate that school finance reform has been a major preoccupation of decision makers within the states in the last few years.

And this reform will continue to pose major policy dilemmas for most state officials in the years to come. Aside from the need to keep funding commitments to finance reforms high, they will also have to make fundamental choices among the funding models that they believe to be most equitable, to make trade-offs between the tax and expenditure equities contained in their finance systems, and to ensure that the equity of their funding systems somehow can be translated into educational reforms that benefit the children of their state. The way in which states are approaching these policy issues is the subject of this chapter.

CHOICE OF FUNDING MODELS

State officials have three basic choices when they are constructing new school finance systems. The first option, which is the least exercised, is full state funding. Though this model produces a high degree of equity between taxes and funding, it has been adopted only in Hawaii.

The next option is the foundation plan, which requires all localities to make a fixed local tax effort to qualify for foundation aid and then guarantees that all school districts will be able to spend at the "foundation" level of expenditure. Though this is still the most widely used state finance plan, its fiscal defects are well known. For example, states often fail to raise the foundation level of expenditures to reflect increased costs. Thus, local districts spend well above the foundation level, drawing on unequalized local tax resources. And traditional foundation plans have rarely provided for the financing of special education or for fields in which costs are especially high. In spite of these limitations, however, foundation plans can produce a high degree of equity between taxes and expenditures.

The third option is that of district power equalization in which the prime emphasis is on school tax equity. Thus, local districts decide upon the level of school tax effort they deem adequate for the education of their children. Once making their tax effort, however, they are guaranteed a revenue yield equal to that of all other school districts making a similar effort. Districts making different tax efforts will, of course, have different revenue yields for their respective tax efforts. This option has been a popular new reform since it is felt to enhance local control over education and since it is supposed to encourage increased school spending by poor districts that have hitherto been unwilling to collect high taxes to support their schools.

State decision makers are continuing to assess the fiscal equity of their funding plans. Considerable equalization of expenditures has been achieved in three foundation states—Iowa, Florida, and New Mexico—and yet this may be attributable as much to the spending and taxing limits placed on local school districts as to the foundation plans in these states. Foundation plans in Minnesota and California have also begun to reduce spending inequities in those states, though more and more communities are holding referenda to authorize exceeding their fiscal limits. Richer communities will, of course, reap more benefits from successful referenda than poorer ones. Sagging state treasuries in New York and Massachusetts have gutted the fiscal equity of their fixed and variable foundation plans. And in some states, such as Iowa, equity in school spending has not greatly affected the school taxing inequities that are caused by local funding of educational programs outside the foundation plan and by relative changes in income and property values of local jurisdictions. In short, foundation plans demand a high level of funding, limits on unequalized local taxing and spending, and greater attention to residual school tax inequities if they are to be fully effective. Most states still have not reached this goal.

A number of states are scrutinizing district power equalization plans. Some states have dropped or modified these plans since they have been criticized as increasing taxes, which is not popular in a time of declining enrollments. Florida has abolished the power equalized portion of its original finance reform. Wisconsin has limited the revenue yield in its school finance plan when tax rates for schools exceed a certain level. Michigan has modified the schedule of revenue guarantees in its aid plan, and Colorado and Kansas have strict limits on expenditures that prevent major increases in local school taxes.

Some critics of district power equalization plans note that poorer districts still suffer under such funding schemes. In Michigan, for example, such districts have not always taken full advantage of the revenue guarantees under the state's aid system. Lack of response to aid incentives can be attributed to many factors, including: rising tax rates for noneducational expenditures, mandated local expenditures for programs funded outside the basic aid plan, and the changing age composition of older, poorer communities. Doubts remain in many states concerning the long-term equity of expenditures of district power equalization plans.

Decision makers will continue to debate the relative equity of these three plans. How this debate is resolved will shape many state fiscal policies in the future. Those who are more concerned about equity in school spending will be inclined to support foundation plans guaranteeing a high level of basic expenditures. Those who are more concerned about equity in school taxing and local fiscal control over school spending will be inclined to support district power equalization plans.

TRADE-OFFS BETWEEN SCHOOL TAX AND SPENDING EQUITY

Recent analyses of new state school finance reforms suggest that inequities in school taxes, rather than in school spending, have been the major concern at the state level. In five states such reforms produced actual declines in local property revenues in their first year of implementation. Limits on taxes and spending in local school districts have held down school spending in many other states. Moreover, many states adopted major property tax credit programs simultaneously with their finance reforms. These programs, now funded at over $1.5 billion per year, have done much to ease the burden of local school property taxes. Property tax "recapture" provisions in new state laws in Montana, Maine, and Utah also highlight the lengths to which some states have gone in order to ensure the overall school tax equity of their new plans.

The main reason for the great emphasis on tax equity has been the perception that rising school property taxes were beginning to erode severely the increased support for education. When school taxes are high in poor communities, this prevents them from increasing their commitment to education. Rising taxes that were often tied to major inflationary increases in property values were beginning to out-strip citizens' ability to pay. Before new spending patterns could be es-tablished, the public resentment of these rising fiscal pressures would need to be ameliorated. Moreover, state officials became concerned that major increases in school revenues in many communities, particu-larly those in which spending is low, could not be efficiently spent in a very short time. Thus, several states have made plans to level off gradually the expenditures of such districts.

Spending equity, however, has been achieved in other ways. At least three states have plans that allocate more money for pupils whose cost of education is high. Adjustments for municipal overburdens in Michigan and cost-of-living adjustments in Florida channel more money into high-cost urban areas. Rural districts in many western states received additional school aid because of their higher spending levels, which are attributable to diseconomies of scale. Programs in special and vocational education direct more monies to high-cost stu-dents. New programs in which the state assumes full responsibility for the costs of retirement and construction of new buildings also have removed a major source of spending disparities among local units.

And yet there continues to be major resistance to unhindered equalization of spending. State decisionmakers still do not understand the educational ramifications of a spending disparity of two hundred dollars per pupil between a high- and low-spending district. Many are questioning the effectiveness of putting more money into special education, especially into learning disabilities, which is the area of greatest growth in that field. Compensatory education also has yet to find a ready constituency in many states. In a recent survey by the National Conference of State Legislatures most of the state education chairmen indicated that they prefer major funding improvements that work to the benefit of the "regular" schoolchild.

Another source of resistance to major improvements in the equity of spending patterns has been the federal government's education aid policies. Impact aid disrupts the fiscal stability and equity of aid policies in several states. The new program for the handicapped creates major mandates for spending that the federal government is unlikely to fund; it also provides for unequalized funding for special education among local districts. In most states federal and state compensatory education programs have little fiscal coordination. All this has produced major state support for education block grants, though passage of such legislation by Congress is deemed unlikely in the near future.

In summary, additional research is needed to determine the changes that might occur with rising spending in poor school districts and the substantive gains that might be accomplished with increased spending in special, vocational, and compensatory education. Until the results of that research are available, the primary concern of state decisionmakers will be to ensure greater equity in school tax policies.

FINANCIAL SYSTEMS AND EDUCATIONAL REFORM: UNEASY ALLIES?

The foregoing suggests that revisions in basic educational practices have not been a major factor in school finance reform. Except in New Jersey, where the debate concerning the fiscal ramifications of the "thorough and efficient" clause of the state constitution prompted a new finance plan, this has usually been the case.

States have, of course, been making strides in some areas of educational reform. Laws requiring minimal competency for high school graduation have been passed in three states: Oregon, California, and Florida. Florida has also instituted an educational testing and accountability system that gives individual communities control over educational policies. Legislation concerned with students' rights has been passed in Minnesota, and most states are improving procedures whereby children can be placed in special education programs. Systems for testing and assessing students are increasing, and in California new laws regarding evaluation of teachers have been proposed. All these developments suggest that state officials realize the necessity of changes in school administration and governance if school finance reform is to have full impact.

It seems logical that educational reform should precede financial reform. As in New Jersey, equitable changes in educational programs and procedures that meet the needs of poorer communities should be costed out and equitably financed in a new state school aid system. And yet, this conceptual approach runs counter to the growing problems in school administration and labor-management relations, which work against a positive alliance between financial and educational reform.

With declining enrollments, most school districts are not able to recruit new teachers. When older and more experienced, but not necessarily more able, teachers continue to teach, costs increase without commensurate increases in educational productivity. In most school systems lack of provision for merit pay increases prevents geographic mobility of better teachers. Because of rising labor and retirement costs, most schools are unable to afford technological innovations that might increase educational effectiveness. In many cases the continued pressure exerted on schools to provide noneducational services to children also may lessen the effectiveness of basic educational programs.

In spite of all the problems, however, school finance reform often directs new monies to those school districts most in need of reform. Large cities, which could benefit from decentralized school management and more effective teachers for minority pupils, and poor suburban and rural school districts, which need to increase salaries and sometimes to hire more qualified teachers, are often the prime recipients of new aid.

It must be recognized, however, that if schools do not change their governance and administrative policies, funds for reform will be used primarily for reduction in property taxes and for across-the-board increases in salaries of the present teaching staffs. Unless such money is used to produce changes in educational policies and programs, new reforms are unlikely to materialize, and those already achieved will be jeopardized.

CONCLUSION

States have made major strides in devising more equitable school finance plans. Constructive debates still occur, however, over the choice of basic funding plans, the balancing of taxes and expenditures in new finance plans, and the need and feasibility of coordinating financial and educational reform movements. The resolution of these debates at the state level should determine, among other things, whether state funding of basic aid programs will continue to maintain the fiscal integrity of new finance reforms, whether taxpayers or schoolchildren will be the main beneficiaries of reform, and whether reform can produce new policies in governance and administration that will enhance public confidence in spending for education.

SELECTED REFERENCES

Benson, Charles S., *et al. Planning for Educational Reform: Financial and Social Alternatives.* New York: Dodd, Mead, 1974.

Bursley, Gilbert E. "The Political Strategies of Educational Finance Reform." *Journal of Education Finance* 1 (Summer 1975): 1-18.

Coons, John E., *et al. Private Wealth and Public Education.* Cambridge, Mass.: Belknap Press of Harvard University Press, 1970.

Grubb, W. Norton, and Michelson, Stephan. *States and Schools.* Lexington, Mass.: D.C. Heath, 1974.

National Conference of State Legislatures. *School Finance Reform: A Legislators' Handbook.* Washington, D.C.: the Conference, 1976.

National Educational Finance Project. *Status and Impact of Educational Finance Programs.* Vol. 4. Gainesville, Fla.: the Project, 1971.

National Legislative Conference. *A Legislators' Guide to School Finance.* Washington, D.C.: the Conference, 1974.

————. *New Programs of State School Aid.* Washington, D.C.: the Conference, 1974.

Pincus, John, ed. *School Finance in Transition: The Courts and Educational Reform.* Cambridge, Mass.: Ballinger Publishing Co., 1974.

Reischauer, Robert, and Hartman, Robert. *Reforming School Finance.* Washington, D.C.: Brookings Institution, 1973.

Coordinating Education and Work: Challenges to Current Thought and Practice

Paul E. Barton

The terminology of "education-work relationships," which appeared on the scene a few years ago, embodies both severe difficulties and large opportunities for education.

The difficulties have become all too familiar. Employers complain about high school graduates who are unable to fill out application forms, high unemployment among youth dampens students' motivation to achieve when jobs are not available, stable or declining enrollments tempt educators to switch academic offerings to vocational training, and college graduates become unwilling recruits into what James O'Toole calls "The Reserve Army of the Underemployed."[1] In this context, it is not surprising that Richard Freeman entitled his latest book *The Overeducated American* and that the publisher made its jacket flaming red.[2]

While education is feeling the pressure of such difficulties, there is emerging a better understanding of education-work relationships. Out of the challenges to current thought and practice comes an opportunity for new growth and broader purpose in education's future. This essay focuses on three aspects of education-work relationships: the time traps into which life has become divided; the transition from education to work; the politics of coordinating education and work.

THE TIME TRAPS

The largest perspective by which one can view education-work relationships is the life cycle. There is increasing recognition of the segmentation that has come to characterize life and the role of education in it. The evolution of the modern life cycle has been such that the period of youth is mostly concerned with education, the middle years are usually devoted to work, and old age has come to be characterized by an absence of productive opportunity in either education or work. This historical development has origins in our still limited concepts of the role of education, in the shaping of human development by the needs of our technological economy, in the impact of an increasingly urban environment on the extended family, and in the American habit of letting matters drift until they become crises rather than simply problems.

There is little doubt that education's largest assignment will continue to be the preparation of the young. In shaping itself to carry out that assignment, however, rigidities in practice and attitude have developed to the point where education itself becomes a barrier to change. There is the expectation that free public education is to be taken at one sitting, with rights to it lapsing shortly after one drops out. There is the isolation of classroom life from the institutions in which young people must find their way. There is the resistance to changing the standard scheduling practices to accommodate planned service and work experiences that would make the movement into the adult period of life less sudden and abrupt.

If, in the past, education concentrated on the young, there is no doubt that this was in response to the needs of a high-technology economy. Industry did not hire young people until they had attained age twenty or twenty-one, which contrasted sharply with the time when the school year was adjusted to the demands of the harvest, and a sixteen-year-old was expected to perform an adult role. Adjustments in industry manning tables have also been made at the other end of the age scale. It is surely progress when hard labor is no longer demanded of an arthritic seventy-five-year-old, but it is increasingly a deprivation when early retirement is invoked on a fifty-five-year-old with unimpaired ability in the workplace.

For the young adult and the person in the middle years, work becomes an unrelenting demand. Economic necessities and social pressures keep one and often two family breadwinners at the work station. The opportunity for education, foregone for a variety of reasons when one is young, usually does not return again. The enforced leisure of later years might be a boon, but there are few opportunities to become skilled in its use. Thus, life becomes separated in three compounds, with barbed wire strung between.

Young people are clearly ready and desirous of adult experiences much earlier than they have them. Adults want and need a chance to resume their education in order to change careers, prepare for retirement, switch from completed child rearing to the service or job sector, or pursue a later developing interest in the theater, art, or music. Those over sixty-five want productive roles in society and the skills to use their time in a rewarding manner.

To a considerable extent this segmentation of life is just a habit and a convention convenient to bureaucratic and economic organization. Although it is not easy to do so, one can change habits and break conventions. There is just enough movement in the direction of making life whole again to ensure that it is more a vision than a hallucination. All of society and its institutions must accept the challenge to change. It is not likely, however, that the change will materialize without strong leadership from the education community. Spreading education more evenly throughout life could become a goal for education that would give it renewed purpose and energy at a time when it now seems defensive and uncertain.

TRANSITION FROM EDUCATION TO WORK

Institutional isolation and the effects of segmentation appear in the period of youth in ways that are concrete enough to identify and to do something about. Though adequate linkages between school and work have somehow failed to develop, putting them into place is getting easier as their absence becomes better understood. This is not just a matter of broad philosophy, but of specific barriers and specific opportunities for overcoming them. These barriers and opportunities are described below.

The Job Shortage

There cannot be a transition to work if there is not enough work to go around. And it is clear that an insufficient amount of work exists. Many more jobs are needed, both for those who leave school and seek full-time work and those who want to go to school and to work part-time simultaneously. Educators see this job shortage as critical for two reasons. First, there is a tendency to blame education for the shortage by confusing a real lack of work with inadequate vocational preparation in the schools. Second, the inability to secure jobs after completing one's education is likely to harm the motivation to learn.

New Opportunities

Traditional means of stimulating economic growth, however, will not produce the needed number of regular jobs for youth. New opportunities will have to be created by identifying the services needed by the community. Policy for youth involves three kinds of opportunities: education, work, and service. The opportunities for service and work must be managed so as to permit integration of all three in the development of youth through the teenage years.

Inadequate Placement Services

Only in a few places are there placement services for students seeking jobs. Neither public employment offices nor schools are providing such services on a systematic basis, although this is a most obvious link in the chain between school and work. Some good models do exist, however, and they provide a firm base on which to build placement services, including a follow-up to see what occurs after the initial job placement is made.

Inadequate Counseling Services

The secondary schools have only the equivalent of one person's time per year of counseling available for each thousand students, and most of that time is spent with college-bound students, aiding them in planning for further education. Not only do counselors not have sufficient time; they also lack information on the functioning of local job markets and how they can be used. Counseling services need to be expanded by drawing more upon resources throughout the community, including businessmen, government employees, union officers, and retired people with both knowledge and time.

Inadequate Occupational Information

Teachers, counselors, parents, and students are greatly handicapped by the lack of information on the kinds of jobs that are available locally, what they pay, what they involve, and what the requirements are to enter them. Some information is available nationally, and a number of promising experimental efforts are being made, but this bridge from education to employment is not erected yet.

Inadequate Opportunities for Integrated Education and Experience

While progress is being made in new work experience models, the Experienced Based Career Education programs of the National Institute of Education, and cooperative education, only a small number of high school students have the option of a program that effectively blends the classroom with experience. Enlarging these opportunities requires both careful planning and changes in the ways schools have traditionally operated. It also means retaining and improving educational quality as the experience component is added, in addition to working with local unions to avoid adverse impact on adult employment.

Inadequate Knowledge of Child Labor Laws

Studies conducted by the National Manpower Institute show that employers and schools do not have accurate knowledge of what child labor laws do and do not permit. Employers frequently refuse to hire youth for fear of violating these laws; this impedes the expansion of work experience programs and hampers youth employment. There is also overlap between state laws and federal laws, which adds to the problem. At present no one is responsible for providing a broader understanding of these laws or for clearly demarcating federal and state jurisdictions.

Inadequate Utilization of Skill Training Resources

Vocational education is still almost wholly identified with training in the public school classroom. The education system does not take advantage of the full range of resources in the community. Arrangements could be made to pay the tuition of high school youth in private vocational schools where the best training is offered or to work with employers and unions to provide training in their establishments.

Inadequate Utilization of Developed Abilities

The title of Freeman's book could as well have been *The Undereducated Economy* as *The Overeducated American*. It is important to ask why the American economy no longer needs the abilities our population is acquiring. We should not accept the passive view that if industry is not using all the educated manpower available, then that manpower will go unused. One of the largest challenges to education is to offer some guidance as to how the economy can utilize the skills of the people available to participate in it.

In none of these possibilities is there any need to reduce the quality of basic education or to switch regular educational curricula to job preparation. Rather, what must be done is to create a number of linkages between education and work institutions, one of the most important being an increase in the number of service and work opportunities for students.

POLITICS OF COORDINATING EDUCATION AND WORK

Large changes such as those described above are possible only when there is consensus about the desirability of making them. Thus, the greater the number of institutions and groups that can see benefit from the changes, the more likely achievement becomes.

The Great Society of the 1960's has demonstrated that singling out the disadvantaged for special benefits did not provide the benefits that were desired. We can also be certain that purely remedial attempts to deal directly with those who are not prospering in our society are less likely to be successful than to change the conditions that cause the failures. At the time expenditures for social programs were decreasing, Mitchell Svirdoff pointed out that social programs that apply universally rather than selectively, such as Social Security and unemployment insurance, were expanding.[3]

Many would benefit from initiatives to remove time traps, improve the transition to work, provide education during the working years, and give larger meaning to the retirement years. Among them are: youth who are looking for their first jobs or their lifelong careers; workers who want to switch careers and need education to do it; the unemployed who are trying to obtain jobs by acquiring new skills; minorities of all ages who are finding education a route to achieving the equal treatment they are promised; women who are seeking occupational equality and need more education to achieve it; mothers who want to reenter the labor market after their children are older; anyone who is facing retirement and wants to make the most of his remaining years.

These groups vary from the powerless to those with at least a modest amount of political clout. Change in the 1980's must involve all groups, not one or two in isolation. As Willard Wirtz has stated, these groups together can constitute an effective "coalition constituency for change."[4]

The engines of change in a vast pluralistic society are not, however, fueled only by what would serve the individual perception of need. High-octane performance comes from mixing individual need and the self-interest of the key institutions in society.

Individual self-interests are involved in a better balance of education, work, and leisure throughout life. This interest is clearly demonstrable in the transition by youth from education to work. An analysis of that situation indicates that no single institution can succeed in bridging this gap alone. What is required is the participation of educators, employers, union leaders, voluntary service agencies, representatives of various levels of government, and parents. The problem was created when these organizations drifted apart in an increasingly complex and urbanized society.

It will be difficult to achieve collaboration among these organizations to solve the problem of transition by youth. There are, however, encouraging beginnings. The National Manpower Institute has called for community education-work councils to bring together the groups mentioned above and is working with the federal government and a number of communities to create an education-work consortium.

The kind of collaboration just described is also advocated by Kenneth Hoyt, director of the Office of Career Education in the Office of Education, and is spelled out in legislation (H.R.7), which has now been passed by the House of Representatives of the Ninety-fourth Congress.

Prospects are increasing for a convergence of interests in the return of the adult to the classroom. Business, unions, and representatives of education have formed a national panel to oversee a study of negotiated tuition-aid plans in industry. The National Institute of Education contracted for the study, which is being carried out by a nonprofit organization with roots in business, labor, and education. The American Association of Community and Junior Colleges has had recent conferences with organized labor to plan for further education of workers. The American Society of Training Directors stays in close communication with all groups involved with furthering adult training and development. A lifelong learning bill that passed Congress in 1975 provides fresh impetus to adult education.

The challenges to current thinking in education-work relationships will be met only through careful attention to the politics of change, and political change is not limited to what happens in legislatures and public education agencies. Any larger purpose calls for a much broader involvement. The educational change discussed here requires coalitions of people and collaboration among private institutions, government, and educational institutions.

NOTES

1. James O'Toole, "The Reserve Army of the Underemployed: Parts I and II," *Change* 7 (May; June 1975).

2. Richard Freeman, *The Overeducated American* (New York: Academic Press, 1976).

3. See Mitchell Svirdoff, "Human Resources and the Pendulum of Power," report to the Ford Foundation, 1976.

4. Willard Wirtz and the National Manpower Institute, *The Boundless Resource: A Prospectus for an Education-Work Policy* (Washington, D.C.: New Republic Book Co., 1975), p. 145.

SELECTED REFERENCES

Barton, Paul E. *Community Councils and the Transitions between Education and Work.* Washington, D.C.: National Manpower Institute, 1976.

———. "Youth Transition to Work: The Problems and Federal Policy Setting." *From School to Work.* Washington, D.C.: National Commission for Manpower Policy, 1976.

Gallagher, Dennis. "Community Efforts to Link Education and Work." *From School to Work.* Washington, D.C.: National Commission for Manpower Policy, 1976.

O'Toole, James. *Work, Learning and the American Future.* San Francisco: Jossey-Bass, 1977.

Silberman, Harry, and Ginzberg, Mark. *Easing the Transition.* San Francisco: Jossey-Bass, 1977.

Organizations Facing Retrenchment:
Guidelines from Economic Theory

David K. Wiles

The issue of retrenchment as an organizational adaptation to changing conditions is discussed below in relation to four interrelated policy questions: What is the economic future of schooling? What economic assumptions underlie the institutional model of school organization? How could economics be interpreted in terms of a human investment model of school organization? What guidelines for organizational retrenchment are suggested by the two models?

WHAT IS THE ECONOMIC FUTURE OF SCHOOLING?

The economic future of schooling can be interpreted as either an institutional phenomenon or a concept of human investment. Further, the particular interpretation helps to delineate the operational meanings of organizational "retrenchment" and the extent to which guidelines become warnings from past experiences.

The institutional perspective of economy defines schooling as an industry for which there are serious indications of decline throughout the 1970's and 1980's. Predictions for institutional decline, as it affects the compulsory public school system, are based upon present and projected birthrates of school-aged children. The 1976-77 school year, for example, reflects an overall national decline in all grades. Further, 4.5 million children five years of age entered public schools in 1966; in 1978, 3.0 million will do so.

Generalizations concerning decline in higher education often are based upon the relationships between the employment of recent college graduates and subsequent enrollments. Evidence, such as that presented by Richard Freeman and J. Herbert Hollomon of the Center for Policy Alternatives of the Massachusetts Institute of Technology,[1] suggests that the extent of downturn represents a long-term change in the functional composition of American society.

Those who are skeptical of predicting general decline on the basis of the institutional perspective predicate their arguments on the fact that past forecasting efforts fail to specify if current conditions indicate a temporary, cyclical, or long-run change. An example of misforecasting caused by interpreting current indicators were the analyses by Seymour Harris[2] in 1949 of the economic value of schooling. Harris predicted a glut of college graduates on the market in the 1950's and 1960's; just the opposite occurred. It is conceivable, therefore, that in the late 1970's and 1980's there could be major shifts in industrial employment, a spurt in spending on research and development, demographic changes leading to expansion, and massive social response to altering the present structure and purpose of schooling.

When, however, schooling is approached as an investment concept, there is a much stronger case, based upon a calculation of economic futures, for a different picture of organizational retrenchment. Arguing that simple assumptions of supply and demand (whether in client availability or employment ratios) will not resolve the issue regarding the value of schooling, proponents of human capital focus upon the interaction between human and physical capital with an appropriate accommodation of the absorption rate created by combining both.[3] Confusion arises over such fundamental questions as, first, whether individuals schooled by a society in which the intellect is highly valued serve as catalysts for production functions or, second, whether the relation of education to future income potential represents a variation in schooling or in the individual. Characteristic of this type of thinking is Professor Riessman's discussion of Victor Fuchs's argument concerning consumer-intensive services (see Chapter 4). Within this context, the extent to which the consumer-client helps the professional-expert is critical. It is obvious that this shift in emphasis has strong implications for economic organization.

This type of approach leads to further issues of economic classification, such as the precise percentage to which schooling influences consumption or investment. Since consumption and investment are complementary and society does not have the option of choosing between the two, the concept of human capital investment cannot be related to them in classic cause-effect terms. Concurrently, the "organization" of schooling also becomes fuzzy, as assumptions of institutional meaning become uncertain. Retrenchment becomes a larger issue, beyond those involved in the policy changes affecting present educational institutions.

WHAT ECONOMIC ASSUMPTIONS UNDERLIE THE
INSTITUTIONAL MODEL OF SCHOOL ORGANIZATION?

The economic assumptions underlying an institutional perspective of our society have implicit philosophical and organizational values in relation to school operations. To address the philosophic position, one must focus upon the particular rationality that ascribes meaning to the term "uneconomic." Meaning focuses on the definition of profit. Profit may be discussed in money or indirect, related references (that is, percent and type of graduates, attendance percentages). Even discussions of activities or assets desired for noneconomic reasons (social, aesthetic, moral, political) are still judged according to an uneconomic character. Thus, meaning that underlies institutional economics is limited necessarily to the "goods" that are supplied and demanded and to those who participate in the market. Methodological limitation of this type (primarily through quantification) allows noneconomic values to be pressed into a framework of calculus (cost-benefit analysis) since all things are assumed, ultimately, to have a price and to be exchangeable.

Also on the philosophical level, one must consider consumption as the sole end and purpose of all economic activity, regarding the factors of production (land, labor, capital) as the means. Thus, in order to maximize human satisfaction it is necessary to find the optimum institutional pattern of productive effort. When maximum production is related to noneconomic values, all materials (renewable and nonrenewable) are equalized in terms of relative cost per equivalent unit and "dollar product value" rationalities. This leads to standard economics of scale and efficiency values. No difference is recognized, therefore, in calculations for renewable and nonrenewable materials. Rather, one automatically chooses the cheapest method, for to do otherwise would be considered irrational and uneconomic.

On the organizational level of anaylsis the prevalent economic perspective assumes certain institutional arrangements for both the public school and for higher education. Most distinguishable is the bureaucratic arrangement that implies institutional stability and hierarchy. Although the "domesticated" nature of compulsory schooling might seem to provide a commonwealth-type of economic classification, this characteristic does not negate the prevalent bureaucratic stipulations. Rather, domestication is regarded as providing additional bureaucratic complexity.[4]

Finally, the economic perspective on providing educational services assumes organizational dimensions influenced by technology, increased complexity, and maturity. Basing his ideas on the assumption that the central feature of economic development is technology, Galbraith[5] argues that there is a concurrent requirement for organization and capital. The more technical and the more organizationally complex production becomes, the longer the gestation period of the final product and the greater the risk of failure between initial decision to invest and realization of return. Thus, the basic motivation of mature organizations is not simply to maximize profit but to minimize risk of in-process failure. This requires that the organization seek to control its social environment by negotiating (or even creating) needs. Again, price does not reflect the consumer's needs, but negotiated interests that manipulate the environment.

HOW COULD ECONOMICS BE INTERPRETED IN TERMS OF A HUMAN INVESTMENT MODEL OF SCHOOL ORGANIZATION?

As with the institutional model, consideration of human investment in providing educational services also involves both philosophical and organizational interpretations. Perhaps the most critical of the former may be the adjustment of the present standards of market rationality that are used to judge institutional stipulations of "uneconomic" policy. Change brought about by the continued scarcity of resources may bend the meaning of consumption of educational services. This recognition would involve the qualitative aspects of growth (Is a larger GNP a good thing?) and expansion (Does schooling actually expand human capital for the individual and society?).

A second philosophical focus may be the further categorization of goods for educational policy. For example, Schumacher[6] calls for the following minimal scheme: primary goods differentiated on a renewable or nonrenewable basis; secondary goods further divided into manufacturers and services classification. This scheme emphasizes the availability of resources and directly affects "cost" calculations when ends are valued above means.

At the organizational level, though the brave new world of a deschooled society may remain a fantasy, reconsideration of resources may well increase th viability of learning networks as present institutions continue to decline.[7] Many writers on the American economy have noted two responses to present uncertainty in policy and risk with regard to investment. First, large organizations once structured in terms of company-wide functions have adopted a product-oriented structure. Second, there has occurred the rise of conglomerates—very large firms that emphasize diversity of products and autonomy of their suborganizations. Are magnet schools and voucher option plans so very different? Fundamental alteration of clients' choices would, of course, affect both the stability and the hierarchy of present school systems.

Finally, there are several alternative explanations to Galbraith's assumption that organizational evolution is due to the imperatives of technological advance.[8] For example, technological knowledge does create specialization and interdependence. In the study of complex organizations under demand for change (that is, specifying the meaning of the "decline" of resources), the great variation in the degree of interdependence among specialists may, however, be much more important than the ultimate connectedness of all roles. The varying time spans in which different roles are necessary to one another may be more critical to understanding the meaning of interdependence than the total organization's technological level of sophistication.

In conclusion, it seems possible to construct an economic model of human investment applicable to the provision of educational services.

WHAT GUIDELINES FOR ORGANIZATIONAL RETRENCHMENT ARE SUGGESTED BY THE TWO MODELS?

From the above discussion, one could conclude that organizations responsible for providing educational services could take very different forms depending upon one's economic perspectives. If one assumes the institutional perspective, the question of retrenchment becomes one of type and degree of organizational adaptation to fewer resources. Change becomes essentially refinement of existing structures and functions of the educational institution. The extent of organizational adaptation becomes a choice between minor changes and the overhaul or termination of functions. The radical impact of major institutional overhaul, such as making schooling noncompulsory or national tracking of students, seems unlikely in the face of political realities based on vested interests.[9] Representative of this assumed reality is Professor Burkhead's perception of "slow-growth" strategies. One such strategy suggests that Congress authorize broad categorical grants conditional on specified state actions in the areas of state planning, local district reorganization, or school finance reform (see Chapter 5).

If one assumes that the adaptation for the 1970's and 1980's will involve minor changes, the institutional perspective of economics may trigger some major unanticipated reorganizational phenomena. For example, the type of economic turbulence created by institutional retrenchment directly challenges prevailing theories of organizational centralization and regional integration. Three core assumptions become less relevant: that a definable institutional pattern must result from the processes of centralization or integration; that conflicts of interests between organizational partners and nonorganizational partners should be resolved in favor of the former; that decisions are to be made on the basis of disjointed incrementalism (perhaps "decomposed" or "loosely coupled," but still assuming general decisional aggregation).

The three assumptions seem clearly evident in the continuing shift in educational policy making to metropolitan, state, and federal levels of activity. These assumptions about interdependence and centralization are, however, called into question by the experiences of certain industries and international consortia (such as the European communities since 1968), which indicate a new trend involving "*novel* [italics mine] kinds and dimensions of independence between organizations, issues and objectives, particularly with reference to policies that . . . unquestionably accept as legitimate . . . the fundamentals of neoclassical growth economy [for example, the existence of general interorganizational unions]."[10] A new type of decisional rationality—"fragmented issue linkage"[11]—may compete with present incremental habits, and it is unlikely to lead to a fixed "set" of institutional arrangements. Thus it may be that prevailing viewpoints concerning organizational integration or interdependence[12] may be misplaced as guidelines for institutional "retrenchment" policy. If interdependence and integration are no longer considered to be covariants, preoccupation with institutional tidiness becomes questionable.

According to the concept of human investment in educational organization, retrenchment means basic reconsideration of the function of schooling. Retrenchment may denote either expansion or shrinkage of present institutional definitions as they relate to various educational services. Focus upon benefits may distinguish further between primary educational benefits (knowledge, skills, standards of

civility); nonschooling, social benefits (income, occupational opportunity, status, prestige); and second-order educational benefits (cer-
tificates, diplomas, transcripts, licenses).

It is interesting that both the "conservative" position of Professor
Glazer (Chapter 3) and the "liberal" one of Professor Riessman
(Chapter 4) seem to support this contention of human investment
economics. Both writers reject the present governmental-institutional
interpretation of economics in our society, but their rationales represent different ends of a philosophical continuum. Glazer views government as an "intrusion into people's lives" and argues for a reduction in
this intrusion (how far is unclear, perhaps to the original social contract). Riessman argues against present mechanisms of economic
policy making on the ground that they do not identify or care for
human needs. It is likely that the extent and the type of actual institutional adaptation will depend upon policy judgments concerning such
commonly overlooked educational benefits as positive, intergenera-
tional transfers of knowledge, neighbors who are affected by favorable
social values, and employers seeking a trained, "brain-intensive" labor
force.[13]

CONCLUSION

This essay has distinguished between two perspectives of economics as they affect the meaning of educational organization and
future retrenchment. The question is whether universal judgments of
appropriate action can be reached when two opposing perspectives
must be considered. The answer is that it probably is not possible. My
view is that philosophies and methodologies for logically determining
"appropriateness" in the formulation of social policy are, and will be,
a striving based upon faith. The process may indeed by grounded in
the "working assumptions" or paradigms that provide the conventional "coherent intellectual framework which is a necessary ingredient for organized scientific endeavor."[14] Nonetheless, how the
economics of consumer-intensive services are interpreted, let alone
assigned policy value, depends upon the a priori judgments of a particular analyst, decision maker, or agency. For example, Riessman
may rationalize the different use of professional experts as a conscious
response to "behavior-related problems" (Chapter 4), while Glazer
may see their value in establishing new "cure expectations" and individualization in the affected population (Chapter 3). At the same

time, Burkhead may make judgments on this subject in light of institutional response to "Baumol's disease" (Chapter 5). If this divergence of views accurately reflects reality, then the choice of appropriate action seems one of prescriptions rather than a logical outgrowth of rational description and prediction.

NOTES

1. Richard Freeman and J. Herbert Hollomon, "The Declining Value of College Going," *Change* 7 (September 1975): 24-31, 62-63.

2. Seymour Harris, *The Market for College Graduates* (Cambridge, Mass.: Harvard University Press, 1949).

3. See, for example, B. Harvat, "The Optimum Rate of Investment," *Economic Journal* 68 (December 1968): 747-767. Although studies of the rate of return of marginal investments are difficult, recent data still suggest the advantages of college graduation in comparison to high school graduation. See Richard Raymond and Michael Sesnowitz, "The Returns to Investment in Higher Education: Some New Evidence," *Journal of Human Resources* 10 (Spring 1975): 139-154.

4. For discussion of increased complexities of determining the meaning of "public order" by relating ideological framework and institutionalization, see Karl Polanyi, *The Great Transformation* (Boston: Beacon Press, 1944). For an example of practical application, see Jennifer Nias, "The Sorcerer's Apprentice: A Case-Study of Complexity in Educational Institutions," in *Organized Social Complexity,* ed. Todd LaPorte (Princeton, N.J.: Princeton University Press, 1975), pp. 256-274.

5. John Galbraith, *The New Industrial State* (New York: Signet, 1968).

6. E. F. Schumacher, *Small Is Beautiful* (New York: Perennial Press, 1975).

7. Donald Schon, *Beyond the Stable State* (New York: Random House, 1971), pp. 180-195.

8. See, for example, the discussion of an industry's maturity cycle in Simon Kuznets, *Economic Change* (New York: W.W. Norton, 1953); or the discussion by J. Serge Taylor of high-low "R & D criticality" industries in "Organizational Complexity in the New Industrial State," in *Organized Social Complexity,* ed. LaPorte, pp. 94-114.

9. An example is the association of interest groups (such as teachers) than "organize domination" of the existing employment structure and whose interests are the present "rules of the game." See David Truman, *The Governmental Process,* 2d ed. (New York: Knopf, 1971).

10. Ernest B. Haas, "The Turbulent Fields and the Theory of Regional Integration," *International Organization* 3 (Spring 1976): 205.

11. *Ibid.,* pp. 190-191.

12. For discussion of the political implications of these two strands of theory, see Robert Keohane and Joseph Nye, "Interdependence and Integration," in *Handbook of Political Science,* Vol. 8, ed. Fred Greenstein and Nelson Polsby (Reading, Mass.: Addison-Wesley, 1975).

13. Kern Alexander, "The Value of an Education," *Journal of Education Finance* 1 (Spring 1976): 429-467.

14. Thomas S. Kuhn, *The Structure of Scientific Revolutions* (Chicago: University of Chicago Press, 1962).

Political Issues in the Expansion of Educational Services for the Exceptional Child

Eleanore C. Westhead
William R. Carriker

In the 1960's, civil rights for minority groups became a major political concern. Many of the issues, however, have not yet been resolved. One of the later groups to be considered a minority are those children and youth designated "exceptional" or "handicapped." Although there have been public residential schooling and day programs for some handicapped since the early 1800's, and a significant effort was made to extend services to the handicapped following the Second World War, federal leadership, through funding, was actually initiated only in 1957.

Since 1957, developments have been rapid; they include funding of demonstration programs, service delivery systems, field research, and development of media. Concurrently, public education became chiefly responsible for accountability, and the rights of children and the family became national concerns. All of these factors crystallized in Section 504 of the Rehabilitation Act of 1973 and in the Education of All the Handicapped Act of 1975 (P.L. 94-142), which now replaces Title B of Education of the Handicapped Act. Though all other federal programs are to continue, they will be critically influenced by both of these laws.

These major legislative advances are, in part, a response to such critical legal actions of the past decade as: *Pennsylvania Association for Retarded Children* v. *Commonwealth of Pennsylvania,* 343 F. Supp. 279 (1971); *Mills* v. *Board of Education of the District of Columbia,* 348 F. Supp. 866 (DC DC, 1972); and *Special Education Division of the Department of Public Instruction* v. *G. H.,* 218 N.W. 2d 441 (ND, 1974).

Among the major changes and additions in the federal legislation are:

1. implications of the right to privacy for students and parents and a clearer definition of what this means;

2. specific due process procedures for students;

3. requirements for long-term program planning and coordination of the plans for school districts (with regard to each child), for colleges and universities (in preparing personnel for careers in special education), for state departments of education (in manpower planning and accountability);

4. an expanded definition of "handicapped" to include "learning disabilities";

5. a limit to 12 percent of the number of "handicapped" in an administrative division for purposes of federal reimbursement;

6. denial of federal funds under any act to school districts not complying with P.L. 94-142 or not eligible for at least $7,500 (which has implications for regionalized programs and defines special districts for the handicapped that are administratively distinct from local districts);

7. equal opportunity for access (both to facilities and programs) throughout the educational spectrum;

8. federal funds authorized to assist agencies in becoming accessible to the handicapped;

9. responsibility of state departments of education to assure the quality and accountability of all agencies serving the handicapped, no matter where a state originally assigned responsibility;

10. commitment to "least restrictive environments" for the handicapped;

11. impetus funding authorized for ages three to five, to be extended by 1980 to ages eighteen to twenty-one.

With the legislation of 1976, professionals in special education received increased resources, authority, and responsibilities. Thus, a number of common and undesirable practices were discouraged. Among them were the inappropriate placement of youth, the consignment of classes to church basements or to the stages of multipurpose rooms, and the refusal to serve the more seriously or multiply handicapped as their educational needs require. Cooperative efforts with all other professionals who can provide assistance will, of course, be necessary in the future.

Rapid expansion and changes in the legal status of special education pose critical issues that must be resolved under the close scrutiny of national political and legal observers, and the problems of implementation will be compounded by unfavorable economic conditions.

CLIENT POPULATION AND "APPROPRIATE EDUCATION"

Fundamental to the field of special education is a clear definition of its client population. Use of the term "learning disabilities" has been helpful; it is critical, however, to define "appropriate education" under the new legislation. This task involves a number of questions. First, how is adaptive behavior, basic to the concept of retardation, to be demonstrated without subcultural or language bias in order to satisfy "informed consent" and the courts? Second, among the severely handicapped and multiply handicapped, how is it to be determined if the government should intervene, and who is to decide upon the "appropriate education"? Third, on what data will a definition of "learning disabled" be based, and how will those who have a mild learning disability be differentiated from those who have a serious one? Fourth, how is the relationship among special education, regular education, and private education to be established, and on whose terms? Fifth, when private diagnosticians and school personnel disagree about a specific plan for an individual's "appropriate education," who will make the final decision?

Legislators, courts, consumers, parents' groups, and professional educators will all be involved in resolving these issues. At least seven major factions with vested interests are included in the last group: elementary education teachers, secondary education teachers, educators of administrative personnel, speech and language specialists, reading specialists, and those in the various divisions of special education. There is, of course, great diversity of philosophic commitments among educators, but if these professionals cannot cooperate, families of handicapped children may turn increasingly to the courts to resolve their demands for their children's education, no matter how unrealistic those demands may be.

Many segments of the educational profession favor a definition of "appropriate education" that will satisfy citizens and the courts and that will strengthen professional practices. Others, however, interpret equality of education as synonymous with equality of funding for each person enrolled. They contend that it would be preferable to rescind mandatory education laws, refuse to accept federal monies, or, through diverse nonactions, fail to consider any of the handicapped in their areas to be in need of special education.

Because of the definitional problems, the federal legislation is yet to be implemented. But the need for accurate definitions cannot be overemphasized. In dealing with the issues of who should benefit and what is appropriate education, broad consequences must be considered. If, for example, a program for handicapped youth could be designed effectively in terms of placement, curriculum, instruction, and ancillary support systems, these advances could also benefit other children. If, on the other hand, youngsters with learning disabilities are sent to regular schools and then require too much individual attention, the other children will be deprived.

CHANGING CLIENTELE

Considerable research has been done on another critical issue: what is the optimum age at which special education should begin? This is tied to the issues concerning definitions, but is not limited to them. More and more states have lowered the mandatory age for the handicapped to three, two, or even birth. "First Chance" projects and special projects in nurseries for the newborn and in universities demonstrate clearly the gains made by even very seriously damaged or maldeveloped children when special educational services are made available to them and their families.

There are, in addition, laws that stipulate the age at which students may leave school. These laws not only allow youth to discontinue formal education at sixteen, seventeen, or eighteen but also permit school officials to dismiss, sometimes arbitrarily, any handicapped individual on the basis of age alone. In some cases, six more months or one or two more years of schooling might have meant full attainment of marketable skills; in others, it might have meant that competence in reading and writing was sufficient for admission to technical schools, community colleges, or even universities.

Though the federal guidelines support appropriate public education of all handicapped from the age of three through the age of twenty-one with no cost to the respective families, a number of problems remain. Among them are the following: Who will decide who enters and who leaves educational programs, and on what basis will the decisions be made? Who can challenge those decisions, who resolves the questions, and on what basis are the questions resolved? While the federal government may offer up to $300 in incentive grants, who commits the state or local districts to full funding? Will communities accept educational services for the handicapped that begin earlier or later than those for the average or gifted? Must facilities for the handicapped be greatly expanded, or can they be cost effective? Can traditional educational systems accommodate diverse programs?

Among the protagonists on these issues are researchers on child development and professional educators who have documented many unprecedented changes in young children. Others include those special educators who know they have reached children too late to be as effective as they might have been. Parents' organizations are a third major protagonist, and the courts, provided the data, generally support them. A recent example was a class action suit in Virginia *(Campbell* v. *Cruse),* in which the parents seeking full funding for youngsters who had been referred to the private sector for their education were granted the "right to prevail."

Too often those who object to the expansion of clienteles are administrators who believe equal means identical; who fear the costs and see no way to meet them; who feel there are more critical needs of education than to increase the number of those among the eligible handicapped population; and who believe these infants, children, and young adults should be the responsibility of agencies other than public schools. Objecting, too, are some legislators who would support rescinding the laws as soon as the climate in the community would permit the change. It will be difficult, however, for them to refute the results of current research. These data indicate that, for handicapped persons, undereducation and help that is too delayed mean unemployment, underemployment, delinquency, and expanded welfare rolls or support by Social Security.

MARSHALING RESOURCES

Education for the handicapped, with its expanded definition, enlarged clientele, and augmented programs, can be likened to an epidemic. The incidence is unknown; the critical geographic areas are unverified; and the cures are unconfirmed. Can there be a national marshaling of resources to meet the challenges? If so, how can competent personnel be trained, funds be collected and allocated, programs be designed and instituted, and effective communications systems be installed and manned?

At this point it has not been determined what resources will be necessary to implement the federal legislation. It is clear, however, that heavy demands will be made on existing educational systems.

This situation may encourage a reversal of the trend or a reordering of priorities with regard to serving the handicapped.

Those who favor the legislation might argue that the electorate has expressed itself and that the national legislation confirms its wishes. Those who disagree might contend that selected individuals and pressure groups were responsible for the legislation, not the electorate.

What could be the consequences? The halfhearted allocation of resources could placate pressure groups for another decade. Lack of support by the public could so discourage the handicapped and their advocates that they withdraw from the struggle. Communities could either gain a degree of support for or deny resources to educational programs for the handicapped. Finally, with the 1980's might come a widespread affirmation of the importance of the individual and a commitment by the community to support its weaker links, regardless of the added costs in the immediate future. In summary, one cannot predict future political developments concerning services for the exceptional child; the subject will merit the closest attention of scholarly observers for some time to come.

SELECTED REFERENCES

Bernstein, C. D., *et al. Financing Educational Services for the Handicapped: An Analysis of Current Research and Practices.* Prepared for the U.S. Office of Education, Bureau of Education for the Handicapped. Palo Alto, Calif.: Management Analysis Center, 1974.

Insight (1972). Published by the Council for Exceptional Children, Reston, Va.

Meyen, E., *et al.*, eds. *Alternatives for Teaching Exceptional Children.* Denver: Love Publishing Co., 1975.

Weintraub, F.J., *et al. Public Policy and the Education of Exceptional Children.* Reston, Va.: Council for Exceptional Children, 1976.

Early Childhood Education: Issues and Prospects

Marjorie G. Elsten
Jenni W. Klein

Education for the preschool child presents issues and problems that differ, in many respects, from those of elementary and secondary education. Projection of need is more difficult, given the present decline in the birthrate and the uncertainty with respect to future birthrates. The percentage of eligible children presently served in preschool programs is very small, and expanding services for a population that has, literally, just come into being must take place with limited time to plan facilities and programs. Coupled with this is recognition of the need for educationally oriented child development programs and for protective care of the young child while the parent (such as the working mother or a single parent) is not able to provide it. Another factor that compounds the problem is the range in cost of preschool services, varying from several hundred dollars for minimal custodial care to thousands of dollars for comprehensive developmental full-time care. Overlaying these concerns is an ideological factor. While many believe that early education and child care should be available for all who want or need it for their children, others view such programs and federal subsidies as improper interventions in family life.

EMERGENT DEMANDS FOR EXPANDED SERVICES

With women continuing to enter the labor market in greater numbers than ever before[1] and the availability of information about the importance of child development in the first years of life, many parents now desire early childhood education and child care services. As a result, the proliferation of public and private early education programs during the past decade has riveted attention on many issues related to the goals and content of such programs, such as: the appropriate setting for early educative ventures; the age and scope of the populations to be served; effective training for teachers and other staff members; and the choice of sponsoring agencies. Such issues are crucial in terms of both practical and political considerations, if early childhood education is to be provided on a scale that meets the comprehensive needs of the young child and his family in the context of a rapidly changing society. A brief review of the history of early childhood education in the United States and of current programs may help to put this policy area into clearer focus.

HISTORY OF PROGRAMS FOR CHILDREN OF PRESCHOOL AGE

Three themes run through the history of early education: the ethic of social reform; the uniqueness and importance of childhood; and the reform of educational practices in the public schools.[2] These themes may be loosely related to the theoretical mainsprings of early childhood education: sociology, psychology, and education. Contemporary programs represent a meshing of these strands within the child development perspective, which now tends to dominate early education. Throughout the 120-year history of formal and informal childhood programs in this country, these themes have resounded in varying intensities in kindergartens, day-care centers, and nursery schools. Some of the variation in these programs grew out of what was frequently seen as a basic dichotomy between educational and social objectives, which has only recently been breeched by such programs as Head Start. They have also reflected, in part, their differing origins.

For the most part, kindergartens were educational in origin. Brought from Germany before the Civil War as private institutions for the relatively affluent, they slowly became part of the public schools. As they multiplied and achieved a secure place in some school systems, preacademic training was increasingly stressed. Age of entrance was generally established at five years, with the goal of getting children ready for first grade. In spite of the gradual acceptance of public support of kindergartens, only twenty-two state governments supported them prior to the 1970's. At present approximately 80 percent of five-year-olds attend kindergartens.

Nursery schools were established during the 1920's at universities, largely for the purpose of studying child development. Most children enrolled in these programs came from families of faculty members. Federally supported nursery schools appeared during the depression of the 1930's, but expired with the gradual economic recovery and the onset of World War II. The nursery school movement, however, continued to grow and to become largely available to middle-class chil-

dren. In general, nursery schools stressed the development of the total
child, including his intellectual, social, emotional, and physical
growth. An interesting part of the nursery school movement was the
establishment of parent cooperatives. In these preschools mothers or
fathers assist the teacher on a regular basis, which not only provides
for active involvement of parents but also keeps tuition lower. Such
nursery schools, by their very nature, cannot, however, enroll children
of working mothers.

Day care in the United States has largely focused on adults rather
than on children. As an institution, day care has frequently been more
closely allied to welfare services than to education. Since the first day-
care center was opened in New York in 1854, the provision of day care
has waxed and waned in response to economic or social crises rather
than to the needs of children. Indeed, the first federally supported
day-care centers were established during World War II to free
mothers for work in war-related industries. In spite of dramatic increases in the percentage of working mothers in recent years, no day
care has been federally supported since defense-related legislation expired in the 1940's, with the exception of Title IV programs of the
Social Security Act. Although the Bureau of the Census estimated in
1975 that approximately one-third of the mothers of children under
six years are now in the work force and a sharp increase in their
numbers is predicted, public support of day care remains a controversial and emotionally charged issue. Much of the controversy is ideological, revolving around differing views of the responsibilities of families
for their children and the traditional roles of the home and other
societal institutions in the nurturance of children.

Heightened awareness of the child's physical, intellectual, and
emotional vulnerability during the early years and the importance of
individualized care began to prompt concern about the general quality of existing day care, particularly the largely custodial nature of
numerous programs designed to serve a great number of children in
the most economically feasible manner. Quality early childhood programs of recent years, such as Head Start, have shown that the needs
of the child and the priorities of society need not be mutually exclusive. Their success in coupling safe supportive environments with
comprehensive activities has promoted the concept of developmental
day care. Fully accepted, this concept means retaining a vision of the
whole child and attempting to meet his present needs and nurture his

future development by comprehensive services that are administered in an individualized manner by a competent and compassionate staff. Basic to developmental day care is the perception of the child as a constant learner. Its goal is to complement the family and to provide and expand on the kind of experiences that a child would encounter in a supportive home environment.

CURRENT STATUS OF PROGRAMS FOR PRESCHOOL-AGED CHILDREN

In recent years, and especially during the 1960's when social awareness was focused on the poor, experimental programs for preschoolers increased dramatically. Research indicating that children's early experiences set the stage for later learning gave special impetus to programs designed to prevent later failure in school. Head Start, the largest national preschool program, was launched by the passage in 1965 of omnibus federal antipoverty legislation. It was conceived by an interdisciplinary team as a comprehensive child development program. Over the years, it has served millions of children and their families, providing a network of services addressed to the child's intellectual, physical, emotional, and social development. All programs require participation of parents and involvement with the community, and their overriding goal—that each child achieve social competence—is now shared by other child development programs. As defined by Head Start, social competence relates to "the child's everyday effectiveness in dealing with his environment and later responsibilities in school and life."[3]

Head Start serves approximately 300,000 children in full-year programs. This is about 15 percent of eligible children (children three to five years old from poverty families). Some Head Start programs are under the jurisdiction of public schools; most of them, however, are carried out under the sponsorship of community agencies. The undertaking addressed many of the issues that would confront any large program for preschool children, including provision of comprehensive services to a multicultural, multiethnic population, home- and center-based programs, curriculum development, helping the handicapped enter the mainstream, staff training, and involvement of parents.[4] Because of its size and innovative force, Head Start has been a prototype, providing both an important fund of experience and a model upon which to base broadly conceived programs.

As this brief summary indicates, early childhood programs have existed for many decades; a focus of public policy on preschool-aged children has, however, developed only during the last decade. Public school systems in many states now require local governments to have kindergarten. If and when enacted in California, the Riles plan would be the only state-wide program to date to include four-year-olds in public education. Federal legislation now funds a variety of early childhood programs under the auspices of education, health, welfare, and community action agencies. A few local schools provide services for preschool-aged children with funds from Title I of the Elementary and Secondary Education Act, and, under the provisions of P.L. 94-142, they may also assume some responsibility for handicapped children in this age group. Perhaps the most far-reaching federal policy with regard to child care services is the recently enacted tax legislation that permits working parents to deduct the cost of such services in the computation of their income tax.

Private organizations, ranging from "mom and pop" nursery schools to elaborate programs sponsored by industry and labor unions, provide a combination of educational and other services, either on a fee basis or as an employee's fringe benefit. State and local education, health, and welfare agencies set standards and supervise to a greater or lesser extent the operation of these programs. It is estimated that in 1974 about 38 percent of four-year-olds and 20 percent of three-year-olds were involved in preschool programs. The majority of these children are, however, in unlicensed programs providing minimal custodial care. The capacity of licensed centers is about 1.2 million, but the number of children requiring day care exceeds that number many times. In sum, a variety of services presently exists, and they are indicative of the range of children's needs, of choices available for some parents, and of types of public and private support.

SHAPE OF THE FUTURE

Public pressure to increase early childhood programs comes from a number of sources. For example, teachers' unions, faced with unemployed members, see the early childhood area as one of employment opportunity. Working mothers and other parents are interested in maximizing the developmental aspects of their children's early years, and women's groups view such programs as essential to furthering their goals for women. Virtually all the interest groups involved have tended to concentrate their efforts to obtain public support on Washington, in part because the accomplishments of the states in pre-school education have been so limited and the needs were perceived to be national in scope, and in part because support was forthcoming from such key congressional sponsors as Vice-President Walter F. Mondale. He was, in fact, the principal architect of the legislation that Congress passed in 1971 and that President Nixon vetoed.[5] This legislation would have substantially expanded financial assistance for the creation of a broad range of child care programs, with emphasis on the preschool child. In 1974 and 1975, bills were again introduced in Congress (S. 626, H.R. 2966) to expand the federal role on a smaller financial scale. This legislation, even more than the 1971 bill, was the subject of extensive opposition, which largely misrepresented the bills as removing parental responsibility for child rearing and "turning it over to the government." These bills are now part of history, but new legislation that will address the extent to which the federal government should subsidize and require standards for pre-school programs is likely be considered in the future.

Experience to date indicates that some key issues will dominate the debate and must be resolved or satisfactorily compromised. The most predictable one is the locus and type of control, which is endemic for all categories of grant-in-aid, intergovernmental pro-grams. What level of government—federal, state, or local—should set standards for preschool programs—and, more specifically, should such regulations be limited only to health and safety standards? Other cogent issues relate to the sponsorship and scope of the programs, the role to be taken by parents, and the qualifications to be established for personnel in the publicly funded programs.

Sponsorship

In 1975 Albert Shanker, president of the National Federation of Teachers, testified before congressional committees that child care legislation should not be supported unless the education establishment was designated to operate the authorized programs. Other witnesses, concerned with the needs of young children and their families, expressed the belief that education, health, social services, and other community organizations should receive federal grants, but that no one type of organization should have exclusive nation-wide responsibility for providing these services. Their position was based on the argument that early childhood programs are likely to focus not only on education but also on such social services as health and nutrition and on involvement of parents.

Many proponents of early childhood education regard flexibility in program design—the ability to respond to the particular needs of the child and his family—to be of paramount importance; for this reason, they do not consider the public schools to be the most suitable primary sponsors of the programs. Flexibility is concerned not only with site (in a school or center, in a family setting or in a home, part-time or full-time) but also with the design of the curriculum and with the varying needs of the child and the social and economic levels of the family. Thus, the medical and nutritional needs of a middle-class family might be met without assistance from the child care program, while families with limited incomes could obtain more extensive help, if only by referral to other providers of services.

Role of Parents

From a philosophical point of view, early childhood programs can be considered extensions of the family's responsibility to rear a child to be a socially competent individual. Early education programs have traditionally tended to work with both parents and children. Many programs that emphasize the involvement of parents, such as Head Start, have used these programs as a point of intervention to assist parents in becoming more competent in the rearing of their children. Such programs have stressed the fact that children learn from the time of birth and that parents are the child's first and fore-most educator. Early childhood is not only an opportune time to pro-vide such aid to parents, but also lends itself to preventive approaches. Present programs vary in the extent to which parental involvement and participation are encouraged or even permitted, but this factor must be weighed in the development of future programs.[6]

Personnel

The issue of staffing—what kinds and how many adults are needed in relation to a group of young children—is the key to the questions not only of quality but also of cost. Some see early childhood education programs as a means of employing the surplus number of elementary and secondary school teachers who are unemployed be-cause of declining school enrollments. At the other end of the spec-trum are those, among them some members of Congress, who see the programs as a means of employing nonprofessionally trained persons on welfare. The Office of Child Development within HEW and professionals in early childhood education take the position that special competencies and traits are required for those dealing with the young child. As a result, a major program to develop Child Development Associates has been initiated. These are persons who, on the basis of training and experience, demonstrate the skills and capabilities required for early childhood programs. The Child Development Associates Consortium, a private nonprofit corporation representing thirty-nine national organizations interested in child development and early education, recently initiated a formal process by which individuals can earn credentials, and at present nine states have incorporated the CDA credential into their child care regulations.[7]

CONCLUSION

In spite of the difficulties in resolving many controversial issues, it is likely that early childhood programs will continue to expand. Public demand comes as a result of profound changes in society, including the rising trend in women's employment, and services of the desired scope and quality are still largely unavailable. As the issues surrounding early education continue to be thrashed out, one principle seems to emerge most clearly: the need for flexible programs that focus squarely on the child without violating the values of the family. Experience to date indicates that there are many ways to provide coherent programs that meet this objective, but new mechanisms must be developed for the millions of preschoolers whose parents want such service. If the public supports the value, as it has in the past, that the worth of a nation can be found in its concern for its children, then it seems reasonable to conclude that it will insist on the extension of services for preschool-aged children.

NOTES

1. Statistics compiled by the Bureau of Labor project that 12 million more women will enter the labor force between 1975 and 1990. Of the 79.5 million women in the United States, 46.3 percent work. Of those, 39 percent have children, and approximately 15 percent (about 5.5 million) have children under six years of age.

2. Marvin Lazerson, "The Historical Antecedents of Early Childhood Education," in *Early Childhood Education,* ed. Ira Gordon (Chicago: University of Chicago Press, 1972).

3. *Head Start Program Performance Standards,* OCD N30-364-4, Department

of Health, Education, and Welfare, Office of Child Development (Washington, D.C.: Government Printing Office, 1975).

4. See *ibid.;* Julius Richmond, Deborah Stipek, and Edward Zigler, "A Decade of Head Start" (manuscript in preparation); Jenni W. Klein, "Head Start: National Focus on Young Children," *National Elementary Principal* 51 (September 1971): 98-104.

5. See Klein, "Head Start."

6. See *id.,* "Parent Involvement—Can It Succeed?" *1976 Comment, Education: A Family Affair* (Toledo, Ohio: University of Toledo, 1976).

7. *Id.,* "Towards Competency in Child Care," *Educational Leadership* 31 (October 1973): 45-49.

SELECTED REFERENCES

Advisory Committee on Child Development, Assembly of Behavioral and Social Sciences, National Research Council. *Toward a National Policy for Children and Families.* Washington, D.C.: National Academy of Sciences, 1976.

Colemen, Joseph G., and Sandoval, Corogon. *Preprimary Education: Needs, Alternatives and Costs 1971-1980.* Prepared for the President's Committee on School Finance. Washington, D.C.: Government Printing Office, 1971.

Education Commission of the States. *Early Childhood Programs: A State Survey 1974-75.* State Report No. 65. Denver: the Commission, 1975.

Schultz, Charles L., *et al. Setting National Priorities, the 1973 Budget* (Chapter 8). Washington, D.C.: Brookings Institution, 1972.

Steiner, Gilbert Y., with the assistance of Pauline H. Milner. *The Children's Cause.* Washington, D.C.: Brookings Institution, 1976.

Steinfels, Margaret O. *Who's Minding the Children? The History and Politics of Day Care in America.* New York: Simon and Schuster, 1973.

Stephen, Mae. *Policy Issues in Early Childhood Education.* Menlo Park, Calif.: Stanford Research Institute, Educational Policy Research Center, 1973.

U.S. Congress, Senate, Statement and Testimony before the Joint Hearing of the Subcommittee on Children and Youth and the Subcommittee on Employment, Manpower and Poverty of the Committee on Labor and Public Welfare by Ernest Van Den Haag and Dale Meers, 92nd Cong., 2d sess., March 27, 1972, pp. 15-22, 3-15.

PART IV
The Changing Politics of Elementary and Secondary Education

Part IV concentrates on contemporary and prospective changes in the politics of education at precollegiate levels—the long-established and, in the eye of some observers, entrenched K-12 structure of American schooling. As a public enterprise its dimensions are staggering: about 17,000 special governmental jurisdictions, 45 million students, and annual expenditures of $57 billion. Although elementary and secondary education is notable as the most costly and pervasive of public services, the study—or even the acknowledgment—of its essentially political character is relatively recent. Until about 1960, research activity was impeded by a formidable obstruction, namely, the arguments successfully employed by educators and many politicians that education was somehow less profane than other public services, and that it appropriately remained aloof from the rough-and-tumble, unsavory world of political victories and defeats. The shift that has taken place in this conception of educational governance has been one of the most telling aspects of the changing politics of education in the 1970's.

For example, Frederick M. Wirt ("The Uses of Political Science in the Study of Education Administration," invited paper prepared for the University Council for Educational Administration, University of Rochester Career Development Seminar on Research in Education Administration, May 15-18, 1977, pp. 12-14) has recently provided an authoritative assessment of research productivity in the politics of

education during the past two decades. He offers the following summary of the relatively few generalizations that are widely supported
and accepted:

1. Educational Administration is political. There is agreement that this concept of
"political" means authority over the allocation of resources and values. . . . Educational administration is both the *object* of political activity from influences outside the
school walls and the *subject* of political activity in that its practitioners can shape policies and behaviors within the school system.
2. Educational administration is increasingly subject to a turbulent environment.
3. School politics show variety, based on community differences in size and status.
4. This new school politics is reshaping the behavior of school administrators.

These statements set forth succinctly the underlying assumptions
common to the contributions in Part IV. It is important to remember
that they are not reports of empirical or field studies by their authors.
They are derivative forms of inquiry — distillations of numerous reports and studies from diverse sources. They are creative, however, in
the sense that the authors have selected the events, issues, and data
germane to their specific topics that they consider to have the greatest
importance in the coming decade. Such interpretative analyses are
periodically desirable in emergent cross-disciplinary fields of study
such as the politics of education, but their preparation is a demanding
task. This is because the field has developed sporadically and unevenly. Wirt points out (pp. 6, 3) that researchers choose and formulate
problems "as the winds of swirling preferences move them" and that
"there are many vineyards in the house of intellect in the politics of
education at this time."

It is not in the least surprising that practitioners and teachers of
practitioners might be perplexed and repelled by what appear to be
such disorganized and even unscientific academic prescriptions, in
comparison with the forms of educational and psychological research
and theorizing with which they are more familiar. At the same time
they are aware that the study and practice of both educational administration and politics are not bounded, or even well served, by the
canons of scientific productivity accepted in other fields. More meaningful communication between the communities of research and practice is long overdue, and Wirt suggests (p. 23) that, as a methodology,
educational policy analysis offers promise for "serving the needs both
of theory and utility." He points out that policy analysis usually involves four aspects, though they are not often distinguished: *descrip-*

tion (reporting behavior and values of actors and resources); *explana-tion* (evaluating the influence of implementation conditions upon the impacts of policy); *criticism* (beyond explanation to questioning of policy in terms of alternative choices that could or should have been made); and *forecast* (predicting to the future from observation of past and current patterns of events).

The chapters in Part IV have a dual purpose. They are analytical treatments of a number of substantive aspects of the politics of educa-tion, and they exemplify, in varying ways, the use of educational policy analysis. The authors have been eclectic in the emphasis they place on one or more of the elements set forth by Wirt; some rely almost exclusively on description and explanation, while others em-phasize criticism or venture into forecasting future developments.

In Chapter 7, Michael Kirst provides a panoramic view of the current and prospective scene in educational politics, utilizing all four of the elements of policy analysis listed by Wirt. The first section of his chapter describes and explains the issues and strategies apparent at federal, state, and local levels of activity, and the second section takes a critical and futuristic perspective, suggesting a broad reform agenda for governance at all three levels. His synthesis of a wealth of informa-tion and personal insights is pointed, bold, and provocative. It carries weight because of his exceptional credentials as a researcher, practi-tioner, policymaker, and professor of educational administration.

Kirst's concern with the allocation of resources for education and the effects of anticipated retrenchments dovetails with the more detailed treatment of economic issues in Part III, and his presentation also serves as a link or "staging area" for the collection of topical papers in Chapter 8. He demonstrates the complexity of interactions occurring among multiple actors, institutions, and interest groups in the educational policy-making process. He introduces and employs some of the familiar concepts and research focuses of political science: conflict, control, legitimacy, coalition building, representation, citi-zens' participation, accountability, executive-legislative relations, and federalism. He makes explicit use of the formulation by Herbert Kaufman concerning evolution in the structure of state and local gov-ernments as a framework for the "new directions" suggested in the later part of his chapter. The reader will also find here the most de-tailed treatment in the book of two highly important developments in the politics of education: the impact of collective bargaining, and the prospects for greater decentralization of policy-making responsibilities to individual school sites.

In policy analysis the conflicts associated with distribution of scarce resources among competing claimants and the processes for resolving such conflicts are central concerns. Analysts comparing the various sectors of governmental action found that education in the past showed relatively high consensus among the parties at interest and low visibility in the public scene. Disputes sometimes made the headlines, but, in general, the operation of the schools was remarkably free of deep-seated conflict. As Wirt concluded in the assessment of research findings referred to above, a turbulent environment has produced highly divisive confrontations over a wide range of issues and transformed the once placid "meeting of minds" into battles between acrimonious factions.

In Chapter 8, Mike Milstein points out that the intrusion of adversarial relationships in education is a highly disturbing development whose implications and effects are not well understood by the protagonists. He shows that the sources of conflict are many, diverse, and clouded by biased rhetoric. The contenders do not even agree on whether the processes of "choosing up sides" and searching for viable compromises are desirable ways to ensure the vitality of educational policy making. The newly emergent adversarial relationships derive from environmental influences with which educational managers, relying on past practice, cannot cope. Their problem is not simply devising new strategies for resolving conflicts within existing structures and rules, but of reexamining some basic assumptions about society and schooling. Milstein suggests that an array of different perspectives on conflict would result from making novel or alternative assumptions about current and future value preferences and trends. He provides a series of questions and comments to stimulate the search for alternative ways to diagnose and manage conflict.

No issue in the politics of education has generated more protracted and heated controversy than that concerning the role of the national government in educational policy making. A long history of public and official debate preceded the enactment of landmark federal legislation and massive grants-in-aid to the states and localities beginning in the mid-1960's. This development admitted national government into far more than a token partnership with the subnational entities. The evolution of intergovernmental relationships in the other functional areas has characteristically been an uncertain and improvisational exercise. In the case of federal aid to education, however, the multiplicity of independent local school districts and strong grass-roots ideology have created unusual tension and conflict among the protagonists, intensifying the adversarial relationships discussed by Milstein. Events have moved faster than the ability of policymakers and researchers to generate and communicate necessary information, devise workable procedures, and develop negotiating skills.

Harold Burbach points out the need to analyze these problems, stating that the experience of nearly two decades provides a basis for stocktaking and developing a better understanding of the federal role. Like Milstein, he casts his recommendations for analysis in the form of questions that suggest the still open-ended and unsettled aspects of the evolving partnership.

Related to greater competition for scarce resources and the emergence of more turbulent and visible forms of educational politics has been the remarkable growth during the past decade of what is commonly termed "the accountability movement." This extends beyond traditional concerns with procedures of ensuring that public funds are legally appropriated and expended to a preoccupation with whether the public funds are bringing about the intended results. For example, taxpayers, school patrons, and legislators are beginning to probe such questions as: "Are children learning the skills and competencies they need to have?" "Are the teachers qualified to teach these competencies?" These questions and their solution were entrusted in earlier times to the expert judgment of professional educators. "Accountability" means that the educators are expected to demonstrate and defend the effectiveness of their activities to the public.

Two essays in Chapter 8 treat different aspects of this trend. Michael Timpane focuses on the activities of the federal and state governments in setting requirements for localities to initiate testing of students' achievement and various other forms of educational program planning and assessment. Much of his contribution is devoted to explaining the problems involved in implementing such programs — "the disuse and misuse of accountability," as he terms it — and to forecasting the future of the movement, with its associated requirements for successful policy management.

Carl Ashbaugh describes recent proposals for the reform of teachers' education and certification, which are referred to as "per-

formance-based" or "PBTE." The accountability element of programs of this type is that goals of performance are specified in advance
of the instructional-learning process for prospective teachers, and such
persons must attain predetermined levels of competence to complete
the training program successfully and to qualify for a teaching credential. Ashbaugh points out that the idea of PBTE may appear to be
straightforward and innocuous to many people, but it has stirred
heated controversy among the key groups involved in the present system of awarding degrees and credentials. The contending groups are
found in public and private universities and colleges; accrediting associations; teachers' unions; state departments of education; and local
school systems. The debate about the pros and cons of PBTE is not
just limited to curriculum and pedagogical issues. It is political in
character because efforts to modify the present system would redistribute important resources of money and control. In addition to his explanation of the stakes perceived by the numerous contenders, Ashbaugh also offers some forecasts concerning the future of PBTE.

The remaining three essays in Chapter 8 are devoted to various
aspects of educational politics and administration at the local community level. Richard Saxe and Elmer Gish take a broad perspective
in their analysis of the problems of public participation in educational
policy making, but they recognize that the influence of the public will
be largely manifested in the operations of local school districts. They
discuss the factors that explain much current public dissatisfaction
with schools and professional educators, including the backlash deriv-
ing from teachers' collective bargaining. They also see some counter-
ing forces at work to stimulate greater and more effective public participation in educational policy making, including the activities of national citizens' organizations, the requirements of federally funded
programs, and the growth of the community education movement.

The contributions of William Boyd and of Michael Kaplan and
John Warden explore important community-based characteristics and
problems that have not yet received adequate attention. These authors
also have in common an extensive use of research-based concepts and
information. Boyd concentrates on the dynamics of changes in the
community and the discernment of developmental patterns associated
with externally and internally induced forms of change in local school
politics. He notes that a significant limitation of the extensive earlier
studies of suburban school districts is that they sampled only those that

were young, expanding in population, and rising in socioeconomic status. Their projection of developmental patterns based on qualitative changes in the social and economic character of a community is, however, supported by more recent research on suburban politics in general, and Boyd points out that more attention needs to be paid to the effects of the "aging process" on the nature of school politics and administration. Since growth and decline are distributed unevenly within metropolitan areas and around the country, it is important to learn more about the community dynamics of each and to trace the way individual school systems are changing in relation to recognizable stages of development. Boyd feels that there is a particularly pressing need for research on the differential impact of community growth and decline upon the responsiveness of school systems to the desires of their clients.

In their discussion of the problems of coordinating the delivery of human services at the community level, Kaplan and Warden deal with a history less of conflict among those who provide and utilize services than with a history of the avoidance of conflict, at least as far as public school systems are concerned. The provision of appropriately related and efficient governmental services for individuals and families is certainly one of the most intractable problems in American community life. It is greatly complicated by the increasing specialization of services and by multiple channels of controlling and funding programs. More than the other public agencies—health, welfare, and housing, for example—the schools have successfully restricted their area of service and displayed great caution in their involvement in joint undertakings. Kaplan and Warden attribute this largely to the political separation of the schools from general government and their ability to finesse the leadership efforts of local governing officials. The pressure on educators to abandon this posture of aloofness has greatly increased during the turbulence of the past decade.

The development of interdependent working relationships among all human service agencies is such an obviously desirable goal that it would appear to be readily attainable if public servants performed with sufficient ingenuity, energy, and goodwill. Kaplan and Warden demonstrate, however, that the process is not a simple matter of organizational change, but involves complex and sometimes subtle issues of communication, control, and the power of various agencies. These agencies are basically political in character, and they generate confrontations more readily than they foster collaboration. They are, however, sensitive and potentially responsive to political pressures for change, such as public demand and program retrenchment imperatives. The authors note that models of active school involvement in interagency coordination at the community level are now beginning to develop; they will bear watching.

7 The Changing Politics of Education: Actions and Strategies

Michael W. Kirst

Public education currently is undergoing a series of shocks from internal and external forces that will result in some important changes in its governance. The most profound shock is the change from a growth psychology—a pattern of governance formulated during an era of steady increase in enrollment and in the scope of the public school curriculum. Expenditures for education grew considerably faster than inflation in prices or the gross national product (two and a half times faster than the GNP from 1960 to 1970). Voters supported substantial increases in state and local taxes for education, and public school teachers remained aloof from collective bargaining under a halo of harmony in the unified education profession. All this has changed, and we now confront steady state or, in many school districts, program retrenchment.[1]

The change has occurred with great intensity. Enrollments will drop substantially by 1985, and population projections are continually revised downward. A surplus of teachers is evident in many large states. Inflation has outrun the growth in school expenditures. Politicians have lost faith in the ability of education to solve a wide range of social problems, including poverty, unemployment, and drug addiction. More and more citizens without children in school are voting to limit increases in public expenditures. Approval by local voters of funds for schools has been declining since the 1960's. In California, for example, local tax referenda for current operations reached an all-time low in 1976 of 24 percent approval. Local voters are bombarded with articles in the media on declining achievement in basic skills — not only can Johnny not read, but he also cannot write. Perhaps we are witnessing a change in voters' priorities, with education of less importance than health or the environment.

The response to all this appears to be a more aggressive political campaign and lobbying strategy by educational interest groups. Since education has lost some of its public luster and traditional priority, political muscle must be substituted. This chapter argues that the best place to use this muscle is at the state and local levels. At whatever level, however, the key to success is building coalitions among educational interest groups and potential allies in services related to human resources, such as health and child nutrition. The worst strategy would be internecine warfare between teachers and "management," or levels of education in competition for scarce education dollars. The art of political leadership in this future context then is formation of coalitions, a practice that currently receives scant attention in preparatory programs for future administrators.

The economic and political context of the next decade raises questions about the present structure and patterns of governance. For example, are the same institutional arrangements appropriate for a decade of explosive growth and a period of stability or decline? Are the state codes and regulations designed effectively for a new period of collective organizations and an old era of "professional harmony" among all educators? I think the answer is no and will suggest some specific changes in my concluding section.

Although we can discover national trends, we must be careful not to generalize for 17,000 local districts and 50 states because the diversity of these areas is striking and important. For example, while enrollments are dropping nationally, they are still growing in Florida and Arizona. We also must be careful not to predict the impact of educational governance or of strategic changes in the behavior of various actors on policy outcomes. We lack theory and empirical data to do so. Education is governed within a complex federal system with numerous interactions and levels. The key actors for curriculum policy making, for example, are detailed in Table 7-1, which shows the numerous governmental levels and actors through which influence must work. Cutting across the grid is the pervasive impact of ideologies, journalists, and producers of educational textbooks and hardware. Education is essentially a bottom-heavy enterprise of over 2 million teachers with considerable autonomy; key policy decisions are made at the local level.

**Table 7-1. Illustrative typology of input sources
for curricular decision making**

	National	State	Local
General legislative	Congress	State legislature	(City councils have minimal influence.)
Educational legislative	House Committee on Education and Labor	State school board	Local school board
Executive	President	Governor	(Mayor has no influence.)
Administrative	HEW-USOE	State department	School superintendent
Bureaucratic	OE (Bureau of Research); National Science Foundation (Division of Curriculum Improvement)	State department (division of vocational education)	Department chairmen, teachers
Professional association	National testing agencies	Accrediting associations and NEA state subject matter affiliates	County association of superintendents
Other private interests	Foundations and business corporations	Council for basic education	John Birch Society, NAACP

Source: Frederick M. Wirt and Michael W. Kirst, *Political and Social Foundations of Education* (Berkeley, Calif.: McCutchan Publishing Corp., 1975), p. 222.

THE LIMITED FUTURE ROLE OF THE
FEDERAL GOVERNMENT IN EDUCATION

In the last decade, the federal government has strikingly expanded its monetary commitment to education. This increased commitment is demonstrated by the Office of Education's budget, which grew from $477 million in 1962 to $5.5 billion in 1972. The federal share of overall expenditures for elementary and secondary education, however, displayed only a slight increase, from 4.4 percent in 1962 to more than 7 percent in 1976. In aggregate terms, most annual growth in expenditures for the lower educational levels has been provided by state and local funds, particularly the latter. For example, from 1960 to 1970 federal expenditures increased by $1.9 billion, state expenditures by $9.86 billion, and local expenditures by $11.74 billion. But the federal government also plays an important indirect role in education through categorical funds, regulations, and related policies in transportation and housing. Thus, the Federal Housing Administration helped to create many of today's suburbs, with crucial implications for urban education.

There are basically six modes through which higher levels of government can affect local schools:

1. Provide general aid—furnish aid on which no restrictions are placed to states and localities or general support for teachers' salaries and for construction. General revenue sharing fits into the former category; the 1961-1963 bills of the Kennedy administration into the latter. Recent proposals for federal assumption of one-third of total school costs would employ this model.

2. Stimulate through differential funding—earmark categories of aid, provide financial incentives, fund demonstration projects, purchase specific services. This is the orientation of the Elementary and Secondary Education Act of 1965 (ESEA).

3. Regulate—legally specify behavior, impose standards, certify and license, enforce accountability procedures. Title IX, which requires women's equity, provides much regulation and no added federal funds.

4. Discover and make available knowledge—have research done, gather and make available statistical and other data.

5. Provide services—furnish technical assistance and consultants in specialized subjects or areas.

6. Exert moral suasion—develop vision and question educational

assumptions through publications, speeches by top officials, and so forth. A recent example of this is advocacy of career education by U.S. Commissioner of Education Marland.

The Office of Education traditionally (1867-1958) stressed the fifth mode, with very minor efforts through the second mode. State governments historically emphasized the first and third. In 1965, differential funding became the key mode for federal influence through bigger and bolder categorical programs and demonstrations. Recently, federal policy has relied more on the third, fourth, and sixth modes as the growth of categorical funding has increased less than annual inflation rates.

Any analysis of federal influence must emphasize the crucial role of the federal judiciary. In the field of education, no single public decision has had more impact than the 1954 Supreme Court decision to desegregate the schools. The recent spate of court decisions on students' rights has resulted in large part from suits brought by federally funded lawyers. Consequently, federal influence now includes such areas of local operations as students' discipline and records.

Every election generates a certain amount of hope that the federal government will be the financial savior of hard-pressed state and local educators and taxpayers. These hopes have not been realistic in the past and probably will not be realized in the future. For example, in the 1972 State of the Union Message and accompanying tentative proposals, President Nixon hinted at a "revolutionary" new program for relieving the burden of property tax and providing fair and adequate financing for education. But the President's revolutionary plan was never seen. Michael Timpane contends that pressures responsible for the growth in federal aid from 1958 to 1968 are diminishing, making it unlikely that there will be any major increase in federal money.[2] Increases in public school enrollment peaked in 1970-1972, as did the demand for teachers. The total fertility rate now stands at its lowest point in U.S. history. State-level school finance reforms have continued despite the *Rodriguez* decision, which ended intervention by the federal courts. Finally, the academic public finance community has recently begun to view the property tax with less disdain; some even see it as progressive.[3]

Overall trends in federal policy have, moreover, reduced the ability of the federal government to intervene in a major way. As employment rates and personal income improve, more money flows into the federal treasury. The fiscal surplus generated by full employment

(4 percent unemployment compared to the current 8 percent) has become very modest. Past federal legislation has resulted in huge future commitments to "uncontrollable" cash income maintenance programs (Social Security, unemployment, Aid to Families with Dependent Children, medicare, and so on). The 1976 presidential campaign indicated much more interest in health care and welfare reform; indeed, education was rarely mentioned except for the issue of busing. If the federal full employment budget only yields a surplus of about $35 billion a year, most of this will probably disappear in tax cuts and new income maintenance programs. We are currently facing a deficit of $70 billion that leaves little flexibility for expanded federal education funds unless cuts are made in other areas. In sum, the initial policies of the Carter administration indicate that the creation of jobs, health insurance, Social Security, welfare reform, and the energy crisis are higher on the federal agenda than a major effort to finance elementary and secondary education.[4] Assumption by the federal government of one-third of school costs as advocated by teachers' organizations would necessitate an increase of about $18-20 billion.

President Carter's overriding fiscal goal is to balance the budget by 1981. Since education's chances of moving up the domestic priority list do not look good, redistributions within the federal budget could free federal resources for education. A chief candidate would be less defense spending (over $120 billion annually). But Carter's first budget only restores the rate of growth in new weapons systems to the rate prior to the speedup inspired by the 1976 campaign. Educators have an important stake in disarmament negotiations.

In sum, the outlook is for a continuation of existing federal policy with marginal dollar increases. Michael Timpane sums up the current federal role:

It consists of an equal opportunity objective which operates both through elementary education programs to enrich programs for disadvantaged students, and through grant and loan programs for college students from poor families. There is also consistent support for reform in educational practice—either reform of a general, locally selective type, through programs like Title III of ESEA, or specific reforms like bilingual education, university community services or career education. Finally, the federal government supports research—research about education and research in educational institutions.

. . . Now, the great change would be for someone to say "let the federal government take the responsibility of underwriting X percent of educational expenditures." That would be a big change, almost the only big change I can think of. Anything else would be telling the President how to exercise the existing federal role.[5]

Given the objective of a balanced 1981 budget, the marginal increases in existing categories will be larger in the initial years of the Carter administration than prior to the 1980 election.

During his 1976 campaign, Carter supported a department of education. Lobbyists for education think this is the essential first step in obtaining more money. USOE is currently an area of controllable expenditures in the Department of Health, Education, and Welfare, dominated by areas of uncontrollable increases—welfare, Social Security, medical care. These programs have increases required by statute or increases in claimants. Since the federal budget uses ceilings for departments, USOE takes the brunt of the cuts of HEW to meet the department's ceiling. It remains to be seen whether even a department of education could compete favorably in view of the broader forces discussed above.

TRENDS IN STATE GOVERNANCE

Recently, there has been a shift in the balance of power toward the state level and away from the federal and local levels. Federal revenue sharing and conversion of federal categorical money to state bloc grants are giving states more influence. At the same time, states are taking policy prerogatives from local governments through school finance reform, accountability, and other areas of state regulation. State governments have become more aggressive in trying to influence local priorities through assessment and testing.[6]

The most dramatic new state initiative has been in the area of school finance reform, accompanied in some states by several other types of policy initiatives, such as accountability and new state categorical programs for the handicapped, disadvantaged, and so forth. Some analysts argue that assumption by the state of the primary share of all costs of education will lead to state-wide collective bargaining. If only the state can provide the money for expanded benefits for teachers, then the logical place for collective negotiations is at the state level.[7] In those states having state-wide agreements with state employees (such as prison guards and state police), negotiations are conducted by representatives of the governor's office. The legislator's role is merely that of ratifying or, infrequently, of rejecting the contract. Special legislative committees often serve as liaison with the governor's bargaining team. In Hawaii, the governor appointed two members of the state board of education and a representative of the

Office of Budget and State Personnel to supplement his own chief
education negotiator. It is interesting that no representatives from the
State Department of Education were involved. There is nothing, however, to prevent a teachers' organization from appealing to the state
legislature.

A number of labor-management experts foresee that assumption
by the state of full financial responsibility may stimulate "two-tier
bargaining." Thus, some issues such as salary schedules and fringe
benefits would be bargained at the state level, and other issues would
be negotiated locally. Two tiers, however, restrict compromise by excluding trade-offs between the issues of salary and noneconomic considerations such as teachers' preparation periods.

The right to strike is an equally difficult area in state-wide bargaining. In the event of a state-wide strike, could the governor stand
the pressure to get children back in school and also give priority to the
future impact of increased state costs? Probably most legislatures ini-
tially would find the strike issue untenable and opt for binding state
arbitration. A related issue is the supposed negative impact bargaining would have on educational experimentation and flexibility because state-wide negotiated agreements would tend to be uniform.
Though regional bargaining may provide more flexibility, regional
boundaries are exceedingly difficult to devise.

Another recent area of state initiative and influence is a system of
certification of teachers grounded on performance-based criteria
(PBTE). Before PBTE, in the 1950's, certification was controlled
largely by the National Council for Accreditation of Teacher Education (NCATE), which was dominated by college professors. Certification was based on completion of college courses rather than on demonstrated competence in the classroom. Teachers who graduated from
institutions accredited by the NCATE were granted reciprocal certification when they crossed state lines.

After this system favoring universities and state education departments was institutionalized, several interest groups—teachers' organizations, parents' groups, ethnic minorities, state legislators, state
boards—gained in strength and demanded a larger share of influence.
The resultant redistribution of influence brought with it a diminution
of control by the NCATE and a more balanced representation on the
NCATE's board. PBTE was evolving at the same time, thus demon-
strating the interaction between private voluntary organizations and
state governance. PBTE, however, lacks a solid empirical base
because we do not know how to define, inculcate, and measure prior-

ity competencies. Consequently, competencies required by the state will be resolved politically through negotiations, bargaining, and coalitions. The outcome will vary according to the state political culture, the structure of state-wide interest groups, and other factors unique to the state. While the popularity of PBTE is diminishing somewhat, a new national mechanism such as certification by the NCATE is unlikely because professional educators will probably split into such adversary groups as humanists versus behaviorists, classroom teachers versus professors, and ethnic minorities versus state education officials.

Even if state-wide collective bargaining and PBTE do not become prevalent, many observers believe that there will be excessive state control of local education. Local schools are already regulated by a complex network of state constitutional requirements, statutes, and administrative rules, and large costs result from unnecessarily high state requirements for personnel certification, tenure, and the length of compulsory schooling. As financial pressure mounts on the local schools, inefficiencies and inflexibility caused by the state may become a major issue.

Myron Lieberman identifies six areas of possible changes in state-local governance:

1. Because state legislatures frequently control educational costs that are paid from local funds, there is inadequate pressure on the legislatures to evaluate costs and benefits carefully.

2. Prior to the 1960's, teachers' organizations emphasized state legislation instead of collective bargaining as the way to improve the welfare of teachers. This emphasis resulted in considerable legislation authorizing teachers' benefits and restricting managerial authority at the district level.

3. Some educational legislation authorizes expenditures, directly or indirectly, to meet problems that no longer exist.

4. Educational legislation often contributes to establishing or strengthening an interest group. Such groups have a stake in maintaining the legislation regardless of its ineffectiveness or inefficiency in ameliorating the problems it was enacted to solve.

5. Some legislation has an unanticipated adverse impact on productivity. There is, for example, no reason for instructors in driver education to have a teacher's certificate.

6. Educational productivity may be inadvertently impeded by

legislation that is not directly concerned with education; thus, child labor laws may discourage youth from entering work-study programs.[8]

A few states have completely revamped the traditional notion of a state department of education. In these states (Massachusetts, Pennsylvania, South Dakota, and Virginia) the secretary of education is in the governor's office. The department is founded on the concept of a unified, centralized system for preschool through graduate school, and the advantage of the new system is, supposedly, the secretary's access to the governor's political confidence and influence. The secretary, through the governor, is also in a better position to coordinate all agencies related to education. A state board of education must, however, live with the ambiguity that the secretary is their chief executive officer and also a spokesman for the governor.

Pennsylvania provides a good example of how the concept works. In that state, the governor appoints the secretary and the seventeen-member board to overlapping six-year terms. The board does most of its work through two councils: basic and higher education. The first secretary of education, John Pittenger, advocated central authority and a consistent philosophy throughout the system. He cited examples of off-campus education and nongraded high school courses that were accepted by the universities because of his ability to coordinate the several levels of education. His opponents, however, decry the close linkage of educational policy to an elected governor and feel competition among the levels of education is desirable.[9]

STATE-LEVEL INTEREST GROUPS

Since state board members have few strong views on specific policies and most state departments of education have traditionally responded to, rather than exercised, leadership, the impact of interest groups has been substantial. These groups have not only been the principal advocates of increased state aid, but have supported the views of professional educators in such regulatory areas as curriculum and certification.

The most important single interest group has been the state teachers' association — the affiliate of the National Education Association (NEA). Although it has grown rapidly in big cities, the American Federation of Teachers has not concentrated its lobbying or organizational efforts at the state level. As in other areas of state politics, the state affiliates of the NEA differ considerably in the amount of political pressure they can exert. The Texas State Teachers Association, for example, is strong enough to commit state legislators to salary proposals during campaigns or primary elections; it has been notably successful in overriding the governor's budget recommendations. The California Teachers Association, on the other hand, has been unable to commit a majority of the state legislature to its school finance proposals.

In most states at various points in history, interest groups favoring state assistance have formed temporary coalitions and in some cases long-standing alliances. These coalitions may develop into permanent organizations, may be ad hoc, one-time affairs, or may be the strategic devices of the state department of education. The aim is to combine political resources in order to maximize influence for a bill or an issue. The strategy is usually to achieve consensus among the various interest groups outside the maneuvering of the state legislature. In effect, coalitions modify competing programs and compromise values so that a united demand is presented to the legislature and the governor. In this way, coalitions are performing one of the functions of political parties.[10]

The outlook for coalitions in many states is hazardous. Local disputes over collective bargaining could make it more difficult for organized teachers to align with administrators and parents at the state level. Cities and suburbs have different socioeconomic compositions that may result in disparate policy interests. Some states have witnessed open conflict among various levels of education for scarce dollars. In California, all levels of education compete aggressively for state legislation that enables them to enroll adults—the only "market" not affected by declining birthrates. Attempts at the state level to coordinate postsecondary education bog down in struggles among various segments to enlarge their share of the market.

The outlook for coalitions, however, need not be completely pessimistic. The Committee for Full Funding in Washington is an excellent example of a group whose strategy is based on the lowest common denominator. In the past various educational lobbies in Washington have attempted on their own to persuade Congress to increase the President's budget request. The outcome has been that a few popular programs have received some increases, but other programs were never able to amass a sufficient number of votes. The Committee for

Full Funding, however, hammered out one omnibus bill that coalesces the favorite programs of a majority of Congress. Each group gets a little more money, with the politically popular impacted areas and vocational education programs getting the most. The latter two programs appeal to the "swing vote" in rural areas that can provide the two-thirds margin necessary to override a presidential veto. Other examples of successful coalitions are big-city interest groups in Pennsylvania and Illinois that have agreed on a salary package and then informed the state that it must help meet the cost or else take responsibility for closing city schools. Moreover, umbrella interest groups such as the Texas State Teachers Association remain united and continue to coordinate their demands to the state legislature.

LOCAL GOVERNANCE IN TRANSITION

The basic administrative structure and pattern for current school policy making were established around the turn of the twentieth century. During this period separation of education from community politics was reinforced (even though political action can effectively transmit community preferences), and there were several key impacts on the lay school board, which was the formal structure for community influence. Around 1900, a national group of opinion makers emerged, including university presidents, school superintendents, and lay allies from the urban business and professional elites. One of their prime aims was to emancipate the schools from what they contended was excessive decentralization and partisan politics. Indeed, many politicians at the time regarded the schools as a useful support for the spoils system and awarded teaching jobs and contracts in return for political favors.[11] A decentralized, ward-based committee system for administering the public schools provided effective linkages to community opinion, but was also an administrative nightmare with tinges of corruption. For example, Philadelphia in 1905 had 43 elected school district boards consisting of 559 members.[12]

The reformers contended that boards elected by wards injected pernicious policies and special interests at the expense of the needs of the entire school district. What was needed to offset this splintering of the public interest was at-large election of board members, smaller school boards, and different kinds of board members. A good school system is good for everyone, not just a part of the community, they said. This viewpoint institutionalized what Robert Salisbury has termed "the myth of the unitary community."[13] Since there are no legitimate "special" group interests in education, there is no reason to give particular groups or areas in the community a seat. To give a seat to labor or design a district for an ethnic minority would be wrong because it would constitute recognition of a special-group perspective on educational policy.

The primary prerequisite for better management was thought to be centralization of power in a chief executive who had considerable delegated authority from a school board elected at-large. The watchwords of reform became centralization, expertise, professionalism, nonpolitical control, and efficiency. Civil service bureaucracies of certified professionals were granted the extensive powers once held by subcommittees of the school board. The preferred model was the large-scale industrial bureaucracy that rapidly emerged in the turn-of-the-century economy.

For several years now, political analysts have contended that education is a relatively closed policy-making system compared to Congress or city councils.[14] By "closed," these analysts mean that education is not open on a continuous basis to influence from its environment. Professional educators and, to a lesser extent, school board members have predominant influence and do not systematically seek views of the lay community. There is no two-party system to institutionalize opposition and to generate alternatives. The government of education is thus characterized by periods of stability under dominance of education officials with little influence from the community and shorter periods of abrupt change that often destroy professional careers when community concerns finally penetrate the insulated influence structure.[15] These short periods of public interest are characterized by a turnover of boards and superintendents.

A 1968 questionnaire by Harmon Ziegler and M. Kent Jennings has offered empirical support for the above assertions. Ziegler surveyed, through both interviews and standardized questionnaires, a national sample of local school districts. He found that the reformers' dream of an educational system had been realized. With regard to school boards, he found that:

Only half the school board members accept the legitimacy of demands originating from community groups. The other half regards community pressure groups as outside the proper school influence system.

There is a strong tendency for boards to perpetuate themselves. Only about half of the board members were elected in a contest with an incumbent. Board recruitment and socialization processes stress traditional approaches to the "proper role."

Most board members can cite only one difference with their electorate opponents and the differences rarely relate directly to the educational program.[16]

For superintendents, expertise has become not only a resource but a way of life learned early and essential for occupational survival. Lacking staff, information, and linkages to the community, school boards find themselves reacting to a superintendent's agenda that highlights expertise and routine as much as possible. But because the board selects and fires the superintendent, it may not need to restate its policy orientation for every issue.

What groups do school boards hear from? The results of several surveys show that the most active voice is the PTA. Almost two-thirds of the board members in the study by Jennings and Ziegler cited the PTA, followed by one-third of the members who mentioned communication with teachers' groups. After that, contact drops off rapidly: civil rights groups (20 percent), business groups (13 percent), right-wing groups (13 percent), and labor organizations (3 percent). In short, in-house and supportive groups (the PTA and teachers) have the most intense interaction with board members by a large margin. Two-thirds of the board members and three-fourths of the superintendents do not think the board's role should be that of a representative of the public desires; they stress, instead, the role of trustee.

The thesis of the closed system, however, can be overstated. Local citizens tend to have more influence in external (school desegregation), redistributive (school closing), and strategic (such as the building of a regional vocation center) decisions. In smaller and more homogeneous communities, professional educators are inclined to anticipate or reflect (especially in middle- and upper-class communities) the desires of the community. In effect, the superintendent operates within a "zone of consent" where negative reaction by the community will not be provoked. Professionals usually have more influence on internal issues and in large and more heterogeneous communities. Professionals also will continue to define many strategic issues (a new curriculum or alternative school) as a technical decision that should be made by professionals. In many large cities the bureaucratic subunits will have more influence than any other participant. Actually, then, school governing agencies do not appear to be any more closed systems than many other agencies of local government. They are clearly more closed, however, than the state and federal legislatures.

THE RISE OF TEACHER ORGANIZATIONS:
A NEW IMBALANCE?

Collective bargaining promises to produce some dramatic changes in the governance of American schools, particularly in regard to the influence by administrators. But even before collective bargaining, the role of the administrator was changing, as William O'Dell noted in 1971:

The most important single thing that is happening today is the shift in the power structure. What we used to conceive of as the role of a board of education and the superintendent is greatly truncated. The federal funds generally add new programs to the schools, not aid old programs; it adds burdens which it doesn't fully finance. But at the bottom is the organization of teachers which is at least three years ahead in its demands of any available resources. The ceiling moves down as the floor moves up, and the administration gets squeezed in the middle along with the school board.

It used to be that a school superintendent, if he was at all successful, would have the feeling that he had the ability to mount a program and carry it through successfully. I think at the present time very few superintendents would be able to say honestly that they have this feeling. They are at the beck and call of every pressure that is brought to them. They have lost initiative. They don't control their own time. . . . Midadministration is very much floundering. They don't know whether they are teachers or administrators.

There has been a change in the role of the superintendent from one who plans and carries through to one who works with groups of people in joint planning and ultimate realization of something the group can agree on.[17]

In the 1950's, teachers found themselves cut off from the school board and the public. They were increasingly told how to conduct their classrooms by business managers, administrative assistants, subject-matter coordinators, and department heads. Collective bargaining was a logical outcome of this and other factors that changed the perception of teachers about their "proper professional role." There are several possible advantages in collective bargaining.[18]

1. Students will learn more about democracy if they experience more democratic decision making in the schools.

2. The right to control one's working conditions is a fundamental American right.

3. Collective bargaining may increase teachers' commitment to their profession.

4. Collective bargaining will force some districts to develop more effective management.

Critics of collective bargaining by teachers such as Pierce and

Wellington contend that the wholesale adoption of the bargaining model used by the private sector will give teachers a disproportionate amount of power. Weak school boards will find themselves with a formidable opponent and inadequate resources to bargain effectively. For example, the private bargaining model assumes that the behavior of both employers and employees is constrained by consumers in the marketplace. The consumer can choose not to buy a product, postpone purchase, or turn to a cheaper substitute. Consequently, unions in the private sector are presented with a rough trade-off between larger benefits for some employees and unemployment for others. In the public sector, however, it is unclear who is the ultimate consumer of education. Also, students do not have the option of changing schools or consuming a smaller quantity of education.[19] Public schools receive tax support even when they are closed by strikes; by withholding public services the unions put pressure on the consumers rather than on management. Strikes are designed to create public pressure for a settlement. Politicians can pass future costs of large settlements on to future officeholders.

This viewpoint leads to Pierce's conclusion that citizens must assert control directly in the negotiating process; they cannot influence the outcome through the marketplace. Moreover, labor organizations that bargain in the private sector rarely ask for control over decisions concerning product and pricing. In public education, however, teachers are seeking control over all areas of educational policy. The solution to the above problems is hindered by the traditional view that negotiations must be kept secret. Even school boards in large districts do not have time to follow the proceedings, and members of the press and public are generally barred.

Administrators also have been successful in expanding collective bargaining. In San Francisco, for example, elementary school administrators are represented by the Teamsters Union. Salary arrangements for middle management are tied closely to teachers' salaries, creating a lockstep ratio. If teachers' salaries are increased by 5 percent, then administrators' salaries go up by the same percentage. This suggests a tacit alliance between the school bureaucracy and teachers' organizations. One possibility for solving this problem is to separate the management team and to bargain independently with regard to administrators' compensation. Principals in New York City refuse to participate in negotiating the teachers' contract and bargain separately. But where does this leave the principals? If they are not part of management, why are they necessary? The following section proposes a major reorientation of the role of the principal to prevent the principals' organization from becoming a de facto adjunct of the teachers' organization.

Teachers' organizations will continue to have an impact on school governance through federal electoral activities. The NEA spent $3 million for their endorsed candidates in the 1976 federal elections. (And teachers' organizations spent more than any other interest group in the 1974 California state election.) At the state level, teachers will have few peers in terms of workers to perform precinct political chores, to raise dollars for campaigns, and to hire lobbyists. The recent increase in teachers' activity in local school board elections, however, raises particularly interesting issues. Given the small turnouts and low public visibility of local board races, the employees may be able to dominate the local election of the school boards as representing school management. In my view, teachers' organizations would derive more benefit from local elections than from their current large-scale efforts at the federal level. Few groups of employees have such great potential to elect both sides of the bargaining table!

NEW DIRECTIONS FOR SCHOOL GOVERNANCE: A FUTURISTIC PERSPECTIVE

Herbert Kaufman discerns in the evolution of the structure of state and local governments a search for an accommodation among three competing values (objectives): representativeness; technical, nonpartisan competence; and leadership. The first objective refers to the election of public officials, the use of referenda, and the preferred effectiveness of the legislative branch in determining educational policy. The second refers to the demand for officials to be trained and qualified for their jobs and a preference for educational decisions based on technical and professional considerations rather than on partisan political premises. The third refers to executive coordination through some central mechanism that ensures reasonably consistent and efficient educational programs.[20]

Our present educational governance structure reflects elements of all three of these values. But at various stages of development one has received more emphasis than the other, partly because new conditions required new methods, and partly because excessive emphasis on one of the values tends to set in motion demands for redressing the balance. Which of these values one now wants to stress depends in part on one's personal bias and in part on analysis of the most pressing governance problems. For example, a 1975 Citizens Commission report on the San Francisco schools concluded that the superintendents did not have enough authority: "The superintendents have directed the executive superstructure as if they were medieval dukes governing a feudal hierarchy of barons, each with their own constituencies and private access to higher authorities."[21] Some reformers advocate changes in governance to provide more executive leadership, not unlike the themes of the turn-of-the-century reformers.

Teachers' organizations in San Francisco contend, however, that the main problem is a lack of decision-making discretion for competent professionals. Teachers are unable to bargain and strike. Consequently, the central office supplies inadequate resources and flexibility at the classroom level. And it is at this level where children come in contact with educational institutions. Accordingly, Kaufman's second value needs to be emphasized in the governance structure.

In direct contrast to these first two perspectives is the 1975 report by the National Committee for Citizens in Education (NCCE). After nationwide hearings, the committee published a report. It contended that: "The American public school system does not operate as part of the democratic process; and . . . . There are so many actors in educational policymaking that (the person) who makes decisions is not clear and citizens are unable to secure their legitimate rights to influence policy decisions."[22]

The NCCE charges that the administrative role in school governance is inordinately strong and urges revitalization of the legislative process—from the school site to the state legislature—to inject more democracy. One alternative to this suggestion would be to increase the governance potential of all three of the competing orientations. We could provide collective bargaining laws based on the model of the private sector, enhance the central management capacity of the superintendent, and give parents at each school site increased resources and formal power to approve major decisions. It is likely, however, that this approach of fighting power with power would lead to paralysis and stalemate similar to the French Fourth Republic. Thus, it appears that we must choose a priority among the three values.

Part of this choice will reflect individual preference. If one accepts, however, a steady state or a declining industry scenario for public education, the choice can be made on different criteria. USOE projects an overall drop of 9.3 percent (4.6 million) students for grades K-12 from 1975 to 1984. In this context neither executive leadership nor professional neutral competence will bring about sufficient change in education to meet current educational deficiencies. Consequently, reform of governance should take the direction of democratic representativeness. James March posits three phases in the history of a social institution:

Education is a declining industry. We have apparently entered the third natural phase in the history of a social institution. The first stage is a period of dynamic growth. Social expectations rise; the institution is able to meet those expectations; there is excitement, expansion, and self-confidence. The second stage is a period of conflict. In the period of neglect social expectations outrun capabilities. Social expectations decline; the institution remains able to meet many of the reduced expectations; there is indifference, passivity, and stagnation.[23]

An institution in a declining or steady state has certain regular administrative characteristics. The age of those in positions of leadership tends to increase as promotions and mobility decrease. There are fewer resources and occasions of success. An oversupply of trained manpower encourages additional bureaucratic superstructure to make room for it. The loss of slack resources eliminates buffers between contending groups in the institution. Internal conflict becomes overt, and executive wheeling and dealing seems less effective in moving the institution. Innovation and change through incremental additions of personnel and programs become less feasible. Ambitious employees leave to find other ways to meet their ambitions. In education, the various levels compete for students. Since the potential number of adult enrollees depends less on birthrates, competition for such students among levels of education will become particularly keen. City and county agencies begin to absorb school functions such as athletics and the arts.

It is unlikely in this context that better administrative analysis and skill in interpersonal implementation can make much of a difference. Problems may not have solutions. Degrees of freedom are lacking to implement new approaches in a declining industry. Conflict will not yield to resolution if resources are scarce. Difficulties will probably persist for reasons that have nothing to do with administration.

The basic reflex of teachers' organizations will be to protect job security, seniority, due process, restricted entry, and stable procedures. School employees will feel threatened by cutbacks in resources and demands of minorities and community groups for a piece of a smaller pie. For example, Affirmative Action in hiring and in new bilingual-bicultural programs will have to give way to the need to preserve the jobs of senior teachers. Classroom aides will quickly join unions in order to safeguard their jobs. Improvements in educational technology could be resisted because they decrease the labor-capital ratio and generate even more surplus teachers.

Educational change, however, cannot be imposed from the top down or through parents' pressure on uncommitted and reluctant teachers. The cutting edge of education is at the school and classroom level—the point where the child comes in contact with the educational process. Consequently, we need to give teachers more ability to plan and evaluate educational reforms at the individual school level. At that level, principal, parents, and teachers can best ensure implementation of educational ideas. Our analysis of governance has underlined the necessary but not sufficient influence of higher levels of policymakers.

In sum, improved representation through enhanced legislative governance and decision making at individual school sites promise the most flexible, adaptable school system for probable future conditions. Emphasis on such representation is most likely to provide new approaches to the historic problems of public education, such as low attainment by minority groups and inadequate career education. With this goal in mind, I propose the following changes in educational governance.

NEEDED CHANGES IN FEDERAL-STATE POLICY MAKING

The limited impact of federal-state categorical programs suggests a strategy focusing on reform in local governance. Federal and state governments can, however, provide grants to stimulate this. Within the federal context, the legislative branch should be strengthened in terms of information, analysis, and oversight. The Congressional Budget Office may help some. A prime candidate for congressional oversight is the vocational education program that has remained largely immune from any attempts by Congress to reform it through statutes. Despite congressional funds earmarked for the disadvantaged and handicapped in vocational education, state distribution formulas and accounting systems are often not precise enough to utilize these funds effectively.

A drastic reform at the state level would be the establishment of a secretary of education in the governor's office. It is desirable, however, to wait for more experience with this concept before it can be proposed as a blanket solution. Indeed, the secretary of education would probably be effective in some states and be unsuitable in others. At this point we have little guidance on which states would prove most promising. I would favor as an interim step augmenting the educational personnel for the legislature and the governor's office. Recent case studies suggest several possibilities for state governance that would assist the overall strategy endorsed in this chapter.[24]

An urgent need is to rethink the balance between state and local control. The governance plan for school sites advocated below requires great local flexibility. In many states, however, the state code has built up incrementally over many years until local authorities have little discretion over the budget. One unfortunate reaction to increased competition for resources in a declining industry could be detailed allocation and procedural rules prescribed by the state. As education loses favor with state politicians, the wrong kind of statutes dealing with accountability could result. On the other hand, states may want to insulate several areas from local collective bargaining. Reforms in collective bargaining and governance of school sites would do much to overcome the need for detailed state regulations.

The following guidelines outline a structure of shared powers.

State Collective Bargaining Laws

1. Binding arbitration should not be required by state law because both sides must recognize that they have something to gain and something to lose from the bargaining process.

2. States should review the preemption of personnel issues in the state code. Some personnel decisions could be returned to the local bargaining table.

3. State law specifying the length of the school year should be eliminated or relaxed. Under present state law, teachers know that any salary they lose during a strike will be made up at the end of the school year.

4. States should open some parts of the bargaining process to the public in order that it might react to the proposals of labor and management. States should not intervene in local disputes by using the governor as the mediator or arbitrator.

5. Some areas of education policy (not wages or fringe benefits)

that are negotiated centrally can be reserved for discussion at the school site. This implies other changes to enhance teachers' influence at the school site, discussed in "Needed Changes in Local Governance," below.

State Boards of Education

1. Members should be compensated.
2. Members should have preservice and in-service training.
3. Members should be more aggressive in developing channels of personal access to state lawmakers.
4. Boards should have additional staff members to identify problems and to analyze data.

Chief State School Officers

1. Recruitment for these positions should be open and nation-wide in scope.
2. The salaries for these officers should be comparable to those of other top educational leaders in the state.
3. Chief state school officers should have the flexibility to appoint their own administrative team.

Needed Changes in Local Governance

The primary role of the federal and state governments should be to provide resources and stimulation for the major decisions and changes at the school site. A first step toward achieving this goal would be a reorientation of priorities from the turn-of-the-century reforms of centralization, depoliticization, expertise, and civil service competence. The new priorities would be increased representation, the school as the unit of governance, and decentralization. Conflicting values inherent in education would be brought into the open, not obscured behind a facade of professional expertise. The dismantling of the reforms should begin with:

1. board elections by subcommunity districts rather than at-large;
2. all members of a school board running at once;
3. optional use of partisan endorsements.

The school board could enhance its effectiveness through its own independent staff. In large districts, decentralization would accompany the above measure. Also in large districts, school board members would receive salaries and would be expected to surrender part of their outside activities, and a new approach to school site decision making would be phased in.

How would school site decision making work specifically? There is no one best system, and various localities might use different forms. One version would work as follows. A prerequisite step would be a complete overhaul and pruning of the state education code to permit more local choice. Then each school would elect a citizen-staff council composed of parents, teachers, administrators, and perhaps high school students. Large amounts of state and local unrestricted funds would be allocated to each school to spend as they chose. Newport-Mesa, California, has a small-scale version of this. It results in markedly different funding patterns; some schools stress more books, others more counselors. The site council would decide the instructional priorities (how much time for "basics") and school organization (open or traditional classrooms). At the end of a three-five-year contract, the council would recommend to the central authorities the retention or replacement of the principal. Collective bargaining with teachers would be at the central level (for example, wages), but some issues (curriculum or choice of textbooks) would be reserved for the school site council. As in San Jose, California, the teachers may want to form a faculty senate at each school that would elect representatives to the school site council and discuss other major site issues. This would help overcome isolation of teachers that has impeded cooperative school planning. Education policies cannot be imposed on unwilling teachers. Moreover, if school site decision making is viewed as a device to undermine teachers' rights and collective bargaining, it will surely fail.

We now have a profusion of overlapping and uncoordinated parent advisory groups at each school mandated by federal or state law. Most of these could be eliminated. For the remainder, the citizen members of the school site council could meet separately and approve applications for federal and state categorical aid. An annual report of school performance would be sent to each home, including program expenditures, educational processes, pupils' test data, and other outcomes such as pupils' self-concept and vandalism.

The central district has a crucial support role for staff and parents' training, evaluation, and oversight. The role of the central district will probably be more extensive for high schools because of such needs as work-study and off-campus programs that can best be coordinated centrally. Experience in other states such as Florida demonstrates that school site decision making requires preparation for principals, teachers, and parents.

This type of governance plan embodies the recognition that it is the individual school, rather than the entire district, that is the critical nexus between the child and the substance of education. The school site is also large enough to have relevance for state aid formulas. We need to know whether money for special federal and state programs is reaching the schools with the most needy pupils. We need to know, moreover, whether these schools are receiving an equitable share of the local district's budget for "regular" programs. Even in school districts with three or more schools, it is the local school site that is the biggest concern to many parents. Even where community participation is not great at all school sites, this plan would have beneficial effects. In addition to what is done in government, the issue of how things are done and how people feel about their governance is crucial.

We must rethink the reformer's assumption that the community is a unity for educational policy and that, consequently, there should be a uniform educational program in all schools. With safeguards to prevent racial and economic segregation, this emphasis on the school site can be linked to the concept of clusters selected by parents. Schools in the same geographical area could feature different programmatic approaches—open classrooms, self-contained classrooms, schools without walls—and parents could choose the approach they deemed appropriate for their children. All alternatives could be within the public sector to avoid the difficulties of an unregulated voucher scheme. A plan with choices would provide parents greater leverage over school policy. Schools that experienced declining enrollment would lose part of their funding. We found that within one school district in Florida the percentage of students in elementary schools who did poorly on tests ranged from 22 percent in one school to 78 percent in another. It is clear that this diversity in skills requires diversity in the practices, programs, and instructional methods of schools.

A CONCLUDING NOTE OF CAUTION

All of these recommendations are formulated from a viewpoint that believes the schools need to be part of a governance system that provides stimulus for innovation and responsiveness. Today, schools are a de facto monopoly with multiple goals and technology. Unlike private enterprise, they are not subjected to everyday market forces (such as competition and profit) that furnish incentives for response to clients, changing programs and diverse resources, or cutting of costs. John Pincus points out, consequently, three factors—bureaucratic safety, response to external pressure, and approval of peer elites—that are likely to make schools adopt innovations.[25] The governance recommendations endorsed in this chapter will increase external and school site pressures on decisionmakers.

The politics of education changes because of internal conditions within the school system and external conditions. For example, much of the preceding argument relies upon stabilization and decline of enrollments; this trend could be reversed. Values have changed quickly before and can do so again. The 1960's demonstrated that fertility can decline dramatically within a single decade. Any decade may contain an equal but opposite surprise.[26]

Proposed reform in school governance, however, should be approached with some caution. Research has demonstrated the complexity of the present governance structure. There is no accepted theory to predict what changes will result in influence or policies from specific school governance reforms. It has been the assumption in federal and state categorical programs that certain changes would result from earmarked money and regulations; as we have seen, their expectations were often not realized. Such experiences suggest that governance changes should take place gradually, with careful evaluation at each stage of change.

NOTES

1. Parts of the argument developed in this chapter are derived from Michael W. Kirst, *Governance of Elementary and Secondary Education* (Palo Alto, Calif.: Aspen Institute for Humanistic Studies, 1977).

2. Michael Timpane, "Federal Aid to Schools: Its Limited Future," *Law and Contemporary Problems* 38 (Winter 1974): 493-512.

3. Dick Netzer, "The Incidence of the Property Tax Revisited," *National Tax Journal* 26 (December 1973): 515-535.

4. See "Different Democrat," *Wall Street Journal,* January 20, 1977; and Michael W. Kirst, "The Future Federal Role in Education," *Phi Delta Kappan* 58 (October 1976): 155-158.

5. Institute for Educational Leadership, *Perspectives on Federal Education Policy* (Washington, D.C.: the Institute, 1976), p. 2.

6. For an overview of the issue of accountability, see Henry Levin, "A Conceptual Framework for Accountability in Education," *School Review* 82 (May 1974): 363-389. For an analysis of school finance reform politics, see J. Berke, M. Kirst, and M. Usdan, *The New State Politics of Education* (Cambridge, Mass.: Ballinger Foundation, 1976).

7. Robert E. Doherty, "State Assumption of School Costs and Collective Bargaining Structure," n.p., August 1973. A preliminary study by Betsy Levin, *Levels of State Aid Related to State Restrictions on Local Decision Making* (Washington, D.C.: Urban Institute, 1972), indicates no relationship between the level of state funding and the amount or type of state control.

8. Myron Lieberman, unpublished research proposal to the National Institute of Education, University of Southern California, 1974.

9. See J. C. Pittenger and L. K. Ginger, "Should States Have Secretaries of Education?" *Compact* 8 (January 1974): 14-18.

10. Discussions of state political coalitions are included in Laurence Iannaccone, *Politics in Education* (New York: Center for Applied Research in Education, 1967); Stephen K. Bailey *et al., Schoolmen and Politics* (Syracuse, N.Y.: Syracuse University Press, 1962); N. A. Masters, R. H. Salisbury, and T. H. Eliot, *State Politics and the Public Schools* (New York: Knopf, 1964); and more recently by Laurence Iannaccone, "Norms Governing Urban-State Politics of Education," in *Toward Improved Urban Education*, ed. Frank Lutz (Worthington, Ohio: Charles Jones, 1970), pp. 233-253.

11. See David B. Tyack, "Needed: The Reform of a Reform," *New Dimensions of School Board Leadership* (Evanston, Ill.: National School Boards Association, 1969), pp. 29-51.

12. *Ibid.*

13. Robert Salisbury, "Schools and Politics in the Big City," in *The Politics of Education at the Local, State and Federal Levels*, ed. Michael Kirst (Berkeley, Calif.: McCutchan Publishing Corp., 1970).

14. See, for instance, Iannaccone, *Politics in Education.* Education appears more accessible and responsive, however, than many other areas of local government such as health, welfare, and housing.

15. *Ibid.*

16. See Harmon Ziegler and M. Kent Jennings, *Governing American Education* (Scituate, Mass.: Duxbury Press, 1974).

17. Interview with Professor William O'Dell by the Stanford University Faculty Committee, May 1971.

18. Lawrence Pierce, "Teachers' Organizations and Bargaining: Power Imbalance in the Public Sphere," in National Committee for Citizens in Education, *Public Testimony on Public Schools* (Berkeley, Calif.: McCutchan Publishing Corp., 1975), Chapter 6.

19. See Harry H. Wellington and Ralph Winger, *The Unions and the Cities* (Washington, D.C.: Brookings Institution, 1971).

20. For an elaboration, see Herbert Kaufman, *Politics and Policies in State and Local Government* (Englewood Cliffs, N.J.: Prentice-Hall, 1963).

21. *San Francisco Chronicle,* May 15, 1975.

22. National Committee for Citizens in Education, *Public Testimony on Public Schools, passim.*

23. James G. March, "Commitment and Competence in Educational Administration," in *Educational Leadership and Declining Enrollments*, ed. Lewis B. Mayhew (Berkeley, Calif.: McCutchan Publishing Corp., 1974), p. 133.

24. Roald F. Campbell and Tim L. Mazzoni, Jr., *State Policy Making for the Public Schools* (Berkeley, Calif.: McCutchan Publishing Corp., 1976).

25. John Pincus, *Incentives for Innovation in Public Schools* (Santa Monica, Calif.: RAND Corp., 1973), p. 49.

26. See Peter Morrison, *The Demographic Context of Educational Policy Planning* (Princeton, N.J.: Aspen Institute, 1976).

8 Priority Issues in the Politics of Elementary and Secondary Education

Analyzing the Impact of Adversarial Relations on the Management of Educational Systems

Mike M. Milstein

Ever since the turbulent 1960's America appears to have been rushing headlong toward the politics of confrontation. Activism generated by the civil rights movement and subsequent movements left us with a new set of influencing mechanisms, ranging from sit-ins, walk-outs, boycotts, and strikes to petitions and countercultural experiments. It is not surprising, therefore, that within this societal context, the actions of those who seek to influence the allocation of scarce resources in education are also marked by turbulence. What is more, an increasing array of issues is being contended, and it is probable that the situation will become further exacerbated in the foreseeable future.

"Adversary" is defined as "one turned against another or others with a design to oppose or resist him or them . . . . An antagonist; an enemy; foe." Managing educational systems, if the early retirement and short tenure of superintendents can be taken as behavioral indicators, is becoming increasingly difficult because of adversarial relations. Unless the policy issues related to adversarial relationships are confronted, there is little likelihood that the situation will change. The intent of this brief treatment is to provide a catalog of these trends in education and to pose a series of policy-related questions that derive from them.

SOURCES OF ADVERSARIAL RELATIONS

Although many policy-related trends contribute to adversarial relations in education, a far from exhaustive listing, by levels of governance, must suffice for present purposes.

Federal

Among these trends are: legislation aimed at achieving national
preferences, even if these preferences differ from those of states and
school districts; involvement of federal courts in decisions regarding
segregation and, more recently, in questions of financial equity and
accountability for educational achievement; and rules, regulations,
and guidelines spawned by the Department of Health, Education, and
Welfare and the Office of Education, which often require states and
school districts to implement programs in ways that federal officials
feel are appropriate.

State

Trends prevalent within the states include: legislatures demanding greater educational accountability, developing internal expertise,
and giving less credence to representatives of the educational community; state education agencies, albeit often unwillingly, requiring
comprehensive data on planning and results for categorical grant programs; infighting among interest groups at the state level, which has
reduced their effectiveness in dealing with policymakers; and state
courts intervening in school issues, often preceding and leading to the
involvement of the federal courts.

Local

At the local level are found such trends as the following: students
and parents becoming adept at influencing the schools; community
interest groups becoming less predictable and harder to identify,
changing, it seems, in form and substance so easily that it is difficult to
cope with confrontational tactics like school boycotts and packed
board meetings; collective negotiations hardening the roles of administrators and teachers to the point that they view each other as opposing forces; and the early retirement of superintendents and other
school administrators, sometimes in spirit if not in fact. The last may
be regarded as a symptom of the malaise, but it also affects policy
choices because subordinate administrators are less likely to take risks
if their superiors are timid.

The participants in these conflicts tend to explain the attendant adversarial relationships in heated rhetoric that reflects their particular interests and points of view. The analytical questions that should guide policy research, however, must be both more searching and conducive to orderly presentation of varying perspectives. Such questions may be usefully organized in two categories: societal-based and school-based. The range of questions also recognizes that divergence will exist among observers.

SOCIETAL-BASED QUESTIONS ABOUT ADVERSARIAL RELATIONS

Societal-based questions are conditioned by alternative assumptions about the future. One view is that the fourth quarter of the twentieth century will be a mere extension of the third quarter. If this is an accurate perception, one can still rely on responses to conflict that were adequate in the past. The other view is that we are currently witnessing a significant break with the past. If this is an accurate perception, unique strategies for resolving conflict must be fashioned.

1. Is our present short-range experience an indicator of a linear trend? Or is it likely that, when viewed by future historians, the present era will be typified as but one of a series of adversarial peaks? Racial, ethnic, religious, and economically based confrontations have existed from the time of the Pilgrims, through the Indian wars and conflicts between sheepmen and cattlemen during frontier days, through the Civil War, on to the union riots of the early 1900's, and culminating in the civil rights movement and Watergate. Our country has been typified as prone to confrontation. In short, are the dynamics of today the same as, or different from, those of the past?

2. Associated with the above question is the question of whether adversarial relations are mere reflections of a growing recognition of cultural pluralism. The notion of the American melting pot proved attractive in the past; the melting pot may have been, however, more rhetoric than fact. As long as there were geographical and industrial frontiers, America was able to find room for almost all newcomers. Today, we are a mature society; thus, we have fewer frontiers to which we can disperse, and so we must confront each other within dwindling spaces. The schools become natural public grounds for this confrontation. If this is an accurate observation, then adversarial relations in education are more explainable. Cultural pluralism is bound to be accompanied by normative diversity and increasingly diverse interest groups.

3. Some observers would typify the present scene as marked more by apathy than by adversarial relations. They argue that those who manned the picket lines yesterday seem strangely subdued today. Is this due perhaps to a large dose of disillusionment? Where such apathy does indeed exist, it may be viewed either as smoldering sparks that can reignite at any time or as an indicator of a return to a calmer period.

4. There is an even more disturbing possibility than apathy: Is participation in adversarial relations becoming a way of life? Do participants view the process itself as the payoff rather than as the means to modifying policies? Are they becoming enamored of the confrontational power game? If so, attempts to resolve their dissatisfactions with policies or programs are unlikely to moderate the intensity of their involvement.

5. Has the general public, or at least significant elements of that public, come to think of public education as less than centrally relevant to their lives? Are we entering an era where education beyond the basics is considered unimportant? If so, then we have the makings of a different set of dynamics, and the current adversarial trends may merely be symptoms of a major change in our valuing of education. Strategies that are devised to mitigate adversarial relations must take this possibility into account, if there is to be any hope of moving educational organizations into a compatible juxtaposition with their environments.

6. On the other hand, have the tasks of education undergone such extensive redefinitions that educators are incapable of making adequate responses? From educating elites around 1900, to focusing on vocational preparation by the 1920's, to the admission and retention of all school-age youngsters since the 1940's, and, finally, to present demands that students in schools actually receive an adequate education, the pressures have increased. Perhaps the expectations are outpacing our ability to respond. The back-to-basics movement may be a first indicator of this possibility.

SCHOOL-BASED QUESTIONS ABOUT ADVERSARIAL RELATIONS

Educational leaders are often referred to as "crisis oriented." That is, they are said to wait until the proverbial alligators are upon them before taking any measured (or unmeasured) actions. Given the contextual setting in which they operate and the related unclarity of the schools' role, it is not surprising that their responses are often less than adequate. Attributes of the organizational setting of education itself probably contribute greatly to the tardy and often inadequate responses of educators.

1. Studies of change in education tend to conclude that educators resist change efforts, at least in part because they are not convinced that making adaptations in structure, process, technology, or pedagogical methods will have any major impact on educational outcomes. Does this sense of equifinality truly exist? If so, does this mindset give educators pause when they are dealing with adversarial situations? That is, do educators assume that what is actually going on in the world is really peripheral to their tasks and thus should be ignored? Are educators incapable, therefore, of responding to changing social conditions?

2. Have we moved so far away from the fabled little red schoolhouse that we have devised an organizationally based, built-in incapacity to respond to conflict situations? We are now an army of specialists, but is anyone in charge? Is there a sense of proprietorship on the part of the professionals, or has specialization made it impossible for them to have a sense of overall purpose?

3. Does the rising tempo of criticism from society cause educators to react ever more defensively? Are they, in effect, becoming locked into their present incapacities because of their defensiveness? Do they think that if they take the criticism seriously they might reach the undesirable conclusion that what they are presently doing is not adequate?

4. Have collective negotiations, which lead administrators and teachers to join in combat over dwindling economic rewards, precluded the possibility that intrinsic rewards can be satisfying for these participants? Teachers seem to have an increasing need to receive intrinsic rewards, but there are fewer formal mechanisms to assure that such rewards will be forthcoming. In light of the present situation, is it feasible for managers of the educational enterprise to move toward self-fulfilling experiences for teachers and themselves? If not, it is probable that the adversarial nature of the situation will intensify.

ADVERSARIAL RELATIONS AS A RESEARCH FOCUS

The result of adversarial relations on educational systems is far from clear. There are those, such as students of organizational change, who conclude that conflictual or adversarial relations, especially resulting from demands made by external sources, may be a necessary ingredient to bring about needed changes in education. There are others, especially spokesmen for administrator groups and school boards, who argue that the potential for changing educational organizations has been negatively affected because we are witnessing an adversarial overload situation. There is much that research concerning adversarial relations in education can do to resolve this very important argument.

The Federal Government and Education:
Problems and Prospects

Harold J. Burbach

Although the role of the national government in public education has expanded greatly over the past two decades, critics are just now beginning to examine seriously the question of what this trend means for educational policy making. The reasons for this scholarly lapse are not nearly so important as the current pressing need for more and better information on the subject. Preparatory to fulfilling this need, theorists, empirical researchers, and policymakers would do well to delineate the questions they consider to be most relevant in terms of developing a better understanding of the issue at hand. Following are but a few of those that beg for attention.

WHY AND HOW DOES THE NATIONAL GOVERNMENT INVOLVE ITSELF IN PUBLIC EDUCATION?

Stephen Bailey and Edith Mosher made one of the most cogent statements on the question of why the federal government is interested in public education: "The federal government is logically concerned with education whenever questions arise about disparities in publicly supported educational opportunities and whenever it can be shown that educational activity bears significantly upon such issues of national value as unity, justice, domestic tranquility, the common defense, the general welfare, and the liberties of present and future generations."[1]

While the actual purposes served by federal educational programs up to this point have been generally consistent with this rationale, one can readily see from the foregoing quotation that there is almost no limit to the ways in which the national government could justify its involvement in educational matters. For those who believe that there are and, indeed, should be some limitations on federal influence, it is thus important to examine in greater detail the question of exactly why and under what specific conditions the national government is justified in exerting its authority in educational decision making.

Michael Kirst's delineation in Chapter 7 of the six basic ways in which higher levels of government can affect local school districts offers a good beginning in determining how the national government actually may involve itself in public education. In abbreviated and slightly altered form, these actions are:

1. Provides general aid—furnishes aid on which no restrictions are placed to states and localities or general support for teachers' salaries and for construction.
2. Stimulates through differential funding—earmarks categories of aid, provides financial incentives, funds demonstration projects, purchases specific services.
3. Regulates—legally specifies behavior, imposes standards, certifies and licenses, enforces accountability procedures.
4. Discovers and makes available knowledge—has research done, gathers and makes available statistical and other data.
5. Provides services—furnishes technical assistance and consultants in specialized subjects or areas.
6. Exerts moral suasion—develops vision and questions educational assumptions through publications, speeches by top officials, and so forth.[2]

One could use this descriptive categorization as a common frame of reference for analyzing various policies and programs in greater detail in order to determine their effectiveness and the full range of their consequences. At the present time, for example, there is a need for some cogent discussion of the pros and cons of block grants versus categorical aids. In attempting to frame this issue, Samuel Halperin[3] says that there are simply no commonly agreed upon definitions, that one person's block grant is another's categorical program. He seeks to clarify this situation by offering a series of background statements that he hopes will stimulate discussion and ultimately lead to a focusing of the areas of disagreement over values and objectives. Concluding what

I consider to be required reading on the subject, Halperin writes: "Block Grants or Categorical Aids? Rather than get hung up in that tired rhetoric, let's ask ourselves: What *objectives* are important in federal aid to education? With objectives more clearly understood, the means to attain them should be more easily discerned in today's muddled atmosphere."[4] This, then, leaves us with a reminder that the question of "how" cannot be answered independently of the question of "why."

WHAT IS THE EXTENT OF FEDERAL INFLUENCE ON PUBLIC EDUCATION?

The answer in purely financial terms is that the federal government contributes only about 7 or 8 percent of the total amount expended for public education. The larger issue, however, is not how much the government is spending on education. It is, rather, how much influence over education its dollars are buying. Within the educational community, answers to this question range from "too much" to "no problem." Those who believe that the federal government is taking over education argue that federal regulation has increased in ways disproportionate to the amount of dollars expended. Citing the need for more federal monies, others contend that Washington is increasingly aware of the limits of federal intervention and, in fact, does not interfere with state and local control of education.

Blocking the way to a more objective examination of this question are the widespread confusion and contradictions regarding the appropriate responsibilities of the various levels of government in public education. Hence, it is important to develop a clearer understanding of the legitimate roles of the federal, state, and local governments in educational matters. While recognizing the difficulties of separating the responsibilities of each level of government under the new federalism, the Education Commission of the States concludes that certain "prime" responsibilities can be assigned to each level. Of immediate interest are those assigned to the federal government:

1. Identify national goals and areas of critical need in education;
2. Provide substantial educational funding to the states in the form of general aid so as to make educational services more nearly equal between and within states;
3. Consolidate the many federal categorical aids into a few "block grants" consistent with the areas of critical need;
4. Complete the annual appropriations process in time to permit effective planning by state and local education agencies;

5. Assume primary responsibility for financing and coordinating research and development; and

6. Develop and help finance, in cooperation with state and local education agencies, a system of educational data and information collection.[5]

With this as a starting point, one would hope for a continued discussion among educators and politicians as to what functions comprise an appropriate role for the federal government in public education. Such a discussion, it seems reasonable to assume, would ultimately contribute to a clearer delineation of the role of the federal government in education and provide a set of criteria against which to judge whether federal policymakers are operating within the limits of their legitimate sphere of influence.

WHAT KINDS OF ISSUES ARISE FROM FEDERAL INVOLVEMENT IN PUBLIC EDUCATION?

Federal involvement in education is, for the most part, a top-down phenomenon. This means that the rating of needs, the definition of problems, and the subsequent solutions emanate not from those who "own" the problem or have the need but from those who seek to solve the problem or satisfy the need. Since the federal government has justified this kind of involvement on the grounds that educators cannot or will not solve their own problems, it is not surprising that many issues and conflicts have arisen between the educational community and the national government.

A number of policymaking issues have also arisen within the federal government itself. According to Michael Timpane, most of the educational policy debate over the past decade has centered on five issues: "education's position in national social policy; priorities among federal education programs; recurring problems of race and religion; the division of intergovernmental responsibilities; and the implementation and management of federal education programs."[6]

WHAT ARE THE PROSPECTS FOR THE FUTURE FEDERAL ROLE IN EDUCATION?

Timpane sees in the future several broad implications for the federal government, as the perennial legislative and budgetary issues are reshaped but not replaced by a changing policy context. He states that:

—pressures for large-scale general aid will remain moderate; progress will depend greatly upon the political effectiveness of organized teachers;

—reliance on the federal government to insure equity for high cost target groups and to stimulate improved educational practice may increase, even if federal resources remain quite limited;

—state/local satisfaction of federal program priorities may become a more difficult problem, and will highlight the need for (a) intergovernmental clarification of educational roles and missions, and (b) improved design;

—urban school districts will continue to fight for special financial assistance from both state and federal sources; and

—organized teachers and other interest groups may press for national solutions to pervasive issues of indirect but substantial interest to education, like public employee bargaining rights and pension portability.[7]

Adding still another view, Kirst sees the future role of the federal government as expanding in three major areas: school finance reform, comprehensive child care, and educational television.[8]

While there are some differences of opinion on the federal government's future role in public education, nearly all writers agree that its emerging role will be an important one. What is needed from this point forward is an evolving body of theory and research to help policymakers understand how the federal government can best contribute to the improvement of the system of public education in our society.

NOTES

1. Stephen K. Bailey and Edith K. Mosher, *ESEA: The Office of Education Administers a Law* (Syracuse, N.Y.: Syracuse University Press, 1968), pp. viii-ix.

2. See Chapter 7 of this volume.

3. Samuel Halperin, "Block Grants or Categorical Aids? What Do We Really Want—Consolidation, Simplification, Decentralization?" in Institute for Educational Leadership, *Federalism at the Crossroads: Improving Educational Policymaking* (Washington, D.C.: George Washington University, 1976), pp. 67-71.

4. *Ibid.*, p. 70.

5. Education Commission of the States, "Sorting out the Roles: Federal, State, and Local Responsibilities in Education," *ibid.*, pp. 57-59.

6. Michael Timpane, *Federal Aid to Education: Prologue and Prospects* (Santa Monica, Calif.: RAND Corp., 1977).

7. *Ibid.*, p. 25.

8. Michael W. Kirst, "The Growth and Limits of Federal Influence in Education," Occasional Papers in the Economics and Politics of Education, School of Education, Stanford University, 1972, pp. 32-46.

SELECTED REFERENCES

Arons, Stephen. "The Separation of School and State: Pierce Reconsidered." *Harvard Educational Review* 46 (February 1976): 76-105.

Campbell, Roald F., and Bunnell, Robert A., eds. *Nationalizing Influences on Secondary Education.* Chicago: Midwest Administration Center, 1963.

Cronin, Joseph M. "The Federal Takeover: Should the Junior Partner Run the Firm?" *Phi Delta Kappan* 57 (April 1976): 499-502.

Merrow, John. "The Politics of Federal Educational Policy: The Case of Educational Renewal." *Teachers College Record* 76 (September 1974): 19-39.

Ornstein, Allan C., and Berlin, Barney. "Social Policy and Federal Funding." *Journal of Research and Development in Education* 8 (Spring 1975): 82-92.

Summerfield, Harry L. "The Limits of Federal Educational Policy." *Teachers College Record* 76 (September 1974): 7-19.

Some Political Aspects of Accountability Mandates

Michael Timpane

There has always been some form of accountability in education. Taxpayers have wanted assurance that their funds were honestly and well spent. The community has set forth standards, educational and often moral, that it expected teachers and students to meet. The teaching profession has complained, however, that most demands for accountability were dangerously reductionist intrusions upon their ineffable art, and social critics have worried that such accountability was a tool of the majoritarian establishment to enforce inequitable status quo norms of educational development. In recent decades, to be sure, the processes of accountability have become more sophisticated and pervasive, but the nature of the political imperatives has changed little. The question has not been and will not be "whether accountability" but, rather, "whither accountability?"

THE RECENT PAST

The experience of the last decade has brought a new order of accountability to the American educational system. Today, every state but two has a state-wide assessment system in operation or in the planning phase, and many other states and school systems have new comprehensive planning schemes designed in one way or another to assure that local educational programs measure up to some standard of performance.

These new accountability programs can be viewed, in one sense, as a logical extension of the principles of management control, which educators have been consistently importing from private enterprise for most of this century. There is no doubt, though, that new political factors have contributed to these developments.

First, the federal government has become an important participant in national educational activities. With its participation has come a greater emphasis on management controls, including the propagation of PPBS, the relentless evaluation of federal programs, the subsidization and encouragement of state and local planning and evaluation processes, and the promotion of citizens' participation in federal programs. The federal emphasis on equal opportunity has also focused attention on several specific performance characteristics of the schools (such as the performance of basic skills by disadvantaged and minority group students), which seem to lend themselves to measurement and accountability. And, what was least helpful of all, early federal forays into policy research and evaluation fueled a growing skepticism concerning the effectiveness of additional resources for education.

Second, partly with federal encouragement and partly for reasons of their own, the state legislatures throughout the nation have, in an astonishingly short period of time, enacted ambitious accountability systems. The immediate motive was often to justify additional state-level expenditures for education (usually under court mandate) to a dubious taxpaying public. In these legislators' view, they were acting nobly to improve the financing of education, but owed the citizenry an assurance that the new funds would be more wisely spent. The state laws usually took one or both of the following forms:

—State-wide testing programs, utilizing standardized achievement tests, often at several grade levels. (More recently mandated assessments have shifted to criterion measures.)

—Comprehensive planning processes designed to ensure that school districts develop specific plans and allocations of resources to meet basic objectives (for example, improved reading performance, lower dropout rates, expanded aesthetic sensibility) through stated program developments over a period of years. Some of the most ambitious states, such as Michigan, attempted to merge the processes of testing and planning and to use some results of assessment for the

purpose of allocating program resources. A number of accountability laws also called for at least modest participation by citizens
and the community in the development of objectives and improvements for the programs.

Third, many localities installed their own planning and testing
programs, as well as those of their state. They also promote citizens'
participation in local planning and yet another form of accountability: expanded parental choice in policies of school attendance (through
open enrollments, pairings, alternative schools, and so forth).

The most massive and explicit accountability programs have been
those devised by the states, and experience under these programs has
been disappointing to their advocates. It appears that state or local
policymakers do not use the state-wide assessments for any identifiable
decision-making purposes and that comprehensive planning has had a
largely mechanical character. The disuse and misuse can be attributed to several factors, discussed below.

Ambiguity of Purpose

Most accountability programs were rushed into practice without
a clear idea of how they were to be used over time. For example,
"accountable behavior" of teachers or school districts should logically
be a function of the contribution that the schools or teachers can make
to the educational performance of children. Such a definition was and
is beyond the state of the art in educational theory *or* measurement;
thus, "success" or "failure" could rarely be defined.

Significance of Variation

Differences in performance among similar school districts or
school sites on measured accountable characteristics are common, but
they are now largely ascribed to differences in the local implementation process (how the whole school community develops and manages
its program) rather than to the effectiveness of any given actor in the
process. The realities of implementation, therefore, cloud the issue of
who is accountable.

Political Resistance

Any form of intergovernmental regulation would be difficult in
our already stress-ridden federal structure. With state accountability
plans, the problems are compounded in that few persons at the local
level have found it in their interest to support vigorous accountability
programs. For the administrator, accountability is a source of conten-

tion within the community, angering some citizens and pleasing others. It also increases work load and specifies bureaucratic responsibilities in a system that has survived on bonhomie and warm rhetoric. For organized teachers, accountability is often seen as a threat to the professional autonomy of the teachers or to union influence. Comprehensive planning processes are greatly constrained by collective bargaining agreements that incorporate existing educational practice as "working conditions." Individual teachers performing in the classroom find the testing aspects of accountability programs totally inappropriate to their needs for diagnosis and prescription. Thus, the bywords of many localities have been: resist, ignore, complain. State officials, once they have exhausted themselves in the paroxysm of creation, have rarely stood behind their programs and have, when faced with strong political opposition, backed off from enforcement. When, in the recent recession, some states failed to meet the financial commitments, which were the original justification for the new accountability requirements, their credibility suffered more. All in all, one has the impression that many features of recently enacted accountability systems are rotting away and that the basements of many state departments of education have two large storage areas—one for statewide testing results and one for mandated local education plans.

THE IMMEDIATE FUTURE

All of these disappointments should not be interpreted as saying that the accountability movement is likely to disappear. Some foolish and grandiose schemes have been erected. Though many have been blown over or undermined, the original impetus for accountability remains relatively intact. There are, in the experiences of the past decade, glimmerings of a workable accountability system for American education. There is, moreover, in the emerging policy context for states and school districts, potential basis for an intelligent system of educational accountability.

The first element is the public. Parents and taxpayers are and will remain skeptical about the value of additional resources for education. Their doubts result only partly from the general disillusionment of the past decade, fed by the availability to the public of disturbing trends in achievement test scores. The doubts arise also (ironically) from the very success of our educational system in creating a questioning citizenry. Citizens themselves are increasingly forced to plan and account in their professional and occupational lives; they will insist that education do no less and often that they participate in the process.

The second element is teachers, who have to cope with accountability. They will not rush to embrace it. They will, in fact, rightly resist it when the measures of their performance are inappropriate or distort the educational process or when the standards of progress are impossible to achieve. But the burden of public disillusionment rests on them, and it has been reinforced, rightly or wrongly, by their organizing to bargain collectively. Teachers can especially not refuse to participate in the planning aspects of accountability programs. There they may achieve appropriate measures of performance, but, what is more important, a greater degree of influence in educational decisions. And they may retrieve some lost professional status from the community and acquire some new professional norms for themselves. Accountability may not be industrial democracy, but it need not be Taylorism-for-teachers, either.

The final element is the policymakers. Can those who raise taxes and allocate resources devise an accountability system that will satisfy the public and the profession? The answer is a ringing "maybe." There are developments in the design and utilization of state-level accountability programs that offer some hope, but these same developments also reveal the associated requirements for successful policy management.

— In most recent accountability systems, states are moving away from state-wide assessments of achievement toward criterion-referenced tests and toward a new connection with policy. A major example here is the push for tests of minimum competency for graduation from high school. The requirement revealed by this or any policy connection is for clarity in goals, objectives, and consequences. In the example, what is competency? What is a proper minimum? What are the equity ramifications? How shall the instances of incompetence be dealt with? Such questions demand answers in a successful accountability system.

— Some of the more sophisticated states use state-wide testing data, in their ongoing process of policy development, to spotlight for review and possible correction areas where performance is weak. Thus, they may ask if writing skills are up to par, if new math is an effective curriculum, and if new, more effective programs can be devised in these areas. The requirement revealed by this development is for analytical capacity. Assessment data will not speak for themselves on these questions. The answers will be found in careful analysis of the results, accompanied by extensive exploration of literature in associated fields.

— Finally, and what is most ambitious, a few states are moving toward site-oriented accountability systems. Here, a local educational plan and measures of performance are developed together, with the encouragement and reward of the state. The requirements revealed are the ability to monitor and assist local projects and the resources (above and beyond basic levels of support) to subsidize local educational improvements.

The requirements for extensive utilization of accountability systems are rather severe. Thus, the question remains: can the ingredients be assembled and mass-produced for accountability systems that will alleviate the anxiety of taxpayers and enhance the performance of schools?

SELECTED REFERENCES

Barro, Stephen M. *An Approach to Developing Accountability Measures for the Public Schools.* Santa Monica, Calif.: RAND Corp., 1970.

Clasby, Miriam, *et al. Laws, Tests, and Schooling.* Syracuse, N.Y.: Educational Policy Research Center, 1973.

Hall, Mary. "Statewide Assessment of Student Performance: A Comprehensive Survey." Paper presented at the American Educational Research Association meeting, April 1975.

Kirst, Michael, and Bass, Gail. *Accountability: What Is the Federal Role?* Santa Monica, Calif.: RAND Corp., 1976.

Legislation by the States: Accountability and Assessment in Education. Denver: Cooperative Accountability Project, 1974.

Levin, Henry. "A Conceptual Framework for Accountability." *School Review* 82 (May 1974): 363-393.

Martin, Don T., *et al. Accountability in American Education: A Critique.* Princeton, N.J.: Princeton Book Co., 1976.

The Politics of Performance-Based
Teacher Education and Certification

Carl R. Ashbaugh

The principle underlying a performance-based program or process is deceptively simple. In performance-based programs, goals are specified and agreed to in advance of the instruction-learning process. Thus the person who wants to receive a teaching certificate or to complete a teacher-training program must attain a predetermined level of competency in performing certain essential teaching tasks. The mere accumulation of credits, courses, and degrees would not serve as evidence of one's ability to assume professional roles. Instead, demonstrated competency determines professional readiness.

The principle of performance-based teacher education and certification (PBTE) may sound rather appealing and innocuous on its face, but it has been the source of much controversy and the arena in which several key groups have been vying for control. Because PBTE involves decisions concerning the allocation of resources for teacher education and certification, the movement has become highly political.

THE POLITICAL IMPORTANCE OF PBTE

In order to deal adequately with this subject, it is necessary to reconstruct some of the foundations of the movement. Writers who document the historical development of PBTE usually point out that no single event marks its genesis. Rather, it has evolved and developed over a number of years in concert with the concepts of accountability and cost-effectiveness. Observers of the evolution of PBTE also equate its growth with the increased federal role in education. Augmented federal funding for research and development in the 1960's brought about advances in educational technology that focused on the systematizing of classroom instruction.

Federal money was also used in the late 1960's for a variety of experimental programs, including investigations of performance-based certification by state departments of education. Other efforts backed by the federal government, such as the ten Elementary Teacher Education Models Program and the Teacher Corps, emphasized a more systematic and more field-based teacher-training process than was prevalent prior to that. These programs and the entire individualized instruction movement have increasingly stressed instructional modes tailored to specified outcomes and thus facilitated evaluation.

Finally, and perhaps most significant for this discussion, has been the development of the concept of shared decision making. For example, the USOE-sponsored Triple T (Trainers of Teacher Trainers) project focused attention on the possibility and desirability of undertaking educational programs that flowed from agreements made by a group of classroom teachers, school administrators, university educators, community representatives, and students. Shared decision making is a complex undertaking in a policy arena such as teacher education and certification, which involves many agencies: federal, state, and local governments; professional organizations; national accrediting associations (NCATE); foundations; and institutions of higher education, both academic and professional. Each of these agencies seeks to maintain a parity with all others.

The evolution of the influence system of shared powers has traditionally produced the following relationships among the agencies involved. The formal power to determine certification resides with state governments. States have also established certification standards and then designated individual universities to employ these standards in the preparation of teachers. Professional influence came about after this basic state legal structure was developed, but the profession, largely through the National Council for Accreditation of Teacher Education (NCATE), has been able, nevertheless, to set the fundamental criteria and general standards state governments use for teacher education and certification programs.

Currently, with the increased influence of the federal government and of organized teachers' groups in educational governance, the traditional balance of power among the aforementioned agencies threatens to be upset. Introducing a concept as controversial as PBTE further accelerates the unbalancing process. Though some have argued that the time is ripe for PBTE, most participants in the teacher education system have not wanted the concept applied directly to them. They recognize that widespread application of PBTE would threaten the traditional systems of teacher education and certification and of governance.

THE PRINCIPAL CONTENDERS

In the political realm, PBTE is a symbol around which desires and interests far removed from its ostensible purpose—rationalizing the preparatory and continuing education for professionals—tend to cluster. On the university campus, where no external compulsion is evident, the merits or demerits of PBTE are not intellectual concerns alone; they soon become rallying points for long-cherished defenses and eagerly sought acquisitions of power. Heavy reliance upon field experience to cultivate competencies, for example, threatens professors and departments whose livelihoods depend on classroom instruction. Some view the ever-present specter of being judged on the basis of what their students can do, rather than on what they are exposed to, as an incursion on academic freedom.

Attempts to activate PBTE on a college or university campus meet the same difficulties confronting any complex innovation, including the inevitable embroilment with the formal political system of the institution. Schools or departments of education seldom enjoy the autonomy typically bestowed upon professional schools such as those of law or engineering. Other schools and departments make policy decisions about the undergraduate curricula that comprise the pre-service preparation of professionals. Thus, the division of education controls only a small proportion of the content of teacher education programs. In short, proposals for PBTE must be processed through academic authorities representing constituencies whose basic loyalties are often contrary to the competency ethos of PBTE. Conflict results not only with respect to ideologies espoused by representatives of the humanities and the quantitative sciences but also with respect to such mundane matters as budgetary allocations, credit hours, and evaluation of teaching. Resolution of such conflicts is in large measure an exercise in the politics of bargaining, of building coalitions, and of lobbying within the confines of the institution.

When external compulsion is present, such as that emanating from a state education agency with sanctions such as disaccreditation, PBTE becomes a magnet for disputes about the exercise of power: Who should govern access to professional positions in a school system? Who should judge the achievements of individuals holding such positions? Hence, as a symbol, PBTE is not only a point of contention but stimulates a host of contenders to use political as well as other means to resolve jurisdictional problems. At state and national levels politics enters most strongly into consideration of PBTE, which is manifest in debates about its validity, practicability, and efficacy in the professional education of educators.

Governmental licensing of educators has become slowly, but not quietly, a potent control upon public education in the United States. At every step of policy determination concerning who is fit to be employed, who can hold hundreds of specialized positions, who can design and execute training, and what that training shall be like, vigorous contenders, both pro and con, have appeared. State legislatures and, more recently, state education agencies have been the chief governmental processors of competing contenders, but federal government agencies have been involved also. Increment after increment has been added to the professional equipment obligatory for educators. Since about 1960, however, this has occurred with increasing difficulty because contenders have become so numerous, well organized, and diverse in their advocacies and defenses. New concerns have surfaced and intensified. The educational establishment, which is sanctioned in existing law, is under attack for alleged poor performances by educators in its employment. Militant and organized educators assert that licensure and its accompaniments are too vital to be controlled by those outside the organized profession. Such concerns tend to override the merits and demerits of PBTE as a reform technology. Efforts to consider PBTE are often deflected because they reactivate broader controversies that resist any final resolution.

As indicated, the organized profession, notably the National Education Association and corresponding state associations, is a principal party at interest. It wants a strong voice in determining what it takes to be and remain a certified educator. It took a leading role in establishing, promoting, and operating the NCATE, but encountered some disillusionment with that approach, especially after the more broadly based National Commission on Accrediting forced a reconstitution of membership in the NCATE. It later used its lobby in Washington to influence USOE's TTT project to bring about mandatory professional participation in teacher training. It seems to have abandoned hope recently for access through teacher training and is concentrating on obtaining a statutory role in determining the requisites for certification and in having a potent voice in passing judgment on the fitness of candidates for certification. NEA has resisted any policy that is couched in terms denoting accountability, a concept usually interpreted as embracing PBTE.

Other primary contenders are the central city school districts. Having been made aware of shortcomings in teachers' performance, urban districts are increasingly forming alliances to do their own training and their own certification. Many aspects of PBTE would apparently appeal to them, but they would be highly critical of its administration by the "university cartel" and those they perceive to be rigid and obstinate in applying regulations concerning training and certification.

Institutions of higher learning accredited to teach educators in a state occasionally speak with a single voice, but only rarely. Instead, they embrace several disparate and divergent contenders, the most potent of which are the associated spokesmen for colleges and departments of education. During the last fifty years, they have successfully influenced governmental actions toward licensure and accreditation of programs. Predominantly members of the American Association of Colleges for Teacher Education, these groups have advocated high quality in the training of teachers, and they have built strong coalitions with state education agencies. It was they, for example, who shifted certification from a course-by-course evaluation of transcripts to the "approved program" basis. PBTE originated from within those ranks, as did advocacy for it to be made compulsory. It must be noted, however, that this contender, which represents the establishment, is suspect in many circles and that its potency within the political system had decreased. Also, in few, if any, states can it speak with one voice on behalf of PBTE; dissenters are quite numerous.

A relative newcomer among contenders in higher education is the state agency for higher education (or, in some states, those governing bodies for multiunit university systems). These agencies are looking askance at the dual governance of education for educators: governance by certification and accreditation of programs emanating from state departments of education, and governance by authorities for all higher education. This skepticism has recently been directed toward the role of the collegiate institution in the licensing of professional educators. The approved program approach is being challenged, and the examples of the licensing procedures for the professions of law, engineering, and medicine are seen as a more proper approach. Governing boards for higher education argue that the state department of education should examine the fitness of candidates, not shift the responsibility back to them. It is likely that this contender, a powerful one in most states, will be adamantly opposed to many features of PBTE.

Only lack of organization prevents the spokesmen for academic disciplines from being a weighty contender. Their power over professional educators has been demonstrated in several instances, such as in California and Texas when so-called reforms in standards for education of educators were in governmental debate. PBTE does not appeal to those in the academic disciplines for a wide variety of reasons, most of which revolve around perceived invasion of established domains or financial threats.

Another veteran contender in higher education is the small institution, typically in the nonpublic sector. These institutions have limited fiscal resources, must attract students in order to survive, and have a high stake in being able to offer certification to their graduates. The history of governmental constraints upon programs to prepare educators demonstrates the ability of the small institution to modify significantly the compulsory reforms adopted. PBTE is a reform that calls for high expenditures of resources, that impressed many as a betrayal of the ideal of a liberal education, and that subjects an institution to complex regulation by external forces. It would be a decided break with tradition if small institutions, who in the past have had remarkably successful communication with persons in government, rally to the support of compulsory PBTE.

The USOE, a government agency itself, is frequently listed as a contender on behalf of PBTE. In the past, however, the USOE has acted essentially as a processor of input pressures. The demise of the Education Professions Development Act demonstrates the directionality of pressures in Washington and indicates that the USOE will hardly be a strong ally of the PBTE movement in the immediate future. This is especially true since its chief weapon—dollars for grants—is largely a memory from earlier years.

THE ANTICIPATED EFFECTS ON EDUCATIONAL SERVICE AND PROGRAMMING

Effects of PBTE are difficult to assess at this time because the concept appears to have peaked in terms of a national movement. Certain of the common characteristics of PBTE, however, have become evident in many teacher-training programs, although they have avoided the PBTE label. Among these characteristics are the following: that program content and the development of learners' objectives show more specificity; that an increasing number of courses for intending teachers are field based; that more feedback from professionals in the field is encouraged; and that broader participation in program planning for teacher education is provided.

If PBTE receives widespread acceptance, the governance structure for teacher training will be markedly affected. On the other hand, current activities and actions of the organized profession are already upsetting the balance of power in educational governance. The result will be less dominance by universities and state education agencies in determining the character of teacher preparation programs. The type of governance mechanism that eventuates may differ from state to state. Because of the many conflicting professional interests, it may be impossible to construct a nation-wide body that will exercise overall professional control with respect to accreditation standards for teacher-training institutions.

PBTE may become an issue for bargaining or negotiating between the organized teaching profession and local school districts and state departments of education. At present the PBTE reform movement is highly criticized for proceeding on a research base that does not yet demonstrate that PBTE is more effective than the traditional preparation process. This fact provides ammunition at the bargaining table.

Finally, this is an expensive reform. Expense is, as a matter of fact, one of the major considerations arising from proposals to install by government decree a system of PBTE. No one yet knows how expensive it would be to implement fully a PBTE scheme. Only modest steps toward PBTE have been reported thus far, and most of these place a heavy burden upon existing resources by diverting personnel. Procurement of requisite resources, whether at institutional or state levels, is essentially a political exercise. In this exercise, as is well known, the merits of a proposed reform may have relatively little weight in allocative decisions. Acquiring the funds may well be the greatest political challenge to the advocates of PBTE.

SELECTED REFERENCES

American Association of Colleges for Teacher Education. *Implementing Performance-Based Teacher Education at the State Level.* Washington, D.C.: American Association of Colleges for Teacher Education, 1973.

Elam, Stanley. *Performance-Based Teacher Education: What Is the State of the Art?*
    Washington, D.C.: American Association of Colleges for Teacher Education,
    1971.
Howsam, R.B. *The Governance of Teacher Education.* Washington, D.C.: ERIC
    Clearinghouse on Teacher Education, 1972. ERIC: ED 062 270.
Kirst, Michael W. *Issues in Governance for Performance-Based Teacher Education.*
    Washington, D.C.: American Association of Colleges for Teacher Education,
    1973.
Larson, Rolf W. *Accreditation Problems and the Promise of PBTE.* Washington,
    D.C.: American Association of Colleges for Teacher Education, 1974.
Rosner, Benjamin, and Kay, Patricia M. "Will the Promise of C/PBTE Be Fulfilled?"
    Phi Delta Kappan 55 (January 1974): 290-295.
Scribner, Harvey B., and Stevens, Leonard B. "The Politics of Teacher Competency."
    Competency Assessment, Research, and Evaluation. Ed. W. Robert Houston.
    Albany, N.Y.: Multi-State Consortium on Performance Based Teacher Educa-
    tion, 1974.

Public Participation in Educational Policy Making:

Trends and Portents

Richard W. Saxe
Elmer H. Gish

Few would disagree that public schools belong to the public and
were established to serve a unique function in society. The rhetoric has
clearly supported this concept as well as the principle that active and
sustained participation of citizens in determining policy for the public
schools is essential to the maintenance and growth of our democratic
society. It is unfortunate that practice has not followed this principle
in public education. There is a serious gap between those who control
educational policy making and the general public.

The pattern of control for public education was set by the early
settlers of America. Lay citizens formulated policy, administered the
schools, and planned the curriculum. Later, as the nation grew,
representatives from the community were appointed to serve on school
boards and were given primary responsibility for formulating policy
and for securing teachers to run the schools. Citizens were still expected to share in the policy-making process for educating the young.
As society became increasingly complex, control of the schools shifted

first to the community representatives and then to the professional educators.

For our purposes here, the participants in educational policy making will be considered as three components: public representatives, professional educators, and the general public.

PUBLIC REPRESENTATIVES

Duly elected or appointed representatives have a responsibility in setting policy to guide and support education as a function of democratic government. Major decisions affecting education are made at the local level by the school board (and governing body); at the state level by the state board of education (and legislature); and, at the federal level by Congress (and the executive branch).

However these decisionmakers may be judged, they are, or at least are intended to be, the representatives or delegates of the public. They are usually lay persons who are called upon to make educational policy decisions as well as to cope with financial crises, militant unions, militant community groups, and other conflict-producing pressures. At the local and state levels, particularly, the policymakers are generally unpaid, they work only part time, and they are untrained for their positions of responsibility. And yet they must provide answers to questions concerning educational policy.

Two major criticisms are leveled at boards of education and legislative bodies. First, they are ineffective because they are not responsive to public opinion. Second, owing to the complexity of world affairs, technology, and so forth, boards delegate more and more power to superintendents, and it is axiomatic in public affairs that responsibility tends to flow to the nearest available *paid* authority.

PROFESSIONAL EDUCATORS

Much has been written about the domination of public education by professional educators and administrators. They have been blamed for the lack of citizens' participation and involvement in the schools because, as professionals, they are responsible for providing the necessary climate and leadership for participation by the community. Because of the closed patterns of their administrations, they are also blamed by some for their rubber stamp school boards.

If the processes of policy formation and decision making in public education are to be open and responsive to the wishes of the public, professional educators and administrators must provide mechanisms for hearing the debates, arguments, persuasions, demands, support, and opposition of individuals and groups as they contemplate the issues. It should be recognized that as public education has grown and become more complex, professional educators and administrators have found it less and less convenient and more and more time consuming to provide for broad participation in school affairs by the public, or even by the public's representatives. At the same time, it appears that the public has become increasingly apathetic about schools.

THE PUBLIC

The ordinary citizen is, at the present time, relatively inactive in the educational policy-making process beyond voting for elected officials, school budgets, and bond referendums. The principal form of public participation is through special interest groups that serve, generally, in advocacy roles. These groups are active participants. It is through them that the most pressure is exerted upon those in power. Also, because special interest groups are heavily dependent on persuasion to exert influence, they serve as major sources of information and analysis for policymakers. Such groups are important to effective decision making. The education profession itself, through its own organizations, has become a strong force in educational policy making. These organizations exert pressures in various ways at the national, state, and local levels.

Throughout the history of American education, the balance of control has shifted among the various participants in the policy-making process. Contemporary problems being faced in the public schools have stimulated the public to participate in solving these problems. Don Davies of the Institute for Responsive Education stated: "Yes, there lies the main hope for educational change—in the citizens, parents, students, and employers emerging as a 'third force' to overcome the inertia of school bureaucracies and teacher organizations, much in the same way [that] they occasionally have overcome other problems by becoming more active, more vocal, more informed, and more demonstrative on community and national issues."[1]

TRENDS AND PORTENTS

The dynamic growth of schools in the late 1950's and early 1960's led to high expectations for education. Unprecedented resources were made available to public schools, and the professional educators were in control. By the late 1960's, however, court-ordered desegration of schools, campus riots, rebellions by youths against authority and the establishment, and other controversies brought the future of public schools into question. Although legislation was enacted at each level of government in an attempt to cope with the basic problems of the public schools, citizens were generally apathetic and disillusioned. Public schools came under attack from all sectors—students, teachers, parents, public, news media, and minorities. Some questioned whether the public schools would survive, and others advocated the dismantling of the public systems in response to suggestions that society be "deschooled." Many called for massive changes in the system.

There are currently forces at work that seem to have the potential for revitalizing the nation's educational system. Among these forces is the tendency toward a larger role for broad public participation in educational policy making. Citizens, as individuals and as groups, are beginning to demand a part in rebuilding the public schools. Present conditions indicate, however, that there is a difficult time ahead.

Inflation, recession, high prices, and unemployment, especially in the big cities, have lessened the desire and the ability of citizens to increase funding for schools. As a matter of fact, in many cases where citizens have the opportunity to vote on regular operating levies, they have demonstrated their unwillingness to support schools at the old rates, much less to approve an increase. This trend seems likely to endure at least as long as the unfavorable economic situation persists.

Teachers, collectively, are coming under attack at a time when the concept of teachers' power is not yet clearly understood or when those who are able to mobilize this power are not yet confident of appropriate strategies and tactics. Although teachers have become more powerful in their bargaining-adversary role, changing conditions are making them more vulnerable to criticism and to counterpressures from parents, taxpayers, and other members of the community.

Teachers and school administrators are accused of cheating all children, but especially poor children, of their right to an adequate education. The concept of professional control of the procedures and substance of public education is being questioned with increasing vigor. Educators are perceived as demanding higher salaries than most of the parents make in many communities to do an easy job that negotiated contracts are making easier every year. Though about 70 percent of school budgets goes into salaries, taxpayers do not see increased services, improved programs, or even more effort exerted by the professionals. They are even told that the relationship between their taxes and the achievement of students is too mysterious and complex for them to understand.

The hallowed concept of local public participation in educational policy making has been frequently forced into opposition to the collective power of teachers. When, in some cities, local community groups, buttressed by court orders and facilitated by support from foundations, sought a measure of control over the resources—personnel and money—going into schools, they met this power head-on. There are few acknowledged heroes among the veterans of those early encounters and a surfeit of inept "leaders" on both sides.

Local citizens, even with outside support, often seemed inadequate to contend with the political acumen and considerable resources of organized teachers. And, from time to time, all participants were forced to regroup and change their strategy when the courts responded to petitions or intervened by issuing guidelines and plans.

Time after time decisions were made away from the local scenes of conflict. Some beleaguered school board members have even come to favor transferring the difficult bargaining and negotiating functions to some more distant agency at the state level. Most board members, however, seek better ways of "fighting it out" with teachers' organizations at the district level.

At least two national organizations with the usual support from foundations have sought to aid the public in making the professionals accountable for more effective education and fair and humane treatment of students. These are the Institute for Responsive Education (IRE) and the National Committee for Citizens in Education (NCCE).

The IRE is attempting to discover alternative forms of participation by citizens and is working with agencies and individuals in an effort to improve tactics. It is the IRE's position that increased power for citizens in educational governance (localism) will help create more effective, responsive schools. The IRE seemingly wishes to serve as a key source of technical assistance, information, and even influence for parents and others seeking to affect the substance and the process of education.[2]

The NCCE is an action-oriented public interest organization seeking to create a broad-based constituency to demand educational reforms and to help citizens act on alternative educational choices. The NCCE seems more likely to press issues and to act as a citizens' lobby at the national level than the IRE, which attempts to offer technical assistance to local units.

The NCCE lobbies for individual rights and has met with some success in the campaign to secure the privacy of school records (the Buckley Amendment). As of September 1976 the NCCE membership included 140 organizations. Louisiana has the most NCCE member organizations with nineteen, all in New Orleans; Illinois is next with fourteen, all in Chicago.

The effectiveness and the role of these organizations, and of other less prominent ones, are not yet clear. They are in the awkward position of seeking to enhance public education at the same time as they attack it. This ambiguity is apparent in the style of their materials and in their tactics. They have denied themselves the luxury of the "deschooling" approach that condemns and attacks the educational establishment without restraint. Their constituency is diverse and transitory. It seems unlikely that they will wield great influence so long as they maintain their present umbrella-type structures and focus their efforts almost exclusively on the schools.

With the establishment of federal requirements for citizens' participation and the rise of citizens' groups and networks, educators themselves have concurrently acknowledged and (at least rhetorically) embraced the notion of increased and improved public participation in educational policy making. This participation has typically begun at a level of public "involvement," which is limited to understanding and supporting schools. Citizens' "participation," implying the active collection and consideration of the people's wishes, is the level of participation prescribed by most federal programs. The main source of influence here is the power of the Parent Advisory Committee to deny support or to block the influx of governmental resources for their children. Citizen "control" or community control is the direct participation of citizens (not the members of the regular board of education) in the formation of educational policy. Control, especially of personnel and budget, is the usual parting of the ways for educators and citizens.

Another force can be seen in political campaigns. Competition for office leads political parties and their candidates to study the concerns of citizens, thereby possibly making elected officials more responsive to the demands and desires of the citizenry.

The community education concept that has developed over the past decade holds great potential for increasing citizens' participation in education for all ages, as well as in civic, cultural, health, and social service activities. It calls for sharing resources in order to maintain a total community program through the use of facilities all day, every day, and throughout the year.

SUMMARY

The pattern suggested by this brief analysis is that educational policy is established through the interaction of various influential forces with the duly constituted decisionmakers, generally without the active participation of the ordinary citizen. Lay participation in educational planning and policy making is growing at the present time, and the need for such public attention to education is increasingly apparent. The problems of our youth, as manifested in deviant behavior patterns, demand solutions. Low academic achievement, violent and rebellious behavior, and general lack of purpose in youngsters are symptomatic of the inadequacy of the schools' solutions. Active collaboration among parents, students, teachers, administrators, and citizens appears to provide the greatest potential for improving the educational opportunities of youth.

NOTES

1. Don Davies, "Notes," *Citizen Action in Education* 1 (Fall 1974): 1.

2. For those who wish to increase their understanding of the processes of public participation, the IRE is a source for some practical ideas. They have recently produced a series of five books called, collectively, *Factual Politics*. The separate titles are: *Facts for a Change: Citizen Action Research for Better Schools; Words, Pictures, Media: Communication in Educational Politics; Facts and Figures: A Layman's Guide; You Can Look It up: Finding Educational Documents; Collecting Evidence: A Layman's Guide to Participatory Observation*. The IRE journal, *Citizen Action in Education*, is an informative publication. Inquiries may be sent to Institute for Responsive Education, 704 Commonwealth Avenue, Boston, Massachusetts 02215.

SELECTED REFERENCES

Center for Law and Education. "Citizen Voice in the Public Schools." *Inequality in Education* 15 (November 1973).

Davies, Don, ed. *Schools Where Parents Make a Difference.* Boston: Institute for Responsive Education, 1977.

Institute for Responsive Education. *Citizen Action in Education, 1974-1977.*

Jackson, Kathleen O'Brien. *The Politics of School-Community Relations.* Eugene, Ore.: ERIC, 1971.

Lindbloom, Charles E. *The Policy-Making Process.* Englewood Cliffs, N.J.: Prentice-Hall, 1968.

Mann, Dale. *The Politics of Administrative Representation.* Lexington, Mass.: Lexington Books, 1976.

National Committee for Citizens in Education. *Public Testimony on Public Schools.* Berkeley, Calif.: McCutchan Publishing Corp., 1975.

Saxe, Richard W. *School-Community Interaction.* Berkeley, Calif.: McCutchan Publishing Corp., 1975.

The Changing Politics of Changing Communities:
The Impact of Evolutionary Factors on
Educational Policy Making

William L. Boyd

It is—or should be—a platitude that politics (educational or otherwise) are heavily influenced by social change. Yet, strangely enough, despite the early and seminal efforts of Laurence Iannaccone to establish a dynamic theoretical approach to educational politics,[1] most attempts to understand school politics have shown little recognition of the significance of change or even of the somewhat predictable impact of evolutionary, developmental factors. Sadly, this shortsightedness seems to have afflicted scholars and practicing administrators alike.

Among scholars, there has been a decided tendency for research to have a static perspective, to be time and place bound, and to be inclined to become fixated on oversimplified themes—such as the overwhelming dominance of school administrators in the policy-making process—which a dynamic, longitudinal approach would call into question.[2] On the other hand, while one might suppose that practitioners would be more sensitive than scholars to the consequences of change because they have to live with its consequences, there is a good deal of disconcerting evidence that administrators often have been remarkably slow to grasp the significance of changes occurring in their communities.[3] Now, however, the dramatic and far-reaching changes which have been occurring recently have forced our attention to the dynamic aspects of educational politics and have raised the general question: how can we better understand and anticipate the changing politics of our communities and their implications for educational administration?

To begin with, there are two distinct types of change that impinge upon local educational policy making and substantially shape its agenda. First, and perhaps most striking, there are the increasingly important developments and forces *external* to the local district (state and federal mandates, court decisions, and so forth) that create demands and constraints to which the local district must attend. Second, there are the often slower and less obvious *internal* developments within the school district that are related to the life cycle and aging process of the community. As Iannaccone and others have shown, these developments also create unavoidable demands and constraints.[4] Usually, the two types of change, internal and external, are dealt with separately in analyses of school politics; however, one of our goals should be to try to relate them, for there is ample reason to think that external developments complicate and exacerbate the problems posed by internal developments.

It would be ideal, then, to overlay or to combine models of externally stimulated developments affecting local educational politics, such as Frederick Wirt's paradigm of turbulent school politics,[5] with models of internal developmental patterns. But the external developments are so complex, and our space here so limited, that we must confine our discussion to a consideration of an overarching developmental pattern that highlights the tensions between internal and external trends. That pattern involves the shifting emphasis over time among three values in government: representativeness; technical, nonpartisan competence; and leadership.[6] The first value refers to the public's demand for "voice" through popularly elected officials; the second to the virtues of professionally trained officials who base their decisions on technical and substantive, rather than partisan, considerations; and the third to "the demand that the actions and decisions of officials be coordinated at some central point so that government programs are reasonably consistent and efficient."[7] As Herbert Kaufman observes, the creation of special districts, such as school districts, mainly reflects a concern for *nonpartisan competence*. But, in the consideration of internal developmental patterns, to which we now turn, we need to note the tensions created by the simultaneous, but *divergent,* trends toward more emphasis in educational governance on *representativeness* (such as in parent advisory councils and school site management schemes) and external *leadership* (through increasing assumption of authority over educational policy by all three branches of state and federal government).

The internal evolutionary or developmental patterns that have been most systematically studied in educational politics are those which have been observed in suburban school districts.[8] Because of the current difficulties with declining enrollments and aging suburbs that are beginning to experience "urban problems," a significant limitation of most of this research is that it has dealt with school districts that were young, expanding in population, and rising in socioeconomic status. In their pioneering work, Iannaccone and his associates found that communities undergoing substantial social and economic change ultimately tend to experience a significant shift in the balance of community power that decisively affects educational policy making. While they found that school officials typically tend to become autonomous and isolated from the community, they discovered that a significant socioeconomic change in the community usually will lead in a few years to electoral conflict, then to the defeat of an incumbent school board member, and finally to a change in the control of the board followed by the involuntary separation of the superintendent and his replacement by an outsider in accord with the values of the new school board. By this series of developments, communities reassert their control over school policy-making structures that have failed to respond adequately to the desires of a changed constituency.

There have been a number of replication studies based upon the Iannaccone and Lutz model as well as attempts to refine and improve the model.[9] Although the findings have been mixed, and raise some serious questions about the model that demand further research, the general notion of a developmental pattern based upon qualitative changes in the social or economic character of a community is supported by research on suburban politics generally.[10] In an insightful recent synthesis of this research, Joseph Zikmund has shown how the origin of the suburban community and the subsequent phases in its aging process influence both the form and style of community politics and the dominant issues receiving attention.[11] Figure 8-1 summarizes the aging process delineated by Zikmund.

Space limitations prohibit a complete explanation of Zikmund's analysis, but the flavor of it can be conveyed. Thus, the suburbaniza- tion of small towns tends to make issues related to the future character of the community dominant—especially zoning and schools—and usually ends with new residents dominating old ones. By contrast, the

Figure 8-1. Successive steps in the aging of suburban communities

1	2	3	4
A	B	C	D

Steps in aging process
1. Beginning of suburbanization
2. Saturation of the land
3. Beginning of invasion-succession
4. Dominance by new residents

Transition periods
A. Massive suburbanization
B. Community stability
C. Conversion and change
D. New community stability

Source: Joseph Zikmund II, "A Theoretical Structure for the Study of Suburban Politics," *The Annals of the American Academy of Political and Social Science* 422 (November 1975): 51.

suburbanization of larger existing satellite cities tends to produce more emphasis on issues related to the impact of the new suburbanites on community service levels and taxation and usually ends with the newcomers being assimilated into the existing power structure. In terms of our concern with aging and declining communities, one of Zikmund's insights is that the social class composition of a community affects the speed at which it passes through the phases of the aging process. For example, when the middle class is threatened by in- migration of groups with incompatible life-styles, they are more likely than members of the working class to be both inclined and financially able to leave the community quickly.

Having briefly outlined two notions of the developmental pattern in the life cycle or aging process of suburban communities, we can now consider some of the important questions that come to mind in the "retrenchment" mood of today. In the first place, as suggested earlier, we know less about the later stages in the community aging process than about the earlier stages. But, because growth and decline are dis- tributed unevenly within metropolitan areas and about the country, we need to know more about the community dynamics of both. We need to ask in what ways school districts are changing (for example, in total population, school-age population, assessed valuation per pupil, socioeconomic status, and ethnocultural composition) and pay close attention to the implications and possible interrelations of these changes. And, of course, we need research on change and the developmental process in urban and rural, as well as suburban, communities.[12]

It is also necessary to explore the changes in educational services that are likely to be required by certain kinds of transformations in the community. For instance, do newcomers to communities that are undergoing socioeconomic change invariably demand changes in educational services, as the Iannaccone and Lutz model suggests? Or is it the case, as David Eblen found, that new residents in communities declining (as opposed to rising) in status often prefer a continuation of the services the schools are already providing? Indeed, may they have moved to the community in order to obtain those services?[13] And, if Eblen's findings are representative, how willing and able are these newcomers to pay the existing level of taxes to maintain these services?

In terms of the public interest, there is a particularly pressing need for research on the differential impact of the community's growth or decline upon the responsiveness of school systems to the desires of their clients. While in some circles it has been fashionable for some time to argue that the schools have been "unresponsive," the new view of public education as a declining industry, analogous to such "classic" declining industries as the railroads, has produced an even grimmer outlook concerning the responsiveness of the schools. In other words, to what extent in the past has the responsiveness of the public schools to public desires been *contingent* upon the opportunities for innovation created by growth conditions (for example, by the opportunity to develop new educational programs in new schools with new teachers)?[14]

If, as seems logical, the opportunities for responsiveness to the public are fewer in declining than in growing school districts, are there ways to channel the scarcity that accompanies declining resources to create competition among school districts (or school buildings or teachers and administrators) that would benefit consumers of educational services? In other words, could adversity beget competition that would beget responsiveness? One line of research here might probe the consequences of competition for students already occurring beween public and nonpublic schools that are facing declining enrollments.[15] The expense of abandoning the public school system may make most parents reluctant to exercise their "exit" option, thereby muting the effects of competition for the public school. On the other hand, the inclination of parents to remain loyal to the public schools could promote their use of political action ("voice") to gain more responsiveness from these schools.[16]

It is interesting to note, however, that Eblen found some evidence that the political action and conflict, which the Iannaccone and Lutz model suggests are necessary to produce responsiveness, in fact may not be so frequently required. Eblen discovered, specifically, that the selection of an outsider as the new superintendent was more strongly associated with the fact that a district's social status was changing than it was with the involuntary nature of the separation of the previous superintendent. As he notes, this finding suggests "a less conflictual and more adaptive response by schools to social change in the community."[17]

However the problems of change are managed in local school districts, external forces, along with declining resources and opportunities for growth, are narrowing the latitude available for responsiveness to clients' desires. With the increasing centralization of authority over educational policy (for example, state accountability schemes, competency tests, and other external forces increasingly shaping the curriculum), and with the national teachers' union movement becoming more successful in imposing contractual constraints, what ultimately will be left to be managed at the school board and school site levels?[18] One thing, at least, that will be left to manage is conflict. The struggles to define or redefine the character of a community's schools during the conversion and change phase of the community aging process are being complicated, and sometimes exacerbated, by the cosmopolitan curriculum reforms (sex education, bilingual-bicultural education, the "new" biology and "new" social studies) encouraged, and sometimes imposed, by professional reformers and their state and national level organizations and agencies.[19] Similarly, conflicts over community service levels and taxation—which are influenced by developments in the community aging process—are being complicated and exacerbated by the imposition from outside the community of expensive mandated educational reforms (such as new special education and bilingual education requirements), and by the strain placed upon local fiscal resources by the demands of nationally coordinated public employee unions.

Taken separately, these developments certainly are not all bad, and the rather grim trends they produce in combination perhaps need not reach their fruition. If they are to be deflected, from such ends, however, it appears that we shall have to act on the future more effectively than we have on the past.

NOTES

1. Laurence Iannaccone, *Politics in Education* (New York: Center for Applied Research in Education, 1967); *id.* and Frank Lutz, *Politics, Power, and Policy* (Columbus, Ohio: Charles E. Merrill, 1970).

2. See, for example, L. Harmon Zeigler and M. Kent Jennings, *Governing American Schools* (North Scituate, Mass.: Duxbury Press, 1974); and the critique of that study in William L. Boyd, "The Public, the Professionals, and Educational Policy-Making: Who Governs?" *Teachers College Record* 77 (May 1976): 539-577.

3. See, for example, John C. Walden, "School Board Changes and Superintendent Turnover," *Administrator's Notebook* 15 (January 1967); Philip Meranto, *School Politics in the Metropolis* (Columbus, Ohio: Charles E. Merrill, 1970), p. 57; Kenneth E. Boulding, "The Management of Decline," *Change* 7 (June 1975): 9.

4. Iannaccone and Lutz, *Politics, Power, and Policy;* Frederick M. Wirt *et al.*, *On the City's Rim: Politics and Policy in Suburbia* (Lexington, Mass.: D. C. Heath, 1972), pp. 161-174.

5. Frederick M. Wirt, "Contemporary School Turbulence and Administrative Authority," in *Toward a New Urban Theory*, ed. Robert Lineberry and Louis Masotti (Boston: Ballinger Press, forthcoming).

6. Herbert Kaufman, *Politics and Policies in State and Local Governments* (Englewood Cliffs, N.J.: Prentice-Hall, 1963).

7. *Ibid.,* p. 34.

8. The evolution of urban districts, while also receiving much attention, usually has not been systematically researched in a comparative framework. Knowledge about suburban school politics, however, is valuable in itself because over one-third (37 percent) of the total U.S. population now lives in suburban communities.

9. These studies include Eugene P. LeDoux and Martin Burlingame, "The Iannaccone and Lutz Model of School Board Change: A Replication in New Mexico," *Educational Administration Quarterly* 9 (Autumn 1973): 48-65; Richard R. Thorsted, "Predicting School Board Member Defeat: Demographic and Political Variables That Influence School Board Elections, doctoral diss., University of California, Riverside, 1974; Douglas E. Mitchell and Richard R. Thorsted, "Incumbent School Board Member Defeat Reconsidered: New Evidence for Its Political Meaning," *Educational Administration Quarterly* 12 (Fall 1976): 31-48; and David R. Eblen, "Local School District Politics: A Reassessment of the Iannaccone and Lutz Model," *Administrator's Notebook* 24 (No. 9, 1976). Iannaccone and Lutz soon will be publishing a new book that will present additional research utilizing the model.

10. The findings by Eblen, Thorsted, and Mitchell and Thorsted are especially challenging to the Iannaccone and Lutz model. Neither Thorsted nor Eblen was able to substantiate the linkage between demographic changes in the community and subsequent defeat of incumbent board members. Mitchell and Thorsted propose (p. 45) that "the defeat of incumbent school board members may have roots in [changes in] political ideology rather than in demographic or sociological variables." What seems more probable, in light of theory and research on community conflict, is that defeat of incumbents may stem from *either* source. (See, for example, James S. Coleman, *Community Conflict* [Glencoe, Ill.: Free Press, 1957].) Because of various sampling and methodological limitations of the various replication studies, it cannot be said that the Iannaccone and Lutz model has been completely and definitively tested. But, at the least, it seems clear that the model needs to be modified and qualified.

11. Joseph Zikmund II, "A Theoretical Structure for the Study of Suburban Politics," *Annals* 422 (November 1975): 45-60.

12. On the need for research on change in rural communities, see Frederick M. Wirt, "Reassessment Needs in the Study of the Politics of Education," paper presented at the meeting of the American Educational Research Association, San Francisco, April 1976.

13. See Eblen, "Local School District Politics."

14. See Robert F. Lyke, "Suburban School Politics," doctoral diss., Yale University, 1968, pp. 225-231.

15. It is regrettable that in many communities the parochial school systems seem to have been so weakened by financial pressures that they may not be able to provide much competition for the public school systems. The situation is complicated, of course, in those communities where whites are abandoning public schools to avoid racial desegregation and its accompanying effects.

16. See Albert O. Hirschman, *Exit, Voice, and Loyalty* (Cambridge, Mass.: Harvard University Press, 1970).

17. Eblen, "Local School District Politics," p. 3.

18. Concerning these centralizing trends, see Tyll van Geel, *Authority to Control the School Program* (Lexington, Mass.: D.C. Heath, 1976).

19. See William L. Boyd, "The Changing Politics of Curriculum Policy-Making for American Schools," paper prepared for the National Institute of Education, U.S. Department of Health, Education, and Welfare, October 1976.

The Public School and the Politics of Coordinating Human Service Delivery Systems

Michael H. Kaplan
John W. Warden

The issue of the school's role in coordinating human service delivery systems is becoming an increasingly timely subject for discussion. The "economics of scarcity" and the competition for financial resources among all human service organizations suggest that an exploration of the policy questions and political issues regarding the school's relationship to other human service organizations is both appropriate and vital. Jesse Burkhead, for example, has pointed out in Chapter 5 that the state of the economy and relationships among agencies are closely interrelated. In Chapter 7 Michael Kirst has outlined a strong case for building alliances at both the federal and local levels with other fields, services, and agencies. From Kirst's perspective, the changing political context of education will increase the external pressures on school decisionmakers. While public schools are not alone with regard to these pressures, educators often view themselves and the world from a narrow perspective. If they continue to do so, they are more likely to face organizational and programmatic retrenchments than to undertake creative political action. The growing concern of communities regarding the use of tax dollars and the recent rejections of property tax increases to support basic school services indicate that educators are already feeling the effects of public demands for more effective human service delivery systems.

DIFFICULTIES IN CONCEPTUALIZING HUMAN SERVICE DELIVERY SYSTEMS

The educational literature related to the overall design and integration of school services with other human services at the community level is vague and lacks a research base. Textbooks in education and graduate classes in educational administration generally have focused on "community-school relations," a concept of interaction that is no longer responsive to organizational and political realities. Researchers must study the experience in health, social work, business, community mental health, and other related fields to find evidence concerning broader conceptual understandings and political insights concerning coordinated service delivery systems.

Experts in the field of interorganizational research, for example, have focused upon three different but related interactional levels: environment-organization; interorganizational activities; and social systems. Attention to these three levels can amplify perceptions of policy design requirements.[1] Eugene Litwak and Lydia Hylton have identified eighteen mechanisms that can be developed with regard to interorganizational coordination, depending upon the nature of the interaction.[2] Michael Aiken and his colleagues have described such coordinative agencies as professional associations, parents' groups, private organizations, governmental agencies, and traditional welfare federations.[3] Their findings reveal that in no case was there ever an attempt to coordinate all the basic variables of resources, programs, clients, and information. Instead, each coordinative body quickly narrowed its focus to one or two of the components and failed to deal with the others — a form of selective coordination.

Professionals in the health field found that in order to serve clients who had a number of problems, it was necessary to develop interrelationships with professionals in other fields, even if they did not wish to pursue such an approach. The field of social work has long attempted to address broad organizational and policy issues with regard to both centralized and decentralized services.[4]

Collaboration between public schools and other agencies commonly has resulted from outside pressure applied by the public and special interest groups. Such pressure has forced the schools to work with the police on the issue of vandalism, for example, and to develop other cooperative relationships in combating drug abuse. Groups with a special interest in child abuse and services to the handicapped are likely to give educators the next big push. A relationship between local public schools and other agencies and organizations still tends to be fragmentary at best and often takes place in a hostile environment when a crisis has occurred.

The development of sustained, effective interdependence with other organizations in the delivery of human services will raise complex and sometimes subtle issues of communication, control, and power. John Tropman has noted that interorganizational mechanisms are based upon a combination of exchanges within the context of power.[5] The school officials and teachers' groups who almost universally have shunned intimate involvement in city- or county-wide cooperative efforts have yet to define and come to grips with these issues. To do so requires that diverse actors — parents' groups, school boards, school administrators, teachers, neighborhood associations, officials and special interest groups from other agencies — come together in various political forums to confront each other about differences and to encourage the emergence of more closely linked goals.

The school's involvement would focus upon questions concerning the level and the groups that would undertake such coordinated services, including the realities of joint funding of client services. Roland Warren has noted three differing "political" strategies employed by organizations in such problematic situations: an ad hoc approach; a coalition approach; a mobilization approach.[6] He concluded that a significant proportion of coordinative instances occur outside the formal coordinative structure and in the context of contest rather than cooperation. Indeed, coordination is not the same as cooperation.

It may be noted that the actions of the federal government display much ambivalence concerning coordinated delivery of services at the local level. School districts and other agencies are now eligible for a host of diverse grant categories, each grant serving a specialized clientele and monitored by a different arm of the federal government. While deploring this situation, the Senate and House committees, each with differing areas of jurisdiction, actually have contributed to the proliferation of grants. Efforts to consolidate federal programs through the once proposed allied services act, which would give states the tools to encourage interagency coordination, have been resisted by congressmen of both parties who wish to "protect" special projects and programs. On the other hand, the federal government lately has stimulated integrative social service approaches in the funding of educational acts, such as that for community schools (P.L. 93-380, Section 405) and for lifelong learning (P.L. 94-482, Part B of Title I of the Higher Education Act).

It is safe to conclude that there are vigorous and widespread analysis and advocacy of the concept of coordinated human service delivery systems. Public and professional understanding or willingness to accept the changes in policy direction and implementing actions that it would impose, however, is more limited and cautious. And educators are especially cautious.

FUNCTIONS AND DOMAIN OF THE SCHOOL
THAT IMPEDE COORDINATED EFFORTS

Michael Aiken and Jerald Hage state that any form of agency co-ordination must focus upon comprehensiveness, compatibility, and cooperation among human service agencies in arriving at decisions related to programs, resources, clients, and sharing of information.[7] George Eyster identified numerous obstacles that impede interorganizational relationships: territorialism, "place-boundness," differences in staffing, and misunderstanding of institutional goals.[8] It is unfortunate that the operations of local educational agencies typically make collaboration with other agencies an obstacle-ridden course to pursue. Perhaps the most fundamental barrier is that a well-developed ideology and entrenched political processes have separated educational government from general government.[9] The situation is generally characterized by an attitude of separatism by educational professionals and an uncritical acceptance of professional educational expertise by the community. There are also legal, fiscal, and psychological constraints that obstruct partnership arrangements.

The domain of schools has traditionally been regulated by lengthy and detailed state educational codes. Recent federal regulations have also had direct impact on local school systems, a development that confirms Warren's prediction that the "vertical patterns" of a community, its external commitments and relationships, will continue to increase. Education has yet to benefit from such federal programs as revenue sharing, which have the potential to strengthen local authority and decision making.

Schools confront many legal constraints in collaborating with other agencies, among the most controversial of which is the manner in which school facilities may be used. Most school boards can permit utilization of school facilities for a variety of purposes, but they must be cautious not to allow interference with the instructional program. The public investment in school buildings is enormous, and it has been argued for years that school facilities should be utilized as fully as possible. Expenditures escalate in situations where schools are operating with empty rooms and offices. One method by which to broaden the acceptable purposes for which school buildings may be used is embodied in the community schools legislation, which includes the schools among the public facilities that are of minimal expense in a community education program. Erica Wood noted, however, that educators may refuse to allow the community to use school facilities if the proposed activity might disrupt the school's educational function.[10] The tendency to be cautious in this regard may be reinforced by an awareness of the political hazards that may accompany extensively shared activities. Keith Goldhammer warned that the community will probably view negatively any radical shift in the school's role, which can erode the support that educators have assiduously cultivated.[11]

Contemporary pressure on schools to expand services and the use of their facilities is certainly not a new phenomenon. In the past, schools played a larger role in community affairs than they do today. Better-trained personnel and subject-matter specialization accelerated emphasis on formalized schooling, especially at the secondary level. Schools in many areas have, nonetheless, actively responded to the community's needs. Programs for which they are typically responsible include: driver education, programs for the gifted, special education, and vocational and technical education. Colleges and universities have cooperated by developing programs to train people to teach in these specialized areas.

Local sources of revenue still supply most aid to public education, although federal and state funding of many programs has been increasing for nearly two decades. The unwillingness of local citizens to pay higher taxes demonstrates to school administrators and boards the necessity of finding new sources of revenue to support existing programs and to establish new ones. Some of this revenue could be provided by other community agencies through combined or shared functions and facilities.

State statutes are amended yearly and localities are expected to alter educational programs accordingly. Rather broad latitude exists regarding how and to what extent many guidelines are implemented, and localities retain extensive freedom to explore potential relationships with other community agencies. They can determine, moreover, whether or not services to their clients can be enhanced through integrated delivery of services.

The conservative approach of schools regarding collaborative efforts is perhaps explicable because they, like many established institutions, display what Eyster called "place-boundness." Educators cling to their own visions of what education means. Teachers' organizations have gained strength and power, but in the process have failed to explore fully the possible options for dealing with declining enrollments and expanded educational services. Eleanor McGowan and David Cohen described the effects that "professional self-interest" has had on attempts by "career educators" actually to change existing school structures.[12] In order to create an interinstitutional human service delivery system, it would be necessary for the schools to share in the adoption of broader community goals and to remove legal barriers to attaining them. Educators, like other professionals, need to explore ways of pooling human resources and not be overly concerned about getting the credit for providing a specific service. They will have to be willing, moreover, to encourage the growth of common ground.

EVIDENCE OF NEED AND POTENTIAL FOR CHANGE

Schools could benefit by integrating certain of their efforts with similar ones of other human service agencies. A sharing of psychologists and social workers could benefit an entire area served by an elementary school. Furthermore, schools might be better off financially if they subcontract for certain services. In Chapter 1, Stephen Bailey stresses the need to cope with the day-to-day problems that emerge in an ever-increasing societal malaise. Schools, for example, are clearly not equipped to handle all the problems associated with alcohol and drug abuse. It is advantageous for schools to enter into appropriate interagency liaisons that will benefit K-12 youngsters, and there is evidence to suggest that they are becoming more willing to do so. This is particularly evident in recent efforts with youth service bureaus, recreation agencies, and the courts.

The expansion of services to new populations is receiving impetus from several forces: the development of some six hundred "community schools" based on an expanded and integrative service model; new and existing legislation related to older Americans; current experiments in the health care field, especially community psychology; and an increasing number of self-help groups and voluntary associations. The greatest impetus may very well come from adult-oriented power bases. The adult and continuing education lobby is becoming stronger in Congress and in some states. Adults may indeed be the learners of the future in terms of numbers to be served.

Where the school as an institution is beginning to serve new populations, it is being done to perpetuate its existence. The domain of the school has fluctuated mainly in response to outside pressures. Today these pressures entail developing broader service boundaries that are based on a revitalized definition of what it means to educate.

Recent actions in Oregon and Ohio, where schools have closed because they ran out of operating capital, clearly demonstrate the need to find new ways of supplying schools with the funds necessary to operate them. When the boundaries and domain of the school change, there are likely to be organizational consequences. Susan Baillie and her colleagues discovered that interprofessional and professional-paraprofessional rivalry raises problems when the school assumes an expanded role.[13]

A major question facing educators relates to how far they should go in providing services to their clientele. As planned, voucher systems were to supplement an educational program; they sought, rather, to replace the program. The Parkway School and others suggest, however, that educational services can be provided in cooperation with other community agencies and institutions by both formal contract and informal agreement. Just how far the school goes will be contingent upon the needs of its clientele, the existing resources in the community, and the extent to which policymakers support such approaches.

Conflict is a factor affecting how agencies build relationships. Litwak and Hylton suggested that interagency coordination is characterized by the need to maintain both conflict and cooperation.[14] If conflict is indeed healthy and should be part of an organization's growth pattern, the potential for organizational change in schools is to a certain extent dependent on effectively coping with conflictive issues. Educators will, in consequence, find that traditional consensus politics is nonproductive.

HAZARDS AND PAYOFFS OF CHANGE

Perhaps the biggest gap in coordinating human service systems is the lack of leadership exhibited among human service organizations, particularly in the area of appointing staff members whose primary function is to build creative linkages with other organizations. Most schools and other organizations have simply paid lip service to forging interagency relationships, but have failed to commit the necessary time or adequate funds. And yet, if we examine the roots of education, we discover that such has not always been the case. Indeed, the first public high school in the United States (English High School, Boston, 1821) shared its building with the town watch.

Available research indicates the need for strong advocates to assist the development of coordinative efforts despite obstacles. What are the school's options? What are the ensuing payoffs and corresponding drawbacks associated with the role identified? What are the legal constraints on schools regarding the provision of services that are not necessarily educational in scope?

First, the school has the option to do nothing, to ride with the times and hope a favorable solution to the emerging economic and political issues will be resolved. The disadvantages of this course appear to outweigh any payoffs. The energy shortage gave us a hint of what is likely to occur: schools will be closed. Second, schools have the option to take advantage of the present scarcity of resources. Aiken and Hage have documented clearly that a scarcity of resources may force organizations to enter into more cooperative activities with other organizations, thus creating better integration of all the organizations in a community structure.[15] Various school models have been described by Joseph Ringers, including service contracts, landlord-tenant agreements, combined budget options, and community education.[16] Writers in the field of community education have identified the following payoffs for a school that takes an active role in such interagency coordination efforts: more positive response by voters to school bond elections; improved accessibility for clients to services; greater degree of citizens' interest and involvement in school affairs; new sources for volunteer and professional help for daytime curriculum; reduction in school vandalism; development of interdependence. Indeed, available research in the field of interagency coordination points to the critical need for mechanisms that promote cooperation and facilitate interdependence.[17]

A corresponding list of drawbacks involved in the school's undertaking a more active role includes: loss of organizational autonomy; conflicts among teachers associated with their work roles; conflicts among professionals and paraprofessionals; conflicts among professionals working in different service areas; and conflicts among professionals and the community. Teachers, for example, may find that the specialization of others in the community exceeds their own; thus, they may feel threatened. Aiken and his colleagues further indicated that schools may be inappropriate organizations for fostering interagency cooperation because of their low level of interorganizational interdependence, a factor that is critical to long-term interagency relationships.[18]

The report by Baillie and her colleagues clearly indicated that schools do have the legal flexibility and latitude to seek changes regarding legal constraints. Legal problems are characterized, accordingly, as "hurdles rather than outright barriers."[19] As Wood's report indicated, the law will probably not hinder such cooperative efforts, but may begin to show signs of creatively encouraging it.[20] Indeed, community education has the potential for creating a whole new dimension of public education law, one that will bind the school closer to the community.

Models of active involvement by the schools in interagency coordination are frequently reprinted in the *Community Education Journal*. The evolution of "human resource centers" already has begun in Atlanta, Georgia, Washington, D.C., and Pontiac, Michigan. The hiring of community education coordinators by school districts and other organizations to build linkages among agencies is, likewise, an emerging trend that needs further investigation. Research in the field, such as that by Peter Cwik and his colleagues, also has uncovered the possibility of interfacing three existing models: the community school, the neighborhood service center, and the educational park.[21]

CONCLUSION

The future role of the school as part of an expanded human service system is dependent on several key factors. First, community agencies must recognize that the declining availability of funds can be turned into an advantage regarding truly collaborative ventures. Second, to meet the challenges of tomorrow, individuals in all the service professions may have to become learning facilitators, as Frank Riessman suggested in Chapter 4. Consumers will be the key agents of change in the delivery of services, while professionals will give direction and evaluate results. Finally, all professional and lay groups must recognize that their own self-interest is directly tied to the self-interest of others. Then teachers' unions, school boards, administrators, citizens' groups, and agency personnel alike can join together in creative programs and political actions designed to serve joint, rather than narrowly conceived, service goals.

NOTES

1. *Interorganization Theory,* ed. Anant R. Negandhi (Kent, Ohio: Kent State University, 1975).

2. Eugene Litwak and Lydia F. Hylton, "Interorganizational Analysis: A Synthesis on Co-ordinating Agencies," *Adminstrative Science Quarterly* 6 (March 1962): 395-420.

3. Michael Aiken et al., *Coordinating Human Services* (San Francisco: Jossey-Bass, 1975).

4. Alfred J. Kahn, "Service Delivery at the Neighborhood Level: Experience, Theory, and Fads," *Social Service Review* 50 (March 1976): 23-57.

5. John E. Tropman, "Conceptual Approaches to Interorganization Analysis," in *Strategies of Community Organization,* ed. F. Cox et al. (Itasca, Ill.: Peacock Publishers, 1974).

6. Roland L. Warren, *The Community in America,* 2d ed. (Chicago: Rand-McNally, 1972).

7. Michael Aiken and Jerald Hage, "Interdependence and Intra-organizational Structure," in *Human Service Organizations,* ed. Yeheskel Hasenfield and Richard A. English (Ann Arbor: University of Michigan Press, 1974).

8. George W. Eyster, "Interagency Collaboration—The Keystone of Community Education," *Community Education Journal* 5 (September-October 1975): 24-27.

9. Frederick M. Wirt and Michael W. Kirst, *Political and Social Foundations of Education* (Berkeley, Calif.: McCutchan Publishing Corp., 1975); Laurence Iannaccone and Peter Cistone, *The Politics of Education* (Eugene: ERIC Clearinghouse on Educational Management, University of Oregon, 1974).

10. Erica F. Wood, "An Identification and Analysis of the Legal Environment for Community Education," *Journal of Law and Education* 3 (January 1974): 1-33.

11. Keith Goldhammer, *Issues and Strategies in the Public Acceptance of Educational Change* (Eugene: Center for Advanced Study of Educational Administration, University of Oregon, 1972).

12. Eleanor F. McGowan and David K. Cohen, " 'Career Education'—Reforming School through Work," *Public Interest* 46 (Winter 1977): 28-48.

13. Susan Baillie, Laurence DeWitt, and Linda O'Leary, *Potential Role of the School as a Site for Integrating Social Services* (Syracuse, N.Y.: Educational Policy Research Center, 1972).

14. Litwak and Hylton, "Interorganizational Analysis."

15. Aiken and Hage, "Interdependence and Inter-organizational Structure."

16. Joseph Ringers, *Community Schools and Interagency Programs, A Guide* (Midland, Mich.: Pendell Publishing Co., 1976).

17. Baillie et al., *Potential Role of the School.*

18. Aiken et al., *Coordinating Human Services.*

19. Baillie et al., *Potential Role of the School.*

20. Wood, "An Identification and Analysis of the Legal Environment for Community Education."

21. *Community Education and Inter-Agency Cooperation,* ed. Peter J. Cwik, Marilyn J. King, Curtis Van Voorhees (Flint: Office of Community Education Research, University of Michigan, and the National Community Education Association, 1976).

SELECTED REFERENCES

Bremer, John. *A Matrix for Modern Education.* Toronto: McClelland and Stewart Ltd., 1975.

Community Education Journal 5 (September-October 1975): 5-53. Entire issue devoted to interagency cooperation and collaboration.

Davidson, Stephen M. "Planning and Coordination of Social Services in Multi-organizational Contexts." *Social Service Review* 50 (March 1976): 117-138.

Levine, Sol. "Organizational and Professional Barriers to Interagency Planning." *A Handbook of Human Service Organizations.* Ed. H. Demone and D. Harshbarger. New York: Behavioral Publications, 1974.

———— and White, Paul E. "Exchange as a Conceptual Framework for the Study of Interorganizational Relationships." *Administrative Science Quarterly* 5 (March 1961): 583-601.

Reid, William J. "Inter-organizational Coordination in Social Welfare: A Theoretical Approach to Analysis and Intervention." *Readings in Community Organization Practice.* Ed. E. G. Brager and H. Sprecht. Englewood Cliffs, N.J.: Prentice-Hall, 1969.

Shoop, Robert J. *Developing Interagency Cooperation.* Midland, Mich.: Pendell Publishing Co., 1976.

Social Policy 7 (September-October 1976): 2-81. Entire issue devoted to "self-help."

Sumrall, Raymond O. "The Educational Park, the Community School and the Multi-Service Community Center: An Attempt toward Holistic Model Interface." Doctoral diss., University of Alabama, 1974.

Warren, Roland L., Rose, Stephen M., and Bergunder, Ann F. *The Structure of Urban Reform.* Lexington, Mass.: Lexington Books, 1974.

White, P. E., and Vlasak, G., eds. *Interorganizational Research in Health.* Baltimore: Johns Hopkins Press, 1970.

PART V
The Changing Politics
of Higher Education

Conflict, crisis, decline, scarcity, retrenchment—such are the themes that in recent years seem to have dominated discussions of the present condition and uncertain future of higher education. Whatever the immediate point of concern—trends in enrollments, academic standards, institutional autonomy, federal and state governmental relations, sources of support, public confidence, or a host of other issues that by now make an all too familiar litany—the outlook, more often than not, has been one of caution if not of stark pessimism.

There have indeed been other periods in the history of higher education when prospects for the future looked dim. As was discussed in Part I, Thomas Jefferson surely had grounds, on more than one occasion, for dismay when he compared what was with what he thought could and should be. On balance, however, we tend to remove "crisis periods" from center stage and to remember instead only the best from the (often embellished) "good old days."

No matter how great the tendency to romanticize history, however, the pressure of present concerns and gloomy forecasts of conditions in the coming decade allow for little complacency. In retrospect we can recall that the periods of greatest reform and change in higher education occurred during times of rapid growth, such as during the decades 1870-1880 and 1960-1970. We are reminded by the Carnegie Foundation for the Advancement of Teaching, however, that the next decade of substantial growth will be from 2000-2010 *(The States and*

Higher Education: A Proud Past and a Vital Future [San Francisco: Jossey-Bass, 1976], p. 7). The Carnegie Foundation projects that, in the first decade of the next century, 40 percent or more of all college and university faculties will be replaced, thus creating "enormous possibilities for changing programs, introducing new disciplines, and setting new priorities" *(ibid.)*. But neither a retreat into the world of past accomplishments nor flights into the possibilities awaiting in the twenty-first century will do much to ease the dilemmas facing higher education in the years immediately ahead. The problems confronting the academy in a changing political world seem, moreover, to be compounded by the fact that, as Stephen Bailey observed a few years ago, "we scarcely know who we are, let alone who's in charge. We no longer are 'higher,' we are simply — or perhaps, less grandly — postsecondary" (Stephen K. Bailey, "Education and the State," in *Education and the State,* ed. John F. Hughes [Washington, D.C.: American Council on Education, 1975], p. 5).

The essays in Part V invite attention to some of the most pressing dimensions of the changing politics of higher — and postsecondary — education. As with the analyses of elementary-secondary priority issues in Part IV, these essays combine elements of description, explanation, criticism, and forecast. Central to each analysis is a pointed assessment of the conflicts and contests for power that are being generated by the unsettled boundaries and uneasy relationships that characterize educational-political problems in the postsecondary arena.

In Chapter 9, Robert Berdahl analyzes the strains in the politics of accommodation sparked by the shifting base of relationship between postsecondary education and federal and state governments and by a changing interface between the elementary-secondary and postsecondary sectors. Berdahl's assessment provides a broad overview of the dynamics underlying the more specific priority issues attended to in Chapter 10.

Berdahl's review of the federal-state interface with postsecondary education underscores the political significance of the recently expanded (post-World War II) federal "supplementary" role in higher and postsecondary educational affairs. The present situation, which involves multiple federal departments and agencies selectively distributing funds and directives to varied components of the postsecondary sector, has resulted in a "messy pluralism" which, while perhaps aiding in the preservation of some degree of institutional autonomy, nonetheless proves a bane to those who seek greater effectiveness of programs. Lacking a clear understanding of the proper dimensions of a "partnership" between the federal government and postsecondary education, we are likely to take faltering and inconsistent steps toward accommodation.

Conflict within and between the major sectors of education further complicates the tangled strategies of accommodation. While the elementary-secondary and postsecondary sectors have much in common, including problems of federal-state relationships, the differences between the two sectors, Berdahl contends, are of kind rather than degree. Further, as the once solid power base of the K-12 "educational establishment" has weakened in recent years, the forces of higher education have tended to become somewhat more consolidated. Although overt conflict between these sectors may for the moment be muted, the potential for competition — over appropriations, over control of the thirteenth and fourteenth grades, and over control of variously defined postsecondary and adult education programs — remains great. Berdahl's examination of current structures and informal arrangements for accommodation existing in various states lays bare the tensions between advocates of a tighter "unitary system" versus those who resist more formal controls and favor informal liaison.

Berdahl devotes special attention to the changing relationship between institutions of postsecondary education and the state. As a consequence of the dynamic growth, expansion of functions, and rising costs and complexity that have transformed "higher education" into "postsecondary education," the historical laissez-faire arrangement between the states and tertiary educational institutions has undergone significant modification. The "self-denying ordinance," by which state governments agreed to provide financial support for public institutions while leaving governance matters in the hands of boards of trustees, proved ineffective when dealing with such issues as changing institutional missions and steadily increasing budget requests in support of new or expanded (and sometimes overlapping) programs. Given the growth of other state agencies and functions, the problems faced by state officials forced to allocate scarce resources on the basis of competing claims and some fuzzy perception of the "public good" became all the more perplexing. Thus, by the mid-1970's, all but two states had adopted some type of formal state-wide board of higher education empowered with coordinating or regulatory functions.

The erosion of the self-denying ordinance and the partial but significant shift of power from institutional trustees to state "super-boards" and to various executive and legislative agencies and commissions have placed severe strains upon the concept of institutional autonomy. Berdahl notes that while intellectual independence (academic freedom) remains firmly entrenched and reasonably well protected, administrative independence (procedural autonomy) has been markedly reduced as states have imposed numerous controls in order to regulate administrative procedures. It is in the area of academic independence (substantive autonomy), however, that tensions between postsecondary institutions and state policymakers are most acute. Questions concerning such sensitive areas as admissions standards, the ratio of resident versus out-of-state students, tuition fees, the vitality of existing programs or the merits of adding new programs are among those matters that relate directly to the heart of the academic enterprise. The boundaries and procedures involved in the struggle for power between campus and capitol over issues in the substantive policy realm remain unclear, and Berdahl observes that some adjustments are being made by both sides. The apparently growing tendency, however, is toward an escalation of state control over matters of substantive importance, a development Berdahl warns is "neither normal nor necessarily inevitable."

In Chapter 10, David Leslie introduces yet another variable — court decisions — that is dramatically redefining the context and conduct of affairs in all sectors of education. Leslie's analysis of "The Courts and the Rules of the Game" concentrates on litigation in three areas: equal protection, due process, and standards of good faith. In reviewing recent court decisions based on these principles, Leslie points repeatedly to the procedural and substantive implications of judicial interpretations. He notes that as conflicts or contests of will between individuals or groups and educational institutions become translated into issues of "rights," it is increasingly difficult for educators to justify their practices and procedures by making general appeals to tradition or conventional standards of "academic wisdom." Although one cannot forecast how much farther the courts might go in terms of challenging the wide range of discretionary freedom institutional decisionmakers have in the past enjoyed, there seems to be little doubt that court-imposed accountability will continue to alter the rules of the game and likely restrict even more the declining autonomy of education officials.

Perhaps the most optimistic contribution in Chapter 10 is Lawrence Gladieux's "Appraising the Influence of the Educational Lobbies." Noting that sustained and sophisticated representation in the political sphere is vital to the future of higher education, Gladieux suggests that within the last few years, at least, there is evidence that the higher education lobby has become better organized, more aggressive, and more effective. He cautions, however, that the inherent pluralism of the postsecondary arena often complicates the desire for a united front before Congress or other policy-making bodies. Special interests and objectives among various elements within the postsecondary orbit will cause, perhaps unavoidably, fluctuations in the degree of cooperation and solidarity manifested by the associations comprising the higher education lobby.

The diversity that prevents a consistently uniform lobbying posture at the federal level also influences governance issues at the state level. James Nickerson and Jacob Stampen reinforce the observations made by Berdahl in Chapter 9 with respect to the factors that have led to a shift of power away from individual campuses and toward concentration of powers in coordinating boards and executive and legislative branches of state government. Acknowledging that a return to full institutional autonomy is most unlikely and yet convinced that the "danger of overpoliticizing higher education is real," the authors suggest that ways may be found to sustain and to strengthen the role of institutions in state-wide governance of postsecondary education. They point, in particular, to approaches involving decentralized management; state-level, long-range planning; greater participation by institutions and their constituencies in publicizing the benefits and services of higher education; and to the role courts are playing in terms of resolving many disputes between state governments and institutions in favor of the latter.

An example of the impact of recent legislation on policies and procedures affecting all sectors of education is described in the essay by Patrick Bird. He explains the major provisions of Title IX regulations and points to some of the problems associated with the administration, financing, implementation, and enforcement of this comprehensive law prohibiting sexual discrimination in educational programs receiving federal support. Notice is also taken of recent steps toward the reorganization of the Department of Health, Education, and Welfare, a move that Secretary Joseph Califano hopes will make civil rights objectives and enforcement "an integral part of every grant, contract, and program that HEW administers."

In the final essay in Chapter 10, Virgil Ward and Robert

Templin examine the implications of the rather sudden and quickening interest in the concept of lifelong learning. The authors discuss the major tenets underlying the concept of lifelong learning and highlight the leading social, psychological, and demographic factors that are providing momentum to the "adult education" movement.

Given the uncertainties occasioned by declining enrollments, increasing expenditures, and shrinking financial support, it is understandable that many see the path to the salvation of educational institutions in terms of the recruitment of the vast and long-ignored armies of "adult learners." Ward and Templin soberly warn, however, that such optimism may indeed by unwarranted. Part-time enrollment of adults in high school and college programs has actually declined within recent years, and current projections suggest that adult part-time registrations in community colleges and technical institutes are stabilizing. On the other hand, adult participation in "nonschool" educational programs is steadily increasing. Competition between secondary and postsecondary institutions for adult learners is thus complicated by the fact that business and industry, governmental agencies, labor unions, professional organizations, community organizations, and other nonschool sponsors are attending more and more to the needs and desires of adult learners. There are, in fact, a growing lack of confidence in and growing impatience with traditional educational institutions on the part of some advocates of lifelong learning.

The political issues associated with the multifaceted movement in adult education thus further tangle the confused web of relationships in the postsecondary arena. Unraveling the strands that hold the most promise for accommodation in the years ahead will be no easy task. It is to be hoped that the essays in this section will serve to intensify our awareness of the possibilities as well as the problems that await us in the 1980's.

9 Secondary and Postsecondary Education: The Politics of Accommodation

Robert O. Berdahl

The establishment of parameters is essential when one is given a topic of this magnitude. Accordingly, my attention will be focused on three areas—the federal-state interface and postsecondary education; relations between elementary and secondary and postsecondary education; and state policies and postsecondary education. The links between and among all three of these areas will be explored, but the major emphasis will be on state policies, with the other two areas merely described in order to provide some context and to point to some needed areas of research.

FEDERAL-STATE INTERFACE AND POSTSECONDARY EDUCATION

By both tradition and the Constitution the states have been given a primary role in the establishment, maintenance, and control of public institutions of postsecondary education. The federal government has, particularly since 1945, come to play so important a part, however, that efforts to understand state policy making in postsecondary education must obviously take it into account.

Despite a variety of federal programs in higher education over the course of the nation's history, it has only been in the last twenty years that such programs have become massive and have directly involved the states. From the federal land grants in the Northwest Ordinance of 1787 to World War II, the national government played a minor role in higher education. The first and second Morrill Acts (1862 and 1890) led to the establishment and support of state land-grant institutions; the Hatch Act of 1887 and the Adams Act of 1906 initiated and increased federal support for agricultural research and experimentation; and, during the First World War, Woodrow Wilson created a National Research Council to mobilize the academic, industrial, and governmental resources of the country, with some federal funds going to universities for defense-related research.

But it took the massive effort of the Second World War to forge the strong, continuing links between universities conducting research and the national government. "In 1940, almost all of the approximately $15 million spent by the federal government for research was controlled by the Department of Agriculture. Ten years later, more than a dozen agencies were spending in excess of $150 million a year for contract research."[1]

The National Science Foundation was established in 1950 to bring maximum coherence to this new federal-institutional linkage, and its bilateral mode of operations did not directly involve state units of government. In a similar fashion, the so-called GI Bill of Rights of 1944 provided grants for veterans directly to the institutions without going through state administrative channels. The third major piece of postwar legislation relating to higher education was the National Defense Education Act (NDEA) of 1958. Reacting to fears of lagging American science in the face of Soviet Sputniks, the NDEA authorized federal loans and graduate fellowships, again administered by universities. Then, in a new departure, the act provided grants to the states for the purchase of equipment to use in teaching science, mathematics, and foreign languages, and the establishment of programs for testing, guiding, and counseling in secondary schools.

By the 1960's, legislation on higher education emerged that was not directly linked to defense measures, indicating a federal interest in a broader set of purposes. Furthermore, many of the provisions of the Higher Education Facilities Act of 1963 and the Higher Education Act of 1965 involved the use of state agencies to administer the federal programs in question. The changes in the size and nature of these federal programs led some observers, such as Alan Pifer, president of the Carnegie Corporation, to predict that by the turn of the century all postsecondary education would be supported by the federal government.

Passage of the Higher Education Amendments of 1972, following protracted debate, seemed, however, to point to the probable emergence of a different relationship. These amendments rejected major federal aid to institutions in favor of aid to students. This factor, combined with a decrease in federal research funds going to universities and an increase in federal pressures for Affirmative Action programs, all seemed to point to a supplementary federal role. Thus, the national government would use its powers and funds selectively to promote students' access to higher education, increase social justice, and support somewhat less research.

With multiple federal departments involved at the disbursing end, and with the recipients of federal funds and pressures scattered among many constituencies—students, faculties, institutions, and sometimes even multiple state agencies (for example, facilities, scholarships, and 1202 commissions)—current realities are fuzzy and incoherent. Questions obviously arise as to the desirability of greater integration of programs at either the federal or the state level and to the conscious agreement concerning which level of government would play the primary role for which sphere of activity.

In regard to the integration of programs, one senses that many academics and administrators would favor a continuance of "messy pluralism" as a greater protection of institutional freedoms than "tight integration." In contrast, political and staff personnel at both the state and national levels would probably tend to favor more integration as a means to enhance the effectiveness of programs and to reinforce the powers of the agency administering the several programs.

It is clearly time now to see whether the findings of Lanier Cox and Lester Harrell in 1969 concerning general satisfaction with the multiple state channels are still true.[2] Furthermore, with the suggestion by President Carter of creating a separate cabinet department of education, this could be the moment to examine the federal side as well. The Carnegie Council on Policy Studies in Higher Education is studying this aspect, and Rufus Miles has recently published a study on this topic for the American Council on Education.[3]

Concerning the division of labor between the federal and state governments (for example, in the area of assistance to students, the national government could concentrate on interstate grants while state governments concentrate on intrastate ones), it can be argued that there never has really been a theory of federalism, a "federal" understanding, or much of a federal "partnership" in postsecondary education.[4] Honey and Hartle have urged that the federal government assume leadership in creating a more conscious institutional-state-federal partnership.[5] Their work reviews the relationship in detail and describes relevant research in progress. Two particularly good examples are reports by the USOE on the partnership in the areas of student assistance programs and private higher education.[6]

The time may fast be approaching when a small but effective invitational conference could put these various pieces together into some pattern and then allow participants to assess the gains and losses of either resting with the status quo or of establishing some more systematized set of relationships. Once such problems are clarified, it should be possible to analyze much more exactly both the national and state politics of postsecondary education. A quick survey of the former reveals considerable research in recent years, most notably the studies by H.L. Summerfield, Harland and Sue Bloland, Chester Finn, Daniel Moynihan, Stephen Bailey, and Thomas Wolanin and Lawrence Gladieux. The section "Literature on the Politics of Higher Education at the State Level," below, discusses research on the latter subject.

STATE POLITICS AND INTERLEVEL ISSUES BETWEEN THE SCHOOLS AND POSTSECONDARY EDUCATION

Before we can profitably deal with the general area of "the politics of education," we must carefully distinguish what the elementary-secondary and postsecondary sectors have in common and how they differ. If, as I tentatively now believe, the differences are of kind rather than degree, there would be important implications for the way that we prepare teachers, researchers, and administrators for the two sectors, and in the way that we recommend state structures deal with policy making in the two sectors. Let me emphasize that I do not equate differences in kind with concepts of superior and inferior. One can recognize the generally greater prestige accorded by society to universities and colleges and still insist, as I do, that probably the most challenging and complex tasks await the professional within the elementary-secondary sector.

Unless my recent survey has missed some major sources, however, there does not seem to be much research relevant to this general concern. I could find no directly pertinent sources in the excellent bibliographical monograph on the politics of education by Laurence Iannaccone and Peter Cistone or the earlier similar essay by Michael Kirst and Edith Mosher.[8] Lester Anderson has established a framework for analysis in a brief essay arguing that the two sectors are significantly different in a number of ways. James Perkins' book for the Carnegie Commission on *The University as an Organization* contains some excellent chapters that distinguish institutions of higher education from those in business and government, but there is no comparable contrast with schools in the elementary-secondary sector.[9] Another Carnegie Commission study, however, does go partway down this road. In *Continuity and Discontinuity: Higher Education and the Schools,* the following paragraphs describe certain differences between the two sectors:

The two worlds of school and college tend to be quite different . . . . [T]heir purposes have not been the same. Even today, school teachers distrust the academic elitism of the colleges, and college teachers are often disdainful of anti-intellectualism in the schools. School teachers and administrators are activists and practical problem-solvers on a day-to-day basis. University faculty members like to study problems over time. In oversimplified terms, these differences reflect the teaching emphasis of the schools and the theoretical and research interests of the universities.

But there are many other differences as well. The difference of status in the student-professor relationship often leads to diffidence on the part of school teachers in the company of university faculty members. The school teacher typically has a master's degree, and the professor has a doctorate. This diffidence is also the result of sex stereotyping; school teachers tend to be female, college teachers male. While university faculty tend to be more liberal than the general community, public school faculty reflect more traditional, middle-class, moderately conservative values.

There are differences of style in modes of operation. University faculty members are accustomed to making policy decisions; in school systems, the administrators make most major decisions. University people work primarily with the written word in formal drafts, proposals, statements, and plans, while school teachers rely principally upon the spoken word and on informal writing style. In their daily activities, university faculty members control their own time and priorities; school teachers adhere to strict schedules and are often unavailable when university people are free to meet. School teachers work alone and are often uncomfortable in the frank and critical give-and-take style of committee activities that characterize university life. Status within universities is often difficult for outsiders to judge, since it often does not relate directly to rank, salary, duties, or size of office. In public schools, status is clear within a hierarchical system complete with titles, degrees, and lines of responsibility. In like manner, college faculty members are much more relaxed about budgetary details and expenditures than school personnel. School systems reserve expenditure decisions to relatively few people.[10]

One may take exception to many points in this general statement. From the perspective of political science, I find most disturbing the failure to underline the radically different patterns of accountability applied to universities and colleges, where autonomy and academic freedom are much in evidence. To be fair to the Carnegie Commission, one must admit that these paragraphs do not constitute a central part in the analysis. No claim is made that the generalizations are based on empirical data. Perhaps the limitations in this and other studies will inspire some scholar to begin research on the philosophical, psychological, sociological, political, and economic differences and similarities of the two sectors.

In the meantime we must make do with the primitive state of our knowledge concerning the political relations between the two sectors. The book by M. Usdan, D. Minar, and E. Hurwitz on *Education and State Politics* examined four major issues that cut across the two sectors: control of the so-called thirteenth and fourteenth grades; public funding; technical education; and teachers' education.[11] In their survey of twelve states, the authors found that there was little evidence of overt conflict between the two sectors in any widespread or continuing sense. There was, however, enough potential trouble in some of the issues to warrant careful attention by the state in order to improve relations between the two sectors. Looking at the two sectors' respective power bases in state politics, Usdan and his colleagues noted a relative decline in that of elementary-secondary education and a relative increase in that of higher education. These changes were linked to two major factors: the internal coherence and impact of each sector and the evolving balance of power between the legislative and executive branches of state government.

In regard to the first factor, the authors pointed out that increased militancy and unionization by teachers had lessened to some degree the solidity of the coalition that had earlier constituted the politically powerful "educational establishment"—the alliances in some states of groups representing classroom teachers, school administrators, school boards, and parent-teacher organizations. At the same time that internal splits were appearing within the teachers' ranks and between them and some of their former allies, forces in higher education were growing stronger. Not only were there rapidly increasing numbers of both students and institutions, but some of the bitter rivalries that had existed between various colleges—in state capitals for funds as well as on football fields—were lessened in some states by the creation of voluntary or statutory state-wide coordinating groups that often labored to reduce the conflicts over state budgeting.

In regard to the second factor, the authors judged that political ties were usually stronger between the elementary-secondary sector and the state legislatures and between higher education and the executive branch. To the extent that this was true, the strengthening of the executive branch vis-à-vis the legislative also resulted in a strengthening of the political power of the postsecondary sector.

The authors then applied the following analysis to an examination of the four issues. First, concerning the control of the thirteenth and fourteenth grades, they found that patterns in their twelve states varied markedly. In some areas two-year colleges functioned as part of the public school system; in others they were part of higher education, whether as community colleges or branch campuses of four-year institutions. Though there has been a general trend to move the two-year institutions into higher education, the authors found no evidence that such transitions have caused major conflict between the two sectors. (There were, however, consequences related to fiscal and technical education; they will be discussed below.)

Second, as regards funding, Usdan and his colleagues noted that, whereas formerly the two sectors had largely drawn from different sources of public funding (the elementary-secondary sector from local funding, and higher education from state), two developments were acting to change the situation. In the first place, as the local property taxes supporting schools approached levels considered intolerable by taxpayers' groups, many states moved to reorganize their financing of schools and, in the process, began to draw more on general state revenues. In the second place, as the community colleges moved from school systems to higher education, their partial reliance on local financing resulted in a blurring of the separate funding sources and in increased competition for the same monies, both local and state.

Third, in relation to the issue of technical education, the authors found the field to be suffering from "lack of direction, lack of commitment, underemphasis and general confusion . . . the problem is less conflict over an issue than the absence of issue substance around which conflict might revolve."[12] In those states where the community colleges moved from the school system to higher education, the job of coordinating vocational-technical education became even more difficult.

Finally, on the issue of teachers' education, the authors found no widespread friction between the two sectors.

The general conclusions of Usdan and his colleagues were that state policymakers were rarely aware of the potential for interlevel conflicts in education and that most seemed content to handle whatever problems emerged in the traditional piecemeal manner. The authors felt that a continuation of such ad hoc patterns of problem solving would not suffice for the future. They then reviewed formal structures existing in a few states for dealing with interlevel coordination of educational problems; recommended no particular structure as best, but urged each state to adopt some formal or informal mode of attacking the issue; and added the usual caution about the limits of structural reform: "Political scientists have discovered reasons to doubt, in recent years, that the structure or form of government is a very important independent determinant of output in the political system. It may, however, exert an influence on the shape of political activity, and it probably can delay or redirect the force of social demands. In many circumstances it is probably an important intervening factor in the overall operation of systems of politics."[13]

In the years since Usdan and his colleagues published their book, I have not come across any comparable research. And yet my impression is that most of the issues continue to be pressing. Certainly recent state fiscal problems have exacerbated tensions associated with a zero-sum game approach to state funding of various educational levels.[14] Certainly, also, increased federal funding and intervention in state structures for the planning of vocational-technical education have raised interlevel tensions in that area. The increase in collective bargaining at both the school and college levels (sometimes involving the same parent unions) also raises interesting issues concerning interlevel politics.

Another issue cutting across both sectors that has increased in importance in terms of future state policy making is the planning and funding of adult education. Governor Edmund Brown's often quoted remark about the state's subsidizing "macrame for Mommy while Johnny can't read" is a direct indication of a funding dilemma between elementary-secondary and postsecondary education.

Finally, one notes that during the intervening years four states have established the office of secretary of education. This pattern should certainly be included in any new examination of states' interlevel coordination in education.

If such an examination were undertaken today, what structures would be found? For "mapping" purposes only, I shall briefly list the major alternatives:

1. *Secretary of Education.* This office has been established in Massachusetts, Pennsylvania, South Dakota, and Virginia. Its nature varies somewhat from state to state (for example, in Pennsylvania, it is

concerned more with line functions, and, in Virginia, more with staff), but its underlying philosophy is the same: to allow the governor to integrate the planning and funding of all education by appointing a senior officer of cabinet rank to preside over the various levels and sub-boards in education. Because the position is so new, I found little relevant literature on it, particularly as it applies to improving interlevel educational coordination. My book published in 1971 dealt briefly with some of the documents relating to the reorganization of the executive branch in Massachusetts. Roald Campbell's evaluation of state boards of education included material on the secretary of education. L.V. Ginger and J. C. Pittenger debated the pros and cons of the new office in an article in *Compact*. Fred Harcleroad also devoted some attention to the emergence of the position, and in Virginia a Commission on State Governmental Management recently issued a document analyzing the role of the several secretaries of education in that state.[15]

2. *State Board of Education.* Here, again, one finds variety in the same type of structure. The jurisdiction of the board ranges from kindergarten to postdoctoral levels. In New York, Michigan, and Pennsylvania the state board (by whatever title it may be called) coordinates but does not govern postsecondary education; in Rhode Island and Idaho the board governs the public institutions of postsecondary education, and, with some technical qualifications, this could also be said of Florida and Montana. But, in any case, in these seven states the potential exists for resolving interlevel problems within a single umbrella structure, whether it governs or merely coordinates. Campbell evaluates all types of state boards of education, including those with jurisdiction broadened to include postsecondary education, but his focus is not on how well such boards handle the interlevel problems. My book and that by Usdan and his colleagues do, however, include some analysis of these boards in that context.

3. *Interlevel Liaison Structures.* Such structures involve some formal type of liaison to promote interlevel coordination. In 1971 I identified four states using this pattern—Georgia, Massachusetts, New Jersey, and Oregon—but these groups may have been altered or eliminated in the intervening years. In the case of Oregon, for example, the Education Coordinating Council[16] has been reformed and strengthened. It has now replaced the Oregon State Board of Higher Education, which still governs the public senior institutions, as the state's official member of SHEEO, the national organization of State Higher Education Executive Officers.

It is clearly time for a major study of the various modes for promoting interlevel coordination. This study should address two main questions. First, are the interlevel problems now large enough, or likely to become so, to require more than informal liaison and consultation? Over the past decade, several state political figures have urged that elementary-secondary and postsecondary policies and funding be more closely linked. In addition to general statements by Robert Graham and Mark Hatfield,[17] L.W. Newbry, a legislator in Oregon, tied his concerns to an explicit zero-sum game analysis: "Primary and secondary education people, community college people, and higher education people are all competing for a limited number of dollars that are available to the legislature . . . . To consider higher education's problem alone is to ignore some of the other major problems that do exist. What we have to do in solving higher education's problem is to set our whole educational program in order."[18] Most higher education circles do not seem anxious, however, to solve this problem by establishing new formal structures. The Carnegie Commission, for example, endorses informal liaison and joint interlevel committees rather than any type of "unitary system" whose control would be "too great."[19]

Second, if formal structures are created, should they be designed to increase or decrease the distance between education and politics in the state? John Pittenger, secretary of education in Pennsylvania, has strong feelings on the subject:

The criticism most frequently made—that [my position] "puts education into politics"—is a strength, not a weakness. In fact, education is always in politics. It concerns money and power, and these are what politicians fight about. I see no advantage in concealing from the public the fact that educational decisions are in fact political decisions and that support for education requires political skills.

In Pennsylvania's system, if the governor and the secretary of education are on good terms—and the system makes it likely that they will be—the secretary has access to the governor's political power. He can get the governor's support for legislative and budgetary initiatives. He can, when necessary, enlist the governor's assistance in persuading other cabinet officers to do what has to be done. And he can exercise some influence over the governor's policies in fields relating to education, to see to it that they are not inconsistent with his own.[20]

Pittenger weakens his case, however, by admitting that, in order for the assets to be realized in such a system, the governor must be strong, and good relations must exist between him and his secretary of education. If we have learned anything about structural reforms, it is that they must not be linked to benign personalities or be subject to severe abuse if less well-intentioned persons arrive on the scene.

Pittenger's views are not unique among state officials. Terry Sanford, former governor of North Carolina and now president of Duke University, said earlier: "More universities have suffered from political indifference than have ever been upset by political interference."[21] A new study of the type prepared by Usdan and his colleagues could investigate this aspect also.

STATE POLICIES AND POSTSECONDARY EDUCATION

Given a primary role in higher education by tradition and the U.S. Constitution, the states, from some early support for private colleges in the colonial period to the emergence of large public systems over the past hundred years, have invested vast sums of public tax funds to support broader access, greater diversity, and higher quality. Some may protest this generalization and point to lingering injustices concerning those who are able to attend college, to various signs of the decline of diversity, and to assorted evidence of the threats to academic standards. But for those who put matters in perspective, either historically or in terms of systems of higher education abroad, the overall verdict must be that, by and large, the states have done well. This is particularly true when another important variable is added to the picture: for most of the time in most of the states, the support of higher education by public tax funds has been accompanied by a "self-denying ordinance" by which the state paid but did not dictate policy.[22]

States and the Self-Denying Ordinance

Instrumentalities of state governments were normally required to operate under some fiscal controls in order to ensure that their activities and expenditures were in strict conformity with their established legal base. When the states began to found public universities, however, they did not turn to their normal models of public accountability. They turned, rather, to precedents in the private sector in which state charters had been granted to legal entities known as boards of trustees (or some variation of this term) who thereby gained the power to govern the institutions largely free of state controls. The exact powers granted to the public institutions varied somewhat, of course, from state to state, and as time passed and more colleges were established, they varied even within a state from one type of institution to another. The following summary attempts, however, to provide some common characteristics of the self-denying ordinance.[23]

1. Twenty-three states give some form of constitutional recognition to higher education whereas few state departments, other than constitutional offices, are so recognized.

2. Forty states confer corporate powers on their highest educational boards (few other departments have them).

3. Elections or appointments of board members are for a longer period than for most public offices, and it is often specified that selection of board members be on a nonpolitical basis.

4. Many boards have been given direct borrowing power, which is rarely granted to state agencies.

5. Many are given power to appoint treasurers, select their own depositories, and disburse funds, especially institutional funds, directly (also rare in other state agencies).

6. Many higher education boards are granted wide discretion and in many instances complete autonomy on policy matters, such as requirements for admission and for graduation, programs, courses, and degrees to be offered.

7. In almost every state, the boards have full authority over all matters relating to academic and professional personnel.

8. Most states require the boards to keep more or less complete personnel records in connection with the budget, but leave final determination to the boards after the appropriation is made. Few boards are given complete authority over administrative and clerical personnel other than over the highest administrative position.

The Dartmouth College case in 1819 established the legal sanctity of state charters to private colleges. A major difference between charters to private institutions and those to public ones is that, except for the few instances in which such agreements were incorporated into state constitutions,[24] grants of power to governing boards of public institutions could later be altered by state legislation. And, of course, even state constitutional provisions can be amended, albeit with greater difficulty. The impressive thing is that, given the pressures that emerged, so many essentials of the self-denying ordinance survived as long as they did. The increasing size, cost, and complexity of both higher education and other activities of state government over the past century have ultimately caused nearly all states to modify the self-denying ordinance.

Increasing complexity has, of course, been a major factor in modifying the self-denying ordinance. When, in a given state, there was only one state university, its lay board of trustees could advise the governor and state legislators on what programmatic and fiscal policies they considered to be in the best interests of both the university and the state. There were relatively few students, the costs involved were modest, and curricular issues in the early days of classical studies were so straightforward that most problems between the early university and state government could be worked out on a direct bilateral basis. The trustees, after all, had been appointed partly on the basis of their ability to consider the public interest in their deliberations. Furthermore, such trustees often had strong political connections with which to back up their advice.

But during the century following the Civil War basic changes occurred in several aspects of American life that were ultimately to have major impact on higher education. The economy gradually shifted from agricultural to industrial; society similarly moved from rural to urban; state governments left behind laissez-faire for extensive regulatory and welfare activities; and the national government grew in power and functions even more than the states. Responding to these changes, higher education developed from an elite to a mass system (now poised on the brink of universal access) with accompanying increases in number and diversity of institutions, in costs, and in complexity of curriculum.

These additional layers of complexity can be examined one by one. First, following the Morrill Act of 1862, a number of states established separate land-grant institutions to teach agriculture and mechanical arts, although, in some cases, these functions were simply assumed by the existing state university or contracted to private colleges. In any case, the curriculum was broadened, more students were attracted, and both diversity and costs increased.

Next, to the traditional offerings of the state university were added increased interest in graduate education and research, heavily influenced by German science, and new programs in public service, a distinctly American contribution to higher education, exemplified by the practice of the "Wisconsin Idea" at Madison by President Charles Van Hise. The richness of the program that resulted has been well described:

Universities began extensive research programs in the physical and biological sciences;

provided new services for the farmers, industries, and other special-interest groups; added professional schools in new areas such as social work, public administration, industrial relations, and municipal management; further specialized in agriculture, medicine, and dentistry; and increased course offerings in almost all previously existing academic fields. Land-grant colleges began to extend their programs into academic and professional disciplines which had traditionally been offered only by the state university.[25]

Another layer of complexity resulted from the spread of normal schools, accelerated by steps to make secondary education compulsory. Soon many of these institutions became state teachers colleges; then some became state colleges with programs through the master's degree in liberal arts and business administration as well as education; and, finally, an increasing minority have even been designated as state universities, with expansion into doctoral-level work occasionally permitted.

Another major source of growth and diversity has been the American community college movement. Catering particularly to urban areas relatively neglected by earlier established universities and colleges, the junior colleges widened access to large new groups of young people: those who could not meet the admissions standards of some four-year institutions and those who lived in areas without such four-year institutions and who could not afford to attend college unless they lived at home. As time passed, these institutions also broadened their functions and became "community colleges" where college transfer, two-year technical, and adult education programs were all combined. Although these institutions began as products of local government, problems of funding, planning, and coordination gradually brought them more and more into the state-wide orbit as well.

State problems with higher education were not confined merely to appropriating adequate funds to provide the necessary facilities for students, as difficult as even this probably was. In addition, thorny questions arose about the overlapping programs of state universities and land-grant colleges, about the wisdom of normal schools' evolving toward university status, about the educational rationale for two-year institutions' becoming four-year ones.

In dealing with these various issues, the device of traditional lay trustees was something less than totally effective. The same boosting spirit that made each local chamber of commerce work to make its city more prominent also caused most governing boards to push aggressively for bigger and better facilities and programs. Often such requests were justified, but sometimes they were not. While governors and state legislators had considerable experience with budgetary fights—even bitter ones—they lacked any frame of reference by which to judge the increasingly complex questions relating to allocations for new programs and changed institutional missions.

The problem of responding to the competing and contradictory advice of lay trustees was compounded by the expansion of their other functions of state governments at the same time: agriculture, highways, police protection and prisons, public health and hospitals, parks and recreation, welfare, and industrial regulation. All these and others demanded time, attention, and state funds. During the years when suspicions by the legislature of excessive gubernatorial power still lingered, the part-time legislators tended to piecemeal, ad hoc responses to these various pressures. A maze of overlapping boards, commissions, and agencies were thus created, each with its own goals and budgetary needs. Relative political strength rather than relative needs usually determined the results. It gradually became evident that only a greatly strengthened executive office could bring some coherence out of this haphazard mode of operations. Beginning with Illinois in 1917, state after state undertook a comprehensive reorganization and consolidation of government. The following five principles were generally observed:

1. Consolidate all operating state agencies into a small number of departments, each organized around a function of the government.
2. Establish clear lines of authority from the governor to all departments and state agencies.
3. Establish staff offices and controls to provide the governor with the administrative techniques necessary for effective direction.
4. Eliminate as many administrative boards and commissions as possible.
5. Provide a postaudit system under the legislative branch.[26]

As a consequence of such a reorganization, state policy-making power was concentrated in the executive budgetary process. Supplementary controls over most state activities evolved in other staff offices: a controller would preaudit expenditures for "legality" and sometimes for "propriety"; a central purchasing office would order all major supplies and equipment; a civil service commission would control the hiring, remuneration, and administration of personnel; a state planning or public works office would exert detailed controls over the design and construction of public buildings. The basic idea (often imperfectly realized) was for the governor to be given both the power and the responsibility to run a coherent administration.

To retain some check on this burgeoning executive power, states provided for a postaudit, and a number of state legislatures created their own review and research agencies, with substantial staff to provide careful analysis of executive fiscal and program proposals. State activities, then, would often receive rigorous examination from both executive and legislative branches.

State Responses to Increased
Complexity and Cost in Higher Education

At a time, then, when many other independent and quasi-independent state activities were being brought under more direct executive control and legislative scrutiny, how did higher education fare? In light of the general weakening in the ability of trustees to cope with increased state costs and complexity in higher education, the self-denying ordinance was generally modified. The particular extent of the modification varies from state to state and from period to period. A safe generalization, however, is that by the mid-1970's all states except two had supplemented the original bilateral relationships involving great institutional freedom of action, with some type of formal state-wide board of higher education dealing with the institutions on a multilateral basis and narrowing sometimes more, sometimes less, their former freedom of action. It is also true, nevertheless, that the creation of these state-wide boards with their special status (several are even established constitutionally) represents a distinct continuing concession from state government. Thus, higher education remains exempt from some of the controls imposed on other state activities.

The detailed nature of these state-wide boards need not concern us here. Richard Millard's monograph and the commentary in 1976 by the Carnegie Foundation for the Advancement of Teaching both point out the tremendous diversity existing within the two major types: *coordinating boards,* which exist in twenty-nine states, plan and coordinate the institutions under their jurisdiction, but do not supersede the campus or system governing boards; and consolidated *governing boards,* which exist in nineteen states, combine governance with planning and coordination.[27]

These various boards differ markedly with respect to details of jurisdiction, powers, and membership, but three observations at least indicate general trends: all but seven of the forty-eight boards include jurisdiction over all public institutions of higher education in their state; all but nine of the forty-eight boards have at least final powers to approve or disapprove new academic programs; and all but about twelve of the forty-eight boards are composed exclusively of public members who do not represent the institutions involved.

Delaware and Vermont are the two states without statutory state-wide boards in the above sense, although each now has a state 1202 commission recently created by executive order of their governors.[28]

A Closer Look at Institutional Independence

It is useful to discuss separately three different dimensions of the relations between public institutions and state governments even though, in practice, they are often intermingled. These dimensions have received various labels, but the terms used are less important than the realities they represent. The Carnegie Commission called them intellectual, academic, and administrative independence; Berdahl used academic freedom, substantive autonomy, and procedural autonomy.[29] Below is an explanation of why intellectual and administrative independence are treated briefly and academic independence is emphasized.

Intellectual Independence. Best known among the three dimensions, and probably the best protected, is intellectual independence (or academic freedom). Because American society over the years has come to accept the basic principle of the scholar's need for freedom of inquiry, most faculty members at most public institutions in most states have operated most of the time essentially free of state efforts to circumscribe their professional freedoms. There have been efforts now and then, of course, to impose some kind of orthodox constraints, but they have rarely emanated directly from organs of state government. In the past fifty years, however, an effective countervailing force has emerged: Committee A of the American Association of University Professors, which has the ability to recommend censure of institutions judged to have allowed serious breaches of this intellectual independence. In any case, this dimension has been well studied and analyzed.[30]

Administrative Independence. Second best understood among the three, and probably the least protected, is administrative independence (or procedural autonomy). This refers to the freedom to choose the administrative means by which institutional policies will be pursued. It is here that the self-denying ordinance has been most modified, as most states other than the thirteen in which their state universities are mentioned in their constitutions (and even in some of them) have imposed a number of procedural controls. They include: central purchasing; central personnel administration for non-academic staff; central approval of capital outlays for sites, plans, architects, and so forth; central control of out-of-state travel; line-item budgets with central controls over transfers between items; preaudits for propriety as well as legality of proposed expenditures; tight central controls over institutional use of overhead funds and revolving funds; and increasing use of fiscal and management postaudits.

In no state were all of these controls employed, but Alexander Brody, the Committee on Government and Higher Education, Malcolm Moos and Francis Rourke, Glenny and Dalglish, and Harcleroad have documented the vast extent of this kind of state oversight.[31]

Because both these areas have been well researched and the problems are accordingly fairly well understood (even if people representing the state and individuals in higher education do not always agree on them), I will emphasize the dimension of academic independence.

Academic Independence. Academic independence (or substantive autonomy) deals with the "what" of academe rather than the "how." From one end of the scale dealing with ends, goals, and objectives to the other dealing with discrete programs, faculty, students, and facilities, this particular dimension is permeated with sensitive considerations of academic values. Should a campus add a law school, or a new doctoral program in Asian studies, or a new undergraduate major in communications? Should admissions standards and tuition fees be juggled to attract different kinds of students? Should faculty salaries or teaching loads be altered to attract and retain improved teaching staff? What role should out-of-state students play in promoting academic quality? Questions such as these constitute some of the agenda of academic substance. Because of the intimate bearing of these questions on the heart of the enterprise, most states until recently have, under the terms of the self-denying ordinance, deferred to trustee-endorsed internal priorities — at least within the limits of appropriated funds. And the nature of the early budgetary process was such that most internal academic priorities could be protected. In the first place, requests for funds were not all assembled side by side in the state capitol, with the resulting temptation to try to compare relative value to the state of proposed programs in higher education with those in other sectors. Second, budgetary staff in the executive and legislative branches rarely included specialists in higher education, and the nonspecialists usually dealt only with marginal issues. Finally, even if such specialists would later begin to recommend major funding priorities in education, many legislators revealed a preference for adhering to the practice that A. Wildavsky has termed "incrementalism."[32] This is the time-honored system by which politicians trade off modest budgetary increases or cuts because they dislike having to make global policy decisions via budgetary review. Within such a budgetary context, a good institutional administrator could learn how to protect favored programs, even in the face of line-item budgets.

The transition from an elite to a mass system of higher education increased, however, the temptation for the state to intervene in matters of substance. Not only were overall costs rapidly soaring, but even "costs at the margin" involved millions of dollars as when new campuses required larger amounts of the taxpayers' money. And, with increasing numbers of students enrolling in higher education, and with research and public service activities bringing universities and colleges more into the public eye, some of the exotic aspects of higher education that had encouraged the earlier deference of the state to academe began to diminish. Because this is a relatively recent phenomenon, its precise boundaries and procedural relationships are not yet fully defined, and much confusion and dissatisfaction remain. Academics, viewing the flow of power away from their institutions toward the state, tend to generalize that all has been lost. State officials have learned with dismay how ingrained and how effective academic resistance can be to coordination within the system. Thus, they continue to threaten further escalation of state intervention.

Escalation of Controls

In the face of the confusion and dissatisfaction from both sides concerning existing relationships, there have been some adjustments in both directions and much tinkering with structure in an unreal search for procedural perfection.

The smaller movement by far has been that of weakening the state-wide board or other state controls. Institutions succeeded in doing this in North Carolina and Virginia in the 1950's; in the 1960's the Ohio Board of Regents was able to get state procedural controls over public institutions lessened, and South Carolina reduced somewhat the powers of its state-wide board; and in the 1970's both the Univer-

sity of Michigan and the Montana Board of Regents undertook successful lawsuits to repel what they regarded as excessive state interference in their internal affairs.

On the other hand, a great number of state-wide boards, executive offices, and legislatures have grown in power over higher
education during the past decade. At least five coordinating boards
with advisory power have received some regulatory powers, and, according to Millard, fourteen regulatory boards have had their powers
strengthened. The boards received additional powers mainly in the
areas of approving new academic programs (now widespread) and
reviewing existing academic programs (just beginning to spread).[33]

Many institutions are uneasy about this increasing power over
programs by state-wide boards. In New York, for example, the State
University of New York and the state-wide coordinating agency, the
Board of Regents, have gone to court in a dispute over the latter's
right to terminate doctoral programs at SUNY-Albany.

But if apprehensions exist over increasing functions by state-wide
boards, even worse news is coming in the form of developments in state
executive and legislative branches. Some of these increasing state controls may reflect a loss in confidence concerning the operations of
higher education and a growing unwillingness to treat higher education differently from other state activities. It is also important to
recognize, however, that some of the enlarged role of the state may be
a product of intense rivalry between the executive and legislative
branches (or even between the upper and lower house) in which higher
education gets involved quite incidentally as a pawn in a broader
power struggle.

Two current studies (by Lyman Glenny and his colleagues and by
the Education Commission of the States) are producing important
evidence that confirms the significantly larger roles of both the executive and legislative branches of state government. (And earlier
studies revealed a similar conclusion about state courts of law.) Glenny
and the staff at the Center for Research and Development in Higher
Education at the University of California, Berkeley, are completing a
massive multivolume study of state budgeting for higher education.
Visiting seventeen states and surveying all fifty, Glenny's group found
convincing evidence that the large growth in the budget analysis staff
of both the executive and legislative branches pointed to much more
rigorous budgetary analysis, to increased attention to evaluation of
programs in a fiscal context, and to a decreasing budgetary role for

state-wide coordinating boards. Glenny and his colleagues predicted that, even in states where coordinating boards now play a strong role in budgetary review, an increase in executive or legislative budget staff would soon produce an unwillingness to defer much longer to fiscal recommendations of a board. The reports of Glenny's group will urge, instead, that state-wide boards give primary emphasis to the following activities: continuous long-range planning and broad policy analyses; state information system on higher education and special studies; development of formulas for budgeting; special nontechnical budgetary review for conformity to a master plan and conformity of programs to such a plan; and audit and review of new and existing programs.

Steering state-wide boards away from a preoccupation with technical budgeting toward emphases on planning and review of programs certainly coincides with my own judgment about the optimum priorities of boards, but it also runs into a new problem of possible overlap with the increasingly prevalent practice of program evaluation by state legislatures. I recently finished, as part of an overall study by the Education Commission of the States (ECS) of performance measures in higher education, a set of two case studies and commentary on program evaluation by state legislatures.[34] The following comments draw heavily from this material. I am devoting considerable attention to this topic because I feel that, whereas escalating state interest in the budget is both normal and inevitable, state assessment of substantive issues in higher education is neither normal nor necessarily inevitable.

This relatively new function of the state is one of several ways the legislature can oversee the activities of a strengthened executive branch. Moos and Rourke, Sanford, Millett, and John Lederle have all discussed the larger role of "strong governors."[35] The powers of the office have grown along several different lines: governors' terms have been lengthened from two to four years; prohibitions against second terms have been removed; stronger executive budgets have been instituted; veto powers over separate items have been given; governmental reorganizations have brought under executive control more independent and quasi-independent commissions and have converted some senior elective offices to gubernatorially appointed ones. Though minor limitations have occasionally been applied, the movement has basically given governors increased powers to match their responsibilities in achieving coherence in state programs.

At the same time, however, state legislatures have taken steps to improve their ability to hold the executive branch accountable. Legislative budget committees have learned better how to analyze the executive budget; legislative subject-matter committees have strengthened their staffs and have undertaken careful studies of the need for new legislation. In this regard the recent study by the Citizens Conference on State Legislatures argues for an even stronger legislative policy role in postsecondary education.[36] The state postaudit function has gradually been moved from independent status or from the executive branch to the legislative branch and has often been broadened in scope to include audits of performance or programs. It is this last phenomenon with which we are concerned here.

As late as the 1940's, nearly all states placed the postaudit function with a popularly elected independent state auditor or with the executive branch. By 1960 fifteen states had made the legislature responsible for the function, and by 1975 thirty-six states had done so. These postaudit functions concerned, for the most part, fiscal and management analyses of legality and efficiency. But the largely unsuccessful efforts in the 1960's to encourage widespread state adoption of PPBS (planning, programming, budgeting systems) resulted in a recognition of the importance of program evaluation, which was, in turn, incorporated in the postaudit movement.

It might be said that PPBS collapsed because of its own excessive demands to gather the enormous amount of information and to fund the extensive staff time needed for detailed cost-benefit analyses of alternative programs. To do this on an annual or biennial basis for large parts of the entire state budget proved too much of a burden, and many state legislators found they preferred the incremental budget trade-off processes so well described by Wildavsky. The more sophisticated observers noted, furthermore, that PPBS theory did not pay adequate attention to the need for evaluation of outcomes.

The postaudit function, however, lent itself to this general mode of analysis — allowing selective studies that were relatively narrow and deep and that stressed evaluation of outcomes by identifying goals and objectives and finding appropriate measurement indicators. In the past seven years, over twenty states have introduced some form of legislative program audit. In a few cases (such as New York, Illinois, Connecticut, and Virginia), special nonpartisan legislative program audit committees have been formed; in other cases, the legislative auditor's functions have been broadened to include program evaluations; and, in still other cases, legislative fiscal or subject committees have assumed the tasks of program evaluation.

E.G. Crane has produced the major overview of the state of the art of this emerging field.[37] He ably documents the enormous range and locations of activities labeled state legislative program evaluation and points out some of the semantic problems connected with such terms as program, performance, audit, and review. What is clear, though, is that current state efforts to go beyond the traditional postaudit concerns with legality and efficiency raise serious questions about whose criteria will determine the effectiveness of programs and how much legitimacy may be attached to them. This is particularly true when program evaluations (as distinct from fiscal and management audits) are attempted in higher education. It takes no seasoned cynic to observe that all fields seeking public funds or resisting public controls engage in special pleading. But, in the case of higher education, there are well-founded arguments based on history, law, and logic as to why it should not be treated as just another state function. Moos and Rourke had some excellent passages arguing the uniqueness of higher education, and Stephen Bailey has waxed eloquent on this subject on several occasions.[38] (All staff concerned with performance audit should, as a matter of fact, be required to read Bailey.)

The future, however, appears ominous. When legislators considered friendly to, and understanding of, higher education call firmly for more assessment of outcomes, the implications are obvious. Howard Klebanoff of Connecticut and Robert Graham of Florida are two such widely respected figures, and each one has sounded the call. Klebanoff, for example, states:

> Outcome data should include not just the number of graduates produced, but quality—a follow-up of what happens to the graduates in terms of becoming contributing members of society.
>
> Legislators and educators must realize that for some programs, it is unlikely that they can ever collect the right data. Under these circumstances, the proper approach is to design less perfect measures for which data are available or can be acquired. Often we cannot wait for the ideal. Some data bearing on program effectiveness are better than none at all. [Order of paragraphs transposed.][39]

One may or may not agree with Klebanoff's statement that imperfect performance data are better than none at all, but this is no mere rhetorical position. Already, even though the movement for legislative evaluation of programs is less than a decade old, twenty studies among more than 150 conducted in twenty states have examined some part of higher education. Most of these studies do not focus on whole systems but on some, often technical, aspect of the system, and few seem to have attempted genuine evaluations of academic programs. The studies are significant enough, however, for the warning by D.H. Pingree, J.T. Murphy, and D.B. Weatherspoon in their review of legislative program evaluation (LPE) and higher education to be taken seriously:

What will develop in the future will depend in large measure on how the higher education community responds to these pressures. If administrators don't begin now to provide relevant and useful program data, state legislatures may well attempt to impose various sanctions, such as eliminating or drastically reducing programs which do not exhibit positive effects. The legislatures may fail in these efforts, but the result will not be a public relations bonanza for higher education . . . public higher education might best be served by accepting, however reluctantly, the legitimacy of LPE and by meeting appropriate criticism with speedy remedial action.[40]

All parties in higher education may not, however, be ready to take this advice. Some will find the very idea of state measurement of quality in programs anathema; others will insist that if such evaluations are to be done, they must be only self-evaluations; and still others will agree with Howard Bowen's insights.

To evaluate outcomes is difficult partly because it is hard to sort out causes and effects, partly because the final outcomes may not be known for decades and partly because some of the most significant outcomes may be impossible to identify or measure in objective terms. Yet, despite the difficulties, educators have an obligation to assess outcomes as best they can, not only to appease outsiders who demand accountability but also to improve internal management . . . . There are some useful procedures for obtaining quantitative data on outcomes, and ongoing research (which should be multiplied many times) will produce more ways of measuring outcomes. Inevitably, however, the assessment of outcomes will require large elements of judgment. One of the problems is to bring to bear on evaluation the judgment of professionally qualified but disinterested persons.[41]

If Bowen's analysis is correct — and I find it closest to my own thinking — it would reinforce the earlier suggestion that state-wide boards have a much more appropriate role to play in review of programs and evaluation of academic outcomes than they can ever hope to achieve in the crowded arena of budgeting. One must quickly acknowledge, however, three major problems, any one of which could prevent a board's playing this role successfully.

First, most state-wide boards may have to be dragged from their relatively comfortable preoccupation with quantitative analyses of budgets (where Glenny and his colleagues are predicting that their roles will increasingly be duplicative and relatively unimportant) into efforts to make qualitative assessments of academic outcomes (where they are in a unique position to play a role of leadership by virtue of combining sensitivities to the nuances of academic values and procedures with an appreciation of state-wide perspectives). Such boards will consider the political and methodological problems of assessing academic outcomes enormous. Emphases by the state on manpower links will cause some faculty and students to complain that universities are being turned into handmaidens of the capitalist economy. Some citizens will see attempts by faculty to make students more rational and autonomous as efforts to alienate their children from home and religion. This is clearly an area filled with problems, and yet if someone must try to solve them, why not the state-wide boards?

Second, even if some boards can be persuaded to cope with these problems, another consideration is the failure of the universities and colleges to cooperate. One may expect that these institutions will not sense that they are dealing with the lesser of evils. Past performance in other areas indicates, rather, that they will actively or passively resist initiatives by the boards and that, as a consequence, such efforts may fail. In a perceptive address, Roger Heyns, former president of the American Council on Education, observed that American higher education "now lives with the consequences of its earlier attitudes toward the coordinating agencies. The delicate issues, complicated enough in themselves, are made more difficult by accumulated distrust, scars from previous battles, and a continuous combativeness."[42]

Finally, if, by some miracle, both the state-wide board and the institutions in a given state decide to cooperate on this task, it remains to be seen whether the performance-oriented staff in the legislative and executive branches will agree not to interfere. In program issues related to budgeting it is clear that they will interfere. In matters relating to intensive program evaluation, the power to intervene will obviously be there. It is to be hoped that there will be enough credibility in the board-institutional evaluations and enough residual understanding of the general desirability of keeping state organs out of internal academic matters to make the state exercise self-restraint.

State governments are not generally known for their self-restraint, however, and so the prospects for success are not good, particularly because of the usual institutional shortsightedness in this area and because of chronic problems in attracting and retaining high-quality leadership on the state-wide boards. The above scenario is, nevertheless, more likely to materialize in the current state of the politics of higher education than those calling for: all institutions voluntarily to embrace rigorous self-evaluation; regional accrediting associations to measure outcomes and to publish their results; or state governments to defer more readily to either institutional self-evaluation or regional accreditation.

Any judgments regarding possible developments along these lines must be based on a knowledge of the key personalities holding leading positions in the states in question. For, to restate the obvious, personal relationships will play a more important role than structures in determining the politics of higher education. Samuel Gould, former chancellor of the State University of New York, has probably done an admirable job of capturing this important point.

> . . . the more subtle personal contacts which are the warp and woof of the fabric of this relationship defy rules and definitions and formulas . . . . they are the true means by which the delicate balance of authority, responsibility, and interdependence existing between the university and state government is maintained, or, when matters go awry, is upset. They represent the interplay of personalities, the development of attitudes on the part of these personalities reflecting a clear understanding of respective roles and motivations, and most of all the creation of a climate of mutual trust and respect.[43]

Gould later warns of the damage that caricaturing and stereotyping can do to both sides of the relationship between education and politics and notes that each side has "charlatans and hacks."

Samuel Halperin has produced, more recently, a brief but provocative list of perceptions that politicians and educators have about each other.[44] To say that there is a "great divide" would be an understatement. And yet attempts must be made to understand each other. Klebanoff, Graham, and John Vasconcellos are three state legislators who have communicated the need for such understanding.[45] Donald McNeil and Lee Kerschner are educators who have spoken plainly before a legislative group about problems in the politics of higher education.[46]

It would be helpful, of course, if persons of goodwill from both sides could turn for guidance to a competent literature on the politics of higher education. As the next section indicates, however, although there have been some improvements during the last decade, the state of the art is still quite primitive.

LITERATURE ON THE POLITICS OF HIGHER EDUCATION AT THE STATE LEVEL

For someone needing a quick grasp of the subject, Leonard Goodall's book of readings, which includes a bibliographical review article, by S.K. Gove and C.E. Floyd, is helpful.[47] This review article analyzes the literature from 1968, when a similar article by Gove and Barbara Solomon appeared, to 1975. The recent listing covers fifty-two citations, most of them post-1970. But if one looks for sources combining essentially political analyses and state policy-making perspectives, he will find few indeed: Leon Epstein; Heinz Eulau and Harold Quinley; Goodall, J.B. Holderman, and J.D. Nowlan; Gladys Kammerer; Lederle; Joseph Tucker, Gove and Floyd, C.R. McKibbon, A. Rosenbaum; and, of course, Usdan, Minar, and Hurwitz.[48]

We also have Millett's interesting autobiographical monograph of his years spent deep in the politics of higher education in Ohio and an equally interesting earlier parallel in Arthur Coons's book on his years in California higher education when he headed the survey team that produced the Master Plan in 1960 and later when he participated on the state Coordinating Council for Higher Education.[49] Both Coons and Millett employed an anecdotal rather than a theoretical approach to analysis, but there may be more understanding in the anecdotal hills than in the present theoretical peaks. Certainly both authors offered many rich insights into the politics of higher education in their states.

Somewhat more sensitive to conceptual concerns were the three authors who joined Tucker in presenting the case studies of four states (Illinois, Wisconsin, Nebraska, and Ohio) in the *AAUP Bulletin* in 1973.[50] Each author made an effort to answer the same general questions posed by Tucker in an introductory note. What was missing was any essay that compared the four states, which I, myself, would have had difficulty preparing. This may be a comment on my lack of grounding in systems analysis,[51] or it may be a comment on general weaknesses in the state of the art.

One book from a related field that suggests some interesting procedural ideas is Graham Allison's *Essence of Decision*.[52] In this fascinating work Allison reviews the events of the Cuban missile crisis of 1962 three times from three different, carefully elaborated, theoretical perspectives: a classical perspective of unitary organizations pursuing rational goals; an organizational perspective by which results are viewed as outputs of internal and external forces impinging on complex social organisms; and a political pluralist perspective focusing primarily on actors striving for advantage (power, money, fame, and so forth) in a highly competitive environment. The reader is treated to a literary variation of *Roshomon,* the Japanese film in which the same traumatic event is pictured from three very different subjective perspectives. The results in both cases are very rewarding.

Would it be possible in the future to build a repertoire of good case studies in the politics of state policy making in higher education, using the Allison conceptual models as frameworks for analysis? Then, perhaps, future assessments will report more cheerful news concerning the literature on the politics of higher education.

NOTES

1. John C. Honey and T.W. Hartle, *Federal-State-Institutional Relations in Postsecondary Education* (Washington, D.C.: Syracuse University Research Corp., 1974), p.13.

2. Lanier Cox and Lester Harrell, Jr., *The Impact of Federal Programs on State Planning and Coordination of Higher Education* (Atlanta: Southern Regional Education Board, 1969).

3. Fred Bohen, unpublished staff paper, Carnegie Council, Berkeley, Calif., 1975; Rufus E. Miles, Jr., *A Cabinet Department of Education* (Washington, D.C.: American Council on Education, 1976).

4. See Bohen, staff paper.

5. See Honey and Hartle, *Federal-State-Institutional Relations.*

6. U.S. Office of Education, *Institutional-State-Federal Partnership in Student Assistance* (Washington, D.C.: Government Printing Office, 1974); John Folger, Aims McGuiness, and Richard Millard, *Towards a More Effective Federal/State Partnership Related to Private Higher Education,* prepared by the Education Commission of the States (Washington, D.C.: U.S. Office of Education, 1975).

7. H.L. Summerfield, *Power and Process: The Formulation and Limits of Federal Educational Policy* (Berkeley, Calif.: McCutchan Publishing Corp., 1974); Harland G. and Sue M. Bloland, *American Learned Societies in Transition* (New York: McGraw-Hill, 1974); Chester Finn, "The National Foundation for Higher Education: Death of an Idea," *Change* 4 (March 1972): 22-32; Daniel Moynihan, "Higher Education — The Worst Lobby in Washington," *Public Policy for the Financing of Higher Education,* conference proceedings (Wellesley, Mass.: New England Board of Higher Education, 1971); Stephen K. Bailey, *Education Interest Groups in the Nation's Capital* (Washington, D.C.: American Council on Education, 1975); Thomas Wolanin and Lawrence Gladieux, "The Political Culture of a Policy Arena: Higher Education," in *What Government Does,* ed. Matthew Holden, Jr., and Dennis Dresang (Beverly Hills, Calif.: Sage Publications, 1975).

8. Laurence Iannaccone and Peter J. Cistone, *The Politics of Education,* ERIC

Clearinghouse on Educational Management (Eugene: University of Oregon, 1974); Michael W. Kirst and Edith K. Mosher, "Politics of Education," *Review of Educational Research* 39 (December 1969): 623-641.

9. Lester G. Anderson, "Does the Difference Make a Difference?" in *Reflections on University Values and the American Scholar,* ed. Lester G. Anderson *et al.* (University Park: Center for the Study of Higher Education, Pennsylvania State University, 1976); Carnegie Commission on Higher Education, *The University as an Organization,* ed. James Perkins (New York: McGraw-Hill, 1973).

10. Carnegie Commission on Higher Education, *Continuity and Discontinuity: Higher Education and the Schools* (New York: McGraw-Hill, 1973), pp. 101-102.

11. M. Usdan, D. Minar, and E. Hurwitz, *Education and State Politics* (New York: Teachers College Press, 1969).

12. *Ibid.,* p. 182.

13. *Ibid.,* p. 171.

14. For a direct reference to a recent "fight" between public schools and higher education over $10 million in Ohio, see John D. Millett, *Politics and Higher Education* (University: University of Alabama Press, 1974).

15. Robert Berdahl, *Statewide Coordination of Higher Education* (Washington, D.C.: American Council on Education, 1971); Roald F. Campbell and Tim L. Mazzoni, Jr., *State Governance Models for the Public Schools* (Columbus: Educational Governance Project, Ohio State University, 1974); L.V. Ginger and J.C. Pittenger, "Should the States Have Secretaries of Education?" *Compact* 8 (January-February 1974): 14-16; Fred Harcleroad, *Institutional Efficiency in State Systems of Public Higher Education* (Tucson: University of Arizona, 1975), p. 6; Virginia Commission on State Governmental Management, *Staff Documents: Executive Management Responsibilities,* vol. 1 (Richmond: the Commission, 1975), Part 5.

16. Since 1975 this has been called the Educational Coordinating Commission.

17. D. Robert Graham, *Politics and Higher Education Coordination,* Occasional Paper No. 2 (Denver: Education Commission of the States, 1969); Mark Hatfield, as cited in Berdahl, *Statewide Coordination,* p. 235.

18. *Partnership for Progress,* ed. R.H. Kroepsch and D.P. Buck (Boulder, Colo.: Western Interstate Commission for Higher Education, 1967), p. 15.

19. Carnegie Commission on Higher Education, *Governance of Higher Education* (New York: McGraw-Hill, 1973), pp. 106-107.

20. Ginger and Pittenger, "Should the States?" p. 15.

21. Terry Sanford, *Storm over the States* (New York: McGraw-Hill, 1967), p. 199.

22. See Earl F. Cheit, "What Price Accountability?" *Change* 7 (November 1975): 30-36.

23. Carnegie Commission on Higher Education, *The Capitol and the Campus* (New York: McGraw-Hill, 1971), pp. 100-101.

24. Lyman A. Glenny and T.K. Dalglish, *Public Universities, State Agencies and the Law* (Berkeley, Calif.: Center for Research and Development in Higher Education, 1973).

25. Lyman A. Glenny, *Autonomy of Public Colleges* (New York: McGraw-Hill, 1959), p. 13.

26. *Ibid.,* p. 15.

27. Richard Millard, *State Boards of Higher Education*, ERIC Higher Education Research Report No. 4 (Washington, D.C.: American Association of Higher Education, 1976); Carnegie Foundation for the Advancement of Teaching, *The States and Higher Education* (San Francisco: Jossey-Bass, 1976).

28. Millard does an excellent job of explaining the complicated ways that the 1202 state planning bodies (authorized but not mandated by Section 1202 of the federal Higher Education Amendments of 1972) were and are related to existing state agencies. Forty-six states have established such bodies since 1974.

29. Carnegie Commission, *Governance of Higher Education*, pp. 17-18; Berdahl, *Statewide Coordination*, pp. 5-12.

30. See Richard Hofstadter and Walter Metzger, *The Development of Academic Freedom in the United States* (New York: Columbia University Press, 1955); Robert M. MacIver, *Academic Freedom in Our Time* (New York: Columbia University Press, 1955); *Academic Freedom: The Scholar's Place in Modern Society*, ed. Hans W. Baade and Robinson O. Everett (Dobbs Ferry, N.Y.: Oceana Publications, 1964); Russell Kirk, *Academic Freedom: An Essay in Definition* (Chicago: Henry Regnery, 1955).

31. Alexander Brody, *The American State and Higher Education: The Legal, Political and Constitutional Relationships* (Washington, D.C.: American Council on Education, 1935); Committee on Government and Higher Education, *The Efficiency of Freedom* (Baltimore: Johns Hopkins Press, 1959); Malcolm Moos and Francis E. Rourke, *The Campus and the State* (Baltimore: Johns Hopkins Press, 1959); Glenny and Dalglish, *Public Universities;* Harcleroad, *Institutional Efficiency.*

32. A. Wildavsky, *The Politics of the Budgetary Process* (Boston: Little, Brown, 1964).

33. Millard, *State Boards*; Robert Barak, "A Survey of State-Level Academic Program Review Politics and Procedures for Higher Education," doctoral dissertation, State University of New York at Buffalo, 1976.

34. See Folger, McGuiness, and Millard, *Towards a More Effective Federal/State Partnership.*

35. Moos and Rourke, *Campus and the State:* Sanford, *Storm;* Millett, *Politics;* John W. Lederle, "Governors and Higher Education," in *The American Governor in Behavioral Perspective*, ed. Thad Beyle and J. Oliver Williams (New York: Harper and Row, 1972).

36. *Report on a Study of Postsecondary Education Policy Development in Four State Legislatures* (Kansas City, Mo.: Citizens Conference on State Legislatures, 1975).

37. E.G. Crane, *Legislative Review of Program Effectiveness* (Albany: Institute for Public Policy Alternatives, State University of New York, 1975).

38. Moos and Rourke, *Campus and the State*; Stephen K. Bailey, "The Limits of Accountability," remarks for Regents Trustees Conference, New York, 1973; *id.,* "Education and the State," in *Education and the State*, ed. John Hughes (Washington, D.C.: American Council on Education, 1974).

39. Howard Klebanoff, "Let's Get Legislators and Educators on the Same Team for a Change," *Compact* 10 (Summer 1976): 10-12.

40. D.H. Pingree, J.T. Murphy, and D.B. Weatherspoon, "Legislative Program Evaluation and Higher Education," *Higher Education in New England* 15 (Spring 1975).

41. *Evaluating Institutions for Accountability,* ed. Howard Bowen (San Francisco: Jossey-Bass, 1974), p. 121.

42. Roger Heyns, "Renewal, Financing, Cooperation: Tasks for Today," *Educational Record* 54 (Winter 1973): 36.

43. Samuel B. Gould, "The University and State Government: Fears and Realities," *Campus and Capitol,* ed. W. Minter (Boulder, Colo.: Western Interstate Commission for Higher Education, 1966), p. 4.

44. Samuel Halperin, "Politicians and Educators: Two World Views," *Phi Delta Kappan* 56 (November 1974): 189-191.

45. Klebanoff, "Let's Get Legislators"; Graham, *Politics and Higher Education*; John Vasconcellos, "Let's Do Something about Distrust between Educators and Politicians," *Compact* 8 (May-June 1974): 2-4.

46. Donald McNeil, "Higher Education Issues and the Legislative Process," *On Target: Key Issues of Region, State and Campus,* Ninth Biennial Legislative Work Conference on Higher Education, Proceedings (Boulder, Colo.: Western Interstate Commission for Higher Education, 1976); Lee R. Kerschner, "Legislation and the Campus: The Relationship of the Political Process to Postsecondary Education — A Plea for Restraint," *ibid.*

47. Leonard E. Goodall, *State Politics and Higher Education* (Ann Arbor, Mich.: Edwards Brothers, 1976).

48. Leon D. Epstein, *Governing the University* (San Francisco: Jossey-Bass, 1974); Heinz Eulau and Harold Quinley, *State Officials and Higher Education* (New York: McGraw-Hill, 1970); Leonard E. Goodall, J.B. Holderman, and J.D. Nowlan, "Legislature and University: The Uneasy Partnership," *Educational Record* 52 (Winter 1971): 36-41; Gladys M. Kammerer, "The State University as a Political System," *Journal of Politics* 31 (May 1969): 289-310; Lederle, "Governors"; Joseph Tucker, "The Politics of Public Higher Education," S.K. Gove and C.E. Floyd, "Illinois," C.R. McKibbon, "Nebraska," A. Rosenbaum, "Wisconsin," and J. Tucker, "Ohio," *AAUP Bulletin* 59 (Autumn 1973): 286-324; Usdan, Minar, and Hurwitz, *Education and State Politics.*

49. Millett, *Politics*; Arthur Coons, *Crises in California Higher Education* (Los Angeles: Ward Ritchie Press, 1968).

50. See *AAUP Bulletin* 59 (Autumn 1973): 286-324.

51. For a careful analysis applied to educational policy making for the schools and the New York legislature, see M.M. Milstein and R.E. Jennings, *Educational Policy-Making and the State Legislature: The New York Experience* (New York: Praeger, 1973).

52. Graham Allison, *Essence of Decision* (Boston: Little, Brown, 1971).

SELECTED REFERENCES

Adrian, Charles R. *State and Local Governments,* 2d edition. New York: McGraw-Hill, 1967.

Basic Facts about Tuition and Educational Opportunity. Washington, D.C.: American Association of State Colleges and Universities, 1976.

Bowen, Howard. "Systems Theory, Excellence and Values: Will They Mix?" Thirty-first National Conference on Higher Education of the American Association for Higher Education, Chicago, 1976.

Budig, Gene A. *Governors and Higher Education.* Lincoln: University of Nebraska Press, 1969.

Conant, James B. *Shaping Educational Policy.* New York: McGraw-Hill, 1964.

Cremin, L.S. *The Genius of American Education.* Pittsburgh: University of Pittsburgh Press, 1965.

Finkelstein, Martin. *The Incentive Grant Approach in Higher Education: A 15 Year Record.* Washington, D.C.: Postsecondary Education Convening Authority, 1975.

Gladieux, Lawrence E., and Wolanin, Thomas R. *Congress and the Colleges: The National Politics of Higher Education.* Lexington, Mass.: Lexington Books, 1976.

————. "The Politics of Private Higher Education in Washington." *Public Policy and Private Higher Education.* Ed. David Breneman and Chester Finn. Washington, D.C.: Brookings Institution, forthcoming.

Halperin, Samuel. "Is the Federal Government Taking over Education?" *Compact* 10 (Summer 1976): 2-4.

Iannaccone, Laurence. *Politics in Education.* New York: Center for Applied Research in Education, 1967.

Ladd, Edward T. *Sources of Tension in School-University Collaboration.* Atlanta: Urban Laboratory in Education, 1969.

Lindblom, Charles. *The Policy-Making Process.* Englewood Cliffs, N.J.: Prentice-Hall, 1968.

Mauer, George. *Crises in Campus Management.* New York: Praeger, 1976.

McKenna, Jon F. "Partisans and Provincials: The Political Milieu of State-Supported Education in Illinois, 1870-1920." Yale Higher Education Program Working Paper, YHEP-5, New Haven, Conn., May 1976.

Riedel, James A., ed. *New Perspectives in State and Local Politics.* Waltham, Mass.: Xerox College Publishing, 1971.

Sharkansky, Ira. *The Maligned States.* New York: McGraw-Hill, 1972.

Wingfield, Clyde J., ed. *The American University: A Public Administration Perspective.* Dallas: Southern Methodist University Press, 1970.

10 Priority Issues in the Politics of Higher Education

The Courts and the Rules of the Game

David W. Leslie

Will the courts alter substantially the way the game of higher education is played? As parties to educational disputes find their interests affected by decisions to economize, reorganize, or reform schools and colleges, they seek increasingly to defend those interests in court. It can be argued that issues of power, around which unmediated conflict frequently revolves, are transmuted and defused once a court is called in, and issues of "right" become the currency used in the test of will. Because the content of rights affects the normatively correct resolution of conflict, the courts have become an extremely important lever for the formerly powerless.

Three important areas of litigation seem to pose challenges to current standards and procedures for operating the nation's schools and colleges. These challenges ultimately confront educators with basic political questions. First, developments in equal protection and related statutory areas suggest reassessment of the distribution of educational finances. Second, due process of law, having been extended to protect students and faculty in public institutions, now poses important challenges to the discretion of school and college officials even where the very substance of the educational process is concerned. And, finally, standards of good faith appear ripe for review in some settings with the potential result that decision making will have to become more open to participation by those affected by administrative action.

EQUAL OPPORTUNITY OR EQUAL EFFECTS?

Developments in the past twenty years suggest that the norms—if imposed from outside—can greatly alter the balance of influence among educational interest groups. The classic cases are now an integral part of current educational reform since many go to the very heart of traditional practice. *Brown* v. *Board of Education*,[1] the most profound of all in terms of cultural and economic effect, provided minority groups with some of the influence they needed to break down separate and unequal school systems. The legal fallout from *Brown* is with us yet, as minorities (and others) push for equal financing, equal treatment of the sexes, and compensatory treatment leading ultimately to equality of effect for the handicapped and for those whose native language hinders achievement in English-speaking schools.

Current doctrine related to equal protection guarantees only equality of treatment and opportunity. Should the arguments in regard to civil liberties prevail, however, the whole map of education might change. The very substance of education may shift from the universal focus to the individual focus. Patricia Cross's ideal of "education for each" will supplant the more traditional "education for all."[2] Special treatment for each student, consistent with his goals and needs, will be required to guarantee equality of result.

Lau v. *Nichols*[3] raised a very close test of the question. The Supreme Court was asked to rule on the rights of Chinese-speaking students in the schools of San Francisco to instruction in their native language. The plaintiffs' petition for certiorari[4] was an eloquent plea for interpreting the equal protection clause in terms of the equality of effect. Justice William Douglas' majority opinion condemned the practice of providing instruction in English to students who could in no way benefit from it. Yet he found a statutory basis,[5] rather than a constitutional one, for invalidating the practice. The effect was to restrict the test to the sensitive area of equal rights for minority racial groups where minimal evidence of discriminatory practices will stimulate close judicial scrutiny.

Against this background, it is increasingly likely that arguments for equality of effect will succeed, whether or not issues of equal protection are raised. Statutes now protect racial minorities, physically and mentally handicapped persons, women, and other groups from discrimination by recipients of federal funds. If a member of any protected group could show an intrinsic inability to benefit from existent programs because of the inherent qualities of that particular group, he or she might force creation of compensatory programs. What *Brown* and the equal protection clause did for racial minorities, statutory protection may well accomplish for other groups.

State courts may provide a second important route to successful litigation in cases concerning the equality of effect. The case related to school finance in New Jersey,[6] for example, provided a closer legal approximation to substantive equality as a criterion for distributing funds to school districts than did *San Antonio Independent School District* v. *Rodriguez*.[7] How far state courts go, however, will naturally depend on the political and legal climate of each state. But it is possible that the revolution begun by the *Brown* decision, having stalled from the top (in some people's view), may find new life in progress from the bottom.

That is an idealistic suggestion, however, because equality of effect requires, virtually by definition, an unequal application of available resources. Redistribution from haves to have-nots is essential if the latter, however defined, are to be treated compensatorily. The practical political questions are immense. Should elite, selective colleges make financial sacrifices to see that open-door colleges have enough to perform remedial work for the large numbers who need it? Should higher levels of education take a backseat to early childhood and elementary education where there is arguably more pedagogical leverage? Should bedroom suburbs subsidize inner cities so that the advantages enjoyed by middle-class children can be more effectively distributed to others who lack them? In a time of economic stress, one suspects that the ethical dimensions of these questions will provide less compelling arguments than will the goring of scarce oxen. All of these questions will doubtless be thrashed out in one form or another across fifty states in the coming years.

DUE PROCESS AND SUBSTANTIVE DISCRETION

A second decision whose full impact has yet to be felt is *Dixon* v. *Alabama State Board of Education*.[8] Foreshadowing the demise of the distinction between rights and privileges and hastening the demise of in loco parentis (particularly in higher education), *Dixon* extended rights of due process to students faced with expulsion from public schools and colleges. Its progeny have gone far beyond the merely procedural model *Dixon* established and have reshaped the relations of students and their parents (as well as of faculty) to the school.

Substantive due process places direct constraints on administrative authority. It requires that policy and practice be founded on an educational rationale as well as on legitimately delegated authority. And, following *Tinker* v. *Des Moines Independent Community School District,* certain forms of behavior by students are untouchable by school disciplinary regulations because the Constitution protects them.[9] Although the courts continue to grant wide discretionary authority to school officials, there are significant signs that the courts will shift the school's burden from procedure to substance and require stricter justification for policy.

David Kirp sounded a warning in 1973 in his article on "schools as sorters," suggesting that substantive due process would be violated where no rational basis existed for sorting decisions.[10] Classifying students, if it results in racial imbalance, has been "strictly scrutinized" in a number of major cities, and the underlying rationale for classification schemes has failed the test, most notably in Washington, D.C.[11] Poor reliability of individual scores and lack of predictive validity in tests have been the villains.

To date, this kind of scrutiny applied to administrative policy has arisen largely from cases concerning equal protection. *Georgia Association of Educators* v. *Nix* suggests that many classification decisions will fail even the test of having a rational basis, a much more lenient standard, and one that would be applied in a substantive due process case.[12] Fairly typical of recent employment testing cases in its factual basis, *Georgia Association of Educators* found a scheme for certification of teachers using the National Teacher Examination to have relied on test scores with no data showing either predictive validity or validity of the cutoff score. The decision is important legally because it points out the failure of the scheme to meet even the rational basis test under traditional equal protection analysis. The door is open — one assumes — to more direct judicial examination of rationales for policy.

Cases of sexual discrimination have led to a similar judicial search for a new level of scrutiny. Because the Supreme Court has thus far failed to declare sex a suspect classification, and because the rational basis test left too many invidiously discriminatory practices intact, lower federal courts seem to have created an intermediate test, called "strict rationality" in *Berkelman* v. *San Francisco Unified School District.*[13] It is referred to elsewhere as the "rationality scrutiny" test.[14] But whatever it is called, it suggests that the judge will apply a "means-based" test to a policy resulting in unequal treatment of the sexes. Does the practice actually foster the accomplishment of legitimate policy goals? Is the method precise enough to accomplish *only* what it is supposed to? Do the side effects of the practice invalidate it? Is it a carefully rationalized method?

The Supreme Court left the status of this emerging test unclear in *Craig* v. *Boren*.[15] Justice William Brennan's majority opinion struck down Oklahoma's law restricting sales of 3.2 percent beer to males twenty-one and over, but allowing sales to females as young as eighteen. Though the opinion was cast in terms that reflected just this line of precedents—beginning with *Reed* v. *Reed*[16]—several concurring justices demurred on the question of whether the opinion should be interpreted to warrant reliance on the test in future cases. Justice Lewis Powell's candid concurrence suggested a continuing disagreement on the Court over this issue.

If substantive due process incorporates these stricter tests of the rationality of administrative acts, at least two important consequences may result. First, the courts will be more open to claims of interest groups that different *means* should be used to accomplish goals of education. Second, even where legitimate ends are a matter of consensus, the public forum may supplant professional discretion as the level at which rationales for practice are hammered out. The need to convince and persuade will become more pronounced. If there are professional reasons for operating in a certain way, they will have to be articulated and defended. If methods are only matters of convention or administrative convenience, they may not withstand attack.

Developments in the area of procedural due process can only reinforce these trends toward stricter scrutiny: the right to decide is coming under increasingly tighter procedural circumscription. *Goss* v. *Lopez*[17] went a long way toward imposing the due process model on even the most trivial of disciplinary situations, but a more recent district court decision clarified the potential of due process for altering the balance of power in matters of policy.[18] This case involved placement of students in special education programs (and out of them as well). Treating education as a property right, the opinion extended to parents certain rights under the Fourteenth Amendment: to notice of the basis on which the classification of their child was made, to inspect the evidence on which the decision concerning their child was based, to introduce additional evidence that might affect the school's evaluation, and to be guaranteed that *all* evidence so gathered would be considered in the final determination. Parents might, therefore, develop an independent medical or psychological profile of their child that could directly controvert that of the school and, thus, could argue for different treatment of the child than what the school had planned. Because of the relatively primitive state of education qua science, the wide disagreements among putative experts, and legitimate differences over the very goals of education, it is not hard to foresee the potential for havoc in this decision. Only a few challenges are needed to expose the weakness of rationales, and the danger is that many practices will appear irrational if challenged on substantive grounds. In any case, due process seems to be the vehicle by which a right to mount such a challenge can be achieved.

Thus, both prongs of the due process clause may serve to challenge administrative discretion that has traditionally enjoyed great judicial deference. A substantive due process challenge might successfully attack discretion directly, and a procedural due process challenge might do so indirectly by forcing the hand of decision-makers into open scrutiny and substantive rebuttal.

DOES "GOOD FAITH" REQUIRE SHARED AUTHORITY?

A final assault on administrative discretion comes from change in the standard of good faith, which has long been construed as protecting administrators in the exercise of their discretionary powers as long as they avoided arbitrary, capricious, irrational, or discriminatory acts. *Wood* v. *Strickland* suggests that demonstration of good faith requires a more positive exercise of responsibility.[19] In qualifying the traditional meaning of "good faith immunity," the Supreme Court imposed a duty on school board officials to respect the substantive and procedural rights of students. Other instances show how the meaning of good faith may change the role of administrators and boards. In the case of *AAUP, Bloomfield College Chapter* v. *Bloomfield College* it was made clear at the trial court level that establishing a "bona fide" financial exigency requires a full accounting of institutional assets and a real effort to expend available resources for basic institutional purposes.[20] The trial judge was overruled for having exceeded his authority to review management decisions regarding disposition of assets, but it is not clear to me to what extent the subsequent bankruptcy of the college persuaded the appeals court that a basically wrong decision had been reached in the lower court. Perhaps another test of the "bona fide" would work out differently. At any rate, the AAUP has argued in at least one amicus curiae brief that joint faculty-administrative consultation on the existence of an exigency is a bedrock requirement of good faith.[21] The argument has been made that *at least* good faith is easier to demonstrate in court where such consultation has occurred.[22] If these developments gain enough momentum, shared authority may supplant administrative discretion on many issues as the most defensible method of decision making.

In short, the traditional presumption of good faith may begin to erode where unilateral decisions affect important interests. It is difficult to predict which model of shared authority would satisfy standards of good faith. Readily available, however, is the model of collective bargaining. Standards of good faith for negotiation of contracts between labor and management have accrued in both private and public sectors. Although the model is widely accepted at the public school level and is gaining acceptance in higher education, it is most suitable where exclusive representation is acceptable. Many educational issues must be resolved in pluralistic settings where neither exclusivity nor stable procedures are available. By implication, then, the alternative is to "go public." Ad hoc sharing of power and responsibility from issue to issue may become an essential ingredient of good faith. It is, however, a singularly inelegant and most unreliable way to manage. Careful rationalization of the need to preserve discretion, if it is to be preserved, will need to present an affirmative account of how such discretion can be assuredly exercised in good faith.

NOTES

1. *Brown* v. *Board of Education,* 347 U.S. 483 (1954).

2. K. Patricia Cross, *Accent on Learning* (San Francisco: Jossey-Bass, 1976).

3. *Lau* v. *Nichols,* 414 U.S. 563 (1974).

4. Petition for writ of certiorari, *Lau* v. *Nichols,* April 5, 1973, in M. Sorgen *et al., State, School and Family: Cases and Materials on Law and Education* (New York: Matthew Bender, 1973).

5. 42 U.S.C. 2000(d) (Title VI of the Civil Rights Act of 1964).

6. *Robinson* v. *Cahill,* 287 A. 2d 187 (1972).

7. *San Antonio Independent School District* v. *Rodriguez,* 411 U.S. 1 (1973).

8. *Dixon* v. *Alabama State Board of Education,* 294 F. 2d 150 (1961).

9. *Tinker* v. *Des Moines Independent Community School District,* 393 U.S. 503 (1969).

10. David L. Kirp, "Schools as Sorters: The Constitutional and Policy Implications of Student Classifications," *University of Pennsylvania Law Review* 121 (1973): 705-797.

11. *Hobson* v. *Hansen,* 269 F. Supp. 401 (1967), aff'd *sub nom Smuck* v. *Hobson,* 408 F. 2d 175 (1969).

12. *Georgia Association of Educators* v. *Nix*, 407 F. Supp. 1102 (1972).

13. *Berkelman* v. *San Francisco Unified School District*, 501 F. 2d 1264 (1974).

14. Linda J. Cochran, "The Emerging Bifurcated Standard for Classifications Based on Sex," *Duke Law Journal* (1975): 163-187.

15. *Craig* v. *Boren*, 45 L.W. 4057 (1976).

16. *Reed* v. *Reed*, 404 U.S. 71 (1971).

17. *Goss* v. *Lopez*, 419 U.S. 565 (1975).

18. *Cuyahoga County Association for Retarded Children and Adults* v. *Essex*, 411 F. Supp. 46 (1976).

19. *Wood* v. *Strickland*, 420 U.S. 308 (1975).

20. *AAUP, Bloomfield College Chapter* v. *Bloomfield College*, 322 A. 2d 846 (1974), aff'd, 346 A. 2d 615 (1975).

21. American Association of University Professors, amicus curiae, in support of the plaintiff-appellant, *Lumpert* v. *University of Dubuque*, Case No. 2-57568, Supreme Court of Iowa (1975).

22. James L. Petersen, "The Dismissal of Tenured Faculty for Reasons of Financial Exigency," *Indiana Law Journal* 51 (1976): 417-432.

SELECTED REFERENCES

Leslie, David W. "Emerging Challenges to the Logic of Selective Admissions Procedures." *Journal of Law and Education* 3 (1974): 203-220.

Lindquist, Robert E., and Wise, Arthur E. "Developments in Education Litigation: Equal Protection." *Journal of Law and Education* 5 (1976): 1-55.

Wilkinson, J. Harvie III. "*Goss* v. *Lopez:* The Supreme Court as School Superintendent." *The Supreme Court Review, 1975*. Ed. P. Kurland. Chicago: University of Chicago Press, 1976.

Appraising the Influence
of the Educational Lobbies:
The Case of Higher Education

Lawrence E. Gladieux

How effectively is higher education geared to represent its interests with the Carter administration and before the Ninety-fifth Congress?

In the early stages of a previous administration, Daniel Moynihan characterized higher education as the worst lobby in Washington, a judgment no doubt colored by annoyance at the unwillingness of the higher education establishment to support Nixon's legislative program for higher education in 1970. But Moynihan's assessment, though rhetorical and probably overstated, has not been unique.

Higher education's performance in the political arena has typically received low marks from political observers and policymakers. There can be no doubt that all sectors of American higher learning, public and private, have much at stake in Washington and in the state capitals. And yet academe's traditional attitude of innocence and aloofness toward politics has militated against an aggressive, creative strategy in its own behalf. Lobbying does not come naturally or easily to the higher education establishment. There are exceptions, of course, and when one considers the historical growth of government patronage of higher education in this country, one must conclude that its leaders must have been doing something right. But, through most of this history, broad public faith in the value of higher education was prevalent. Academe could, perhaps, afford an arm's length, passive relationship with public policy-making bodies. Normal interest group politics were less important than popular aspirations in fueling the expansion of public support for higher education, particularly in the boom era following World War II.

Federal legislative breakthroughs of the 1960's were achieved more in spite of than because of the efforts of the national educational lobby. The indecisiveness of the higher education groups in the early 1960's actually led one member of Congress, Senator Joseph Clark of Pennsylvania, to chide college and university leaders for not being more forthright and energetic in asserting their needs and priorities. A friendly legislator was telling the would-be lobbyists to get organized.

The altered conditions of the 1970's hardly need recounting. The boom years are gone. Demographic trends point to stabilization, if not shrinkage, in the market for postsecondary education. Job prospects for college graduates and Ph.D.'s have dwindled. Public opinion still holds higher learning in a favorable light, but the mystique is not what it was. Confidence in higher education's benefits to the individual and to society has weakened. Competition for public resources has intensified. And relations between government and higher education have become at once more extensive, complex, and troublesome.

Sustained, sophisticated representation in the political sphere is vital to the future of higher education. There is evidence that the higher education lobby, at least at the federal level, is increasingly

alert to the task and is more professional, more energetic than ever
before.

THE DEBACLE OF 1972 AND ITS AFTERMATH

Recent improvements have developed against the background of
heavy criticism touched off by the Education Amendments of 1972 —
the most far-reaching legislation for colleges and students of the current decade. And yet the representatives of higher education in Washington contributed relatively little to its passage.

Ironically, the major higher education associations had for the
first time spoken loudly and clearly with one voice, which at least some
congressional spokesmen had long encouraged them to do. The
associations had united in urging that the federal government undertake a responsibility for general operating support of institutions of
higher education, and they managed to agree on a preferred formula
based on enrollments. But the associations failed to achieve their
supreme objective. After a protracted struggle, Congress in 1972
made a clear choice to direct federal policy and the majority of federal
funds toward students rather than institutions.

The higher education lobby failed for a number of reasons, including twists of fate and personality clashes in the House committee
that were beyond their control. Political miscalculation and inept
follow-through by the associations also played a part. It is clear, in
retrospect, that the associations bet on the wrong horse when they
placed their hopes in Representative Edith Green. Despite her strategic position as head of the House higher education subcommittee and
her vaunted legislative skill, Mrs. Green did not have the strength to
prevail on the issue of institutional aid. While the alliance with her
was a reasonable decision at the time, the associations' almost exclusive reliance on one representative was not. They did little to drum up
broader support on the House and Senate committees, which Mrs.
Green needed. The representatives of higher education were notably
inactive once they had enunciated their priority and found a sponsor.

The associations' strategy rankled other legislators, particularly
the chairman of the Senate Education Subcommittee, Claiborne Pell,
who charged that higher education had ignored what was going on in
the Senate. The single-mindedness of the lobbyists concerning institutional aid caused them, moreover, to overlook other crucial dimen-

sions of the emerging legislation, such as Section 1202 which authorized new state postsecondary planning commissions.

Finally, the higher education establishment was roundly indicted for advancing its position without adequate research and data to back it up. Many legislators complained that the associations were unable to supply the information needed to formulate intelligent policy. The harshest congressional critic was Representative John Brademas, who charged a failure of analysis by the higher education community: "We turned to the citadels of reason. We said, 'Tell us what you need,' and they said, 'We need $150 per student because that's what we've been able to agree on.' "[1] One postmortem on the role of the American Council on Education, higher education's lead group in Washington, faulted its tendency to rely on vague statements of opinion from an elite group of distinguished educators rather than hardheaded, sophisticated analyses and data.[2]

SHORING UP SINCE 1972

During the past four years the associations have made substantial changes. It has been a time of political fence mending and reorientation. New attitudes and new sensitivity are reflected in higher education's relations with Capitol Hill. Efforts have been made to generate better data to meet the needs of policymakers. One Dupont Circle, home of most of the major higher education associations, is the locus of much new "policy research." The American Council on Education now has its Policy Analysis Service, which, in contrast to the academic orientation of the council's old research office, tries to contribute directly to the policy debates on postsecondary education.

The associations are also trying to anticipate and take the initiative on emerging issues, rather than always reacting to and having to catch up with events. And they are striving for better access and greater leverage within the executive branch as well as within Congress. Mutual disregard between higher education and the Nixon administration closed off the associations from key decision points in the executive machinery. Lines of communication began to reopen under Ford. Under the Carter administration the associations have a chance to restore the ease of access they enjoyed during the 1960's.

The associations' efforts to recoup have won them at least a measure of new respect in Washington. Senator Pell, for example, said that he had "received much valuable information from the associations . . . as we have begun to extend and amend the 1972 legislation . . . . The end result has not been an inflexible position such as that which the higher education community presented in 1972. Rather, we have been exposed to what I believe is a healthy clash of issues and ideas."[3]

THE 1976 AMENDMENTS

The "healthy clash" Pell referred to was focused primarily on the federal student aid programs under Title IV of the Higher Education Act. With their top priority—institutional aid—relegated to a back burner, the associations had adjusted their sights and were zeroing in on the intricacies of programs designed to reduce financial barriers for students seeking postsecondary education. The goals of "access" and "choice" became code words in a debate over who gets what, where, and how in federal assistance to students.

The dollars at stake in this area are substantial and growing. Total need-based federal student grants, work-study aid, and direct loan assistance have more than tripled since 1972, reaching over $2.7 billion in the 1977-78 academic year. There were various proposals to recast such aid during the Ninety-third and Ninety-fourth Congresses, but the higher education community found itself divided as each reform scheme created potential winners and losers among different types of institutions.

In the end, Congress chose not to overhaul the student aid programs, but, rather, to extend them for another four years with a series of refinements and provisions designed to curb abuse and strengthen their administration. The relatively noncontroversial Education Amendments of 1976 were signed into law on October 12.

Even though the associations were split on the major issues of student aid, they were much more vitally engaged in the recent legislative round than they had been in 1972. They were part of the mainstream of debate, and they helped shape the result. The higher education community either originated or had a hand in developing a number of legislative improvements in student aid as well as other program areas. Individually and collectively, the associations proved persistent and attentive to detail in pressing their interests.

At the stage where the legislation was being considered in conference committee, the American Council on Education and a number of the other associations issued a statement urging either the House or Senate position on seventy-seven points of difference between the two bills. Of the seventy-seven, sixty-nine were ultimately resolved in line with the associations' preferences.

The concerns of higher education in Washington, of course, extend well beyond the programs administered by the Office of Education as revised in the recent Education Amendments. A host of regulatory and programmatic issues affecting higher education cut across more than forty federal agencies. At any given time, the associations may be operating on several fronts—from appropriations for the National Science Foundation or health manpower to postal regulations, Affirmative Action, reform of the copyright law, problems concerning energy, privacy of student records, or indirect costs on federal research grants.

Led by the American Council on Education, the associations are becoming increasingly aggressive in their response to federal regulatory thrusts, and they have recently won some significant victories. Following heavy pressure from the higher education groups, for example, the Veterans Administration has abandoned its proposed procedures for implementing the "85-15" rule, which would have posed cumbersome problems of data collection and reporting for colleges enrolling recipients of assistance under the GI Bill. Likewise, the Internal Revenue Service has abandoned its plan for taxing tuition remission benefits offered to college employees and their dependents.

THE QUESTION OF STYLE

The political self-consciousness of higher education and its concern for more effective representation in Washington are clearly growing. Further recent evidence is the launching in mid-1976 of the National Association of Independent Colleges and Universities. For the first time, private institutions have an exclusive lobby of their own, designed to be a forceful and clear voice of the independent sector of higher education in the United States. The Association of American Universities is also moving to strengthen its presence in Washington. And students themselves are now on the Washington scene with the effective presence of the National Student Lobby and the Coalition of Independent College and University Students.

The style of the higher education lobby is also changing. The associations, for example, are now full-fledged participants in the

Committee for Full Funding of Education Programs, whereas a few years ago they were skittish about joining this direct-action lobbying coalition. (Representatives of higher education now constitute a near majority on the steering group of the committee.)

And yet political advocacy on behalf of higher education remains low key relative to other claimant groups in society. Professional lobbyists point out that higher education fails to utilize the full range of political resources at its command. There are colleges in nearly every congressional district. There are massive numbers of alumni, trustees, and administrators, not to mention faculty and students, who are affected by governmental action toward higher education. The potential power base of colleges and universities is relatively untapped. And higher education does little to compensate its friends in the legislature. The higher education lobby has taken virtually no initiative in the area of electoral politics. By contrast, the predominant groups representing elementary and secondary teachers, the National Education Association and the American Federation of Teachers, have moved heavily into this area in recent years.

The tax-exempt status of the national higher education associations, which nominally bars lobbying, partly conditions their style. The political undermobilization of higher education, however, has deeper roots. Academic leadership is still in the process of shedding its apolitical and antipolitical attitudes that can be traced far back into the history of education. Distaste for the art and practice of politics is mixed with a genuine concern that aggressive political action would somehow be inappropriate to the academic enterprise and might even be counterproductive.

ONE VOICE VS. MANY

The higher education establishment also faces the perennial question of whether to submerge its internal differences and strive for a united front in appealing to Congress and other policy-making bodies or to let each interest within higher education act independently. Critics of the higher education lobby, including members of Congress, have offered conflicting guidance over the years on which is the more effective strategy.

Given the inherent pluralism of the constituency, it is not surprising that organized representation of higher education in Washington sometimes seems a babble of conflicting voices. Objective interests frequently diverge among higher education's many segments, levels, and professional groups. Patterns of cooperation and solidarity will continue, as in the past, to ebb and flow depending on the issue and the interests involved.

Harold Enarson has noted "a kind of mutual exhaustion in higher education and government, not surprising after a decade of upheaval and rapid change."[4] The representatives of higher education in Washington must carry on, nonetheless, struggling from day to day in what seems to be an ever-widening arena of government relations with academe. It remains to be seen how effective they will be in establishing access to and influence with the Carter administration, but it is clear that higher education no longer qualifies, if it ever once did, as Washington's "worst lobby."

NOTES

1. "Interview with John Brademas," *Higher Education Daily*, July 11, 1975, 2.

2. John Honey and John Crowley, "The Future of the American Council on Education: A Report on Its Governmental and Related Activities," mimeographed (Washington, D.C., September 1972).

3. As cited in William A. McNamara, "The Wallflower Dances: Education Lobbying Steps Out," *CASE Currents* 2 (January 1976): 6.

4. Harold Enarson, "The Endangered Partnership," *ibid.* (September 1976): 8.

SELECTED REFERENCES

Bailey, Stephen K. *Education Interest Groups in the Nation's Capitol.* Washington, D.C.: American Council on Education, 1975.

Gladieux, Lawrence E., and Wolanin, Thomas R. *Congress and the Colleges: The National Politics of Higher Education.* Lexington, Mass.: Lexington Books, 1976.

King, Lauriston R. *The Washington Lobbyists for Higher Education.* Lexington, Mass.: Lexington Books, 1975.

Pease, Donald. "Higher Education Needs to Lobby." *Chronicle of Higher Education,* November 27, 1972.

Wolanin, Thomas R. "The National Higher Education Associations: Political Resources and Style." *Phi Delta Kappan* 58 (October 1976): 181-185.

Political and Programmatic Impacts of
State-wide Governance of Higher Education

James F. Nickerson
Jacob O. Stampen

That winning combination is a yet unidentified balance which would retain most of the advantages of central control with a minimal sacrifice of institutional sovereignty.

D. Kent Halstead
Statewide Planning in Higher Education (HEW, 1974)

It was pointed out that the anti-legislative, anti-government bureaucracy feeling in this country may be as strong as the anti-higher education feeling. In any case, the two groups share a common problem — explaining what their efforts accomplish — which might be the basis for dialogue.

Marvin W. Peterson
"Innovation, Outcomes and the
State Budgeting Process" (Institute for
Educational Leadership, 1976)

The boundaries of higher education are expanding rapidly. The existing forms of governance in higher education are increasingly being overextended by the issues — assuring access, serving new clienteles, supplying new services, providing public aid for private institutions, and dealing with state-wide collective bargaining. There have been, as a consequence, a shift of controls and decision making toward the state level and a consequent lessening of institutional effectiveness and identity.

It seems clear that concentration of controls at the state level cannot continue unchecked. Neither can we foresee a sudden return to the former levels of institutional immunity and autonomy. The restoration and maintenance of a healthy balance between centralized policy and control at state levels and institutional sovereignty are essential for the public purpose and for institutional vitality. It is likely, therefore, that greater efforts will be made to balance the advantages of central control and institutional sovereignty.

This essay examines the political and programmatic impacts of state-wide governance of higher education. Political factors affecting state-wide governance are discussed first. Some observed institutional impacts of current trends and issues in governance are then illustrated. Finally, factors that may lead to changes in state-wide governance are presented.

THE POLITICAL ENVIRONMENT

It is a current paradox that, while the value of higher education and the appropriate level of investment in it are being questioned, the boundaries of governance of state higher education are expanding. As a reflection of this situation, the number of decisionmakers in higher education has increased, as has the number of issues, and resolution of these issues has gravitated toward state political arenas.

Participants

Private colleges and universities, community colleges, vocational-technical schools, K-12 education, and even proprietary schools have increasingly participated in decision making. The list of issues in state-wide governance compiled by the Education Commission of the States and the concerns under review in this volume verify this fact. Also, the federally initiated concept of postsecondary education, of which higher education is only a part, is rapidly becoming a reality. Lyman Glenny and his colleagues document the fact that governors, legislators, and especially their agencies and staffs have become more and more influential in higher education policy making.[1] At the same time, faculty leaders are being eclipsed by managers in higher education.

Carol Van Alstyne and Sharon Coldren document the growing presence of congressmen, new social constituencies, and federal regulatory agencies in higher education decision making.[2] Finally, the new participants have altered relationships among traditional constituencies in higher education.

Governmental Control

Since World War II, the trend has been toward centralizing authority in higher education coordinating and governing boards.[3] In 1976 twenty-one states had governing boards, and the remaining twenty-nine states had coordinating boards. During the period from World War II to the late 1960's the trend was toward coordination to provide increased access. Since then the characteristic pattern has been governance to control costs.

A recent study of budgeting in higher education in the fifty states, however, describes the control of policy passing beyond boards to governors, agencies of the executive branch, legislators, and legislative committee staffs.[4] A survey by the American Association of State Colleges and Universities (AASCU) affirms these conclusions concerning the shifting balance of influence.[5] The AASCU found that in thirty-five states governors and legislators were playing a more active role in policy making. The issues with which they were involved typically ranged from general policy and internal transfers of funds to reporting, staffing, and printing. The study by the AASCU determined that governors and legislators were not specifically trying to influence the content of academic programs, although these programs were often substantially affected by tightening of the parameters for decision making. Thus, though the governors and legislators were mainly concerned with controlling costs, they were also involved with many other kinds of issues. A recent study by S.V. Martorana and W.G. McGuire on state control and community colleges illustrates that state actions are not unidirectional, but rather reflect conflicting themes and a wide array of issues. The net effect of involvement is to increase state control at the expense of institutional policy boards.[6]

Illustrative Issues

Among the wide array of currently active issues, two were selected to illustrate the impact of the state political process on the governance of higher education: access to higher education promoted by public aid to private institutions and state-wide collective bargaining.

Those who believe that higher education should be financed through students (economists advocating systems of high tuition and high student aid and many advocates of private higher education) argue that such policies can assure equitable access to higher education, save state tax revenues, and eliminate much of the need for excessive state regulation of higher education by allowing students, voting with their checkbooks, to determine the viability of institutions. Governors and legislators also hear opposing views that such an approach may not be as equitable or inexpensive as asserted, and might even expand the state's commitment to financing and governing not only private colleges and universities but proprietary schools as well. Richard Millard sums up the current status of this issue: "In spite of what has been a federal thrust toward a 'free market' concept — based in part on the assumption that the structure of higher and postsecondary education should be determined primarily by students and where they take their money — few if any states are willing to go back to institutional laissez faire . . . . The trend is in the opposite direction and the alternative to coordination by a state board is direct control of the postsecondary education system by executive and legislative mandate."[7]

States are cautious about financing what they cannot control, at least to some degree. Most states, however, have compromised in this debate by expanding both aid to students and control over institutions benefiting from such aid. Observers note that this kind of decision can mean that state-wide higher education bodies will have an excessive number of issues to resolve, and failure to resolve them invites increased intervention by governors and legislators.

State-wide or system-wide collective bargaining is another issue that disturbs existing systems of governance. Centralized governance creates the need for centralized response. In states where employee relations boards have ruled that either the governors or the state higher education system is the employer of faculty, the following tendencies have been observed. Faculty organize on a state-wide basis and deal directly with their employers. College presidents tend to lose the choice of leading their institutions either as representatives of the faculty or as representatives of their boards. Students must organize on a state-wide basis to protect their interests. Governing boards, in cases where governors are judged to be the employers, lose important prerogatives, and faculty dealing directly with governors and legislators invite increased state intervention. Institutional governance thus becomes state-wide.

These examples illustrate how state-wide governance of higher education has increasingly become a part of the state political process. In the case of access and aid to private institutions, the issues are too broad and too basic to be dealt with outside the political arena, and they stimulate a more active state role in the governance of higher education. In a similar way, state-wide collective bargaining creates a need for academic constituencies to participate in the political process at the state level, thus altering academic structures all the way down to the departmental level.

Programmatic-Institutional Impacts

A common complaint among institutional leaders is that decisions having the force of law come from many different sources.

Governors and state and federal legislators make decisions. Uncoordinated regulatory agencies, both state and federal, interpret those decisions, and, to protect themselves from the charge of failing to reflect the intent of statutes or directives, they often overregulate or ask for more than is required. As a result, institutions may expend scarce resources for fruitless or duplicative endeavors.

In states where governors and legislators have authorized readjustment of institutional program priorities, governing boards have found their options limited to the elimination or reduction of programs. Authority to reinvest savings in stronger programs or in new programs is not readily given. Donald Smith provides an excellent example of this kind of impact in Wisconsin.[8]

Redirecting funds and resources from programs for traditional constituencies (eighteen to twenty-two-year-olds) to programs for the new constituencies (such as the lifelong learner, the part-time student, the special student sponsored by business, industry, or the military) or to various governmental and community service agencies puts new strains on both institutional and state-wide governance. Institutions, wishing to serve new constituencies in new ways, need the incentive of state-wide support for planning and programs. Yet, as Frank Bowen and Eugene Lee have observed, systems tend to innovate slowly.[9]

Glenny reports that preauditing and the displacement of state funds with nonstate funds have become routine practices in many state budgetary processes. Both practices severely constrain the governance of institutions and negatively affect programs. Studies of the governance of higher education have long opposed preauditing.[10]

In states where coordinating and governing boards have assumed the supervision of private institutions, such as in New York and North Carolina, private institutions have come increasingly under either direct or indirect state control. New York has even ordered elimination of programs in private institutions. In North Carolina the public higher education system has assumed the responsibility of overseeing the requests for appropriations made by private institutions.

The overriding issue of how to retain the advantages of central control with minimal sacrifice of institutional sovereignty, however, is far from being resolved, and tensions appear to be increasing among governors, legislators, and educators. While the negative effects of current developments in governance are not felt equally in every state and while most public and private institutions are fiscally healthy, the majority of students of governance feels that the danger of overpoliticizing higher education is real. And yet, because of the range of issues confronting state higher education, it seems equally clear that existing structures may not be able to deal effectively with the convergence of issues, and few observers expect a return to full institutional autonomy.

How then can state-wide governance evolve? Are the old values of governance at the institutional level obsolete? Can collective bargaining bring a new order? How much of current uncertainty is caused by the nation's own uncertainty about the future? Will legislators and governors reduce their testing and probing once the future becomes more certain? What forms will the governance of higher education take in the future? Will institutions be able to respond quickly and effectively to the demands of changing constituencies? None of these questions can be answered at this time. We can, however, pose one question for which there may be an answer: Can steps be taken to sustain and strengthen the role of institutions in state-wide governance of higher education?

BUILDING BLOCKS FOR CHANGE

Fred Harcleroad believes that one step that can be taken is to decentralize the management of higher education by assigning clear divisions of responsibility to state higher education agencies and institutions.[11] To accomplish this, he suggests selective use of innovations already under way in industry. For the state, they include decentralizing management, information, and planning and accounting systems among institutions and limiting roles of tightly staffed state-wide higher education bodies to master planning, overall policy, large capital costs, and broad fiscal controls. Institutions, in turn, would be given responsibility for the establishment of local planning goals, local standards of achievement, and local budgets, personnel, and purchasing policies, and minor construction projects. To quote Glenny, Robert Berdahl, and others, "it is ironic that the higher education community that slavishly copied models of industrial corporation governance and control in the past should ignore current corporate patterns of decentralization."[12] If this design were followed, there might be a reduction of conflict among institutions and between institutions and state higher education bodies, thus reducing mutually damaging struggles before legislators and governors.

Glenny, Millard, and others believe that commitment to long-range planning at the state level offers a systematic way of avoiding abrupt imbalances caused by short-term changes in the political climate. If long-range goals were established and reviewed frequently, it might be easier to address systematically the issues and programs of higher education. Because planning would be forward looking, it might be easier to deal with emerging issues and to avoid sudden convergences of issues.

Organizing institutions and their constituencies for more effective participation in state political processes is also being tried. In Florida the state higher education system recently made an open effort to demonstrate its value to local constituencies and legislators. This systematic attempt to inform citizens about the services performed by higher education has reduced ambiguity concerning the value of higher education and has increased state appropriations. Last year the University of Missouri undertook a similarly intended effort which, however, was not made public from the beginning. Rumors of covert political activity spread, and the effort was cited in the press as the cause for firing the university's president. The example of Florida, however, suggests that higher education can demonstrate its case in the public arena and that such efforts may even be appreciated at a time when governors and legislators have sincere questions about the social priority of higher education.

Finally, M.M. Chambers suggests that the courts may answer the question as to who shall govern.[13] In an analysis of recent litigation concerning institutional autonomy, Chambers found that in almost every dispute between state governments and higher education institutions the courts ruled in favor of institutional autonomy.

While the preceding discussion has not been able to predict future forms of governance for higher education, it has pointed out some critical weaknesses. The possibility that higher education will be made a permanent part of the formal state political process, such as becoming a department under a governor, is meeting growing opposition from educators and the constituencies they serve. On the other hand, it seems unlikely that higher education will be financed primarily by students or shaped wholly by their choices, whether paid for by personal funds or by voucher. As Millard and others have suggested, states are unwilling to endorse open-ended financing. In addition, we cannot expect or ask for a return to institutional self-determination without regard for the state's plan or purpose.

It is to be hoped that the restoration and maintenance of a healthy balance between centralized policy and control and institutional sovereignty will emerge from the struggles that lie ahead.

NOTES

1. Lyman A. Glenny *et al.*, *State Budgeting for Higher Education* (Berkeley, Calif.: Center for Research and Development in Higher Education, University of California, 1971).

2. Carol Van Alstyne and Sharon L. Coldren, *The Costs of Implementing Federally Mandated Social Programs at Colleges and Universities* (Washington, D.C.: American Council on Education, 1976).

3. Robert O. Berdahl, *Statewide Coordination of Higher Education* (Washington, D.C.: American Council on Education, 1972).

4. Glenny *et al.*, *State Budgeting*.

5. Jacob O. Stampen and Ronald H. Field, "Relations between State Governments and State Colleges and Universities, 1976," draft prepared for the American Association of State Colleges and Universities, 1976.

6. S.V. Martorana and W.G. McGuire, "Survey Confirms Trend towards State Control," *Community and Junior College Journal* 47 (September 1976): 8-10.

7. Richard M. Millard, *State Boards of Higher Education* (Washington, D.C.: American Association for Higher Education, 1976), p. 57.

8. Donald K. Smith, "Coping, Improvising, and Planning for the Future During Fiscal Decline: A Case Study from the University of Wisconsin System," *The Monday Morning Imagination: Report from the Boyer Workshop on State University Systems* (Princeton, N.J.: Aspen Institute, 1976).

9. Frank M. Bowen and Eugene C. Lee, *The Multi-Campus University* (New York: McGraw-Hill, 1971).

10. See *Coordination or Chaos?* (Denver: Education Commission of the States, 1973).

11. Fred F. Harcleroad, *Institutional Efficiency in State System Public Higher Education* (Washington, D.C.: American Association of State Colleges and Universities, 1975).

12. Lyman A. Glenny *et al.*, *Coordinating Higher Education for the 70's* (Berkeley, Calif.: Center for Research and Development in Higher Education, University of California, 1971), p. 3.

13. M. M. Chambers, *Durability of Reasonable Autonomy for State Universities* (Normal: Department of Educational Administration, Illinois State University, 1976).

Political and Programmatic Impact of
Affirmative Action Policy: The Case of Title IX

Patrick J. Bird

One of the most controversial pieces of legislation of the last ten years became effective with the publication in 1975 of the *Final Title IX Regulation Implementing Education Amendments of 1972 Prohibiting Sex Discrimination in Education.*[1] Congress is generally wary about moving too far ahead of public opinion, especially when such action promises to add stress to the country's educational system. In the face of overwhelming evidence that serious inequities between the sexes existed in educational admissions processes, treatment of students, employment of faculty, and educational programs in general, however, Congress enacted laws that have had a widespread and disturbing impact on both school districts and institutions of higher education.

The purpose of this essay is to explore several basic questions concerning Title IX and its implementing regulations: What federal laws and regulations regarding sexual discrimination in educational institutions preceded Title IX? What is covered under the Title IX regulations? How must institutions comply with Title IX? What are some of the conflicting positions on Title IX? Can Title IX be administered, financed, implemented, and enforced?

PREVIOUS LAWS AND REGULATIONS REGARDING SEXUAL DISCRIMINATION

Several laws and regulations preceded Title IX.[2] The first, Executive Order 11246 (as amended by 11375), which became effective October 13, 1968, forbids discrimination because of sex, race, color, religion, or national origin within the entire work force under federal contract projects. This order embodies the concepts of nondiscrimination and Affirmative Action. Nondiscrimination requires the elimination of all existing discriminatory conditions and the examination of all employment policies to be sure that they do not discriminate, while

Affirmative Action compels the employer to recruit, employ, and promote qualified members of groups that were formerly excluded, even if the exclusion cannot be traced to particular discriminatory actions on the employer's part. Personnel policies and practices covered under Executive Order 11246 relate to recruitment, hiring, nepotism, placement, job classification, job assignment, training, promotion, termination, working conditions, rights and benefits, salary, back pay, leave, pregnancy and childbirth, fringe benefits, child care, and grievance procedures.

In 1971 the federal government stepped into the admissions process of educational institutions by passing the Comprehensive Health Manpower and Nurse Training Act. Under this law programs in health personnel training that receive assistance under either Title VII or Title VIII of the Public Health Service Act cannot practice sexual discrimination in admissions or employment.

Four years after Executive Order 11246 became effective, Congress extended its provisions to employees of most other institutions that do not hold federal contracts. This was accomplished through two laws. The Equal Employment Opportunity Act of 1972 amended Title VII of the Civil Rights Act of 1964 to include all institutions with fifteen or more employees and protects against discrimination in employment on the basis of sex, race, color, religion, or national origin, and covers hiring, upgrading, salaries, fringe benefits, training, and other conditions of employment. The Education Amendments of 1972 (Higher Education Act), among other provisions, amended the Equal Pay Act of 1963 to cover all institutions, and they specifically prohibit discrimination in salary and fringe benefits on the basis of sex.

Title IX of the Education Amendments of 1972, which prohibits sexual discrimination in educational programs that receive federal funds, states: "No person in the United States . . . shall, on the basis of sex, be excluded from participation in, be denied the benefits of, or be subjected to discrimination under any education program or activity receiving federal assistance . . . ." This is similar to Title VI of the Civil Rights Act of 1964 except that Title IX applies to discrimination based on sex rather than on race, color, or national origin, is limited to educational programs and activities, and includes employment practices. The Education Amendments of 1972 became Public Law 92-318 (86 Stat. 235) in June of that year. The preparation of the complex implementing regulations for Title IX required, however, an additional three years. On July 21, 1975, Title IX took effect as the first comprehensive antisexual discrimination law covering students.

COVERAGE UNDER TITLE IX

The provisions of Title IX, discussed below under the five subparts of the regulations, clearly indicate the pervasive way in which the mandate affects educational administration and reveals as well the institutional actions and costs that compliance entails.

Subpart A—Introduction

Effective July 21, 1976, each recipient institution is required to take appropriate steps to eliminate policies and practices that discriminate by sex in admissions, treatment of students, and employment in connection with educational programs or activities. Thus, institutions must certify that their programs or activities benefiting from federal funds will be administered in compliance with the act, publish grievance procedures, and assign an employee to coordinate compliance efforts and to investigate complaints.

Subpart B—Coverage

With regard to admissions, this law applies to vocational, professional, and graduate higher education institutions, public undergraduate institutions, and state education agencies receiving federal financial assistance. The law does not apply to institutions in the process of changing from a single-sex institution under a plan approved by the commissioner of education, institutions controlled by religious organizations if the law is inconsistent with the religious tenets of the organizations, military and merchant marine academies, institutions that have traditionally admitted only students of one sex, and certain youth organizations, such as fraternities and the Boy Scouts. Although admissions policies and practices of private undergraduate institutions are exempt, once a student is admitted, he or she must be treated without discrimination on the basis of sex.

Subpart C—Admissions and Recruiting

No person can, on the basis of sex, be denied or subjected to discrimination in admission except as outlined above under "Coverage." A recipient institution cannot, on the basis of sex, give preference or rank applicants, apply numerical limitations, treat individuals differently, administer or operate any test or admissions criteria, apply prohibitions relating to marital or parental status, show favoritism to applicants from schools that admit predominantly a single sex, or discriminate in recruitment.

Even if employment opportunities in the field are limited, the obligation to comply remains. Exemptions do not extend to professional fraternities, sororities, or societies receiving federal assistance or significant institutional assistance if the organization's admission practices might have a discriminatory effect upon future career opportunities. Though "significant assistance" is not defined in the regulations, if an organization could only exist in its present form with that assistance, it would generally be considered "significant." Institutions cannot make preadmission inquiries concerning marital status; they may, however, ask about various responsibilities such as supporting dependents. The requirement that all foreign students complete Immigration and Naturalization Form 1-20A does not violate these regulations.

Subpart D—Educational Programs and Activities

A person cannot be subjected to sexual discrimination under any educational program or activity, including requirements, aid, benefit, or service. Nor can the institution give significant assistance to any organization, agency, or person that discriminates on the basis of sex in providing aid, benefit, or service to students or employees. Institutions can administer single-sex scholarships or awards if reasonable opportunities are available for members of both sexes. Faculty members may not advise societies that are discriminatory, but institutions may rent rooms to such organizations within the context of the meaning of "significant assistance."

A recipient may not, on the basis of sex, apply different housing rules, regulations, fee requirements, services, or benefits. Single-sex housing may be provided, and an institution may assist an agency, organization, or person that is providing such housing where it is proportionate and comparable in quality and cost. In determining "comparability" of housing, one must consider such factors as cost, location, facilities, conditions of property, and contracts, although some flexibility is allowed. Residency requirements that discriminate on the basis of sex are prohibited. Dormitory hours and other regulations must be the same for both sexes except that hours could differ if the occupants of all dormitories were to choose their policy freely. Separate, but comparable, toilets, locker rooms, and the like are allowed.

Course Offerings. Courses and programs cannot be segregated on the basis of sex. Grouping by ability in physical education classes and separation of students in contact sports, human sexuality classes or units, and choruses where vocal range or quality is a factor are permissible. Separate physical education classes offered on the basis of differing rules of a sport and separate departments of physical education for men and women, even if both departments are open to students of both sexes, are prohibited.

Counseling. A recipient institution cannot practice sexual discrimination in counseling or guiding students or applicants for admission.

Financial Assistance. It is not permissible for a recipient institution to provide differential amounts or types of financial assistance, limit eligibility, apply different criteria for assistance, aid any foundation, trust, or organization whose assistance discriminates by sex, or apply any rule concerning eligibility for assistance that treats the sexes differently with regard to marital or parental status. Financial assistance may be awarded on the basis of sex where members of one sex have historically been underrepresented and the purpose of the aid is to overcome the effects of this underrepresentation; such assistance must, however, be part of an overall program of nondiscriminatory financial aid. Reasonable opportunities for athletic scholarships or grants-in-aid must be available to both sexes in proportion to participation. Separate scholarships or grants-in-aid may be provided for members of each sex as part of separate athletic teams.

A recipient institution may administer or assist in the administration of scholarships established pursuant to wills or trusts, that require such awards to be made to a single sex, provided that the overall effect does not discriminate by sex. Thus, once eligible students have been identified and ranked in the order in which they are to receive aid, awards may be made from both restrictive and nonrestrictive sources. If aid restricted to one sex runs out, however, the institution may make no further awards unless it uses alternative financial resources to achieve nondiscrimination. As an example, a school ranks, independent of sex, a hundred students to receive awards. After awards are made to the first seventy-five, the only funds remaining are restricted to males. The seventy-sixth and seventy-seventh students are males; the seventy-eighth is female; the seventy-ninth and eightieth are males. The school may award aid from its financial pool as long as it does not deviate from its list determined independently of sex. And so the seventy-sixth and seventy-seventh students receive awards. But, unless the school uses other funds to aid the seventy-eighth, it may not pass her by and provide assistance to the seventy-ninth and eightieth.

Employment, Health, and Insurance. A recipient may not, on the basis of sex, discriminate in assisting students to secure employment, in employing students, or in providing insurance and health benefits and may not accept requests or refer students to employers who specify one sex or give preferential consideration by sex unless sex is a bona fide occupational qualification. If full-coverage health service is offered, it must include basic gynecological care regardless of the student's marital status.

A school may have a special voluntary class for pregnant students if instruction is comparable to that offered to nonpregnant students. If disability pay to employees is provided, it must be granted for absence owing to pregnancy, childbirth, false pregnancy, or termination of pregnancy. When a school provides leaves of absence to mothers for the purpose of child care, they must also provide them to fathers.

Athletics. In interscholastic, intercollegiate, club, or intramural athletics no one can be discriminated against on the basis of sex, and a recipient is not allowed to provide athletics separately on this basis. Separate teams are permitted, however, where selection is based upon competitive skill or where the activity is a contact sport. Where a recipient has a team for members of one sex and no such team for the other sex, and the athletic opportunities for members of that sex have previously been limited, members of the excluded sex must be allowed to try out for the team, unless a contact sport is involved. As an alternative, because of varying interests, separate teams may be required.

In order to determine if equal athletic opportunity exists, one must consider the following: Do selection and level of sports accommodate the interests and abilities of both sexes? Are equipment and supplies, scheduling, travel, coaching, tutoring, compensation of coaches and tutors, locker rooms and practice facilities, medical and training facilities and services, housing and dining facilities, and publicity provided equally to both sexes? In this area postsecondary schools have until July 1978 to comply.

Because the courts have consistently considered athletics sponsored by educational institutions to be an integral part of the educational program, athletics are covered under Title IX. Revenue-producing sports are treated as any other sport and are subject to all provisions of the athletic section. Unequal aggregate expenditures for male and female teams do not constitute noncompliance; the relevant consideration is opportunity, not cost.

The regulations require that an institution award a reasonable number of athletic scholarships to members of each sex in proportion to the number of students of each sex participating in athletics, but separate scholarships or grants-in-aid may be provided for members of each sex as part of separate athletic teams. The key to the section on athletic scholarships is reasonableness, not strict proportionality. The participation, relative interests, and athletic proficiency of students of both sexes must be considered.

If athletic programs are not operated separately, awards may not be given separately. Thus, if a school has a coeducational diving team, it must give awards to top divers, irrespective of sex. When a training table is provided for athletes on scholarships, all such athletes should have access to it. Separate male and female teams may operate under different rules.

In accord with the stipulations concerning "significant assistance" discussed under "Subpart C," above, an institution may be violating the law if it provides locker space and attendants to a discriminatory group or organization.

Textbooks. The regulation does not require, prohibit, or abridge in any way the use of particular textbooks or curricular materials.

Subpart E—Employment

No person can, on the basis of sex, be excluded from participation in, be denied the benefits of, or be subjected to discrimination in employment or recruitment, whether full-time or part-time, under any educational program or activity operated by a recipient of federal financial assistance. This regulation pertains to decisions regarding employment, contractual agreements with outside groups, and applicant preference and includes recruitment, hiring, upgrading, promotion, pay rates, job assignments, collective bargaining, leaves, fringe benefits, training support, employee-sponsored activities, and so forth.

COMPLIANCE WITH TITLE IX

In order to comply with Title IX an institution has to follow a number of prescribed practices.

First, the institution must evaluate its current policies and practices concerning admission and treatment of students and employment of both academic and nonacademic personnel working in connection with the institution's educational program. Should any policies or practices not meet the requirements of the law, the institution must modify them.

Second, the institution should appoint at least one employee to be responsible in this area, should give this person the authority to investigate complaints, and should inform students and employees about this person.

Third, grievance procedures should be established and publicized. Effective procedures can often result in settlement without the need for intervention by the federal government.

Fourth, the institution should take specific and continuing steps to notify applicants, students, staff, and all other interested parties that it does not discriminate on the basis of sex.[3]

CONFLICTING POSITIONS ON TITLE IX

Of the 10,000 comments received by the Department of Health, Education, and Welfare throughout the process of developing the Title IX regulations, 123 were submitted by major organizations. Seventy-four institutions of higher learning expressed their concerns as well as groups and organizations representing women, higher education associations, elementary and secondary teachers, students, school boards, school administrators, athletic associations, and governmental commissions. Most comments concerned sports and athletic programs, coeducational physical education classes, sexual stereotyping in textbooks, the impact on fraternities and sororities, scholarships, and employment issues.

To assess the positions of a wide variety of groups on selected issues involved in Title IX, comments received by HEW from these organizations were analyzed by Andres Fishel.[4] His specific intent was to determine the extent to which each organization opposed six key recommendations made by the Women's Equity Action League (WEAL) and Representative Bella Abzug. Below are the issues, with representative supporting and opposition statements.

1. *Textbooks.* WEAL and Abzug recommended that the regulations include review and evaluation of textbooks for sexist bias, contending that damaging portraits of females are now contained in

almost all classroom materials. Opponents argued that such a regulation would raise constitutional issues and cause severe financial strain.

2. *Single-Sex Courses.* WEAL and Abzug supported the requirement for integrated physical education classes. They maintained that this is a key issue in assuring equal opportunity in sports and that the present system produces major inequities in physical training. Separate programs, they stated, foster traditional sexual stereotyping. Those who oppose this requirement contended that this regulation infringes on institutional autonomy. It has not been shown, furthermore, that separate courses are inferior or inherently unequal.

3. *Single-Sex Scholarships.* WEAL and Abzug urged that regulations continue to forbid all single-sex financial awards. Since financial assistance is often the key factor in enabling students to attend an educational institution, enrollments can be covertly controlled by excluding certain persons from financial aid. Opponents argued that combining restricted funds with other sources can satisfy the full purpose of the law and that there would be financial and other difficulties in amending single-sex trusts.

4. *Part-Time Employee Fringe Benefits.* WEAL and Abzug advocated that fringe benefits be prorated for permanent part-time employees. This would eliminate covert sexual discrimination caused by the disproportionate utilization of women as part-time employees. Those against this recommendation argued that it makes no economic sense because most part-time employees are students, and the short duration of most such employment makes enrollment in pension plans meaningless.

5. *Equal Contributions and Benefits in Retirement Plans.* WEAL and Abzug recommended that both equal contributions and equal benefits be required (the proposed regulations require one or the other). They maintained that, regardless of actuarial distinctions, women as a class should not be subjected to unequal treatment. They also argued that men should not be treated unequally because of a higher incidence of heart attacks. Those in opposition contended that women outlive men, a circumstance for which an employee should not be penalized and which must necessarily be included in the regulations in order to guarantee fiscal and actuarial soundness.

6. *Treatment of Maternity Leave as a Temporary Disability.* While the preliminary regulations treat pregnancy as a temporary disability, they include several procedural provisions for maternity

leave. WEAL and Abzug recommended the deletion of these provisions in order for pregnancy to be truly considered a temporary disability. Opponents argued that pregnancy should not be associated with accidents or illness and emphasized the need for protection against excessive costs.

Students' groups, national governmental commissions, teachers' groups, and women's groups overwhelmingly supported the WEAL and Abzug positions. Support from other groups was less uniform: 67 percent of chief state school officers favored their recommendations, as did 43 percent of the athletic groups and 40 percent of the elementary and secondary education groups. Only 21 percent of the higher education groups and 14 percent of the college and university administrators approved the measures. State school board associations gave no support.

Of the six WEAL and Abzug positions, only two were incorporated into the regulations: single-sex courses and maternity leave. The four rejected positions concerning coverage, significant assistance, athletics, and reverse discrimination remain as issues still likely to be the center of legal battles.

Some of the most heated debates and intensive lobbying efforts over the regulations were initiated by the powerful National Collegiate Athletic Association (NCAA) and the Association for Intercollegiate Athletics for Women (AIAW), backed by several influential women's groups. The NCAA considers the legislation destructive to intercollegiate sports, and the AIAW dismisses the law as ineffective in providing equal sports opportunities for women. Although the regulation requirements concerning athletics will cause some continued skirmishes, it appears that the major battle in athletics, which has been brought to a head by the Title IX legislation, will be fought over the control of women's sports.

ADMINISTRATION, FINANCING, IMPLEMENTATION, AND ENFORCEMENT OF TITLE IX

Title IX will affect the 16,000 public school systems in the country as well as the 2,700 institutions of postsecondary education currently receiving federal funds. The magnitude of its coverage presents serious questions concerning administration, finance, implementation, and enforcement.

The federal government gives colleges and universities nearly $9

billion a year. With funding come regulations, inspections, conditions, record keeping, and legal costs. It is estimated that federal
regulations now cost colleges and universities about $2 billion a year, a
figure roughly equal to the entire sum the institutions raise through
voluntary donations. One indication of the demands being placed on
universities is Derek Bok's estimate that the Harvard faculty spent
more than 60,000 hours during the 1974-75 school year meeting
record-keeping requirements of federal programs.[5]

Noncompliance and subsequent loss of federal assistance can also
be expensive. In 1976 two institutions, Hillsdale College in Michigan
and Brigham Young University in Utah, refused to comply with Title
IX. These institutions stand to lose federal financial aid to their
students — about $200,000 for Hillsdale and $6 to $7 million for
Brigham Young.

In order for Title IX to be effective, funds must be appropriated
for its implementation. Because of the strong opposition to this legislation expressed by many congressmen from both parties, funds may be
difficult to obtain. The lack of adequate funds has been demonstrated for the past eleven years by the difficulties of the Equal Employment Opportunity Commission (EEOC) in eliminating discrimination in employment. In 1976 the General Accounting Office
(GAO) concluded that progress by the EEOC in this area has been
limited and reported that there is a backlog of more than 100,000
charges on file with the commission. As a matter of fact, the GAO
charged that individuals must wait an average of two years to have
complaints resolved. The EEOC responded that it was staffed to handle only 2,000 charges but that it was faced with 10,000 cases immediately upon passage of the legislation. The National Organization for
Women is suing the agency for "unlawfully abandoning thousands of
cases."[6]

A new consolidated enforcement approach proposed in 1975 by
the Office of Civil Rights (OCR) was intended to alleviate some of the
problems encountered by the EEOC. According to former Secretary of
Health, Education, and Welfare Casper W. Weinberger, these enforcement procedures would focus on the "main, systemic forms of
discrimination, and give priority attention to these cases, rather than
follow the current approach in which priorities are dictated by the
morning's mail, with each complaint, regardless of apparent justification, to be investigated, just because the complaint has been made."[7]
Weinberger also explained that this new approach would not "signal

the end to considering complaints from individuals or groups." However, such complaints would be used by the OCR to "help determine enforcement priorities and to guide the direction of the compliance reviews."[8] Many groups and individuals, both those who favor and those who disapprove of the concept of Title IX and of specific regulations, oppose this approach and steps toward implementation proved ineffective.

It is apparent that the Carter administration has inherited enforcement problems of great magnitude. The new secretary of HEW, Joseph A. Califano, has acknowledged that the job of the OCR is enormous and that it has not, in the past, received the resources needed to carry out its responsibilities. In consequence, the OCR has previously been unable even to examine and catalog the assurance-of-compliance forms filed by educational institutions under Title IX. The size of the enforcement problem becomes even more apparent when it is noted that as of March 1977, 13,576 of the nation's school districts and colleges had failed to submit the required statements attesting to their compliance with Title IX, or filed inadequate assurance statements.[9] These forms were to have been filed by September 30, 1976.

In April 1977, Secretary Califano announced initial steps for the reorganization of the OCR.[10] In addition to the appointment of a new director, he established two new positions in the civil rights office, deputy director for compliance and enforcement and deputy director for program review. The former has been made responsible for complaint investigations, compliance reviews, and regional operations. The latter is charged with the responsibility for coordinating new civil rights compliance programs to be undertaken by each agency within HEW. When announcing these positions, Califano stated his belief that the enforcement of civil rights laws must be decentralized and become an integral part of the mission of each agency within HEW.

According to Califano, 75 percent of the personnel efforts of the OCR go into investigating Title IV (race and national origin) complaints in education, while discrimination in other areas has received very little attention. Perhaps a more decentralized approach to the problem will better ensure the implementation of Title IX, particularly through his plan for "making civil rights objectives and enforcement an integral part of every grant, contract, and program that HEW administers."[11] One thing does seem certain: because Title IX legislation is so controversial and can affect more than 45 to 50 million elementary, secondary, and postsecondary students, its interpretation and enforcement will probably generate considerable litigation and enormous costs for administration and implementation.

NOTES

1. U.S. Department of Health, Education, and Welfare, Office of Civil Rights, *Final Title IX Regulations Implementing Education Amendments of 1972 Prohibiting Sex Discrimination in Education* (Washington, D.C.: Government Printing Office, 1975).

2. "Federal Laws and Regulations Concerning Sex Discrimination in Educational Institutions," *Chronicle of Higher Education* 24 (October 1972): 1. See also U.S. Department of Health, Education, and Welfare, Office of Civil Rights, *Higher Education Guidelines, Executive Order 11246* (Washington, D.C.: Government Printing Office, 1972).

3. See Martha Matthews and Shirley McCune, *Complying with Title IX: Implementing Institutional Self-Evaluation* (Washington, D.C.: National Foundation for the Improvement of Education, 1976).

4. Andres Fishel, "Organizational Positions on Title IX," *Journal of Higher Education* 47 (January-February 1976): 93-105.

5. "Red Tape Blues," *Newsweek,* August 30, 1976, 77.

6. Claudia Levy, "EEOC Disappointed in GAO's Probe," *Washington Post,* October 2, 1976.

7. "Statement by Casper W. Weinberger, Secretary of Health, Education and Welfare," *HEW News,* June 3, 1975, 5.

8. *Ibid.*

9. "Schools Found to Lag in Banning Sex Bias," *New York Times,* March 16, 1977, II, 4:5.

10. American Council on Education, *Higher Education and National Affairs* 26 (April 29, 1977): 6.

11. *Ibid.*

SELECTED REFERENCES

Glazer, Nathan. *Affirmative Discrimination: Ethnic Inequality and Public Policy.* New York: Basic Books, 1976.

Project on Equal Education Rights (PEER). *Summary of the Regulation for Title IX Education Amendments of 1972.* Washington, D.C.: Project on States and Education, University of Virginia, 1975.

Project on Equal Education Rights (PEER). *Summary of the Regulation for Title IX Education Amendments of 1972.* Washington, D.C.: Project on States and Education of Women, 1975.

Taylor, Emily, and Shavlik, Donna. *Institutional Self-Evaluation: The Title IX Requirement.* Washington, D.C.: American Council on Education, Office of Women in Higher Education, 1975.

Timpano, Doris M. "How to Meet Title IX." *American School Board Journal* 163 (March 1976): 30-34.

U.S. Department of Health, Education, and Welfare, Office of Civil Rights. *Elimination of Sex Discrimination in Athletic Programs.* Washington, D.C.: Government Printing Office, 1975.

Lifelong Learning and the
Politics of Education

Virgil S. Ward
Robert G. Templin, Jr.

The sudden and rapidly growing interest in lifelong learning, which only recently has captured the imagination of American teachers and educational leaders, is born in a time of crisis for educational institutions facing declining enrollments, spiraling costs, and waning public support. The discovery that, in the recent past, increasing numbers of adults have been enrolling as part-time students is being heralded as the future economic salvation of many schools, colleges, and universities.

Few American writers, however, have seriously investigated the political and social implications of the concept of lifelong learning for formal educational institutions. At best, lifelong education has been equated with such terms as "nontraditional," "recurrent," "continuing," or "adult" education. Rather than anticipating any fundamental changes in the purposes or processes of education itself, lifelong education often is viewed as the mere programmatic extension of what has been done in the past for children and youths, now adapted and modified for the growing adult population.

THE CONCEPT OF LIFELONG EDUCATION

Although the theme of learning throughout one's life is certainly not a new one, the systematic treatment of education as a lifelong experience owes much of its recent impetus to European educational theorists such as Edgar Faure, R. H. Dave, and Paul Legrand of France and Torsten Husén of Sweden. Popularly introduced to this side of the Atlantic in 1972 by the UNESCO International Commission on the Development of Education, lifelong education was offered as "the master concept for educational policies in the years to come."[1] Maintaining that "lifelong education is not an educational system, but the principle on which the over-all organization of a system is founded,"[2] theorists have proposed five major tenets that undergird the concept and that have important intellectual and political implications affecting the whole of the educational system.

First, proponents of lifelong learning hold that the need for education does not begin with childhood and end with the emergence of adulthood. Recognizing that learning needs begin at birth, they believe that the development of an educative environment for preschool-age infants and children must become a major objective. And, since the rapid social, economic, and cultural changes of the twentieth century demand continuous development throughout life, the educational system must be extended to facilitate learning through the middle and older adult years. They specifically reject the notion that the educational system functions primarily for children and youths.

A second tenet maintains that the purpose of education should be to develop self-directed learners who are not only capable of coping with change, but who also are able to improve the conditions of life through the development of competencies associated with life roles. Education "can no longer constitute a definitive 'whole' handed out to and received by a student before he embarks on adult life . . . ."[3]

According to the third tenet, the processes of education should not be characterized by the transmission of predetermined content representing what is known, but rather by the acquisition of the skills of inquiry, and learning how to learn. The curriculum of education should not, consequently, be determined by the learner's age as the criterion of readiness to learn. It should, instead, be oriented toward developing competencies for life roles and be sequenced as the learner confronts developmental tasks through which he experiences the need to learn.[4]

The fourth tenet asserts that lifelong education is a major societal function and not a monopoly of the schools. Education is too important to be left to "experts" who decide what ought to be done and in what ways while society is relegated to the role of supporting these plans by making available the necessary resources.[5] Greater societal involvement in the design of education through political decision-making processes and through the use of community resources is thought to be imperative.

The final tenet concludes that the importance attached to formal schooling itself is generally exaggerated, as is the presumed relationship between "schooling" and "learning." Rejected is the proposition that teaching is equivalent to learning and that education and schooling are synonymous. It is argued that schooling generally lasts too long, serves to separate rather than integrate youths and society, and, in its present form, does not meet the learning needs of adults. Unlike Ivan Illich, who proposes "deschooling" society, theorists of lifelong education recommend that schools continue to play an important role in education, along with other community resources, though major reforms would be required to integrate schools with society.

FORCES PRODUCING THE NEED FOR LIFELONG EDUCATION

Regardless of the theoretical sources for the concept of lifelong education, the forces that give rise to the demand for and necessity of lifelong education are clearly present in American society and show no signs of abating.

The rapidity of change has found expression in the knowledge explosion where the currency of knowledge in many fields is now less than ten years. Industrial, electronic, cybernetic, communications, and other technological advances continue to impinge upon and transform our daily existence. Increased economic rationalization and occupational mobility, combined with the changes mentioned above, have led to the accelerated occurrence of persons changing jobs five and six times during a lifetime and have increased the probability that today's children will enter careers, and indeed a society, that have yet to be imagined. Because of changing attitudes, values, social roles, and social institutions, continuous learning has become necessary for survival in a society characterized by pluralistic values and a multiplicity of alternatives for thinking, feeling, and acting.

Added to these forces is the growing proportion of the population that has passed the ages once considered appropriate for schooling. By 1980, the population bulge of the postwar baby boom will be entering middle age, a time of life previously thought to be appropriate for adults to concern themselves with activities other than schooling, education, and learning. Other projections estimate that between 1975 and 2000, 80 percent of the population growth will occur in age categories of thirty-five years of age and older.[6] Developmental psychology dealing with the entire life span is yielding evidence suggesting that adults have the capacity and need for continuous growth and learning throughout life without necessarily experiencing a decline in learning abilities after age twenty, thirty, or even sixty.[7]

These interacting forces have given rise to an unprecedented need and demand for educational opportunities for the adult population. According to the National Center for Education Statistics,[8] more than 17 million adults participated in organized instructional activities on less than a full-time basis in 1975, which was more than a 30 percent increase since 1969. This was, thus, the fastest growing segment of education. When adults engaged in both full- and part-time instructional activities are considered together, they represent nearly 20 percent of the total adult population. There is every indication that the demands will expand as a greater proportion of the total population grows older, life expectancy increases, and social change requiring new learning accelerates.

POLITICS OF LIFELONG EDUCATION

Juxtaposed against the growing demand of adults for learning opportunities are schools now facing declining enrollments among their traditional students. Declaring the growing population of adult learners "open game," many community schools, community colleges and technical institutes, and colleges and universities are scrambling to attract these new students, thus hoping to offset the prospect of fewer students.

Evening offerings of these schools have been expanded, new courses devised, and new locations found. Credit is now awarded by many colleges for "life experiences," and institutions without physical campuses or full-time faculty are being established. External and nontraditional degree programs are mushrooming. According to the Educational Testing Service, twenty-six nontraditional degree programs were offered prior to 1970.[9] Since that time, however, 228 new programs have been established, with 105 other programs proposed but not yet implemented as colleges and universities are increasingly attempting to appeal to the growing adult population.

These attempts to attract the part-time adult student have often made it difficult for educational institutions to cooperate in developing comprehensive educational plans and have led to fierce competition between institutions. In Virginia alone, for example, it is estimated that at least twenty-seven out-of-state institutions currently offer degree programs within the commonwealth, much to the aggravation of the state's public and private colleges.[10] This national problem, associated with charges that many such programs are of poor quality, has led the Council on Post-Secondary Accreditation to launch "a major attack" on questionable off-campus degree programs.[11] This internal struggle has set the stage for the first of three emerging political issues related to lifelong education and schools: who will serve the educational needs of the growing numbers of adults, and in what ways will they be served?

The second political issue is the public's growing lack of confidence that schools can appropriately address the needs of our learning society. While it is true the participation of adults in educational programs is increasing rapidly, part-time adult enrollments in high schools, community colleges and technical institutes, and colleges and universities are actually declining or have stabilized despite the myriad of efforts made specifically to attract these persons. High schools have stabilized or have been dropping in adult enrollments since 1969; four-year colleges and universities had 110,000 fewer part-time adults enrolled in 1975 than in 1972; and community college and technical institute enrollments of part-time adults appear to have stabilized in 1975 and 1976.[12]

In contrast to declining enrollments of both full- and part-time students in schools, adult participation in nonschool educational programs has accelerated. Between 1969 and 1975, enrollments in educational programs sponsored by professional organizations, labor unions, employers, governmental agencies, hospitals, community organizations, and other nonschool sponsors have increased by 46 percent.[13] Nearly as many part-time adult learners are being served by this nontraditional segment of educational activity as in all schools combined.

Leaders in business, industry, and the professions are among the most sensitive to the need for continuous development of human resources through education and are perhaps the most critical of the schools' failure to meet the needs of lifelong learning. Illustrative of this attitude is David J. Culbertson, vice-president of Xerox Corporation, who writes: "corporations and society at large have needs that for the most part are not being fulfilled by our colleges and universities — the need, for example, to cope with technological change. Traditionally, our institutions of higher learning have served as part of the pattern in which life is broken into three neat segments — the first devoted to learning, the second to earning, and the third to enjoying the rewards of one's labor. Clearly this pattern has now changed."[14]

Impatient with schools and the growing separation of schools from society, several large corporations, including American Telephone and Telegraph, International Business Machines, and General Electric, now offer their own baccalaureate programs; the Arthur D. Little firm is now authorized to award a master's degree; and virtually all larger corporations support and develop educational activities within their organizations.[15]

The growing crisis in confidence concerning the ability of schools to meet lifelong educational needs is echoed even by teachers when speaking of their own continuous educational development. In 1973 the Second National Assembly of the American Association of Community and Junior Colleges recommended the establishment of teachers' centers separated from universities and their graduate schools as a means of providing more relevant educational opportunities for their faculties.[16] Recent governmental support under the Education Amendments of 1976 for the adoption of teachers' centers for public school teachers can be seen as another indication of the growing lack of confidence.[17]

The third political issue involving lifelong education and the schools focuses on the priority of schooling in relation to other educative needs of society and on pressing social issues that also compete for the shrinking tax dollar. The environment, energy resources, health care, housing, recreation, transportation, care for the aged, unemployment, and poverty are being viewed increasingly as more urgent considerations not only for direct tax support but also for needed educational attention than are considerations for increasing expenditures for new classrooms and teachers' salaries. Thus, while there is a growing realization that the need for education is life long, the view also exists that there is presently too much schooling for too long a period with too little evidence of a valuable return received on the investment made.

IMPLICATIONS OF THE POLITICS
OF LIFELONG EDUCATION

Lifelong education both as a concept and as a movement does not appear to be a passing fancy that will have momentary popularity and then be discarded when its innovative appeal passes. Its theoretical development already has had an international impact, and the social and demographic forces that give rise to the need and demand for lifelong educational opportunities are presently manifested in American society. As the movement develops, it is likely to challenge traditional assumptions regarding the purposes and processes of education; political issues will, in consequence, become more sharply focused and debated, and pressure for a national policy of lifelong education will gain increasing momentum.

Steps toward formulating a national policy regarding lifelong education have already begun with the "Lifelong Learning" legislation passed as part of the Education Amendments of 1976. Included within its scope are a determination to search for educational alternatives outside of schooling, a recognition of the need to integrate schools with society and its problems, and an evaluation of novel procedures for financing continuing educational opportunities.[18] As the author of this legislation has commented, "Education is no longer the theory of schooling; rather it is the interactions of educational institutions with each other and with the world at large."[19]

The political issues identified earlier in this essay are not likely to be resolved by school leaders acting alone but rather through the political processes within the context of the larger society. Though the opportunity for educational leaders to contribute to a national policy of lifelong education exists, it requires a willingness to reexamine fundamental assumptions regarding education and a commitment to alter, in some cases radically, the processes of education in the schools.

It will also require political organization among educational groups, which until now have encountered one another as adversaries in the political arena, particularly when issues revolved around serving the learning needs of adults. Reflecting upon the failures of past attempts to organize politically, William Griffith observes: "Organizational chauvinism made it impossible for adult educators working in one type of institution to welcome the involvement of adult educators from other types of institutions in lobbying for federal support. A fear that the pie might have to be cut into too many institutional portions has plagued the political behavior of adult education lobbyists."[20]

A fundamental question to be confronted is whether school leaders will take lifelong education seriously, contribute to and prepare for changes that are required, and cooperatively organize and participate in the political decision-making processes or whether they will remain reactive and disorganized, be further removed from the educative needs of society, and face the rising tide of obsolescence as a marginally functional social institution.

NOTES

1. Edgar Faure *et al., Learning to Be: The World of Education Today and Tomorrow* (Paris: UNESCO, 1972), p. 182.

2. *Ibid.*

3. *Ibid.,* p. xxxiii.

4. R.H. Dave, *Lifelong Education and School Curriculum* (Hamburg: UNESCO Institute for Education, 1973); Malcolm S. Knowles, "Toward a Model of Lifelong Learning," *The Adult Learner: A Neglected Species* (Houston: Gulf Publishing Co., 1973), pp. 160-161.

5. Torsten Husén, *The Learning Society* (London: Methuen, 1974), p. xvi.

6. U.S. Department of Commerce, Bureau of the Census, "Projections of the Population of the United States, by Age and Sex, 1975 to 2000 with Extension of Total Population to 2025," *Current Population Reports,* Series P-25, No. 541 (Washington, D.C.: Government Printing Office, 1975).

7. Howard McClusky, "What Research Says about Adult Learning Potential and about Teaching Older Adults," *Adult Learning: Issues and Innovations,* ed. Robert M. Smith (DeKalb, Ill.: ERIC Clearinghouse in Career Education, 1976), pp. 116-121.

8. Preliminary data from 1975 Participation in Adult Education Survey, Adult and Vocational Education Surveys Branch, National Center for Education Statistics, U.S. Office of Education.

9. Telephone interview between Paul K. Beebee, University of Virginia, and I. Bruce Hamilton, Office of New Degree Programs, Educational Testing Service, Princeton, N.J., April 1, 1977.

10. State Council for Higher Education in Virginia, "Summary Data: Out-of-State Institutions Offering Instruction in Virginia, Academic Year 1975-76," mimeographed (Richmond, Va.: the Council, 1976).

11. American Council on Education, *Higher Education and National Affairs* 25 (October 29, 1976): 1.

12. Preliminary data from 1975 Participation in Adult Education Survey; American Council on Education, *Higher Education and National Affairs* 36 (February 11, 1977): 5.

13. Preliminary data from 1975 Participation in Adult Education Survey.

14. David J. Culbertson, "Corporate Role in Lifelong Learning," in *Lifelong Learners: A New Clientele for Higher Education,* ed. Dyckman W. Vermilye (San Francisco: Jossey-Bass, 1975), p. 30.

15. *Ibid.*

16. Terry O'Banion, "Alternate Forms of Graduate Education for Community College Staff," in *Graduate Education and Community Colleges,* ed. S. V. Martorana *et al.* (Washington, D.C.: National Board on Graduate Education, 1975), p. 49.

17. U.S. Congress, Education Amendments of 1976, Public Law No. 94-482, 90 Stat. 2154-2155 (1976).

18. *Ibid.,* 90 Stat. 2086-2089 (1976).

19. Walter F. Mondale, "The Next Step: Lifelong Learning," *Change* 8 (October 1976): 45.

20. William S. Griffith, "Adult Educators and Politics," *Adult Education* 26 (Summer 1976): 279.

PART VI
Impact of the Changing Politics of Education on the Training of Educational Administrators

Difficult as it is to generalize about the present and future state of educational affairs, the reader may find that the only unifying sentiment among the authors of the preceding chapters is: things are not what they used to be, and predicting the shape of things to come is hazardous. Their agreement about the upheavals of past practice and of potential realignments applies to the whole spectrum of educational concerns among the citizenry of all ages and conditions—life goals and expectations for schooling; the economic resources and costs of meeting new and diverse needs; the attendant forms of political conflict and of ultimate policy choices. The preceding chapters should also show the reader that mounting uncertainty in recent years did not stifle scholarly curiosity and research. Rather, it may have proved a stimulus for inquiry, since even a cursory examination of the bibliographical references in this volume attests to the variety and range of the issues under study. Further, the topics included are only a few that have the highest priority; the list by no means exhausts the policy changes and problems that educators and administrators encounter in their tasks of operating schools, colleges, and all the other kinds of educational undertakings.

The authors in Part VI direct attention to these beleaguered administrators, whose situation is unenviable today and in the foreseeable future. This is not entirely due to social change and turbulence, but stems also from the unready state of the profession itself.

The knowledge, attitudes, and leadership strategies that assured adequate, even commendable, performance in the past are deeply rooted in the professional training, ethos, and practice of preceding decades. Consonant with the tenets of Ellwood P. Cubberley's influential *Public School Administration,* published in 1916, the superintendency, at least in the larger school systems, became the capstone of a bureaucratic form of school organization that has remained substantially unchanged. Similarly, the internal organization of colleges and universities retains its distinctive and heavily traditional elements.

This is not to say that the tasks of educational administrators previously lacked challenge, ambiguity, or risk. For example, in *Urban School Chiefs under Fire* (Chicago: University of Chicago Press, 1976), Larry Cuban documents the development of the school superintendents' multifaceted and often contradictory roles as teacher-scholars, chief administrators, and negotiator-statesmen. From time to time, in various locales, the essentially political basis of public education became manifest in stormy episodes that threatened professional monopoly of policy and program decision making. Indeed, an important hallmark of a successful superintendent was his mastery of methods to contain and control disruptive influences. One strategy was rhetorical: to lay stress on the evenhanded, politically neutral character of his role.

The administrators of institutions of higher education tended to be less exposed to lay interference, but they also found it expedient to practice unacknowledged arts of political maneuver in dealing with their governing boards and with public agencies. When the post-World War II period brought expansion of student populations and more pervasive federal and state influences, among other changes, all educators faced greatly complicated tasks. With some success, they alerted the public and the politicians to the need for more resources. In spite of growing pains and the periodic spasms of public criticism, the mood of the educational community during the 1950's and early 1960's was relatively euphoric.

Educational administrators continued to advocate and to operate as much as possible in accord with professional values of long standing: autonomy, planned and orderly modifications of policy and programs, and perception of the educational sector as a unique claimant for public support.

In the turbulent mid-1960's and 1970's the utility of these guiding principles was outpaced by the events and political developments described in the preceding chapters. Like other internalized emotional mainstays for human action, however, professional norms are not readily replaced by new habits of mind. This hiatus or lag between social and political changes and the role conceptions held by professionals in policy-making positions is not uncommon. For example, practitioners in medicine and social work are experiencing today the same kind of dissonance that dismays educators. On one hand, they wish to maintain their established professional standards and status, while, on the other, they must try to satisfy an increasingly contentious and skeptical public.

The authors of Chapters 11 and 12 implicitly recognize that the modification of basic attitudes and the redesign of professional training programs are typically arduous and protracted processes, especially with regard to shaping the role that any group of professionals will, or should, assume in devising and implementing public policies related to their sphere of expertise. None of the authors offers a comprehensive or an easy remedy for overcoming the present difficulties of educational administrators. In fact, the processes of planning, mediation, and power brokerage that they address go to the heart of a reinterpretation of the meaning of professionalism in general; on a broad front, these concerns have received much recent attention from social philosophers and commentators, elected and appointed public officials, and social scientists in several disciplines.

The discourse has so many facets that any single analyst must be very selective and set definite limits on his area of inquiry, especially in a brief treatment. The authors of the following chapters have observed this caveat, and they share the further assumption that readers concerned with improving the performance, and allaying the anxieties, of educational administrators will view their recommendations for new initiatives in the context of the analyses and forecasts made by the authors of the preceding chapters. Part VI relates, specifically, to the needs and the potentials for change that may be derived from shared, reliable knowledge about, and open acknowledgment of, education's political aspects and problems.

In Chapter 11, Roald Campbell draws on his exceptional knowledge and experience in the worlds of educational scholarship, school practices, and university training of school administrators to offer a proposal for preentry training of a new breed of top-level or chief administrators, particularly for the elementary and secondary school systems. At the outset, he makes a distinction between the requisite plan-

ning and mediating functions of such officials, choosing to treat power
brokering as an aspect of the latter form of activity. In brief, he
recommends that the responsibility for developing an elite corps of
leaders with cosmopolitan outlook and broad competencies be
assumed by a few of the major universities, and he sets directions for
program design that would depart markedly from present practice.
These include: reduction in the number of institutions presently offering graduate programs in educational administration; the enlargement of the recruitment pool from which trainees are drawn; the personal characteristics to be stressed in choosing such trainees; the
broadened use of university-wide resources; and greater emphasis on
the clinical component in the training experiences.

Campbell's proposal is visionary, but he analyzes realistically
both the obstacles and the encourgements to its implementation. The
difficulties are typical of those to be overcome by initiatives that challenge the status quo: finding adequate resources, overcoming the resistance of those whose prestige and power would be threatened, and
gaining public understanding and acceptance. While he regards the
external impetus to change as very important, he puts the onus of
making initial moves directly on the professoriat now responsible for
training educational administrators.

Campbell's views about present faculties are not entirely
sanguine. His own research revealed the narrow base of their recruitment, their isolation from other professional influences, and their
complacency about their own activities. These characteristics are obviously incompatible with the pluralistic and iconoclastic thrust of
today's social and political developments. He implies, however, that
some faculties can change, and he suggests that an important first step
would be the addition of specialists in diverse policy areas—urban
planning and labor relations, for example—which would provide new
forms of interaction and stimulate the redesign of programs to make
them more responsive to current and future needs.

Kenneth Mortimer's commentary on Campbell's essay provides
for the reader, in microcosm, insight into one of the basic differences
between institutions for elementary and secondary education and
those for higher education, namely, the contrasts to be found in administrative roles and functions, and in generally accepted attitudes
about mangement. Whatever their problems may be, school superintendents, principals, and other supervisory personnel are typically
recognized and rewarded on the basis of specialized competency to

manage the school bureaucracies. Leaders in higher education, where collegial relationships are valued, play much more ambiguous roles. From his vantage point as a professor of higher education, Mortimer states that administration has not been a highly sought or well-rewarded activity among academicians in general, and it is not even a desired badge of specialization among those engaged in the academic study of higher education. Still he finds several points of agreement both with Campbell's general prescriptions for an administrative training program and with his analysis of limiting conditions on its implementation. Mortimer also expresses concern about the parochialism of the many professors recruited on the basis of their experience in school administration who undertake to provide training in the emergent specialized programs in higher education, not the least because, like Campbell, he believes that they lack credibility with their university colleagues. He recommends that such persons should themselves first pursue university-level studies in higher education, and he further outlines the aspects of the study of politics that he considers essential for incorporation into the curriculum of higher education studies.

The other commentator on Campbell's contribution, Aubrey McCutcheon, is a lawyer who is also well versed in the problems of urban school administration and in training school administrators. He is troubled that crucial policy decisions affecting education are currently being made by public officials and representatives of other professions without the informed counsel of educators, and he emphasizes far more than either Campbell or Mortimer the need for school administrators to acquire and employ advocacy skills. He gives higher priority to encouraging and helping those already on the firing line, who are forced to assume activist roles as power brokers, even in the face of unknown risks that this change in professional practice may entail. He offers evidence concerning the perceptions of practitioners about their own needs in this regard, suggesting that short-term as well as long-range programs to provide training assistance are feasible and urgent.

In providing an overview of the entire volume and especially of the contributions in Chapter 11 by Campbell, Mortimer, and McCutcheon, Jack Culbertson performs two valuable services. First, he provides a perspective on the present and future state of educational administration that does not diminish the difficulties, but offers encouragement and guidelines for constructive next steps. His thoughtful analysis of the uses of adversity tends to dispel the notion that the retreat to a "siege mentality" is the only recourse for educational administrators when they must find ways to cope with threats of retrenchment and radically changed working environments. Second, Culbertson draws together in a succinct and coherent summary the diverse emphases of the principal authors, reinforcing one of the major purposes of the volume—to extend the potential influence of educational policy analysis in the teaching and practice of educational administration.

11 Improving the Performance of Educational Administrators as Planners, Mediators, and Power Brokers*

Roald F. Campbell

If, indeed, the politics of education has changed, what do educational administrators do about it? My assignment is a specific one: to discuss how we might improve the performance of these administrators as planners, mediators, and power brokers. Even with this specificity I must further delimit the topic by noting a few assumptions, suggesting a focus for the chapter, and establishing other limitations. The assumptions include the following: that administrative performance, particularly in the areas of planning, mediating, and power brokering, needs improvement; that we have the know-how necessary to effect this improvement; and that the university and professors of educational administration can play a major role in such improvement. One might question each of these assumptions, but I will not do so here.

The focus of this chapter is on the content and feasibility of preparation programs to cope with the changing role of the educational administrator, particularly as a planner, mediator, and power broker. To be sure, the 1980's will not be totally different from the 1970's or the 1960's, but we are confronted, as documented in the other chapters, with some changes. The implications of these changes for the administrator in the areas of planning and mediating will be suggested. I have deliberately combined mediating and power brokering as closely related roles under the one term "mediating." I give this

---

*Useful suggestions were made by Edwin M. Bridges, Tim L. Mazzoni, Jr., and L. Jackson Newell on an earlier draft of this chapter.

term a proactive as well as a reactive meaning, and in no sense do I limit mediating to a specific stage in labor negotiations to which the term is often applied. The processes of planning and mediating differ in a number of respects. Planning seems to be a very logical process. For an organization it usually involves the setting of goals, the generation of alternative ways of reaching those goals, the appraisal of each of the alternatives generated, the selection of the alternative thought to be the most effective strategy, the implementation of that strategy, and finally the evaluation of the outcomes of the program implemented. Ordinarily planning aims to be orderly, objective, logical, and quite impersonal.

Mediation, on the other hand, is clearly a political process. It may occur in any phase of policy making from initiation through enactment, though it is most visible during the support mobilization stage.[1] Central in this process are the interests and influence of competing policy participants. Skills in mediation are undoubtedly many, including facilitating the expression of the policy preferences of relevant participants; sharing information with these participants as to how their preferences relate to one another and to feasible policy options; and identifying points of agreement to serve as the basis for reconciling conflict and developing workable compromises.[2] While mediating, so conceived, may involve the logical process of planning, and planning may take account of the political context, the two are different, albeit related, processes. Planning tends to be more monolithic, data oriented, elitist, and long range. Mediating tends to be more pluralistic, people oriented, democratic, and short range. As William Boyd[3] has noted, the mediating role departs most sharply from the traditional self-image of the school administrator as expert-statesman. While the mediator may have strong convictions of his own, his job is not one of advocating his own position, but, rather, one of helping to effect the most desirable compromises possible.

Planners usually generate many alternatives, are concerned with what ought to be, and may be poor politicians. Politicians settle for few alternatives, are concerned with what is possible, and may be poor planners. We are asking that the educational administrator comprehend and become expert in these two processes, which at times may seem quite antithetical. It may also be worth noting that there are possible hazards involved for any administrator who attempts to become expert in planning and mediating. There are people in our society who associate planning with totalitarian government and not with a free enterprise system. There are also people who look askance at a school adminstrator who deliberately seeks to serve in a mediating or political role.

I have also imposed other limitations on the chapter. In focusing on preparation for planning and mediating, I do not take account of preparation for other managerial roles. For instance, Henry Mintzberg has developed ten roles that, he says, characterize administrative work.[4] Some of these, which I tend to ignore here, include the roles of figurehead, monitor, disseminator, and spokesman. Also, what I have to say will emphasize the preservice preparation program more than the in-service, but this is not meant to deemphasize the importance of in-service or continuing education for administrators. Finally, I shall deal more with top-level or chief administrators of school systems, state agencies, and similar posts than with those in higher education. While much of what is said may apply to higher education, the context surrounding academic administration deserves more treatment than I can give it here.

With the delimitations noted, I shall attempt two major analyses: presentation of a number of preparation program directions; and consideration of some of the obstacles, largely political in nature, that will probably need to be faced in the implementation of a program with these characteristics.

SUGGESTED PROGRAM DIRECTIONS

In my view, few, if any, university training programs for top administrative officers for school districts, state education agencies, and similar posts appear to give adequate attention to the planning and mediating roles demanded of those officers. I shall suggest a number of program directions that, if appropriately implemented, could do much to meet this apparent lack. For each of these directions or recommendations I shall provide some detail, but I cannot set forth complete specifications as they might be developed by a single university. The suggested program directions follow:

1. A small number of university preparation programs should have as a major focus the preparation of top-level or chief administrators for educational agencies. In this country over three hundred universities offer graduate programs in educational administration. At least a third of these give both doctor's and master's degrees in the

field, and many also provide a two-year degree or certificate program as well. The remaining institutions most frequently offer the master's degree only. In a recent year over a thousand doctoral degrees in educational administration were granted by American institutions, about one out of thirty of all doctoral degrees conferred that year.[5] Approximately two thousand persons in the more than three hundred institutions apparently serve as professors of educational administration. This is an extensive program in terms of institutions, program offerings, enrollments, and faculty personnel. In spite of the magnitude of the overall effort, many institutions have one- or two-person departments or areas of educational administration, the programs are inadequately conceptualized, and the offerings are frequently textbook courses taught in late afternoon or evening to part-time students already weary from a full day's work as teachers or quasi-administrators. In most of these programs teachers who wish to obtain certification for a principalship, principals who hope to be promoted to other administrative posts, a few persons with backgrounds in one of the related disciplines who aspire to become researchers in the field, and others whose backgrounds and career goals are less definitive are grouped together. Most such programs are course bound, credit bound, and certificate bound.

One cannot escape the conclusion that too many universities are offering programs in educational administration, that many of these programs are of questionable quality, and that in few places is there a focus on a particular set of career goals. It is true that there may be an advantage in having future practitioners and future researchers in educational administration together for some elements of a preparation program. It should be recognized, moreover, that some persons who prepare for a principalship will eventually wish to prepare for top administrative posts. Nor can the great variability of school systems across the country in terms of organization and size be ignored. Still, despite these conditions, there is need for a few universities, perhaps ten to twenty in the nation, to focus on preparing top-level educational administrators as at least one of their major efforts. Those who design programs in these institutions could then consider realistically the occupational demands of such administrators, including their skills as planners and mediators.

2. Universities with programs in educational administration, particularly those focusing on the preparation of top-level administra-

tors, should enlarge the recruitment pool from which candidates come. Most institutions presently do little by way of recruitment. Thus, their students tend to be self selected. These students most frequently want to meet state requirements for an administrative certificate, and almost without exception they have had teaching and sometimes administrative experience in school systems. These limited recruitment practices seem inadequate even for middle-management positions in educational agencies. They should be completely unacceptable to those institutions proposing to prepare top-level administrators.

In the first place, it is clear that a limited number of students with high intellectual skills choose, while undergraduates, to prepare for teaching in the public schools. To use that population later as the only or chief source for adminstrative candidates means that much intellectual talent is being ignored. In an effort to recruit administrative candidates with high intellectual capacity, those with teaching and administrative experience should not be passed over, but, in addition, persons in business, law, and other occupations should be considered. It also seems desirable to consider persons who have completed bachelor's or master's programs in one of the basic disciplines. Persons with other occupational and academic backgrounds will, of course, have much to learn about educational theory and practice, but that is not impossible for intelligent individuals who are highly motivated.

Enlargement of the recruitment pool will require an active program on the part of an institution. Persons who have demonstrated many of the characteristics needed in administrative posts should be sought out, the challenge of administrative work in education should be presented to them, and those with outstanding ability and motivation should be encouraged to apply for acceptance in a preparation program. It is obvious that this process will be facilitated if scholarships or fellowships of some kind can be provided for those candidates who are accepted.

While education is presently a declining industry, as James March[6] has noted, and recruitment for such an industry may be difficult, there is reason to believe that selective recruitment for top-level positions will appeal to some very competent persons. In this process two large groups have, up to this point, been largely overlooked: women and members of minority groups. Any recruitment program of the kind suggested here might even seek to have such groups somewhat overrepresented at this time.

3. Only those persons who rank high on a number of personal

characteristics should be admitted to the training programs for top administrative officers. I realize that this recommendation requires that a set of criteria be developed and that ways be established for securing evidence on those criteria. Even though these procedures may be imperfect, they should not be bypassed. As to criteria, I propose the following: intellectual ability; demonstrated leadership in group situations; commitment to social and educational improvement; facility in oral and written expression; willingness to take risks; personal stability.

Each of these characteristics deserves some amplification. Thus, some evidence of intellectual capacity can probably be secured from common tests of mental ability or general achievement, such as the graduate record examination. While such evidence alone is not sufficient, very low scores on such instruments would cast doubt upon the intellectual capability of candidates. In addition to test scores, evidence from field records of a candidate's participation in problem-solving situations should be sought. In like manner, demonstrated leadership in group situations can come only from field evidence. If a candidate has frequently been selected by his peers or his superordinates for positions of leadership, one can assume that those who knew the candidate best saw in him or her potential or actual leadership behavior. In terms of the skills central to our consideration here, appropriate probing might also reveal to what extent that behavior demonstrated strength in the mediating role.

Any discussion of a candidate's commitment to social and educational improvement obviously implies a consideration of his or her values, particularly as they apply to society and the place of the school in society. While we seem to be in a period of crisis with respect to our basic values, I contend that persons interested in becoming top educational administrators should have some convictions stemming from a thoughtful examination of our basic documents and the nature of the American experience. R. Freeman Butts has said that the common values of the political community include "freedom, equality, justice, popular consent, and personal obligation for the common good."[7] We might quarrel about the exact meaning of each of these words, but they do appear to represent the essence of the American dream, not completely realized but one still worth working for. Educational opportunity for all has a place in that dream, and the school, particularly the public school, can be an important agency in helping to ensure such opportunity. How does one discover this kind of commitment? I suspect that a face-to-face interview with a candidate could yield some evidence. Even more important would probably be a probe of the values that appear to have motivated a candidate in his or her prior work experience.

Much of the work of top educational administrators requires skill in communication, both oral and written. Though Mintzberg[8] has noted that managers rely heavily on oral communication, that observation should not rule out the need for skill in the written word. Evidence on effective communication can be obtained through interviews with the candidate and through requests for written documents, such as an essay on why the candidate wishes to enter a special training program for administrators.

Any administrative work is risky. For those at the top of the hierarchy the risk is even greater. For the type of administrators being recommended here the risk may be further increased. Those who cherish security above other values should not enter these preparation programs. It should be noted, however, that while the risk in administrative work is great, the satisfactions that come from having made a difference are also great. Evidence of a candidate's willingness to take risks might be secured from personal interviews and, perhaps even more reliably, from an examination of risks taken in his or her life to date.

Closely allied to a willingness to take risks is the personal stability of the candidate. While it seems that no one can escape entirely emotional highs and lows, extreme reactions may adversely affect the relationship between the top administrator and members of the staff. For instance, quickness to anger on the part of the administrator may create problems of morale that reduce the productivity of those in the organization. Also, periods of depression on the part of the chief may tarnish the sense of purpose and thrust necessary to organizational well-being. The best evidence one can get on the emotional stability of a candidate would appear to come from an examination of the candidate's relationships with others, particularly with work groups, concerning his or her prior experience.

Unless candidates bring strength in the above characteristics to the program, there is little such programs can do to build these characteristics. We are faced with what a person has become over thirty years and with what he may become over two or three years. While training programs may sharpen the conceptual and analytical skills of students, no university should become so arrogant as to assume that it can make over completely the people who enter its doors. Evidence of the characteristics noted above might be collected from the field activities of the candidates. I think it incumbent that we improve our capacity to collect and interpret such evidence.

4. Universities with a preparation program for top-level administrators should make better use of the whole university faculty. While it seems desirable to place responsibility for the development and operation of a program in a department or division of educational administration, that division should make appropriate use of the diverse talent found in a major university. For instance, courses in such basic disciplines as political science and sociology may have particular relevance for future administrators. Certain applied courses such as urban planning and labor economics may also be very useful. Only as faculty and students in educational administration work with faculty and students in other areas does the pertinence of university-wide offerings become apparent. When faculty members who teach these germane courses have been identified, they should also be invited to participate in courses and seminars offered in educational administration where the application of their ideas to educational settings can be explored in depth. These auxiliary faculty members should also be invited to serve in advisory roles to future administrators, particularly on their dissertation committees.

Some may question that a division of educational administration can capture the talent of much of the university in the way suggested. But there is nothing unrealistic about such a proposal, provided the program is of high quality. Faculty members in the best universities are attracted to students who have ideas, who are searching for new insights, and who find something challenging in areas removed from their own specialization. There is one other requirement if these productive relationships in the university are to be realized: the faculty in educational administration must command the respect of their colleagues in related fields. This represents a genuine problem in many institutions where some professors of educational administration are oriented more to practice than to scholarly work and where they may be quite complacent about their own field and its progress.[9]

Two other matters require mention. A program designed to prepare top-level educational administrators will require a commitment by the whole university, not merely a commitment by a department or a school. Instructional costs will be high, particularly if the clinical components are to be well done. While the commitment and the teaching resources must be broad, the responsibility for conceptualizing and operating the program must be placed on a faculty in educational administration, a group whose "noses get skinned" if things do not go well.

5. Those who design and operate preparation programs for top-level administrators, with emphasis on planning and mediating, should make more deliberate and skillful use of the socialization process. As noted above, planning and mediating tend to be, respectively, analytical and political processes. While an understanding of these processes may be acquired through organized course work, the attainment of skill in such processes requires emotional as well as intellectual experience and opportunities to share with peers actual performance of these new skills and to have such performance rigorously examined. This appraisal might be shared by peers, faculty members, and selected practitioners in the field. Future administrators are, in a real sense, being subjected to the understandings, attitudes, and skills of a new culture composed of those who value planning and mediating on the part of an administrator and who themselves perform those skills effectively.

At the preservice level this kind of socialization is most apt to be fostered by the creation of a center. Such a center requires physical facilities where each student and faculty member has a place, an office or work space, in close proximity to others in the group. This proximity promotes the kind of informal interchange or sharing that is essential to the socialization process. A conference room or meeting place should also be available. This room should be large enough to accommodate frequent visitors—faculty members from related areas, practicing administrators, community representatives, or others. Beyond its physical arrangements a center should require that genuine responsibilities be carried out by future administrators. For instance, one student might serve as a planning consultant to a district superintendent and his staff. Another might become a resource person in negotiations between management and teachers in a school district. Still another might assist the research staff of a state legislative committee. In each case, the future administrator participates fully in planning the experience, assumes genuine responsibilities, and has the performance of his or her duties examined by associates on campus and in the field. These responsibilities are closely related to clinical experiences about which more will be said later.

Even at the in-service level the power of socialization should be deliberately employed. While practicing administrators should obviously organize and control their own professional groups, there clearly is need for administrators who work at planning and mediating to confer with each other and to provide mutual support as these processes are examined and, it is to be hoped, improved. A tie between groups of practitioners and the campus center discussed above would seem to be advantageous to both bodies. The administrators could insist that those on campus keep their "feet to the fire." Conversely, those on campus might insist that the best insights and analyses possible be brought to the examination and appraisal of planning and mediating activities.

6. As part of the instructional program for future administrators, appropriate use should be made of such devices as cases, simulated materials, management games, and computer-based, decision-making exercises. All of these devices are designed to help bring a greater sense of reality to the curriculum, for our purpose, particularly reality in the areas of planning and mediating. These devices can also supplement the clinical experiences, especially where such experiences are difficult to obtain. For instance, real situations are, at times, so sensitive that observation, much less participation, on the part of outsiders will not be permitted by the responsible persons in charge. Cases involving many of the same elements might serve quite adequately as an instructional tool. In like manner cases or games might be used to demonstrate the possibilities in computer applications to problem situations. In a related development, Lloyd McCleary and his colleagues[10] have developed a series of modules that also appear to be useful approaches in instruction. These devices represent ways of bridging the gap between abstract ideas and field situations. Their use may also involve less risk and more time for analysis than is possible in some field situations.

7. While simulated materials can be useful, preparation programs for administrators should include a substantial clinical component. Skills in many areas, including planning and mediating, cannot be acquired without some observation and participation in real situations. It may be that the clinical component is, at present, the weakest part of most preparation programs. There are at least three ways by which most of these programs can be improved. First, a wide range of situations should be used. In the planning area, for instance, observation and practice might be acquired in such places as a governor's office, a mayor's office, a state planning agency, or a school superintendent's office, provided a genuine planning program is a part of their

operation. In the mediating area, use might be made of such places as the office of the state teachers' association, a legislative staff, the state department of education, a state labor relations agency, or the office of a school superintendent, provided, again, that mediation, anticipated or in process, is part of their activities. Mediation needs to be viewed from the vantage point of a variety of actors, which suggests that there be some variety of clinical experience for each future administrator.

A second requirement for the clinical component involves a careful diagnosis of the kinds of experiences most needed by each student or future administrator and a willingness to tailor-make each program. For instance, one student may need exposure to city government, another to state government, and still another to school government. In planning these clinical experiences there should be a three-way process involving the student, one or more professors, and one or more field supervisors. Such planning should consider the student's needs and should make explicit the kinds of observation and participation activities in which the student is to engage and what responsibilities he is to carry. In terms of observation, the student should have close contact with practicing administrators as role models who demonstrate competence in planning and mediating. But the clinical component must permit future administrators to go from observation to participation, to the assumption of responsibility. To permit the assumption of responsibility by a neophyte means that the field supervisor and his or her associates must be willing to assume the risks involved in such practice.

A third requirement of the clinical component is careful evaluation of each clinical experience. This evaluation should involve the planners of the experience, the student, the professors, and the field supervisors. In addition, it seems desirable that others affected by the experience in the field be involved appropriately in the evaluation and that the student's peers on campus be permitted to share in the appraisal. Such full-scale evaluation permits each clinical experience to provide for all students in the group living case material for their own development.

8. As a final direction, professors should assist in providing for the continuing education of chief educational officers. While space does not permit full elaboration of this point, two reasons behind this recommendation should be mentioned. The first, already alluded to, is supportable from the standpoint of campus-field relationships. The

programs of centers where preservice preparation programs go forward can be enriched if at the same time the in-service problems of administrators also become part of the concern of such centers. Edwin Bridges[11] has suggested three stages of preparation for administrators: the certification stage, the postselection stage, and the employment stage. This chapter deals chiefly with the postselection stage and briefly with the employment stage. It seems clear that some very specific problems can be dealt with best when administrators actually confront them.

A second argument for the in-service education of administrators is based, once again, on the socialization process advocated above. At the in-service level a group of administrators, often in rather close proximity and with common interests, can, over time, with frequent meeting and sharing, build peer relationships that are useful conceptually and in terms of psychological support. It is obvious that the administrators themselves should control and give direction to the activities of these groups. To prevent provincialism or the enshrinement of practice, however, frequent participation by professors from the campus and by other persons should be encouraged. These professors can, in turn, find in these groups much stimulation for the study of administration and the design of preparation programs.

Thus, in summary, these eight recommendations place the responsibility for the training of top-level or chief educational administrators on a few major universities, recognize that recruitment and selection of candidates must be given much greater emphasis than at present, and set forth some ways by which the preparation programs can be substantially improved. These steps should be taken with the objective of improving the performance of educational administrators as planners and mediators. Changes will not, of course, come easily, and so we turn next to some of the roadblocks.

PROBLEMS OF IMPLEMENTATION

A number of obstacles stand in the way of implementing the program suggested above. The first of these concerns the reduction of the number of universities that offer focused and appropriate attention to the training of top-level administrators. A conceptual task is involved here—the problem of getting ten to twenty institutions to consider seriously and constructively what it takes to select and train future administrators to be more effective planners and mediators. Organizations such as the University Council for Educational Administration can encourage this effort but, finally, each institution must consider the problem and make the necessary commitment.

Fully as difficult as the conceptual task is the political one. With over three hundred institutions having programs in educational administration and with at least a third of them offering the doctorate in the field, how do we encourage more than a hundred of them to renounce their purported training programs for top-level administrators? Few college presidents seem ready to concede that there are certain areas with which they should not deal. Most professors of educational administration like to feel, moreover, that they are fully capable of performing the task before them. Then there is the reaction from the field. Citizens and prospective administrators often believe that their own state university, and even the university in their region, can do just as well as universities further away. This is particularly true when the details of the program are not well developed, understood, or accepted.

The development of a few key institutions to train top-level administrators must also cope with the emergence of a number of new, off-campus programs, such as Nova,[12] which permit administrators to remain on their jobs while they seek, on a part-time basis, the doctoral degree.

All of these difficulties might be affected by economic circumstances. Perhaps the budget squeeze can be a vehicle by which universities examine their multiple functions and eliminate those in which their performance is marginal. It appears, on the other hand, that substantial grants, particularly from one or more foundations over a period of at least ten years, could help establish ten to twenty institutions with program standards and reputations for training top-level administrators that could not be matched by other institutions. Without some such impetus, it is doubtful that a limited number of such institutions can emerge.

All of this leads into the second obstacle — provision of more adequate support for programs established in the ten to twenty institutions. Additional resources are needed for at least three purposes: support of students, support of faculty, and the extension of the clinical component. It is doubtful that the most promising students can be recruited for the program without promise of substantial support in the form of fellowships or scholarships. Nearly every institution undertaking the program will require additional or different faculty members in educational administration and in supporting disciplines, a process that can be accelerated with outside support. Also, as noted above, the clinical component in most institutions needs considerable development by way of planning, supervision, and evaluation, steps that require greater financial outlay than is now the case.

These additional resources should come from two sources: the university itself and outside funding agencies. No university should move into a program for training top-level administrators unless it is committed to the kind of program contemplated and is determined to provide financial support to implement such a program. But, if possible, that commitment should be augmented by new, outside money. It is desirable that most of this money should come from foundations because they, as compared with government, do not have to be as concerned with the geographical spread of their grants or to impose as many guidelines.

A third roadblock to the achievement of this program is found in many existing state certification programs for school administrators. These programs are ordinarily developed by state-wide committees whose recommendations are accepted and put in force by the state board of education. Members of these advisory committees are usually school administrators and teachers. Their formulations normally reflect the status quo, and several years of teaching experience are typically required for persons seeking any administrative certificate. These provisions obviously eliminate candidates from such fields as business, law, and public administration, which is opposite from the recommendation made above. In short, the pool of administrative candidates is limited to former teachers, a practice we contend is too restrictive.

There appear to be at least three ways out of this dilemma. In some states where provisions are not too restrictive, present requirements might be seen as minimums only, and the program contemplated here could be built upon them. In many states current certification programs should be substantially revised or eliminated. In some states the state board of education could and should provide the leadership necessary in this revision. In other states the state legislature itself may have to take action to require revision or elimination of the present restrictive provisions. Some legislatures have moved in this direction, and more legislative leaders would probably welcome such an opportunity.

While it may seem somewhat strange, a fourth difficulty in achieving the program recommended concerns the way competency-based training programs have captured the support of many professors of educational administration. Based upon Skinnerian psychology and perhaps prompted in part by the accountability movement, the competency approach seems to be built on the following assumptions: that we know what administrative behaviors should be; that we can define these behaviors objectively; that we can teach these behaviors to prospective administrators; that we can measure the presence of these behaviors in administrators; and that these behaviors when employed by administrators will enhance the organization's performance.

I have at least three reservations regarding the competency approach as it is usually enunciated. First, it seems to take little account of recruitment and selection of appropriate candidates. In actuality, most of what people will be after training they bring to the training program. Second, there is little recognition of the fact that achievement in any situation is as much a product of the situation and the expectations surrounding the situation as it is of the behavior of the person. Third, and most important, it is questionable that the understandings and skills needed in planning and mediating, such as social analysis, organizational diagnosis, and political judgment, can be taught as a combination of minor segments of behavior. In my view, understandings and judgment depend on a psychology of learning that goes beyond mechanisms of conditioned response.

To be sure, one cannot be opposed to competence; it is the typical formulation of the competency-based programs to which I object. I assume that there exist ten to twenty institutions, needed to implement the program recommended here, that have no overpowering dedication to the competency format or that competency can be placed in a much broader context in the universities that undertake such a program. In any case, I urge that planning and mediating skills, sought in such a program, not become victims of what can be simply defined and easily measured.

The employability of graduates of the program may be another roadblock. In the first place, the labor market is now tight. As noted above, education is a declining industry, little expansion of administrative personnel is on the horizon, and administrators tend to hold onto their positions. Superintendents and other top-level administrators may not enjoy the length of tenure suggested above, if one follows the deductions of Larry Cuban,[13] but overall a tight market makes access to positions more difficult.

Even more serious in terms of the employability of this "new breed" of administrator may be the attitudes of boards of education and similar bodies. Members of such groups, when they seek administrative officers, frequently place great importance on the experience of prospective administrators and less on their training. Such employing bodies, moreover, often value administrators who give promise of running the day-to-day operations of the organization, and they may be wary of such terms as planning and mediating. It may be necessary to determine what images those two words conjure up in the minds of board members and possibly to develop some alternative language that carries our meaning to such people. Or, as indicated above, when the terms are fully understood, they may represent to some employing boards functions they do not see as appropriate to an administrative officer. These last reservations may also be shared by other influencial citizens in the community. The program suggested here will, in a sense, have been conceived by an elite group of university persons, and, if successful, it will produce an elite corps of administrators who are quite cosmopolitan in outlook. We are not yet sure whether these planners and mediators will be acceptable to the employing boards and the citizens of the communities where we would like to see them work. I suspect that adequate communication with some members of these boards and communities would, in many cases, permit access, but I do not believe the problem will be solved without considerable liaison effort.

Our final roadblock has to do with limitations in the professoriat itself. I approach this problem with some temerity since I have been a member of that group for over thirty years. I have already noted that in my view too many professors have placed undue faith in the competency-based approach to training, but the problems are even more serious. When L. Jackson Newell and I did our study of over thirteen hundred professors of educational administration we were struck by their seeming complacency. At one point we commented:

With so few professors coming from minority groups, one wonders how almost a third of the professors saw it as no problem. In view of many informal reports about scholarly meetings which professors attend, it seems remarkable that a third of them saw "no problem" with the meetings. Even a larger proportion of the professors saw no problem in the ability of their students or in the intellectual climate of their departments. The relative complacence of professors on many of these problems contrasts dramatically with the dissatisfaction on the part of many citizens about the schools, their effectiveness, and the quality of leadership functioning in them. One wonders how the study and training arm of the profession can be so pleased with itself while the practice arm of the profession is in such difficulty.[14]

We also looked at the recruitment of professors. In terms of personal characteristics, 98 percent were male, and 97 percent were white. There were only twenty-three blacks among the 1,333 who responded to the inquiry. Four out of five professors came from rural, small-town, and small-city backgrounds. Of the total group 43 percent came from the Midwest. In terms of church affiliation, 71 percent were Protestant, 11 percent were Catholic, and 10 percent listed no preference. In their political choice, Democrat outnumbered Republican two to one. Among their professional characteristics it can be noted that only one in ten received his doctorate prior to age thirty, and about a third of them were forty or more. Most professors had held five or six positions in education prior to their present one. In most cases these positions were in the public schools as teachers and administrators. Thus, in short, most professors of educational administration were socialized by the public schools before they became professors, and many of them remained practice oriented even when they entered the academic world. This orientation frequently prevented professors from communicating with scholars on campus and may have contributed to the placing of teaching and field service above scholarly inquiry on the part of such professors.

There are at least two ways out of the dilemma of complacency and isolation. Persons in these positions can be stimulated to change. Whole faculties in the area, under some circumstances, can seek new insights about their own programs and each person's role in such programs. A new chairman, in some departments, might stimulate and guide this type of development. In many cases, however, it will probably require an infusion of new people into the department to bring about changes in conceptualization and implementation of programs. New persons should obviously include those with interests and competence in the areas of our concern. One such person might come out of urban planning, another out of political science, and a third out of labor relations. In the interaction between these new faculty members, who know much about their specialties and perhaps little about their application to school situations, and other faculty members, who know about operating schools, some productive program directions may emerge.

SUMMARY

I have focused this chapter on preparation programs designed for top-level or top administrators of education agencies, particularly in an effort to make those administrators more effective planners and mediators. I have noted that planning is an analytical process, and those who participate in it should apply social and organizational insights to the process. Mediating also requires social and organizational insights, but the process is a political one. While planning asks the question what should be done, mediating is concerned with what can be done. Administrators in top-level posts must act on their analyses. To help us secure persons who can both think and act, I have suggested a number of directions that should be applied to preparation programs. They include the establishment and support of ten to twenty training centers at a few major universities across the nation, active recruitment efforts to secure suitable candidates, the application of rigorous procedures in the selection of those candidates, effective involvement of the entire university faculty, appropriate use of simulated materials and computer-based, decision-making exercises, a substantial increase in the quantity and quality of clinical experiences where planning and mediating are both observed and practiced, and, most of all, a program that clearly recognizes that the teaching of planning and mediating skills can best be done in a milieu where the meaning and application of these skills are shared by members of a small, face-to-face group. Primary members of this group should be fifteen to twenty future administrators and a few responsible faculty members. Faculty members from related areas, selected practicing administrators, and key leaders in the community should augment the primary group on frequent occasions.

To implement a program designed to improve the planning and mediating skills of top-level educational administrators will require a number of changes: many universities will need to discontinue their programs, and substantial new resources, preferably from foundations, should be channeled to those who intend to take the charge seriously; state boards of education or state legislatures will need to revise or eliminate the certification requirements for top-level administrators; substantial attention will have to be given to making persons with competence in planning and mediating acceptable to employing boards; and faculties in educational administration, at least in the ten to twenty institutions required for this program, will need to be substantially reconstituted.

NOTES

1. See Roald F. Campbell and Tim L. Mazzoni, Jr., *State Policy Making for the Public Schools* (Berkeley, Calif.: McCutchan Publishing Corp., 1976), Chapter 2.

2. See T. V. Smith, *The Democratic Tradition in America* (New York: Farrar, Straus and Giroux, 1941).

3. William L. Boyd, "The School Superintendent: Educational Statesman or Political Strategist?" *Administrator's Notebook* 22 (1974).

4. Henry Mintzberg, *The Nature of Managerial Work* (New York: Harper & Row, 1973), Chapter 4.

5. Roald F. Campbell and L. Jackson Newell, *A Study of Professors of Educational Administration* (Columbus, Ohio: University Council for Educational Administration, 1973), Chapter 1.

6. James G. March, "Analytical Skills and the University Training of Educational Administrators," *Journal of Educational Administration* 12 (May 1974): 17-44.

7. R. Freeman Butts, "Once Again the Question for Liberal Public Educators: Whose Twilight?" *Phi Delta Kappan* 58 (September 1976): 12.

8. Mintzberg, *Nature of Managerial Work,* p. 38.

9. See Campbell and Newell, *Study of Professors of Educational Administration.*

10. Lloyd E. McCleary and Kenneth McIntire, "Competency Development and the Methodology of College Teaching: A Model and a Proposal," unpublished paper.

11. Edwin M. Bridges, "Administrative Preparation: A Critical Appraisal," in Association of California School Administrators, *Thrust for Educational Leadership* (Burlingame: the Association, 1976), pp. 3-8.

12. Gerald E. Sroufe, "Nova's Ed.D. Program for Educational Leaders: Looking Backward, Looking Forward," *Phi Delta Kappan* 56 (February 1975): 402-405.

13. Larry Cuban, *The Urban School Superintendency: A Century and a Half of Change* (Bloomington, Ind.: PDK Educational Foundation, 1976).

14. Campbell and Newell, *Study of Professors of Educational Administration,* p. 141.

Preparing Administrators in Higher Education: Some Special Considerations

Kenneth P. Mortimer

Roald Campbell did not speak directly to the arena of higher education with regard to the training and preparation of administrators. As a professor of higher education, I will discuss first the special nature of administration in higher education. I will then describe the various programs that purport to prepare administrators in higher education before proceeding to a discussion of two problems considered in Campbell's contribution—how to raise our credibility with our professional colleagues and how to improve the performance of administrators as planners, mediators, and power brokers. I suggest that a broader awareness of the political perspective of organizations is necessary.

ADMINISTRATION IN HIGHER EDUCATION

I start with the assumption that colleges and universities are somehow different organizations than the public schools, although there is a great debate about the nature of these differences. I think there are differences in the context within which they operate and in the kinds of organizations that they are. The external politics of postsecondary education is quite different, even at the state level, from that of the public schools. Colleges and universities are dominated internally by a professional control structure that is somewhat regulated by the faculty. For example, they often carry out the basic functions of management—planning, organizing, directing, staffing, coordinating, reviewing, and budgeting.

In colleges and universities compliance norms—that is, the reasons why individuals comply with orders or directives—are usually rooted in a professional value structure that attributes great legitimacy to such values as control of knowledge and expertise. To put it another way, administration is not a high-prestige activity in colleges and universities. One does not "aspire" to become the head of a department, at least not overtly, since such behavior would be suspect. In short, we are operating in higher education on the margins of a decision-making process controlled in important ways by the faculty.

A second point is that there are two competing systems of administration in colleges and universities. One is the academic side, including academic administrators, department heads, deans, academic vice-presidents, and presidents. For the most part these administrators are not trained in preservice programs for administration. Higher education operates very much on the Peter Principle. It is somehow assumed that people who are good researchers and scholars will somehow, by the grace of God or other reference to divinity, turn out to be good administrators. Good scholars normally do not aspire to these positions; they may be dragged into them for the good of the institution and because their turn comes up. Anyone who is around long enough and gets promoted in a college or university cannot avoid some administrative tasks. But productive scholars really do not pay attention to that sort of business. Perhaps the best way of training such academic administrators is through in-service programs, workshops, seminars, and a variety of other arrangements to which I think we need to pay more attention.

The second side of administration and the one in which many training programs in higher education tend to concentrate is the administrative or bureaucratic. Students who enroll in college and university administration programs aspire to be planners, budgeters, members of student personnel staffs, directors of admissions, and governmental employees at the federal and state levels. Some of them need and acquire skills that can be taught, such as counseling and student personnel skills. Thus, in programs in higher education we are preparing those administrators who are or will be on the bureaucratic as opposed to the academic side of the organization.

THE NATURE OF HIGHER EDUCATION
TRAINING PROGRAMS

It might be helpful to discuss the present status of training for the "profession" of higher education. About four thousand students are enrolled in graduate programs that purport to specialize in post-secondary education; these programs number approximately eighty or ninety. There are three hundred to four hundred full-time faculty— that is, people whose primary assignment is in higher education programs and courses—and probably another four or five hundred part-time faculty who call themselves professors of higher education. Among the latter are deans or associate deans who teach an occasional course or professors of educational administration who teach the one course in college and university administration that may be offered by their departments.

The study of higher education is cut up a variety of ways and includes not only the study of organization and administration but also the study of history and philosophy, curriculum and instruction, and college students. Higher education programs, then, are broader than the study of administration. These programs cover the full range of activities that are normally associated with a school or college of education. Within the context of higher education there are people, of course, who specialize in community colleges, in professional education, and in adult and continuing education. Some universities offer curricula that specialize in student personnel work or community college leadership programs.

The professional association for professors of higher education is the Association for the Study of Higher Education. It has two hundred fifty to three hundred members and was formerly affiliated with the American Association of Higher Education. We, as a professional group, have all the identity problems of an emerging profession, and we do *not* want to be called professors of educational administration. We are professors of higher education, and we are very proud of it.

Even taking into account the differences in our two perspectives, I can support most of Campbell's eight points as basic ingredients in a program to prepare administrators in postsecondary education. There should be a small number, and, in fact, there are already a small number, of programs that purport to train top-level administrators in postsecondary education. The scope of these programs has been described by Paul Dressel and Lewis Mayhew.[1] Fifteen or twenty programs each have from five to ten faculty, who recruit students on at least a regional basis and give major attention to the study of higher education. In addition, there are a number of programs with two or three professors of higher education who tend to offer instruction to junior administrators at the institution where they are operating and to others who are within commuting distance of the institution. Furthermore, there are many programs where one or two people, adjunct faculty or part-time administrators, teach a few courses in higher education.

TWO BASIC PROBLEMS

It is easy to support the emphasis on internships, on course study, on the socialization process, and on the use of faculty from other areas, advocated by Campbell, because I think they are integral to the training not only of administrators in the K-12 realm but also in the higher education or postsecondary realm. But Campbell raises two basic problems: the lack of prestige of educational administration faculty within the university; and improving the performance of administrators as planners, mediators, and power brokers.

Lack of Prestige of Educational Administration

Over one-half of the professors of higher education operate on the basis of little or no specialized preparation in the field. Many are part-time administrators who teach as a sideline and who, because they want to dabble in the classroom and are no longer competent in their particular fields, decide that they are miraculously competent to teach higher education. Others are former administrators who have had no preparation in the study of higher education or educational administration at the postsecondary level. During the past year we have entertained three visitors from three separate institutions at the Pennsylvania State University Center for the Study of Higher Education. They were leaving administrative posts to "head up" programs in higher education. They asked us, and we were happy to comply with their request, to prepare bibliographies and to identify people with whom they should consult about developing programs in higher education. It is my argument that these people should not control the study of higher education although they can and should be a part of it. I am not eliminating them from the profession. But who should exercise control? The control should come from those who are formally prepared to study higher education.

I should like to offer a proposal: *before any administrator could be allowed in a classroom to teach in the area of higher education, he or she should be given at least a year's leave and asked to go to another institution to study higher education.* This addresses the problem that Campbell has raised concerning the way we are viewed by our colleagues elsewhere in the university. I believe that our programs will lack intellectual credibility with our colleagues as long as these programs are controlled and staffed by those whose preparation is limited to a certain number of years of experience as an administrator. There is, in my opinion, little in the administrative experience to qualify a person to teach doctoral students and to supervise doctoral research. I believe and urge that practitioners should have a strong role in the practicum, in developing internships, and in a variety of other areas that Campbell discussed. But we will never gain the respect of our colleagues in the universities as long as we are dominated by people whose interests are entirely based on experience and who are devoid of conceptual sophistication.

Performance of Administrators as Planners, Mediators, and Power Brokers

On this subject I should like to add a dimension to what Campbell has suggested. We should be concerned about the political dimensions of *all* administrative problems. What is politics? What are power relationships? Many of the chapters in this volume focus on specific aspects of politics: the activities in which governing bodies engage; the relationships between the branches or levels of governments and between collective bargaining agents and school boards. I should like to urge anyone involved in instructional activity to put such matters in the context of a broad conception of politics. As Robert Dahl has stated, a political decision may be construed as one that involves, to a significant extent, power, rule, or authority. With Harold Lasswell we should be emphasizing politics as the study of who gets what, when, where, and how.[2]

There is an element of politics in all aspects of administration, in most decisions with which we deal, and in most problems that educational administrators have to confront. We should be asking ourselves: can we develop a training program for administrators that will create, and sensitize people to, the awareness of the political elements that are almost inevitable in any decision-making environment? Programs for the preparation of higher education administrators should be planned with four political questions in mind.

First, who governs? What is the distribution of power, authority, and influence at all levels of the internal and external environment, from the federal, or even the international, level down to the individual faculty member or employee? For example, questions concerning tenure in colleges and universities should be considered in the context of a variety of external forces, including the guidelines established by the American Association of University Professors and decisions by the United States Supreme Court.

Second, what are the resources of power, and how are they manipulated? Money, charismatic qualities, and political influence, expertise, and skills are the resources, and there are severe limits on the extent to which some of them can be manipulated. I agree with James March, who said that the context of educational administration limits the prospects for *dramatic* administrative success, and I think we should try to create an awareness of the *limits* that the political environment sets on administrative effectiveness.[3]

Third, whose interests are involved in any given decision? In collective bargaining, for example, the employee's interest in job security and economic welfare is of utmost importance. Interests of faculty in decisions regarding tenure quotas, promotions, and work load are governed by the same concerns. What then are the political elements involved in such decisions? To ignore considerations of faculty job security in an argument over tenure quotas seems to me to be the height of folly.

Fourth, how is conflict resolved? We tend to concentrate on how conflict might be managed with the idea that if it is managed properly, it will disappear. I think the more realistic assumption is that conflict is a natural phenomenon, and we have to tolerate certain levels of it. Some conflicts cannot be resolved. And yet in academe the search for consensus is considered the appropriate decision-making style. It is necessary to have more careful analyses of the extent to which this is, in fact, feasible and of the implications of consensus as a style of conflict resolution.

These types of concerns present a formidable agenda for those who are involved with programs devoted to the study of higher education. The relative newness of higher education as a field of disciplined study, combined with the broad spectrum of professors and administrators who appropriate the label "higher education faculty," may suggest that we have not as yet been able to focus our concerns sufficiently on the dynamics of the political considerations raised in this volume. Perhaps it would be timely now for the Association for the Study of Higher Education or the University Council for Educational Administration to undertake a thorough analysis of our successes and failures in this regard. Certainly Campbell's contribution can serve as a useful reference point for a more thorough effort.

NOTES

1. Paul L. Dressel and Lewis B. Mayhew, *Higher Education as a Field of Study* (San Francisco: Jossey-Bass, 1974).

2. Robert A. Dahl, *Modern Political Analysis* (Englewood Cliffs, N.J.: Prentice-Hall, 1963); Harold Lasswell and Abraham Kaplan, *Power and Society* (New Haven, Conn.: Yale University Press, 1950).

3. See Michael D. Cohen and James G. March, *Leadership and Ambiguity,* a General Report prepared for the Carnegie Commission on Higher Education (New York: McGraw-Hill, 1974).

Beyond Mediation:
Administrators as Advocates

Aubrey V. McCutcheon, Jr.

ADVOCACY TRAINING FOR PUBLIC SCHOOL
ADMINISTRATORS: A FELT NEED

If there is reason to complain about the contributions of Roald
Campbell and Kenneth Mortimer I think it must be for their lack of
emphasis upon advocacy training for educational administrators.
Such training was *the* one most important request I received from administrators in public schools in the metropolitan area of Detroit while
I was employed by the Detroit Public Schools. It is still requested of me
more often than any other form of assistance, both in my teaching role
at Wayne State University and as I move around the country engaged
in activities as consultant.

The requests come in many ways, sometimes for direct assistance
in dealing with legislative bodies or with parent groups or executive
agencies. Sometimes the request is made in relationship to a pending
confrontation with individual staff members, union representatives,
superordinate and subordinate administrators, or others who have
found need or desire to challenge otherwise effective administrators.
The same questions are asked: How can I, how do I, forthrightly and
effectively espouse what I believe to be (after careful analysis) the correct position to take regarding *this* issue? In other words, how do I
maintain reasonable relationships while being persuasive? How do I
keep or make friends while exerting influences in areas about which I
really do know best? Administrators want to know how far they can
go, how far they must go, before either giving up or being adamant.
They are saying, "Give me some training, even if it is limited. At least
make me feel comfortable as I stumble."

It is my view that any consideration of the content and feasibility
of preparation programs designed to cope with the changing role of
educational administrators must be substantially weighted to encompass such concerns. It is insufficient to consider means of making
administrators—or remaking them—merely planners and mediators.

We cannot minimize the importance of power brokerage by equating it with the neutrality of mediation, even if mediation is conceived to be a proactive rather than a reactive undertaking. And we need to concentrate not only on preentry training of future recruits for the profession but also on those who are already on the job and are seeking to develop needed skills in doctoral and postdoctoral programs.

ADVOCACY SKILLS IN SCHOOL ADMINISTRATION

While I do not minimize the importance of planning or conciliation efforts, I am inclined to the view that the realization of the best-laid plans or compromises results from a realistic reassessment of a previously presented, strongly advocated position. My legal training causes me to appreciate the value of anticipating the best arguments that can be offered by "the other side" and of making the most effective rebuttal for them. Good lawyers are able to argue persuasively, even vehemently, for the merits of a position, which, at the same time, they recognize will not necessarily become the ultimate resolution of the matter at issue. They expect negotiating and bargaining to be an essential part of the decision-making process. Few experts in other professions adopt, or even condone, such a pragmatic attitude toward problem solving. They normally attempt to assemble and present the best and most authoritative data possible, and then to rely on that evidence to win acceptance of their findings. This strategy, at least in theory, characterized the past relationships of professional school administrators with the public, with politicians and school boards, and with their own staffs.

Some very complex political challenges face public school administrators every day, however, as the chapters in this volume indicate. They are forced to become activists *and* practical problem solvers, and they are beginning to realize that the image of the professional "above the fray" is no longer practicable when they must interact with people in varying degrees of combativeness. Although they may not experience precisely the same kinds of confrontations that engage lawyers, still their cry is for better advocacy skills in dealing with disruptive conflicts and adversary situations.

Let me share with you the results of an actual informal inquiry concerning preparation program needs as perceived by a diverse group of public school administrators: five urban superintendents, three suburban superintendents, one deputy superintendent, three assistant superintendents in specialty areas, three personnel directors, and four school principals. They urged that the type of training be provided at the graduate or postgraduate level that would prepare them to do the following tasks.

1. "Get along with the community." (This statement was variously defined to mean "getting along without necessarily having to go along"; getting the community to listen instead of reacting emotionally; getting the community to recognize "they don't know everything"; and getting the community to understand that all school administrators are not "lazy, dishonest, or dumb.")

2. Develop new ways to motivate staff.

3. Understand and properly engage in collective bargaining.

4. Understand and properly operate "under the law."

5. Develop and implement new staff evaluation plans.

6. Understand and achieve the best way to finance schools and to get more dollars for schools.

7. Work with a "split board."

8. Determine who is "the community."

9. Convince the board and the community you want to work *with* them.

10. Share power and responsibility without abdicating authority.

11. Deal with politicians.

12. Deal with declining enrollments.

13. Convince "people" that schools cannot do "everything."

I approve of this list because it reflects the desire of school administrators to acquire the skills of persuasion, negotiation, and political know-how that fall within the purview of advocacy training.

ADVOCACY SKILLS AS AN AID
TO PUBLIC SCHOOL ADMINISTRATORS

Who is to lobby for more equitable financing of education, or to respond to the lobbying of groups opposed to such reform? Who is to influence the forms of "accountability" that legislators impose on the public schools? Who is to deal with the educational consequences of locating highways, housing projects, shopping centers, or homes for senior citizens? Certainly we no longer debate whether or not all these political decisions affect schools, and we ought not question the need for school administrators to exercise substantial influence when such decisions are made. Further, if more and more decisions regarding education are to be made in the courts or at the bargaining table, advocates of better education are needed at the side of lawyers in court and of trained labor relations specialists at the bargaining table.

An example of the consequences of unsuccessful advocacy on the part of school officials in meeting political challenges illustrates the above point. In August 1976 the superintendents, staff, and the school board in Detroit agreed on the budgetary necessity to reduce certain program offerings and undertook *careful* planning to accomplish them. The state superintendent of public instruction, acting on the basis of complaints from people in the local community, requested that the state board of education deny authority to the Detroit Board of Education and its superintendent to make the planned reduction in service. The rationale given by the community politicians and accepted by the state board of education was that the financial difficulties of the Detroit public schools were not as severe as had been presented. At the same time, the state board admonished the Detroit board that it was illegal to operate under a deficit budget. The superintendent and staff reinstituted some of the planned reductions in services. When school started in September, however, they were still looking for a way to save money so that they would not operate illegally with a deficit budget. It seems safe to say that more effective exercise of some advocacy skills would have avoided this unfortunate dilemma. The administrators in the Detroit public schools might have been more persuasive in describing the fiscal problems of the schools. Some effort to create counterpressure upon the state board of education, through partisan influence or otherwise, might have put the Detroit school officials on a more equal footing with those in the community who would not accept their assessment of the financial situation.

I recognize that there is great risk in exercising the characteristics of a power broker, but I say to university faculty and students, as I say to my peers frequently in the Detroit public schools, that this is the risk we must take if we really want to help the students. Professors of educational administration must prepare practitioners to deal with problems of the real world or suffer with them the failure of educators to be properly heard. Advocacy training must be the first new step in such preparation, particularly if we want to develop effective *power brokers* to cope with and, more often, fashion the changing politics of education.

12 Challenge and Opportunity

Jack Culbertson

It is indeed felicitous that this volume has explored many timely aspects of educational politics and that it has done so in two ways: by looking back to the times of Jefferson and by looking ahead to the 1980's.

Three general themes seem to inform and permeate the chapters in this volume. One theme is centered in the concept of decline—declining enrollments, declining resources (relatively speaking), declining confidence in social institutions, including those responsible for education. It is paradoxical that there is a countertheme—growth—growth in complexity, growth in ambiguity, growth in demands for accountability, growth in professional distress. Implicit in the clashing themes of decline and growth is a third theme: that educational leaders and those responsible for preparing these leaders now find themselves in a new and adverse environment.

I am not going to summarize the contribution of the other authors, but I do want to comment briefly on this new and frequent companion of educational leaders called adversity. It is clear that we are having some difficulty in understanding and accepting the concept. I was interested in a recent study, for example, that examined the problems of declining enrollment within one state (Mark Rodekohr, *Adjustments of Colorado School Districts to Declining Enrollments* [Lincoln: University of Nebraska Printing and Duplication Service, 1975], pp. 1-7). Superintendents were asked in the

339

study whether or not enrollments in their districts were declining. The large majority said that they were not. At the same time, the data submitted to the state agency from their districts indicated that enrollments were, in fact, declining. In this one example is reflected a part of our current difficulty. It is not easy to cope with the unpleasant aspects of adversity, to face it openly and courageously, and to address its underlying problems. At the same time, if we are not able to understand, accept, and adapt to the new reality, we are in danger of trading off short-term political advantages for some long-term losses. This generalization is based upon the assumption supported by most of the chapters in this volume: that the present environment of adversity is not a phenomenon that will pass quickly. In Chapter 5, Jesse Burkhead documented in conclusive and excellent fashion the resource problems likely to face educators in the 1980's, and he provided a basis for viewing these problems in a larger economic context.

Because of our long and relatively prosperous period of educational growth, we may tend to think that ours is the only generation that has confronted adversity or, at least that has confronted it in an environment as unpleasant, threatening, obdurate, or complex as the present one. We were reminded by Jennings Wagoner in Chapter 2, however, that Thomas Jefferson experienced marked adversity in his long struggle for the improvement of education. It is heartening to remember the staying powers of Jefferson, and we need to take stock of the important and tested resources that are available from the past. One of these resources is the lasting set of values that has held us together, including Jefferson's concept of liberty. We are still free to initiate and to seek new alternatives. We also have as an inspiration Jefferson's view concerning the significant relationship between education and a democracy, as Stephen Bailey eloquently demonstrated in Chapter 1.

The tendency to think only of the negative aspects of adversity is a very human one, and yet history offers much wisdom concerning its positive aspects. One of the more pithy sayings, for example, is that of Shakespeare: "Sweet are the uses of adversity, which, like to toad, ugly and venemous, wears yet a precious jewel on her head."

How, then, can we learn to understand, accept, and meet the challenges of today's adversity? What are its "sweet uses"?

NEW VISIONS

One of the most important uses of adversity is found in the opportunity it provides to search its attendant conditions of ambiguity, uncertainty, and conflict for a new and more effective vision. Because of the current malaise, there are likely inadequacies in the nature and clarity of our vision. Here history can provide useful precedents. In 1776, when we declared our independence from England, the Articles of Confederation were devised to serve as the symbol of a new vision and a guide for the nation's future development. But its governance arrangements brought many difficulties. During this period there was a great struggle going on between the states and the national government, and intense conflict took place between the states. All the while, however, our national leaders were at work searching for a better guide. Out of a decade of adversity and a series of almost unbelievable events came the new arrangements and the new vision represented in the Constitution. Nathan Glazer noted in Chapter 3 that we are at a crossroads in considering what the next stage of governmental action will look like and that we are not clear about its "scale," its "form," and its "fundamental principles." The same generalizations can be applied to educational government. Thus, as we move toward the 1980's, we have a special opportunity to generate new visions and to create arrangements to realize them.

A more specific example of this kind of challenge is found in the views Roald Campbell expressed in Chapter 11 concerning the urgency of conceptualizing new training programs for educational leaders that are different and that meet new needs. Given the shift to a climate in which the management of decline predominates, changes in perspective and purpose are imperative. There are, of course, opportunities for all of us to come to terms with the demands of this new climate, whether we are policy analysts, designers of programs, preparers of leaders, or leaders in schools or universities or other settings. The attainment of new purpose and perspectives amidst adversity, then, can be one of the greatest achievements of our generation.

NEW OPPORTUNITIES

Adversity creates pressure for individuals and institutions to move beyond present dissatisfactions to something more desirable — to transcend the status quo. There is latent, if not manifest, motivation to reduce ambiguity, to confront complexity, and to achieve constructive resolutions of conflict. Put another way, adversity creates new opportunities for individuals and institutions to learn and to adapt. Even though unusual leadership is required in adverse conditions, the attendant climate for change can be an ally for those who would want to turn adversity into a positive force. Within such a climate, for example, there can be advocacy of the type referred to by Aubrey McCutcheon. Inventive proposals can receive a hearing because of the need and motivation to find new solutions. Such a climate, even though unsettling, can offer advantages to those interested in improving education and in achieving effective change.

I am told that the Chinese have a word for "crisis" that combines the symbols of danger and opportunity. Thus, whether one looks at educational institutions today from a macro- or a microview, there is, even in the midst of difficulty, much opportunity. If we think of something as specific as closing a school in this era of decline, we can see the potential for new uses of buildings to promote adult learning, for example, even while parents struggle against the closing of the school. Current criticisms of training programs offered by institutions of higher education and the inadequate resources that are brought to bear upon them put policymakers on the defensive. At the same time, opportunities for leadership to achieve adaptations of programs are created, and such adaptations, if effective, will be valued by the clients served. Leaders in one university, for example, looked at the scene four years ago and decided that, given the tremendous change within and around educational institutions and the new questions that were being posed, there was a growing need for effective policy analysts. Therefore, they assigned a much lower priority to their programs designed to prepare superintendents and principals, and, over a period of two years, designed a new, high-priority program for preparing policy analysts. McCutcheon noted that in Michigan administrators had inadequate staff development programs to address the challenge inherent in the management of decline. Leaders responded by creating a new professional development center. Thus, we need to remind ourselves that opportunity resides in adversity. The challenge to leadership is not to be paralyzed by unpleasant conditions, but to search out opportunity and use it to advantage.

GAINS IN EFFICIENCY

Another use of adversity, particularly in its relation to retrenchment, has to do with the attainment of greater efficiencies in education. We are well aware that leaders in the private sector frequently use recessions and retrenchment to examine their organizations, to identify inefficiencies, to study obsolescent practices, and to substitute more efficient technologies or operations. A number of school systems and institutions of higher education in recent years have gone through this process. While such an approach may be unpleasant and create dissatisfactions, opportunity to achieve greater long-range efficiency in school operations is present within the context of retrenchment.

NEW FORMS OF COOPERATION

In Chapter 4, Frank Riessman wrote about concepts of self-help as represented in a host of new organizations to deal with the excess use of such items as tobacco and alcohol, or to address special problems as, for example, divorce or child abuse. He noted that citizens are turning increasingly from traditional institutions and are creating their own arrangements through which they can help themselves. He did not discuss the concept of self-help with regard to the education profession, but I would suggest that we could profitably examine this concept and its implications for change within the field of education and educational leadership.

Implicit in the idea is the ethic of cooperation. In the midst of conflict and differing perspectives, we seem to be moving in the direction of placing relatively greater value upon the ethic of cooperation as compared to the ethic of competition. We are seeing more clearly the power inherent in helping one another achieve objectives that go beyond ourselves and our respective institutions. Thus, we have experienced in this volume an example of the potential for professional self-help. The University of Virginia and its leaders have contributed resources, time, and talent to benefit the participants of the seminar on which the volume was based. By committing themselves to values that transcend their immediate locale, these leaders are serving their fellow educators in school systems, universities, and other settings and regions. They did this by gaining the cooperation of leaders and scholars from many other institutions across the country. Would it not be possible for us to extend this kind of cooperation to more complex problems and, in the process, realize needed professional and educational adaptations?

In Chapter 7, Michael Kirst discussed the need for coalition building within the new political environment in which educators find themselves. In Chapter 9, Robert Berdahl gave us useful insights for the future on the politics of accommodation among leaders in public schools and postsecondary education. Leaders and professors in higher education tend, generally, to have more experience at the state level of politics. Local school administrators and professors of school administration, as a group, are more oriented to the politics of education in local settings. While recognizing, as with Kenneth Mortimer, that the politics of education is different for higher education institutions and for public schools, complementary resources and emergent leadership groups could be joined to achieve new coalitions. In these times of adversity, we can discover ways of professional self-help and, in turn, opportunities to increase the resources available to education.

In sum, then, as enrollments, resources, and confidence decline, complexity, ambiguity, and dissatisfaction increase. This peculiar admixture of growth and decline, in the view of many, creates a new and adverse environment for educational leaders. There can, however, be both challenge and opportunity in adversity; history also shows that it can have important uses and profound advantages. Leaders can use adversity to help define new and more desirable directions for educational institutions. The dissatisfaction created by adverse conditions establishes a readiness for needed change, and this can abet leadership. The adversities of retrenchment can also be used to achieve greater efficiencies in present programs and operations. Finally, because the demands of adversity are marked, new forms of cooperation are encouraged. These forms can facilitate the pooling of a wide range of human and other resources and can help leaders address the complex demands of adversity more effectively.

Those wishing to confront adversity and challenge should find many useful leadership concepts in the chapters of this book. As the University Council for Educational Administration, for example, develops a plan for the period 1979-1984, its leaders will be examining this and other sources for clues to the future. It is already apparent that the attainment of clearer directions for education and leadership, given current ambiguities, poses the major challenge to those who would guide educational institutions. Unless the challenge is met, progress will be limited. The challenge cannot be met unless excellence in the art and science of educational politics is demonstrated. As leaders move to meet future policy-making challenges, the following observation by Seneca assumes significance: "The good things which belong to prosperity are to be wished, but the good things that belong to adversity are to be admired."

Index

347